Diary of a Curable Romantic

Diary of a Curable Romantic

Junius A. Davis

Copyright © 2008 by Junius A. Davis.

Library of Congress Control Number: 2007907971
ISBN: Hardcover   978-1-4257-9318-0
               Softcover   978-1-4257-9317-3

All rights reserved. No part of this book may be reproduced or transmitted in any form or by any means, electronic or mechanical, including photocopying, recording, or by any information storage and retrieval system, without permission in writing from the copyright owner.

This book was printed in the United States of America.

To order additional copies of this book, contact:
Xlibris Corporation
1-888-795-4274
www.Xlibris.com
Orders@Xlibris.com
44553

Contents

Preface	Diary of a Curable Romantic	7
Chapter 1	Grandpa Davis	9
Chapter 2	Camp Kelly	17
Chapter 3	Grandma Johnson	19
Chapter 4	My Parents—The Early Years	27
Chapter 5	Growing Up	30
Chapter 6	The Teen Age Years	38
Chapter 7	Undergraduate Work at the University of North Carolina	45
Chapter 8	Initial Tour in the Navy	56
Chapter 9	The Mating Game	73
Chapter 10	Wedding	77
Chapter 11	Our Life in Atlanta	80
Chapter 12	Our First Residence in Greensboro	83
Chapter 13	Second Tour of Duty in the Navy	88
Chapter 14	Our Life in New York City	94
Chapter 15	Graduate Study at Columbia University	100
Chapter 16	Our Year in Middletown, N.Y.	107
Chapter 17	Life on the Faculty of Princeton University	113
Chapter 18	Our Life at Emory University	123
Chapter 19	Graduate Deaning at UNC-G	140
Chapter 20	Entrance Bigtime into the Testing Movement	150
Chapter 21	Life in Hopewell, New Jersey	162
Chapter 22	Return to North Carolina	171
Chapter 23	Duke University, On the Side	182
Chapter 24	Tenure at the Research Triangle Institute	188
Chapter 25	Family Life in Chapel Hill	198
Chapter 26	Medical History	203
Chapter 27	Inlaws	212
Chapter 28	Pets	218
Chapter 29	My Love with Means of Movement	223
Chapter 30	The Three Children as Adults	236
Chapter 31	Retirement	243

Appendices

Appendix A	Resume for J. A. Davis	255
Appendix B	Paper: "How to Succeed at ETS	277
Appendix C	Remarks: Memorial Service for Charles Edge	285
Appendix D	Funeral Sermon for Claude Morris by the Rev. Mike Davis	291
Appendix E	Selected Published "Letters to the Editor"	295
E1	Letters Concerning Preparation of Teachers	296
E2	Letters Concerning Educational Tests and Measurements	302
E3	The Duke Lacrosse Fiasco and the NAACP	306
E4	Factors That Drive Up Medical Costs	309
E5	Letters to the President, VIA Letters to the Editors	312
E6	Letters about Irritants	317
E7	Letters Responding to Letters	326

Preface

Diary of a Curable Romantic

From the time my Father-in-Law's autobiography, *Seventh Son of a Seventh Son*, was published in June, 1993, I have been bugged to do a similar job for my offspring and theirs. Several dear friends that I have bored with some account of an experience, the most notable being Doris Gold, the First Day Cover artist of national acclaim, have been kind enough to tell me that the experiences I have just recounted to them should be incorporated into a book. I have resisted, not because of any hesitance to deal with words on paper, but because there is so much in my life that is best left unreported.

But as I have expressed this concern as a reason for not providing an account of my life, I have been told that it would be no trick simply to omit those events that I or my heirs would find embarrassing, and focus on the many other things that I consider significant, whether benign, calamitous, or of casual interest. Accordingly, I have now spent some time attempting to put words on paper—starting with several notable ancestors whose example affected me, and moving through my life, stage by stage.

This account is markedly different in tone, if not in substance, from my professional vita, which in my nineteenth year of retirement now I find rather dull. I have placed my vita in the appendix, and there should be no discrepancy in event or dates from the more informal account of experiences that impressed me or that I felt were significant in making me what my good friend, Marty Hamburger, has called "a curable romantic." The appendix also contains copies of a sample of letters to the editor that I have written over the years about things that have upset me sufficiently that I have felt a need to protest publicly.

I have been amazed to find that others who have been with me at the time reported recall different events as significant from those that I recall. Apparently there are personal factors that affect recall, and thus the forthcoming account is a highly personal one, and may differ from what others involved recall. I need to stress, however, that I have made absolutely no attempt to romanticize or to stray from factual accounting; there may be errors in memory or report sources, but there has been no attempt to stray from what I believe to be true. And many of the people and events named can be found and elaborated by using a search engine such as Google.

This account was started in March, 2006, and has progressed in fits and starts since then. I find my memory is not what it used to be, and seldom does a week go by that I do not recall some other event of significance that I have omitted in what has been previously written. Some of these events have been forgotten by the time I could get to a keyboard, and other past events of significance that should have been included will surely be suggested by future day-to-day occurrences. I have also found that in some instances my initial recall was faulty, and have made corrections in these cases. But I am beginning to chafe at the distraction from others and other things I would like to do that work on the manuscript has caused. Therefore, I am putting it to bed, without much remorse for omissions or remaining errors of recall, but with hopes that the frankness sometimes involved does not prove upsetting to any reader. And, most of those who might find something said to be libelous are now deceased. This, then, is an account of a young male who started out in life reveling in the romance of all things, without the scorn of a Miniver Cheevy, but for whom most experience was sobering. Between the lines, the perceptive reader will discover how I learned that life consists of many fantasies that we have created to justify our remarkable existence, but that conceal the aspects that are really there but that we simply do not want to face.

Chapter 1

Grandpa Davis

My paternal grandfather, William Ayers Davis, born July 21, 1865 and died March 9, 1943, in Bladen County, North Carolina, was probably one of the most endearing figures I have ever known. He was huge—six feet six or seven inches tall, broad shoulders and trim waist, well developed biceps from holding mules and an occasional horse immobile while he shod them in his blacksmith shop, and traditionally Welsh in every respect. He could be as completely at ease splitting wet cypress railroad crossties to fuel the tobacco barn at curing time, as he would be sitting with his head bowed in his little church on a Sunday morning.

His father, William Ross Davis, was born April 11, 1835, and died April 1, 1924. William Ross was the son of Isaac Davis, born April 22, 1805, and Edith Hester Davis, born January 12, 1809. William Ross married Catherine McClain, born May 1, 1839, on the Isle of Skye, Scotland, and died in Bladen County May 22, 1924. William Ross is reputed to have hidden out in the Bladen County swamps when the Civil War conscription agents came around, and to have justified this by the statement "I don't own any damned negroes, and I'm not going to fight for them." He became a local hero, however, for the area had a huge population of Lumbee Indians, who took advantage of the absence of men and raped the women and plundered their food supply with considerable abandon. The five notches on the 1850 Henry Parker rifle that was his and that has hung over our fireplaces stand for Lumbees, not Yankees, I was told many years ago by an uncle. The gun was always described by my grandmother, however, as "Pa's old war gun."

My grandfather, the fourth of eleven children of William Ross and Catherine McClain Davis, was deeply religious. Although he did not wear his religion on his sleeve, it nevertheless was an important element in his life. I never heard him utter a word that would not have been appropriate in church, and he was scrupulously honest and straightforward in all his dealings.

William Ross Davis and Catherine McLean Davis, Circa 1920

William Ayers Davis, Circa 1940)

As a young man in his early twenties (he later married Eliza Lennon Kelly on March 28, 1888), he was active in a little Baptist Church, then the only church in Bladenboro, and was appointed a deacon in recognition of his reputation as a man of faith. But there was an unexpected death of a man in the congregation, leaving his widow with debts and no way to pay them. Their farm had several acres of Scuppernong grapes that were ripening, and my grandfather picked them, converted them into wine, selling it to provide cash for the widow. The only problem was that the most opportune setting for the sales was the church steps on a Sunday morning, where contact could be made with every man in the community. The pastor, however, and the deacons felt this was not appropriate for an officer of their church, despite his good intentions, and voted privately to exclude him from office. This hurt him deeply, and his response was to purchase a lot in the center of town, and build a small church there of his own. He was successful in getting an agreement for a nearby Presbyterian college to provide a student minister or faculty member to preach every third Sunday, and thus he returned to his Welsh roots as a Presbyterian. The church was initially illuminated by a series of kerosene lamps attached to the walls on each side (though electric lighting was provided in the late.1930s), and had a series of foot-pump organs provided by my grandfather. My aunts and uncles constituted the church officials and Sunday School teachers, and save for a couple of families (i.e., Hesters and Singletarys) who had snuck in, its members were mostly Davises, or individuals who had married into the family. But I can honestly say that we had our own church. And it was much later that I understood why my mother always asked if the girl I was dating was Baptist, and was much relieved if she was of some other faith such as Catholic or Jewish. Baptists had become anathema throughout our family.

It is rumored that Georgetown University had a basketball player who attained a world record by using the words "you know" two hundred and thirteen times in a single sentence when interviewed. Grandpa Davis loved to talk, and his repeated but superfluous words were "And along like that." He would say something like "Yesterday I was plowing the tobacco field and along like that, and this little bantam rooster came strutting out of the swamp and along like that, and . . ."

When Grandpa Davis died in 1943, he had, counting his eight children, something like 149 children, grandchildren, and great grandchildren. He loved to get a dozen or so of his little grandchildren, most of whom lived on an allotted parcel of land from his farm and were thus nearby, and tell them stories, of which he had an endless repertoire. I recall his account of finding a hollow tree in the swamp that abutted the farm, hearing a scratching noise inside, and climbing down inside to explore. The noise, he said, turned out to be caused by a little bear cub, which he found cuddley and affectionate. His fondling this little fellow was suddenly interrupted by the hollow tree becoming dark inside. It was the mother bear, returning to her nest, and backing down toward him.

He would stop at this point and wait, gazing off into the distance, until one of the little ones, flushed with genuine emotion, would say "Granddaddy, Granddaddy, what did you do then?" "Well," responded my grandfather, "I had this here little old pocket knife in my pocket. I got it out, opened it like this, and along like that, and when that old mama bear got close enough I grabbed her by the tail, jabbed her backside with the pocket knife, and she pulled me right out of there!" It was then, of course, that the children knew that he had been pulling their legs, but their laughter revealed no ill will for being duped.

His story telling skills were but one of many assets. He maintained a large farm of over 100 acres with a single mule and five sons—who, when they reached the age of 10, were old enough to both own their own shotgun and to work in the fields. He was the village blacksmith for the little rural community of Bladenboro, operated it's only grist mill, and built many small houses which the local cotton mill purchased and rented out to its employees. In the 1930s when his blacksmith business began to fall off, he opened a dry cleaning establishment, but left this to his daughters to manage.

His carpentry skills had been honed by his construction of a large log cabin which he planned to serve as the home for him and his bride, Liza Lennon Kelly. He made the walls double thick to ensure that the home would last forever. Unfortunately, however, wharf rats found the spaces between the logs to be a comfortable habitat, not only as a place to live, but also as a place to die. It was not too long after he brought his bride home that the smell of decaying flesh made the log cabin uninhabitable. Sadly, my grandfather set it afire after building a more conventional house nearby.

This was a simple house. It was perched on cypress logs some two feet off the sandy ground. It had a porch across the front with the usual swing, a parlor inside with a red velvet covered sofa and chairs and an organ operated by pumping foot pedals, and then two bedrooms opening on one another on each side of the house, and finally, at the rear end, a large enclosed porch with a pump and a large kitchen/dining area complete with walk-in fireplace that was originally used for all cooking, but which, though replaced by a wood-burning cook stove in the 1920s, frequently saw service for meal preparation into the 1930's. In addition to the cook stove, there was a homemade table about 5 feet by 15 feet, with a long bench on each side. I do not recall ever visiting except when three shifts were required to feed those present—with the first shift involving the children under 12, the second shift the males of 12 or older, and the third and final shift the females 12 or older, who had been involved in the cooking and serving. The house had no electricity, so the table had several kerosene lamps, together with a bowl for salt, and a similar bowl for sugar. One from outside the area had to be very careful in sweetening their coffee or salting their eggs, as I found out the hard way.

There was a screened porch off one side of the kitchen, which had the luxury of a hand pump to provide water for cooking or bathing, so that the trip outside to an overflow (an artesian well common in the swampy area) was unnecessary (one had to leave the house only to use the outhouse some fifty feet away). Saturday was a day for bathing, and this was done in a tin wash tub on the porch and with some unwritten but known code for preventing intrusion by the opposite sex of the one bathing. The soap was homemade lye soap, a tan substance cooked in a large pot outside the kitchen door, and stiff brushes substituted for wash cloths. But I will never forget the sweet ambiance Saturday evening after everyone had had their weekly bath, and were ready to hitch the mule to the wagon the next morning and go the mile into town for Sunday School and church.

My paternal grandmother died on September 24, 1941, and my paternal grandfather on March 9, 1943. Until that time, only my father and his sister Mary, the oldest, had moved away from the homeplace—Mary with her husband to Hamlet, and my father never really returned to live after he had left home for the University of North Carolina—his money taking him as far as Fayetteville, and walking the rest of the way to Chapel Hill.

Being the oldest boy, and with the farm requiring the children to share in the work, my father took on the role of teacher for his brothers and sisters. He enjoyed this role, and his first employment was that of teacher in a little one-room school house in Butters, a dozen miles away. I have a faded picture of him and his students, some twenty in all, and ranging from apparent ages of about six to about 15—together with a goose perched on the shoulders of one of them. He was proud of the fact that one of these pupils later became a dean at Wake Forest University. It was the teaching experience, however, that spurred him to enroll in 1912 in the University of North Carolina, where he supported himself by chopping wood for the student dining hall. He would not be able to finish, for the war took him away when he enlisted in 1914, and was assigned to an Army Gunnery School at Fort Monroe in Norfolk, Virginia, where he attained a rating as a radioman. An order for two pairs of shoes, size 14, could not be filled, and thus when his battalion went overseas, he stayed behind and became a radio communications instructor.

My father's brother Foster, who had served with the Marines in China during WWI, lived with his wife Katie and daughter Hazeline in a little house within sight of the home place, which could be reached by walking in four minutes—two for walking, and two for removing the sand spurs that one's bare feet would collect. Down some four hundred yards from Foster's house was brother Jarvis, who had five children, all girls, and who was clearly my father's favorite sibling. He and my father would talk happily for hours when we visited. My father's sister Ila, and his brother Chester, built their houses a mile away behind the cotton mill that was just across the railroad track from the homeplace, and brother Frank was about a mile to the west where the ground rose out of the swamp and farming in the sandy soil was possible. That accounted for all but my father's sisters Stella and Mary. Stella and her husband and seven children, all girls but two, lived alternately in their own house in Bladenboro or with my grandfather and grandmother when adverse circumstances caused them to lose their residence. Mary, my father's older sister, married a Mercer, and, as noted, lived in Hamlet, NC. I had no contact with her or her family.

My aunts and uncles had so many children that I could not really keep up with them. Ila's oldest son Clyde, one of eleven children, was a good friend, but died in an automobile accident. Their farm was used more for raising animals than growing crops, and I can remember two things about them: Ila's husband "Gumery" (for Montgomery) coming home from whatever work he had been doing, in his old car, driving it up to the kitchen window, and attaching wires from the car battery to a radio inside the kitchen. Everyone would gather around and enjoy this remarkable modern convenience. The other thing I recall was their large Shropshire hog, an animal of considerable ill humor, that we could ride if we were brave enough.

So far as I know, Chester was a railroad engineer all of his working life. At that time I visited them (in the 1930s), Chester had two sons, Chester Jr., and Robert, and two younger daughters, Florence and Eva Gray (another son came much later). The two boys were aged on each side of me by a few months, and they were my favorite cousins by far. I have lost track of them, but during WWII, Chester was assigned as a Seaman to a light cruiser, and in a boxing match at Pearl Harbor was declared the Pacific Fleet champion. He had always been pretty tough, so this was no surprise. What did surprise me was that his younger, smaller, and much more timid brother Robert, whom I had been able to beat up when bested by his brother Chester, and who was also a Navy enlisted man, gained the title of boxing champion of India shortly thereafter.

Stella's husband was a man named Earl Edwards (pronounced "Eddards"). There was a period in the 1930s when he was appointed Bladenboro's lone policeman, and he got into trouble when he shot through the door of the town's General Store because someone inside did not respond to his call to come out, and this act destroyed the masculinity of the store's owner, who, though drunk, had some political clout as well. Earl was sentenced to a two year stretch in the state penitentiary, but escaped, and hid out for a year or so on a desolate and then uninhabited stretch of beach south of Wilmington known as Holden's beach.

Here he lived, in a "Mullet Shack" built by local fishermen, for over a year until he became a "cold case," surviving primarily on seafood that he could acquire from the ocean and the adjoining marshes.

My father's brother Frank was apparently his mother's favorite. But throughout his life he was plagued by bad luck. Money borrowed for crops had to be repaid by my grandfather when Frank's crops failed; his mules had a tendency to die unexpectedly, and although the soil was sandy, burying a mule was a proposition of considerable proportions. He decided one year to plant only okra, which was a cash crop of much promise—but found that the crop matured within a week, and that the market could accommodate but a portion of his crop when it was in its prime, and there was no market for week-old okra. When we visited my grandfather, he would sooner or later hitch up the wagon with his mule, and we would take the one-lane two rut road through the swamps to Frank's house, where the children would dance with joy, saying "Daddy, now we can cut the 'bigun'"—meaning, of course, the huge watermelon that required more than the family to dispose properly of it, and which had been saved for just such an occasion.

One thing that I learned about my grandfather was his prowess in making wine or moonshine. He concealed a jug of something potent in the bottom of a filled corn crib, with an inserted rubber tube just under the surface of the corn where he could find it. My cousins Chester and Robert delighted in sharing their discovery of this marvel, and I although I never joined them in sneaking a "chaw" of tobacco, I recall the sweet taste of the potable in the corn crib.

Making alcoholic beverages was not only a skill, but a prized art form. I recall when prohibition was eased, and beer sales were permitted in some counties in North Carolina. My grandfather, possibly threatened by this "store-bought pizen," took a specimen bottle, filled it with purchased beer, and sent it to the State Agricultural Agent in Raleigh for analysis. He proudly proclaimed the results that he said came back in a couple of weeks: "Dear Sir, your mule has enureses."

But all the stringencies of absence of electricity and plumbing were eased by the remarkable camaraderie at tobacco curing time. The men (meaning males of age 10 or better) would gather at the tobacco barn, where the curing process would require several days of carefully controlling the temperature, but where the requirements for tending the fire were sufficiently lax that there was much time for storytelling and music via guitar or fiddle. These evenings would follow days of preparation where the women bunched and tied the freshly plucked tobacco leaves and strung them on slats for insertion in the tobacco barn for curing, and the toddlers would amuse themselves by playing with the green tobacco worms that were brushed off the tobacco leaves.

Despite inability to remove the stickiness from handling the green tobacco and the constant infestation of gnats and mosquitoes which were sufficient to keep the evening party stag, these were wonderful times. And they were always climaxed by baling the cured tobacco and carting it into town to one of the several tobacco auction barns, and coming home with the cash that would largely sustain the family until the next year's tobacco crop sale.

Chapter 2

Camp Kelly

I made a startling discovery at my father's funeral, in the family church in Bladenboro, North Carolina, in 1964 when I spied a man about his age that I had never seen before, but who was an almost exact duplicate of my father, and who was obviously known to the others present. Persistent questioning revealed who he was.

When my grandfather married, his wife, Eliza Lennon Kelly, had a spinster sister who came to live with them. Somehow the sister got pregnant, and produced a child that she named Campbell or "Camp." The man with the eerie resemblance to my father was, of course, Camp Kelly.

I was intrigued by this discovery, and pressed for information about this man. One of the most significant things that I learned grew out of the fact that in the little rural community of only several hundred people there could be no secrets, and Camp's bastardy was well known. He grew up ostracized and bitter. In fact, he was reported to have read the Bible through seven times looking for contradictions. In the process, however, he apparently became deeply religious.

My grandfather, although now probably faced with a marriage from which the joy had gone, felt it was only right to assure that Camp could make a living, and used him to run a donkey engine and portable sawmill in the swamps, where Camp and a crew of blacks would harvest cypress trees and convert them into planks. One hot August day Camp was unable to get the donkey engine started, and the more he tried without success, the madder he became. The crew of a dozen blacks stood by, waiting for their jobs to begin.

Finally, in desperation, Camp pulled out his Bible from his overall pockets, closed his eyes, pointed his head skyward, and for some fifteen or twenty minutes prayed vigorously for the Good Lord to send a great forked bolt of lightning down to destroy that donkey engine and to strike every one of those God-damned lazy 'niggers' dead." When he finished and opened his eyes, he found that whether the Good Lord had heard his prayer or not, the work force of blacks had not only heard it but had taken its authenticity seriously, and had scattered into the swampy woods.

But it was at my father's funeral, more than two decades after my grandparents' deaths, that I not only acquired a step-uncle, but also began to understand more completely my paternal grandmother. I had never seen her smile during her lifetime, and had assumed that this was a function of her rheumatism, for she kept a jar of "Rub-My-Tisim" liniment on the mantel above the walk-in fireplace in the kitchen. I do not know what happened to her sister, but my grandmother became a grim and stoic woman, and one who resented "Pa's" Sunday afternoon story telling to the children when he should have been "down in the swamps apraying." And, I understood, too, the account of how my father's brother Foster lost his front teeth—as an adolescent, he made the grave mistake of saying "Damn!" one evening while "Ma" was poking up the fire in the kitchen fireplace with the cast iron poker.

Chapter 3

Grandma Johnson

My mother's mother and my grandmother, Lucretia Dundenah Ledbetter Johnson, was no ordinary woman, and, as will become apparent, had an extraordinary influence on my young life.

She was born December 9, 1861, and could recall slightly older peers talking about hearing gunfire from Civil War skirmishes. Her father, born in 1833, was a physician, who had deserted her mother, Elizabeth Craven (b. May 18, 1855) when my grandmother was three months in utero, and until a cousin did some genealogical research 125 years later, I assumed as true the family rumor that he had gone in the service during the Civil War, had served as a physician at Andersonville, and had died in one of the epidemics there. In actuality, it seems he had run off with another woman, an 18 year old beauty named Harriett Carney, but had shortly contracted a fatal disease, believed to be typhoid fever, dying on August 22, 1862—at the tender age of 29. I have a picture of him taken in 1862 in his doctor's office, a skull prominent in the background.

When my grandmother was fifteen, she took food and water to a group of men who were driving sheep through the rural area near Liberty, NC, where she lived. One of the men had been stricken with some strange malady, and she tended him while he was in the area. This act of kindness backfired, for she contracted polio, and was paralyzed, being bedridden for the next two years.

She frequently talked about an older sister named Jesse, who must have been as fiercely determined to keep her world under control as my grandmother was. Jesse decided to try warm baths for the legs several times a day, a treatment later "discovered" by and named for a Sister Kenny. With time, my grandmother responded to this, and began to resume some mobility—though for the rest of her life, she would have to drag one foot when she walked.

Winchester Ledbetter, M.D. Circa 1862

    Both she and Jesse were people that interacted with and influenced greatly other people in the community. I recall the story of a new mother whose infant was simply wasting away. My grandmother discovered that her breast milk was watery, and contrived a paste of flour and water which could be squeezed through a handkerchief as if it were a teat. She had the baby fed this way, and the baby began to gain weight and ultimately thrived.

    I learned many wondrous things from listening to her talk to friends. Her house in Liberty was not underpinned, but on stone joists, and the crawl space was two or three feet high. The house was on the edge of town, and its underside seemed a haven for drunks on Saturday night who could not quite make it home. Grandma assured me that not one of these men ever tried this but once, and from the quiet but confident way in which she expressed this, there could be no doubt that it was true.

    A more telling episode came when she was in her early 20's. A neighbor's child came home from school with welts on her back from a whipping she had received at school. Her offense—she was caught reading Hawthorne's *The Scarlet Letter*. My grandmother did not show any emotion, but borrowed a mule the next morning, rode side saddle to the little one-room school a few miles away, entered and stripped the teacher of her outer garments before the class and horsewhipped her with the prod she had used to keep the mule on course. The community lost a teacher, but gained an advocate for reasonableness and common sense.

Junius Houston Johnson and Lucretia Ledbetter Johnson, Circa 1890

Lucretia married Junius Houston Johnson, a dashing young man born Nov. 19, 1864, on May 11, 1890. He was employed by the railroad, and after several assignments in small North Carolina communities shortly became station master in McColl, SC, a position he held for the rest of his life. There was an abundance of time between trains, and this was invested in practice with the locals that led to his becoming checker champion of South Carolina. My grandmother remembered him for two habits that bugged her but that she could not break. First, he wore his hat except while sleeping, removing it from his head and placing it beside the bed when he retired, and sitting up the next morning, putting the hat back on, and then getting out of the bed. The other habit was sitting by the fireplace in the evening after supper, chewing tobacco, and spitting at—but frequently missing—the fireplace. Restoring the fireplace to a state of grace became a daily chore for my grandmother, but when my grandfather died of causes unreported to me but unexpectedly on September 20, 1912, she said she frequently wished he were still "sitting there a-spitting."

They had built a large house with a wrap-around porch, and kept a milk cow in the fenced in yard. Shortly (in 1891 and 1894), Lucretia had two daughters, the second of whom was my mother, and a younger son (in 1903). But unfortunately, it was on September 20, 1912 when the father died suddenly, leaving my grandmother with the girls, the nine year old boy, a house, and a milk cow. Not to be daunted, my grandmother began to take in boarders, and to market the milk produced by the cow. Her hard work and frugality in the next two decades had remarkable results—she ended up owning much of the business area of the little town of McColl, South Carolina, and my mother had the first automobile owned by anyone in that town, as well as tuition for a fancy boarding school for girls, the Edgefield Academy, where she learned such diverse things as how to play the piano and how to write with one of the new office machines, what we now call a typewriter.

Johnson House, McColl, SC, 1902. From left to right: John Parker; Dempsey Johnson; Cleo Johnson and cat, J.H. Johnson holding Vivian Johnson, Lucretia Johnson, Lady the Cow, and "Uncle Bill."

Upon completion of her studies, my mother moved to another town to become a "typewriter" for a friend of the family who owned a cotton mill. She acquired a room in a private home a block or two from her work station and from the Methodist Church that she dutifully attended each Sunday. My grandmother must have been too occupied to tell her much about the birds and the bees, for one Sunday when she was walking back from church, a young man, whom she had seen shyly eying her throughout the service, caught up with her and offered to help her across the street. In so doing, he held her arm. The next week, she was late with her period, and became terrified that she had gotten herself pregnant by letting this young man touch her as she crossed the street.

My mother's older sister, Cleo, was someone who, although usually wrong, never lacked for an opinion and could be counted on to be outspoken. Cleo married a young textile engineer who had patented several special machines for the manufacture of yarn or yard goods, one of which involved twisting cotton fibers in opposition to one another so that the resulting yarn had an elastic quality. In time, he became superintendent of a large cotton dry goods knitting mill in Burlington, N.C. He was frugal and devout—I recall his old Essex which he modified in some way many times and which he kept running for some 20 years by rebuilding parts that failed. He would stop by the side of the road on every trip of more than a few miles and pray for safe passage. He delighted in providing Christmas presents for the children of each of the some 100 employees of his mill, and dispensed them dressed in a Santa Claus suit the day before Christmas in a large room at the mill. This was in the early 1930's, when men were delighted to have a job, and I recall the average pay at the mill was thirty cents an hour: a wage my father made when he returned from his extended convalescence at Mt. McGregor hospital in New York State, in a job of packing yarns and fabric for shipment that my uncle benevolently provided.

But while this philanthropic manager puttered with improving a knitting machine or modifying the old Essex, his wife (and my aunt) grew more and more eccentric. I recall that she could not resist purchasing any new cook stove that came on the market, and that she could not relinquish the ones she had. Accordingly, her kitchen was packed with five different cook stoves. Unfortunately, they were seldom used, for she disliked cooking, and the family dined on sandwiches, cereal, and fruit. When her husband retired, she had him build several dozen rabbit hutches behind their garage, and she bred rabbits for sale to the local hospital, where they were in considerable demand for pregnancy testing. From her sales, she delighted in keeping careful count of the number of young girls in that community who had risked pregnancy.

My mother's sister also found that after each of her five children were born, she became too sickly to take proper care of them. One died from diphtheria shortly after birth, but my mother took most of them for the first two years. The oldest became a writer and editor for a trade journal and assembled a very fine stamp collection, and treated my mother with the kind of affection one usually reserves for their birth mother.

My grandmother's youngest, a boy, had the handicap of growing up with three dominating females—his mother and his two sisters—directing him about. He tried several business ventures, being financed by my grandmother. One that I recall from visiting him when I was very small was an ice-making plant in Lillington, NC, where 100 pound chunks of ice were produced for commercial and residential use. The major impact on me, however, was the present of a monkey wrench owned originally by his great-uncle, Andrew Johnson. (This was later presented to my dear friend Harvey Estes, M.D. chair of the Family Medicine Department at the Duke University Medical School, research colleague, and collector of antique tools.)

The Andrew Johnson named was President Andrew Johnson. I was unaware of the relationship until long after I had completed college and graduate study, and had stumbled on it one day in perusing the family Bible. I assumed that I had not been told of this illustrious ancestor because of his near-impeachment, but no, I was wrong. My mother told me that we never recognized him as a relative because it was generally known that he wore a pistol in his belt at all times, and (this was the real kicker) *breakfasted on bourbon and eggs.*

But the brother found permanent employment as a radio (and later TV) technician, working for a retail electronic sales firm in Greensboro. I remember visiting him there one day, and finding a bottle of gin in his kitchen. He discovered my discovery, and asked me to be sure not to tell my father, as he was very much against alcohol. This surprised me, for I had always thought that my mother, like my grandmother, was the prohibitionist. His son, and my cousin, became an airport control technician, working at Miami International Airport, but retired to a mobile home in which he and his wife traversed the country—until an accident while on the way to Jimmy Carter's Sunday School Class, which served to ground them in Stuart, Florida. (They now live, in 2007, in a retirement community in Pompano Beach, Florida).

Returning to my recollection of my maternal grandmother: my father developed a serious hyperthyroid condition about the time of the great depression, and this interfered with his work. As a consequence, we moved, in 1928, in with my grandmother, who had purchased a large house in Graham, North Carolina, and my father was hospitalized for almost two years at Mt. McGregor Hospital in New York State. My grandmother never lacked for a strong opinion on everything, and, though partially crippled by her childhood polio, was a personality of such strength that one could sense when she was in the room. We lived with her—not she with us. When my father returned, he shortly secured work as a life insurance salesman, and we moved to Greensboro, where I entered school, and then to High Point, where my sister Sara was born July 19, 1932. But my father's health problems continued, and we moved back in with my grand-mother in 1933, and here my youngest sister was born on November 22 of that year. My grand-mother died in March, 1940, and her house became our house for the lifetime of my parents.

My grandmother had two cats when we moved in—the Papa Cat and the Monkey Cat. The Papa Cat was a huge solid white short hair cat with a large square head, and was complacent unless challenged by a dog. The size of the dog made no impression on the Papa Cat, who seemed to relish any challenge from any dog foolish enough to impinge itself upon him. He would remain motionless and serene until the dog came very close, but must have acquired some characteristics from his mistress for it would then spring into action with his claws and fangs coordinating nicely to dispatch the poor animal that had disturbed him. I recall neighbors moving into the area with large dogs, and their coming to apologize about what their dog would surely do to our cats. But my grandmother never worried about this, and the Papa Cat remained in firm control of his territory. The Monkey Cat was affectionate, and he and I became close buddies, close enough that when it became time to have my portrait taken by a professional photographer at age 4, the Monkey Cat shared the pose (that's us on the front cover). And our block on North Main Street in Graham became known for its neurotic dogs with tattered ears.

As indicated earlier, no one made up my grandmother's mind for her—she could very well do this for herself. She taught, until a few years before her death, a Bible class in the Methodist Protestant Church, a class that bore her name. Several sayings I remember well: in politics, she said she always voted for the man, not the party, but quickly added that she had never known a Republican she would vote for. Another favorite, used to advise on entering arguments not worth having: "Never get in a pissing match with a skunk." And I recall when I reached pubescence, she called me aside and told me to be careful with girls—"It only takes nine months and fifteen minutes to get into trouble."

I recall a time when we were having the planking on the front porch which stretched across the front of the house replaced with new planking. I was eight or nine years old then, and while the workmen were at lunch I decided to explore the damp ground under the house that could be accessed by the hole at one end of the porch where the planking had been removed. My grandmother, who was sitting in a rocking chair on the yet untouched portion of the porch, fiercely forbade me from doing this, but judging her distance from me too great, her handicapped leg too unwieldy, and my movements too quick for her, I jumped down into the opening. When I did, I landed on an electrical cord to a portable light the workmen were using, and given the damp ground received a very considerable shock. I was convinced that my grandmother had somehow reached the opening as I jumped in, and had kicked me hard in the rump as I went down.

In spite of her tendency to make all decisions and to hold strong opinions, she had a heart of gold. I recall that when I was about 10 I wanted an air rifle more than anything I could think of. She had strong feelings about guns of any sort, and lost no opportunity to preach to me about this. Yet, when Christmas came that year, I sneaked into the living room where we had the Christmas tree after the others had gone to bed, and there under the tree was a beautiful Daisy BB gun.

I was sufficiently excited that I could not go to sleep. In desperation, I decided to pass the five or six hours before morning by praying as a diversion. I very quickly ran out of things to pray about, and recall feeling very guilty when I remembered that Moses, for gosh sakes, had prayed for forty days and nights at some similar crisis point in his life. And there I was, pooping out after only a couple of hours!

But morning came, I took proud possession of the air rifle, and questioned my mother and father if either of them had purchased this for me. I can recall saying, when they assured me that they had not, "Then there has to be a Santa Claus, for Grandma would never do such a thing." Grandma, of course, was the one who had dragged one foot into the local hardware store and had purchased the air rifle, concealed it under her skirt, smuggled it home and hid it in her steamer trunk in which she kept the pint bottle of bourbon a nephew doctor had prescribed, a teaspoonful at a time, for tachycardia many years earlier.

There was one other episode with my grandmother that she felt would have an indelible impact on my life. This involved the movie, shown occasionally in the 1930s, entitled "Ten Nights in a Barroom." It was a tear-jerking account of a successful business man who was reduced to a pitiful state by spending ten nights in a barroom on the way home from his business. I recall at day 10 his discovery of a bit of money in his pocket, and his planning to buy his little girl a doll, but on the way to purchase it succumbing to the lure of the barroom, where his little girl found him, in a disheveled array, when he was late getting home, having spent his money on demon rum instead of the promised doll. Although my grandmother was against movies, she was more against alcohol, and had said many times that if one ever dared to take just one drink, they would be hooked. The movie, she felt, was eloquent proof of this. When it came to one of the two cinemas in Graham, she reached into her little pinch-penny purse and gave me money for admission. Thus, I went to see "Ten Nights in a Barroom," but found Tom Mix or Lash LaRue more to my tastes.

My grandmother died at home in her sleep on March 15, 1940.

Chapter 4

My Parents—The Early Years

For some reason unknown to me, my grandmother moved from McCall, SC, to Bladenboro, NC, with my mother (b. July 1, 1897) who secured work in the local bank. My father (b. March 4, 1892) was employed there as a teller. Although she was short (4' 11") and he was tall (6' 5"). They became a couple and ran off on June 18, 1920, to Fayetteville with another couple to get married. My mother noted that she weighed 90 pounds, and that my father weighed 189 pounds; he impressed her by drinking a pint of water before the wedding ceremony so that he could be exactly 100 pounds heavier.

They honeymooned at White Lake, making the trip down the one lane sandy road from Fayetteville in a T Model Ford. Their first purchase was a Victrola and a number of records (I recall vocals by an Irish tenor), and the Victrola lasted until some seventy years later when it was disposed of in their estate auction.

They shortly moved to Raleigh, where my father secured a job with the Raleigh YMCA. They rented a little house not far from Central Prison, where sirens signaling an escapee not infrequently interrupted their sleep. Their house was also infested with honeybees, that had found a home between the siding and the internal paneling, and that ultimately yielded almost a hundred pounds of honey when the siding was removed.

After a brief time at this address, they moved to a better neighborhood where my mother produced her first born, a stillborn female. The birthing was at the home as was the custom then, and this loss weighed heavily on them. Shortly after, they must have tried again, for I was born on February 4, 1925, and given a first and middle name from my maternal ("Junius") and paternal ("Ayers") grandfathers. My father, as the oldest boy in his family, had had the responsibility of teaching his siblings, and his first job had been that of a teacher in a one room schoolhouse at Butters, NC. He had always hankered to be a teacher. So. with the expanded family to support, he resigned the YMCA job, and entered the teacher education program at the University of North Carolina in Chapel Hill.

Vivian Johnson Davis and Roy Davis, Circa 1920

As noted, I was born in February, 1925; it was in the fall of that year that my father reentered the University of North Carolina to obtain a teaching credential. This enabled him to gain a position as Latin teacher and Principal of a high school in a mill district of Burlington, and we moved in with my maternal grandmother in nearby Graham. The school was no prize assignment, and had a history of persistent vandalism. My father was proud of the fact that he solved this quickly by identifying the ring leader of the gang that broke the windows regularly, by calling this young tough into his office and commissioning him to patrol the grounds at night and to beat the stuffing out of any one who damaged school property. Like his father a more earthy description of what would be beaten out of anyone damaging school property was beyond his oral habits. My father told this young man that he would protect him no matter what, and that together they could defeat city hall if necessary. The session must have been convincing, for there was no more vandalism—although some students later showed up at school with black eyes or bruises.

My father was thoroughly conversant in Latin, and at one point told me that my name "Junius" was Latin for the month of June. I asked him why I had been named this when I was born in February. My father simply shared the wise look at which he was so good, and said that one day I would discover the answer. It was not until I was in my forties that I realized it was that I was *conceived* in June.

Unfortunately, thyroid problems and an exothalmic goiter shortly interrupted the new marriage, and my father had a thyroidectomy at the one hospital in the state that at that time was delving into this matter—Charlotte Memorial Hospital in Charlotte, some 150 miles away. He was hospitalized for several weeks prior to the surgery, and I recall visiting him, with my mother, for a half day shortly after his surgery. Like the auto mechanic who promises to return any worn parts that he replaces, the surgeon had put the portion of the thyroid gland that had been removed in a glass dish, and this was on a table near the bed in the hospital room. I remember that it looked to me as if it was something he could very well do without.

His convalescence was not easy. He had lost considerable weight, and felt he could not return to the rigors of the school. Having an interest in footwear probably from difficulties in getting a GI issue of size 14 in his enlistment in the Army in 1914, he answered an ad from Bronson Shoe Company for a salesman, and with a kit provided by the company began peddling shoes to friends and neighbors. This proved to be unsatisfactory, and, with health continuing to be a problem, he entered Mt. McGregor Sanatorium in upstate New York, a charity hospital which specialized in thyroid problems. Here he spent the better part of the next two years. My mother and I continued to live with my maternal grandmother during this time, and though we lived frugally, we had no serious unmet needs that financial resources could resolve.

Chapter 5

Growing Up

The two earliest memories I have were being rocked and comforted by my mother just after a frightening injury. The first was when I was about two years old and lying on a cot with a bottle when I rolled off and apparently broke my nose. I remember distinctly being picked up, mopped up, and rocked until the bleeding had stopped. The second instance was when I was about 4 and was riding in the rear seat of our T-Model Ford touring car in High Point and I leaned on the door handle as my father made a turn and I fell out on the pavement. I was more frightened than hurt, but this accident occurred at a corner where there was a PureOil station, and someone there produced a cane-bottomed chair for my mother to sit in while she held me until I began to have more interest in the crowd of onlookers than in a couple of skinned knees.

My mother had no stomach for the going practices of child rearing, but substituted her own. I found from the family photograph album that I had been garbed in dresses until I was in my third year. My mother later explained that it made it so much easier to change my diaper, and that when she was young this was standard operating procedure. And, of course, she could not understand why other mothers ignored this option with their male children, and thus labored unnecessarily when diaper change was necessary.

My mother was an avid cook, rising at 6 A.M. each morning to mix dough for biscuits in a dish pan that would be used later for washing the breakfast dishes. Although she got considerable joy from her cooking, there were only three techniques that she knew how to apply: these were baking, boiling and frying. But she started each morning with grits and hot homemade biscuits. Another favorite of hers was vegetable soup, seasoned with a ham bone that our grocer would save and sell to her for a nickel. The soup would be started on a Monday, and leftovers during the week would be added and the concoction reheated. Thus, our menu had considerable variety. Things she did not like—tomato catchup, for example—she never purchased, because, I have heard her tell others, "My children do not like it." This she really believed. I recall the surprise I had when years later in graduate study at Columbia University I discovered that the proper cut of steak could be broiled.

But my mother was as honestly and openly as simple as my father was intellectually brilliant. I can remember one day when I was in upper elementary school she suddenly looked up from her sewing machine (she made all her own clothes), and, obviously stunned by an impulsive thought, said to me "Son, do you use profanity?" Probably reflecting genetic makeup from my male parent, I responded "Why, hell no, Mother." But she believed me, and breathed a considerable sigh of relief.

For my mother, cleanliness was not next to Godliness—it WAS Godliness. Giving a deaf ear to any protests from the neighbors: at 5 PM each day, she stripped any little child that happened to be at our house or playing with me in the yard, and dumped us together in a tin washtub just off the back steps. A little girl that I dated when in high school lived two houses down and was a frequent playmate, and accordingly had no secrets from me. At a high school class reunion some 50 years later, she could not attend (she then lived in Texas), but she wrote the group that one of her fondest childhood memories was not the tub, the memory of which I think she repressed, but that she appreciated the fact that although she was afraid she could not find her way from her house to the school, I would always walk with her to assure that she found her way. This I had forgotten.

It was before I started to school that my father had to go to the sanatorium in upstate New York to recuperate from the thyroid condition remaining after surgery. He was gone for almost two years, and my mother and I continued to live with by maternal grandmother. All of us suffered from the separation, but he wrote us daily, and usually had something cheerful to say. It was this period where he began to write poetry under the pen name of "May B. True," and most of his poems were published in a daily column in the *Charlotte Observer* under the title "Fresh Country Verses."

Upon his return from the sanatorium, he secured a job as a life insurance salesman with the Pilot Life Insurance Company, working in the Greensboro area. So, we moved to that city. My mother confessed later that the house was really a shack and she was embarrassed by that as well as the fact that at Christmas time they could afford only one small cast-metal toy truck about 3 inches long, but my memory of the time and house was pure pleasure. My dad was home, for one thing—and for another, the house sat on pillars about three feet tall, and the floors had numerous cracks through which I could poke things into the house from underneath, or vice versa. This was great fun.

I was enrolled in the first grade here, and that led to a situation the memory of which surely shaped my later life. My teacher was a woman with sturdy hips named Miss Hannah, and was good natured enough to let us get away with calling her "Miss Banana." But she was not so condescending when one day I tried out some choice expletives I had picked up somewhere. Miss Hannah yanked me up, dragged me into the girls' washroom, and proceeded to wash my mouth out with soap, using the foul green stuff from the dispenser just over each wash basin. I can still taste the vile and powerful flavor, and the fact that I was hauled into the girls' washroom for this ritual only added insult to injury. But I never again used questionable language before someone for whom I did not know well enough to gauge the probable reaction. Ms. Hannah had achieved what Pavlov would call "One trial conditioning."

My father's physical condition gradually improved, and he was modestly successful in his job as a life insurance agent. During the summer before I was to enter the third grade, we moved to High Point, NC, where he had a better option with Metropolitan Life Insurance Company. But my admission to the third grade was a major hurdle. I had started school when I was five years old, with my 6th birthday in February after admission the previous fall. My third grade teacher, a terror whose name (Miss Frances Ward) I will never forget, simply felt I was not old enough for the third grade, and did what she could to move me back to the second grade. I am not sure what happened, but my father, who had been in public school education, had some hand in getting me back in Miss Ward's classroom after a brief stint in the second grade. She resented this, I am sure, for the school day never ended without some indignity being forced on me. Ms. Ward delighted in getting the other pupils to share in debasing me in every way that eight year olds, and a teacher of the same or lower mentality, can contrive.

(As providential fate might have it, some twenty years later when I was graduate dean at the University of North Carolina in Greensboro, who should apply for admission to graduate study in education for a required course to renew her teaching certificate but one Miss Frances Ward, from Ray Street School in High Point! The fact that she scored below chance on the Miller Analogies Test, which I used as an admissions credential, gave me a wicked but welcome feeling of elation. I rejected her application. I do not know what happened to her, but I lost no sleep over denying her admission.)

It was in High Point, on July 19, 1932, that the oldest of my two sisters was born. This was an occasion of extreme joy for me, and I suspect I was as proud of her as were my parents.

My father was employed in High Point, as noted earlier, as an agent for Metropolitan Life. This was the early thirties, and I recall his gratitude that he, unlike so many others affected by the great depression, had work. (I recall his ejaculation "Hooray" when we encountered on the streets the sign "Men Working."). Many of the policies he was responsible for carried a charge to the holder of a nickel a week, and this sum had to be collected and entered. Most of his policy holders were black, and he frequently let me ride with him as he collected in the evenings. He was warmly received, and we were invited to frequent fish fries at the Negro Baptist Churches, where fish breaded with corn meal and hush puppies were cooked in a large cast-iron pot filled with boiling vegetable oil. The evenings where we dined on this delicious bit of real soul food as he collected from the attendees, and as we joined in the socializing, made later dining on venison at the Nassau Inn in Princeton, NJ, a mediocre event.

Perhaps because of his absence for the considerable period of time when I was of preschool age, we both felt unusually close to each other. He was one of the brightest people I ever knew, and his imposing stature made me not only look up to him but feel, at a mature height of six feet, that I was rather short.

He made up for the time he had missed being at home. I recall many events that not only endeared me to him, but also contributed to my continuing development.

We were on a trip of some 130 miles to the beach below Shalotte, where my Uncle Edwards, the husband of his sister Stella, had escaped from Central Prison and hid out on among the sand dunes until interest was lost in his capture. The circumstances leading to this unusual residence have been recounted in an earlier section.

We found Uncle "Edderds," as he called himself, who invited us to stay for supper. I recall a wonderful evening on an isolated beach, with the surf only yards away, and feasting in near darkness on oysters roasted on a cast iron sheet covered with wet burlap and placed over an abundance of hot driftwood coals.

This wonderful evening almost crowded out of memory our stop on the way to find Uncle Edderds. My father knew the area from having grown up there abouts, and on the way to the beach below Shalotte, he turned into a one-lane sandy road into Deep Swamp where we ended up in a little community called Makatoba. This place had only several dozen inhabitants, who not only were unspoiled by the outside world into which they never ventured, but also had intermarried so that it would take three or four of them to add their IQs together to get a hundred. We spent an evening with perhaps a dozen of the men, who were sitting around a tobacco barn telling stories and drinking some rather potent brew that they had made, I think, from potato peels. The honest acceptance my father and I received was a strong and viable lesson that there are human qualities just as important, if not more so, than intelligence and financial comfort.

It was sometime in 1933 that I remember my father coming home early, sitting down at the kitchen table, and talking in low but obviously sad tones. It was clear that his was a private conversation, but I stood just outside the door. I remember vividly hearing one terrible word—"*FIRED!*" The household took on a quiet and serious aura, despite my new little sister, and within a short period of time, we got our belongings together, and moved back to Graham to live with my maternal grandmother, who was beginning to be in less than vigorous health. My father soon got a job as a postal clerk, and worked in this capacity until he retired sometime in the late 1950s. This was a mundane job for a person of his intelligence, but he made it a challenge by memorizing alternate postal routings and schedules over the country.

When time came for me to make curricular choices in high school, I found other options competing with Latin, and my father offered to solve this dilemma by teaching me himself, using his own textbooks carefully preserved from his days as a Latin teacher in high school. We got Caesar over the bridge before we both gave up on each other.

Although my father was extremely bright, and although for the larger part of his adult life he was handicapped by illness, he stood out among other people by his deep concern for human dignity regardless of race, creed, intelligence, or social position, for a thirst for playing devil's advocate when someone stated a strong opinion about anything, and a penchant for truly creative humor. I will give examples of each of these that I shall never forget.

Although we were in a financial position where we had more grits and potatoes than ham and beef, my father was scandalized in some quarters because he loaned the unmarried town prostitute money for milk for her several illegitimate children. That the children were hungry was all he really concerned himself about—certainly not their illegitimacy. And as I will report elsewhere, he was the driving force in creating an overnight refuge for servicemen caught trying to hitchhike through town but stuck for the night. He became active in the boy scout movement, and when no one could be found to organize a black boy scout troop, he went to work and did it himself, and as scoutmaster took a group of young blacks to a BSA Council camporee where they excelled all the other troops in competition. And I recall a friend who was a son in a mill family who invited me and several classmates to his house for some kind of party. I was the only one to come, and my father pointed out that the others invited were sons of people who considered themselves to be solid middle class, and therefore not proper to associate socially with my friend. My father was not a person who ever made a physical show of anger, but we could tell when he was deeply agitated inside, and my report of the evening where I was the only guest obviously bothered him. He redoubled his efforts to get me to ignore the differences that served as sorting factors among human beings.

My father reveled in debating others during the political campaigns for the nation's presidency. We never knew really who he would vote for, for when he found someone planning to vote for one candidate, he would take the other side and argue for the opponent. He was extremely clever, and could usually get anyone who had made a choice without thinking very much to reexamine his or her motives and decisions.

But overriding all other traits was his capacity for humor. My mother told me of his needling people in the 1920s who were inordinately proud of their pocket watch and chain splayed over their vested tummies, by asking "What time is it by your watch and chain?"

Something unexpected and deeply funny happened most every day. One incident was so very typical of his humor. I had been assigned to the U. S. Navy's Judge Advocate's office in the Charleston Navy Yard after my ship was decommissioned and as I waited for release from the Naval Reserve. Merchant ships were once again going into oriental ports, and the opium trade was flourishing in the nation's ports. Inevitably drunken sailors would get caught up in the traffic in such a way as to end up in the bay, where their bodies came to the surface a couple of weeks later. My most frequent job was to try to trace back and determine if their deaths were accidental, or, if not, the persons responsible for their deaths. In so doing, I found the most prolific source of useful information to be the prostitutes that plied their wares in the waterfront bars.

One prostitute, Lena, who had been most helpful, made it clear that she would like to do something nice for me, and could think of only one thing, something that would be involved in a weekend stay at a beach cottage. I could think of no gracious way to decline except to tell her that I thought too much of her to accept her kind invitation. Lena had never been treated this way, and she backed off in a kind of respectful but loving awe. "Besides," I said, "I plan to visit my parents this next weekend." Her response was immediate and emphatic: "Then I'm going with you!" I have forgotten how I wriggled out of this, but I shared the experience with my father by phone.

I came home to Graham, NC (which was only about 175 miles away) that weekend, alone, of course, and as I entered the living room, I spied a young lady sitting on the couch who seemed somehow quite familiar. Her makeup and dress indicated strongly that she was not a graduate of Vassar. My father came into the room, and said: "Son, this woman from Charleston has told us what you did and about her condition as a consequence, and your mother and I feel the only thing you can rightly do is to marry her." I stood in stunned silence, feeling that I had been set up by one of my informants, but as I stammered to protest, the young lady began to laugh. She was a country cousin, a daughter of my Aunt Stella and Uncle Edderds, that I had not seen since she was a little girl, and who had in passing through town stopped to visit a few minutes before I was expected home.

My father's humor was funny but, as in the example just cited, not necessarily kind. There was a period of time when our neighborhood was troubled by a peeper, who would peer into bedroom windows as people were undressing for bed. My parents slept in a bedroom at the rear of the house, and seldom bothered to draw the shades.

One evening as my mother was undressing for bed and my father was seated on the bed removing his shoes, she saw a face at the window. "Daddy," she said, "There's the peeper!" In his voice that could be clearly heard in the next county, my father quickly replied "Shoot him!" The face disappeared, and there was a loud crash outside. The next morning we found that a climbing rose on a trellis supported by two four by four posts set three feet apart had been hit in the middle with sufficient force that the posts, probably rotted from being in the ground for a number of years, had been broken off at the ground, and the prize climbing rose that had grown to magnificent heights on this trellis over the last dozen years was now on the ground.

The trellis was rebuilt, and the rose nursed back into the latticework. But this proved to be the end of the neighborhood siege by the peeper. My father simply asked the local police to look for a badly scratched young man, and he was shortly apprehended and hauled away to the Dorethea Dix Hospital in Raleigh, the state mental institution.

My father was troubled throughout his adult life by bunions, a consequence of having size 14 feet in a size 12 world. A bunion on his right foot became infected shortly after his retirement, and efforts to heal it failed. As gangrene set in, his leg was amputated just above the knee, and I discovered that this had happened when I was at Emory University in 1957 and learned about it from a post card from him with a brief comment about the surgery buried among other news from home, and signed "Long John Silver."

He had always been physically active, and this was a considerable change. My mother took over driving, and my father gained considerable weight. In 1964, he suffered a minor stroke, and requested to be taken to the VA Hospital in Durham, NC where cost-efficient care could be given. Once there, a young resident just out of Medical School decided that he must immediately verify the stroke, and had him hop on his one good leg for two minutes. Before the test could be completed, my father had a massive heart attack, and went into a coma. I was at ETS then, and on a business trip at the College Board offices in New York City when the phone call came in that he was at the VA hospital and in critical condition. I excused myself and caught the next plane to North Carolina, landing in Greensboro, and making the 70 miles from the Greensboro/High Point Airport to the VA Hospital in Durham by rental car in about 55 minutes. He was comatose when I arrived on July 1, 1964, my mother's birthday, and after sitting by his side briefly, I went out to the waiting area to console my mother. In a few minutes, the resident who had required the stress test called me out of the waiting area and astounded me by asking "Where do you want to send the body?" I am quite sure that that young man learned something that day that he will never forget. But this was the start of my lifelong lack of confidence in doctors, and the validity of the medical advice they so glibly provide.

My last memory of my father was the visitation that followed at the funeral home in Graham, with the open casket at one end. Many relatives and townspeople came, and I recall the noise level of the many conversations among people who had not seen each other for some time, and that indeed were loud and raucous enough to wake the dead. I could not help but rationalize, after first feeling great offense, that this was probably what he would have wanted. That may have triggered what I thought was a slight smile on the face of the corpse. After a brief ceremony at the Graham Presbyterian Church, where he had served as an elder and Sunday School teacher, he was buried in the family plot at Pinecrest Cemetery in Bladenboro, NC, his ancestral home, alongside my still-born sister.

My mother adjusted better than I had suspected she would. She became active with Senior Citizen groups that traveled about the state, and enjoyed the support of friends and neighbors. Some 20 years later, however, she began, in her 80s, to have trouble moving easily, and at one point fell and had to lay where she fell in the house for several hours before someone came in and discovered her. This experience provoked us to get a "Call Alert" system, involving a transmitter that she wore on a chain around her neck, and with a button to call for help in any emergency. No emergencies came after this, although she found several times when she bumped the button by mistake that help came roaring in in two or three minutes after signaling.

She reached a point in 1987 that we felt that living alone was too hazardous, and we moved her to a nursing home in nearby Mebane, owned and operated by the Presbyterian church. Her first year there was reasonably happy: I knew that she had adjusted when she told me that the funniest sight she had ever seen were six or eight old ladies, stripped nude, sitting in a row in the bathing area of the home eagerly waiting for their turn with the contraption that would lift them up and dip them in a large vat of warm water and thus provide a bath.

Her demise, on March 6, 1991 at age 93, was, like that of my father, largely a result of bad medicine. She had suffered from arthritis from her 60s, and the local doctor had prescribed a drug named Feldene, which in the next 30 years virtually destroyed her kidneys. When she suffered a kidney infection at age 93, he prescribed Tetracyclene, a drug my physician research associates said should be used only with great care and on vigorous young people. She died, at Alamance General Hospital, shortly thereafter. My two sisters, one from Columbia, SC, and the other from Blacksburg, VA, were with me at her bedside the last hour, and although she appeared to be in a coma for the last 24 hours, shortly before she died she opened her eyes, looked at us, smiled, and said softly "You are all here!."

Chapter 6

The Teen Age Years

I entered the teens somewhat as a loner. My mother insisted that I wear knickers rather than long pants, and I was certainly the only boy in my class in high school to be so attired. I was at least a year younger than any of my classmates, and was resented for making better grades with ease. Frequent asthma attacks probably occurred when the social situation at school was not tolerable. The teachers were partial to the sons and daughters of the town elite—the bankers, the merchants, the physicians, etc.—and my father, though respected as a Presbyterian elder and a scoutmaster, was only a postal clerk. Although I tried to keep my language simple, I was known—and touted in the school newspaper—as "The Walking Dictionary," a term with decided negative value in the largely mill town of Graham, North Carolina.

I became fast friends with another "loner,' one Mac Cook, the second son of our widowed (private) kindergarten teacher, who had unusual musical talent (he later taught at Juliard). Mac and I would hang out together, frequently with unexpected results. One that neither of us will ever forget had to do with a trip we made to the town cemetery one night, principally to show each other that we had no fears of such. On the way back, in pitch darkness, we took a wooded path that as a shortcut ran behind a Negro church to an avenue that would take us to Mac's house, and fresh from our experience with the interred deceased, stepped on a body lying across the path. It was obviously a drunk who had not made it home, for it emitted grunts when one of us, then the other, stepped on it. Nevertheless, we set a record getting home.

A later shared event came on Halloween. The town's one block of stores, and main street separating the two sides that was about sixty feet across, became the site of festivities and an opportunity for parents to show off their kid's Halloween costumes. Mac and I went down, feeling too grown-up to go in costume, but restless nevertheless. On the way home, we decided that it would be great sport to tie toilet paper bows on the main entrance to the public high school, and procuring a supply of paper from the trees nearby, we crept up the dark steps to the double doors leading inside, with the principal's office on the left, and the music teacher's office on the right. As we finished the bows and were affixing them to the doors, the lights suddenly flashed on, and "Shorty," the unaffectionate name given to our five foot six inch principal, came dashing out and grabbed each of us by the collar. When he saw whom he had caught, however, he roared in laughter, and said something like "You boys, of all people!" And "Boys will be boys." This response was because he had been expecting toughs from the mill district, not the sons of the scoutmaster and the kindergarten teacher who never made less than a "A" in their studies. Although we were grateful for the reprieve, we somehow felt sorry for the prejudices that Shorty exhibited against our classmates whose fathers and mothers worked in the several mills in Graham and nearby Burlington, and were a little angry that family status could absolve one of serious problems.

I had a cousin who lived outside the town in an area surrounded by piney woods. Some of my happiest days were spent exploring the area, and generally communing with nature. This probably led me to join the Boy Scouts, although I carefully avoided the white troop that my father served at that time and that accommodated the sons of the town's elite; instead, I joined Troop 41, where the members were sons of mill workers, and the scoutmaster a textile chemist employed by one of the mills. This troop met in the "Hut" for a Methodist church, which was a building with open space for various gatherings built behind the church itself. It was on a side street and directly faced a home on the other side where our high school English teacher rented an upstairs bedroom.

This teacher had a habit of completely undressing in the early evening, and languishing about in her room. She had a habit of massaging herself while in the altogether, and seldom attended to the blinds, a custom not uncommon in our little town. But in front of the scout hut, and affording an eye level view of her bedroom about 25 feet away across the street, was a climbable maple tree. This feature served, I am sure, as a recruiting device for Troop 41—that is, until one of the scouts, a lad that we called "Linky" instead of Lincoln, which was his real name, climbed up the tree, got a good look at our English teacher, and got sufficiently excited that he fell out of the tree and broke his arm. This let our scoutmaster know our secret, and climbing that tree was strictly forbidden from then on. (We suspected, however, that on nights other than troop meeting nights, he may have sneaked a peek himself, for our teacher had a body that was a perfect "ten," and our scoutmaster was no angel, but a rather regular guy.)

Our scout troop was unique, in that we always had an hour where the game was to wrestle each other to uncomfortable positions, and freeze in position when the scoutmaster blew his whistle. We always acquired a few bruises, but it was pure joy for the particular group that troop attracted. And my membership in the Boy Scouts made me eligible in the summer for attendance at the district scout camp, which was exceedingly well run. It was there that I gained my Red Cross

Water Safety Instructor rating, which was a step above Senior Life Guard. I won in competition for knot tying and surveying, and was inducted into the Order of the Arrow. The pure pleasure of the value-laden activities even made me oblivious to the particular skill of the camp cook, which was taking all the leftovers from the prior meal, adding a little sugar or syrup and cream sauce, and serving it for desert at the next lunch or dinner. Such things as finding a string bean in a pie was commonplace. We were extremely fortunate in having a man named "Pat" Patterson as the district scout executive and the director of the summer camp experience. Unlike many I later found attracted to scout leadership, he was ideally suited for this work, and scores of boys profited as I did from the experience.

I thoroughly enjoyed my two sisters: Sara, born July 19, 1932, in High Point, and Josephine, born November 22, 1933, shortly after we moved back to Graham. By the time I was in high school (fall, 1937), they were old enough to thoroughly enjoy, and we used to go on long hikes along the railroad tracks to Haw River, two or three miles away. My older sister found that she could thoroughly discombobulate me by mimicking the baby Sweetpea in the Popeye comic strip, by squatting and saying "GLOP!" and refusing to budge until thoroughly rested.

In school, she was far brighter than I, and made excellent grades—which was hard on our younger sister, who was only 16 months her junior. Josie, as we came to call her, became something of a rebel, developing an immense sympathy for any downtrodden, and at one point reportedly rebelled at school, climbing to the roof of the three story structure by utilizing the spaces where brick walls joining at an angle left toeholds that any person daring enough to try could use to scale the walls.

Both sisters went to Lees-McRae (Junior) College in Banner Elk. This was a Presbyterian institution that converted into a resort in the summer, employing students as resort employees so that they could pay their way during the academic year. Sara worked as a secretary in the Dean's office during the academic year, and both worked as waitresses in the dining room in the summer when the paying guests were there. Both finished with distinction: Josie as the person who made out like a bandit on tips in the dining room, and Sara, who like her mother made all her own clothes, and who was voted "best dressed" by her classmates. Following this college experience, Sara continued for her AB degree at the University of North Carolina in Chapel Hill, majoring in dance and recreation; she took a job as Director of Recreation for the city of Kinston, then offering primarily activities for service personnel at a base in the area. Josie took a hospital course in medical laboratory technology in Charlotte, and specialized in blood work as a Medical Technologist in hospitals, starting at the UNC Hospital in Chapel Hill.

Sara married Paul Lovingood, a geographer who moved from a faculty position in the Department of Geology at a western NC college to the University of South Carolina, where he served with distinction until retirement several years ago, punctuated by a couple of Fulbrights to African nations. Sara became the director of the kindergarten sponsored by the black YWCA in Columbia, SC, in the 1950s. She later picked up a Ph.D. in the USC School of Education, and then became a specialist in a school operated by the military for service families near Columbia. They reared three children: a boy who turned his mechanical genius into work as an electronics specialist; a daughter who became, like her mother, a specialist in early childhood education, and a daughter who became a Presbyterian minister. The latter has won an amazing number of national sweepstakes or lotteries, resulting in trips for two (her mother has accompanied her) to Germany, Africa, and Hawaii, among other fabulous prizes.

Josie married Jim Shotts, the son of the director of the student YMCA at the University of North Carolina, and Jim became a purchasing agent for Virginia Polytechnical Institute in Blacksburg, VA, where they bought a hundred acres of mountainside, the back parts of which were too rugged to inspect Over the next 30 years they turned a barn into a first class home, raised three highly successful boys and one beautiful daughter, participated in many activities of the Quaker Church, became involved in humanitarian work in an isolated village in internal Guatemala, and traveled in retirement to places like Viet Nam and Cuba.

In our high school in Graham, the teachers clearly favored some students as a function of their parent's role in the little community of Graham. In spite of my grades, which were straight As except for typing (I broke my arm about halfway through the course, and had to finish with one hand, and on which I got a "D"), I was passed over for the Honor Society, whose members were nominated by the teachers, by some individuals with poorer grades than mine. I sought refuge with two special friends, both from modest backgrounds: Tom Coble, and Dan Bulla. We were invincible and inseparable, calling ourselves "The Three Musketeers.". After high school graduation and service, Tom became a pharmaceutical representative, calling on doctors in a two state area, marrying a girl from the other side of town who spent her evenings with girl friends and who left him shortly, and remarrying a girl that looked just like her and settling in South Carolina. He later started a successful printing shop business, but died of a heart attack in his late 50s. Dan Bulla, on the other hand, always enjoyed being a mystery to people. We lost track of him until the word came that he had moved to Virginia and had learned to fly, probably in the service, and had tried to loop his plane without his seat belt fastened, falling to his death about the time the rest of us were overseas in WWII.

Our high school had a policy that anyone with an A average in a course did not have to take the final exam. Except for a typing class, I had a straight A average, and as a consequence never had an exam until my freshman year in college. It was at that point that I began to question sharply the policy of the high school in this regard.

The summer after high school was a significant period for me. I took a job as Life Guard and Boat Boy at a rural recreational locale known as Kimesville Lake, some 15 miles from Graham and only a stone's throw from Liberty, where my maternal grandmother had grown up. It was situated in a rural area, but had cabins that could be rented. The lake was formed by a dam on a rather substantial stream, and there was a swimming area just inside the dam. The backed up water, however, created a navigable stream leading about three miles up into the woods, and it was this course that permitted the lake owner to offer motorboat rides for a fee. I ran a cruise boat of about 20 feet in length, as well as rented out rowboats for those who came to fish or to spoon, and collected boat ramp fees for those who brought their own boats.

I recall a holiness preacher that came weekly with his boat and outboard motor. Frequently he had trouble getting the motor started after the boat was launched, and it was he who added a number of choice expletives to my vocabulary.

The owner of the lake was a genial entrepreneur, who had spent his life going from one money making scheme to another, always making just enough to eke out a sparse living but to invest in some new venture. He had purchased a truck and taken on a rural milk delivery route as a side line, and in one two week period when he was otherwise disposed, I drove the milk truck to all the country stores within a 40 mile radius, as well as served residential customers in the towns of Liberty and Siler City. One of my best customers was a house in Siler City with a red light in the porch fixture, but I knew enough to value their business and to take financial remuneration for my services, not give it for theirs. I was not so lucky with a residential customer in Liberty, where a most attractive girl was generally at home alone when I came with the daily quart of milk. I thoroughly enjoyed being invited in each trip, but unfortunately she came down with the German Measles while I was still on the route, and of course I followed suit.

The lake had a sandwich shop, and the owners left me in charge one day of the counter and their 6 year old daughter while they went somewhere. The little girl fell with a coke bottle in her hand, which shattered, leaving many slivers of glass in her hand. I removed them, applied bandages, and then passed out cold. This taught me that although I was probably appropriately tender, I could be tough when required.

But the Kimesville Lake area was a place unique in the state if not the entire south. Across the dirt road from the entrance to the lake was a combination Gulf station and general store, where some 20 local young men gathered around the pot belly stove inside during the winter, or on benches outside in front of the store and behind the pumps in the summer. On each Monday, one (they took turns) would steal a can of malt, several cakes of yeast, and 10 pounds of sugar, sneak across to the lake and commandeer a rowboat, proceed to the end of the lake several miles upstream, and mix the ingredients to make homebrew. This concoction would be put in loosely capped quart mason jars, and hidden in the stump holes within 100 yards of the end of the navigable waters. On Saturday, the other young men would singly find their way up stream, poke about in the stump holes until they found a mason jar full of homebrew, drink it and return to the Gulf station and general store and generally tear it up in the ensuing party. The proprietor did not seem to mind, for he was always plied with homebrew that someone had fetched for him, and after all, these men were not only his customers but also his companions. And on Sunday morning after church, the young men would come back and put the store back into apple pie order until the next Saturday night.

I remember discovering this local tradition, and being sworn to secrecy, was given advice as to the best utilization. One had to know who had the duty to make the homebrew, for many of the individuals simply dipped water from the lake to use in the brewing process. A twenty year old named Fisher was cited as the one to respect: not only did he have a one-word given name (others were "Billy Bobs" or "John Henrys"), but also was fastidious enough to go to the trouble of taking well water upstream for use in the brewing process. Accordingly, the weekends after he had the Monday duty were special occasions.

The women's bath house provided an outlet that would be served years later by such magazines as *Playboy* or *Penthouse*. The shower areas had plank flooring, with the planks separated by an inch of space to permit the shower water to drain underneath and into the water below the dam. The bathhouse was on pilings some six feet off the ground, permitting easy access to the local young men who at night would relish getting soaked while getting an eyeful through the cracks in the floor under the showers. This practice was known to the owner's wife, who commissioned me to police the area. I am happy that she relaxed upon making the assignment, rather than followed up to see how her orders had been carried out.

An account of my summer after high school cannot be considered complete without mentioning a young lady named Rachael Whiteside, with whom, of course, I fell deeply in love. Her family had purchased a summer cottage on the lake, and moved there for the summer. Rachael and I became inseparable, and I found her brother Frank to be a friend to be admired. Frank was the main lifeguard for the lake, but had left home after high school five or six years earlier, and had worked his way around the world as a seaman on a tramp steamer. These two helped me tremendously to mature quickly, and I aged several years that summer.

This summer was also the occasion for the purchase of my first car. It was a 1932 A Model Ford convertible, which I got for the tidy sum of $25.00. The steering was sufficiently worn that to turn required several spins of the steering wheel. I kept it for several weeks, until crossing the bridge below the dam caused a bump that threw the battery against the frame of the car, burning a nice nick in the frame and exploding the battery. I sold it to Fisher for $25.00, and borrowed the senior lifeguard's car, a 1933 Studebaker with much too many miles, when I had a trip to make. That car had its own problems—for example, only the high beams were operative at night. Frank, the owner, advised me to do what he did: "Blink the lights when an oncoming car approaches, and he will likely think you tried to dim your lights." Thankfully, the summer was soon over, and I returned to my bicycle and to the campus of the University of North Carolina.

Chapter 7

Undergraduate Work at the University of North Carolina

Came the fall of 1941, and both tanned and matured from the summer at Kimesville Lake, I got myself ready for entry into the University of North Carolina at Chapel Hill. This was my father's institution. In fact, my mother had opposed my choice, *believing* that my father got all of his bad habits there; I *knew* that he had, which made it an easy choice. I approached orientation week as if it were heaven that I was entering, and as if Roy Armstrong, the Admissions Director who never forgot a first name, was St. Peter himself. I prepared myself by purchasing a green suit with yellow socks and and a pink shirt, so that I would fit in with the sophisticated student body of which I expected to be a part.

The bicycle that I had had for the four years since I had reached the age of 12 was still quite serviceable, and provided the mechanism for my trek to Chapel Hill from Graham, some 24 miles away. My father had walked to the University from Fayetteville; it seemed only proper that I ride my bicycle from Graham. Remembering that my father had supported himself by chopping wood for the University Dining Hall cookstoves in 1913, I applied for a job at the University owned and operated Carolina Inn, becoming a bus boy for three hours each day in return for three meals each day, thus saving myself the fifteen to thirty cents that meals would cost at the university cafeteria.

This employment almost cost the University its inn. As a cafeteria employee, I had a locker in a dressing room, where staff changed to whatever garb their job required; and, as a cafeteria employee, I had to don a sort of white jump suit. I came in one day smoking my pipe; I put in in the pocket of a sport coat that had a woolen lining, and hung it in a locker; donned my uniform, and reported to the kitchen. Shortly thereafter, a fire alarm went off, and the Chapel Hill fire department came in time to confine the blaze to the dressing room where I had left my jacket, and my not un-lit pipe. Both, of course, were total losses, but they were replaceable. And I joined the others in expressing questions about the possible origins of the fire.

As for my university residence, I got off to an uncertain start, in that the dorm room to which I was assigned had a very surly upperclassman roommate. After the first week, he confided in me that he had contracted syphilis, and I broke all speed records in getting to the office of my academic adviser, Dr. W. D. Perry, and telling him of my concern. He responded immediately by finding me a single garret-type room in another dormitory. And in later years, I began to suspect that my first roommate was not afflicted, but simply crafty in getting a single room for himself. But I enjoyed my independence, and the fact that I could study when I felt like it, without worrying about keeping a roommate awake.

In social as in academic affairs, I was a fast learner, and I do not recall ever putting on the green suit and associated accessories. My first English class was in composition with young teaching assistant George Harper, who assigned frequent themes, and always read what I wrote to the class, which was, of course, a sizable salve to my ego. He thoroughly enjoyed what I wrote, and read it in such a way that the class could only share in that. A current professor in the UNC Department of English, one Daphine Athas, was also in that class, and I recall that Professor Harper said she tried hard but would probably never amount to much. Harper went on to major professorships at the University and Tulane. Athas became a successful novelist with her first novel *Entering Ephesus*; and I abandoned writing for a major in physics, principally because of the technical emphasis that the developing wartime society seemed to value, and accepted a membership in the Naval ROTC. A couple of years ago (in 2005) I found Harper, then in his 90s, in retirement and living in Florida. I wrote him, but had no response.

I had entered the University in the fall of 1941, and had immediately volunteered for assistance in the control room of the University radio station, which broadcast via a phone line feed to a Durham radio station. I was alone on the controls on Sunday afternoon, December 7, 1941, when two UNC professors and two Duke professors were debating "Will we go to war with Japan?" in a half-hour show beginning at 1:00 PM. At about 1:12, I recall a frantic call from the Durham radio station technician that word had just been received that Pearl Harbor was being attacked by the Japanese, and that they had interrupted our show for the announcement. I left the control room, went out into the studio, informed the panelists, and let them resume their debate after a moment of silence. They were shaken but up to the task, though we all unwound afterward by going to Danziger's (a coffee shop downtown) for Viennese coffee and the conversation that should have followed on the air about the breaking news.

During my time at the University, there were two favorite places. One was a basement lounge at the University Presbyterian Church, where students could relax and study in a home-like atmosphere. There were soft chairs, good lamps, an excellent record player which attracted a remarkable collection of records from the students who used it, and a kitchen that for a time some of us used to prepare our food. A favorite friend, a bit older than me who "adopted" me as her little brother, but whose mature perfume nevertheless kept me in a trance, was Fran(ces) Diefendorf, who years later I found had become Fran Mertz and lived on a ranch in Texas with her beloved horses. (We currently share our physical problems via email.)

The other favorite haunt was Danziger's Viennese Candy Kitchen and Coffee Shop, a hole in the one-block length of downtown Chapel Hill stores. The front part of the shop contained glass counters with an amazing array of hand-crafted sweets, and a back part consisted of booths in a room with the walls covered with pleasant graffiti and mottoes such as "Le appetit vient en mange" or something like that. There was also an upright piano which the proprietor, a kindly Viennese refugee that we called "Papa D," tolerated my less than professional playing by ear. The Viennese coffee was delicious—served in a tall glass mug, with a dollop of whipped cream on top. No date was complete until a stop on the way home at Papa D's. Incidentally, Danziger later recorded his experience from childhood in Vienna to ultimate retirement in the North Carolina mountains in a book published in 1963 by John Blair, Winston Salem, NC, entitled *Papa D—A Saga of Love and Cooking.*

Before leaving the matter of the business establishments along the one block business section of Franklin Street at that time, I need to pay proper obeisance to a beer joint named The Porthole, which was on an alley leading from Franklin Street to the section of the campus with the music building. It was here that I threw out my Grandmother's dire prediction of what would happen if I ever took one drink. I have forgotten the occasion, but one day I went there with three friends who were looking for a way to avoid studying. We ordered four bumper (or quart) bottles of beer, one for each of us, and over the next hour, consumed the contents. That done, we ordered another round of four, and, when those had been properly dispatched, still two more rounds of four. We had insisted that the empty bottles be left on the table of the booth, for we were proud of our accomplishment. As the other three made the necessary trip to the Men's Room, I was sitting there alone when Orville Campbell, the editor of the student newspaper who had had his share of the establishment's libation, stumbled to the table, counted the bottles, looked at me (I weighed 110 pounds then), counted the bottles again, looked at me again, gave me a salute, and shaking his head, walked out and down the alley.

Although the university was coeducational, women (unless town students living at home) were allowed only in the junior and senior classes, and I was sixteen when I entered—eager for female companionship, but much too young for schoolmates of the opposite sex in college. I quickly solved this by forays on the Chapel Hill High School seniors of that year, becoming acquainted with a number of young ladies, many of whose fathers were professors at the University. The daughter of basketball coach Bill Lange, one Shroyer Lange, quickly became the love of my life, and although our dating was rather sparse and reserved, I wrote some music and plays dedicated to her. We maintained correspondence throughout WWII after I left the University for active duty in the Navy, and after her father left the "white phantoms" he had coached so successfully and had bought a bowling alley in Ohio and moved the family there. To her, I am sure that I was a valued friend and nothing more; someone to write because it was the duty of every female at home to take an interest in servicemen. But to me, she was the epitome of what I wanted my life to be. Her letters for the most part recounted bridge games with her girl friends, but one out of about every four was signed "Love, Shroy." When those letters came in, the sun always came out, and the Japanese kamikaze planes were a minor irritant.

I had dated other girls, of course, many of whom I found exciting. I was particularly attracted to one petite young lady, a high school senior, with a trim 90 pounds on her five foot frame, and worried when I found that she dated many other college students. I went back for the 30th reunion of my class in the spring of 1975, and could not believe that the delectable young chick that she was had become a 300 pound behemoth. She did not recognize me, for which I was decidedly grateful.

There was a dance weekend in which I invited the girl from Graham that I had been paired with for the social events there, though I had never felt entirely comfortable with her. A large part of this was that she had a mother whose prudish tendencies inevitably landed painfully on any of her daughter's male friends, and I recall vividly that on the fifth or sixth date in high school days I decided that we knew each other sufficiently for a goodnight kiss, and had prepared to kiss her goodnight when we got back to her front door. Perceiving my intent, and probably convinced by her mother that it would lead to all manner of impropriety, she said "Don't spoil it," and darted inside the door. I had felt my interest waning, but she was an attractive young lady, and others were inviting their high school sweethearts to the University for a big band weekend. I think Tommy Dorsey was here that time. Since the affair extended over two days, it was the custom for the boys to arrange with townspeople for overnight rooms for their dates, and usually the houses making themselves available for this were well known as proper havens by the University student personnel people, and generally accommodated six or eight girls, two to a bedroom. My date came in on Friday, and stated a strong preference to have lunch at the Carolina Inn. So, there we went, and (surprise!) so did her mother and father, who suddenly appeared out of nowhere. We had lunch together, and her mother said to her daughter: "I need to powder my nose—could we go to your room?" The weekend was completed without other unexpected events, and my date returned home, with everything intact and her lipstick not smeared. That was my last date with her, although we corresponded occasionally when I shortly went into the Navy. I suspect, from later events, that she considered me her prime and faithful beau until she found me engaged to another young lady in Graham.

I found my classes at the University to be exceptionally easy, and after the first quarter, I registered twice for the next and subsequent quarters—once as "Junius A. Davis," and second as "J Ayers Davis." When the grade reports and bills would come, I would find a dimwitted clerk in the Registrar's office and get a correction, putting all the credits on one transcript, and thus completed degree requirements except for one summer session in two and one half years. My reason for doubling up was that with the war going on, I wanted to get into the service. Colin Kelly, the early war hero for purportedly diving his plane into and sinking a Japanese battleship, was a distant cousin of my mother's, and this added incentive. The campus NROTC expanded for the second quarter of the 1941-42 year, and I had joined in January, 1942, a month before I was 17, with some release from regulations because of our involvement in the war following Pearl Harbor.

It was exhilarating to be on my own, and in the company of some truly outstanding professors, who, like George Harper, took a personal interest in every student. President Frank Graham could call most of the some 2100 students by name, and held an open house at his residence every Sunday afternoon. I remember warmly classes in mathematics at the home of Dean Ernest Mackie. In short, the experience made Princeton University 8 years later seem like a bad dream in comparison, except it was like a nightmare that turned out to be real when one awakened.

I had several professors of international acclaim, but the most memorable was Dr. Archibald Henderson, Professor of Mathematics and George Bernard Shaw scholar, with whom I took a first course in analytic geometry. Henderson was in his seventies at the time, and was begining to show some physical signs of aging. He was exceptionally bright, so much so that he had trouble understanding why his students could not comprehend him (my father had taken a course with him in 1913 when Henderson was a young instructor, and reported that his students then had the same problem). He gave assignments continually that none of us could handle, though I recall one attempt by an eager beaver student who filled a wrapping paper sheet of about 30 by 72 inches with small figures in an attempt to solve a problem he had given us.

On the final exam, there were 10 questions; I attempted only one, ending the course with a gratuitous "C." I suppose I should have been grateful, but with my friend Alexander Littlejohn Feild, III, I put a very well formed toilet paper bow on his office door near the entrance to Phillips Hall. And, I believe that I discovered why this great man retreated from his classes in the Department of Mathematics and thrust himself into GBS.

There were several classes that were particularly memorable, in positive or negative ways. An example of the latter was my first calculus class, taught by a Dr. Garner who was plagued with COPD, and who lectured with his head completely outside the Phillips Hall classroom window in a frantic attempt to absorb some fresh air, presenting a comical sight to passer-bys, but a problem for those of us inside the classroom who could not hear his lecture. A most enjoyable class was one in Shakespeare, taught by a Shakespeare scholar named Professor Taylor. He surprised us by giving, as a final exam, a single question: "Write down all the lines you have memorized from the material we have studied this quarter. Some students left the room after a few minutes, but he had to call time on me in three hours. For me, Shakespeare was a love, and there were many lines that once read I simply could not erase from memory.

Another enjoyable class was a class of early English literature, starting with Chaucer, and featuring other early English writers. I recall one day the instructor asking if there were any questions, and one young lady named Miriam Lawrence, the somewhat naive but eager scholarly daughter of the Episcopal rector, raised her hand, and said "Professor, I have looked in the dictionary for a word I don't understand, and I can't find it. Can you tell me what a 'cunt' is?" After a moment of silence, the class, mostly males, simply got up quietly and filed out, leaving the professor to deal with the student and her problem.

The Department of Music, whose most famous graduate was Kay Kyser, was a favorite haunt. I sang in the University Glee Club, and took several courses in music appreciation. One course that was particularly enjoyable was taught by a visiting professor who was Lily Pons' pianist, and who taught sitting at a Steinway and playing as he lectured. My forays into the Music Building prompted me to try to compose some music of my own. After completing a humorous and atonal piece I labeled "Agony in G," I remember working on a more serious string quartet piece that I named "The Purple Pirate," and music professor Dr. Schenlan offering to get a quartet together to play it. I will never forget his reaction. He knew that I was a Physics major, and in great exasperation after struggling with the harmonics I had written in said, in his thick German accent: "I might come to your physics laboratory and try to make coffee on your calorimeters. You would tell me, 'You can't make coffee on these machines.' I must say to you 'you can't make music on my instruments!'" That was the end of my effort to create serious music.

My closest friend over the college years was Alexander Littlejohn Feild, III, from Baltimore. He was very bright, and a physics major. We studied together, finding that we could enter the locked main lecture hall in the Phillips Building through second floor doors to the balcony, then shinnying down a support to the main level. There in the main physics classroom we could study in quiet and comfort. But our friendship was not all study. I introduced Alex to a girl from my high school class then enrolled at the Woman's College in Greensboro, and one way or another we went on a number of group dates. The girl, Marjorie Bason, was not only the valedictorian of my high school class, she was also very attractive. I remember one time when Alex and I, and another three friends, dated girls that Marjorie picked out for us at the Woman's College in Greensboro, about 50 miles west of Chapel Hill. My home in Graham was about half way between, and the boys came to my house for an extended Friday-Saturday bash, and the girls to Marjorie's house. We partied into the wee hours Friday night, driving around with eight of us in the car I remember driving around Burlington and Alex, in the back seat with Margie and another couple, asked if we had heard the one about the farmer who asked Bessie, his mule, if she would like some oats, whereupon old Bessie raised her tail and said "A f-e-e-e-w." This was met with silence except for Alex's tee-heeing. We tired after a while of the cramped quarters in the car, and took the girls to Marjorie's house, and after that went to my house where the boys and I fell asleep on pallets on the living room floor. But what should occur shortly thereafter at 6 AM but the appearance of my mother, entering and banging on a dishpan to awaken us for the breakfast of grits, country ham, eggs, and biscuits that she had prepared for us. I don't think I have ever seen a sadder group of boys needing a shave and in sagging boxer shorts, looking helplessly at one another. From then on, we partied either in Greensboro or in Chapel Hill.

Although Alex is now deceased, I am sure he remembered to his dying day taking Marjorie to a major college dance in Woolen Gym with a name band, with Marjorie, his date, resplendent in a strapless dress. As his luck and her precarious dress would have it, at one point the top of Marjorie's gown came down, revealing a very nice little booby. Alex, never at a loss for inappropriate words, exclaimed "Pretty little thing, isn't it!" Marjorie was a good sport, and simply stuffed it back in. Alex joined the Navy as an enlisted man and later became a quantum physics expert for Western Electric, and Marjorie married a professor of philosophy who taught at NYU, but she died shortly thereafter (in the 1960s) of a brain tumor.

Another good friend in college was John Fesperman, a music major who later became my best man when Pegge and I married after the war. John, who returned from Navy duty to the University to complete his work as I had done, was one of a group calling itself the Snuffbuckets, and rallying around Reverend Charles Jones, an outspoken liberal later ejected from the Presbyterian Church for "putting brotherhood of man above the fatherhood of God," which translated meant that he did not object to Blacks attending Sunday Services at his church, and indeed welcomed them—usually students from N.C Central University in Durham—to young people's activities at the church. This was long before Martin

Luther King began to make waves in the South, and Jones' behavior was pure heresy in the 1940s.

The Snuffbuckets were organized by a graduate student named Wayne Kernodle, fresh from helping as a student to plan and build Black Mountain College in the western part of the state (and later to become head of the Sociology Department at William and Mary). But having the church lounge area and kitchen as a place to study and a place to cook and eat inexpensively, and being able to join in Rev. Jones' various forays to encourage acceptance of Blacks by the white culture, attracted a number of eager and idealistic students whose common cause bound them together to the extent that those still living, though scattered across the country, still keep up with one another by visiting and by email. Most have held significant posts: viz., Dean Winn, chief of surgery at a major metropolitan hospital; John Anderson, a tenured professor at the University of Pittsburgh; and at least two prominent theologians: Charles McCoy and Zan Harper; and my friend John Fesperman, who went on to a career as a conductor and organist of national acclaim, retiring from an important post with the Smithsonian Institute in 1995. And Jones' impact on the campus community and on the Snuffbuckets has been documented in a 2002 Writers' Showcase book by Mark Prior, entitled *Faith, Grace, and Heresy—the Biography of Charles Jones*.

Most of what Rev. Jones was espousing was fresh and exciting to most of the Snuffbuckets, who frequently went on protest activities. I had little stomach to join them, for indeed what Jones was trying to accomplish, though new to them, involved activity that my father had engaged in as far back as I could remember. It later turned out that when Jones came under fire for his stand on "brotherhood," my father was appointed as one of the committee chaired by a fundamentalist preacher from Greensboro in an attempt to prove the committee was fairly balanced. My father found it simply a *pro forma* device for railroading Jones out, with the committee chairman selected to perform that mission; the chairman's name, Piehoff, became synonymous with that of Satan in our household. Jones resigned from the Presbyterian ministry in July, 1953. I remembered Jones not from his race advocacy, but principally from his sermons, always masterpieces that held everyone in the congregation spellbound.

Jones stayed in Chapel Hill, with a loyal group of parishioners creating a new church for him which was called the "Community Church." This church flourished and Jones attained some notoriety in the national Civil Rights movement, but when he left that ministry in 1966 he became a chief advisor for the sons of Papa Danziger, who had opened several restaurants in Chapel Hill. "I was in the restaurant business before I went into preaching," he told me (for at that time I had returned to residence in Chapel Hill), "and I never quite got the restaurant business out of my system." He remained a good friend, and, in fact, was of considerable help to my son Mike when he was making his decision to enter the ministry and deciding on a seminary.

But back to my undergraduate days. My entry to the church lounge and the Snuffbuckets was more a function of the fact that I taught a Sunday School class of 6 to 9 year olds than of joining in the various protest activities. I recall one little girl of 6, Latishia "Tish" Harrer, the daughter of the chair of the Classics Department, reciting at a parents day "The North wind doth blow, and we shall have snow, and what will poor robin do then—" and then she added, with considerable emphasis and slowly shaking her head: "*Pore thang!*" This, of course, brought the house down. Incidentally, I learned two decades later that Tish had accomplished a childhood dream, by swimming the English Channel.

One experience about a year after I entered the University involved a report of some major victory in the war in the Pacific. John Fesperman and I stole into the main area of the Presbyterian Church shortly before midnight, and precisely at 12 midnight rang the church bell for several minutes. If anyone ever came to see who had created the ruckus, we were too far away to know.

Although tuition in the early 1940s was only $1.50 per credit hour as I recall, and although my parents had given me a check book to use without naming a balance, I knew that they could ill afford to support me. In addition to the bus boy activity at the Carolina Inn that provided three square meals each day, I took a room in town with rent free in exchange for firing the furnace in the winter and doing the necessary yard work in the summer. I did not get along with Maisie, the spinster daughter at this house, who was beyond ready marriageable age, rather plain, and somewhat overweight. Although a lady of uneasy virtue, Maisie had, in addition, a condition that I would call "personality deficit.," or, more precisely, an infinite capacity for vacuity.

I moved from that house to a room on Rosemary Street behind the church that was owned by a Mrs. Abernethy, the mother of a bachelor shop owner in the village who lived in the house with his mother. Each Saturday night, he would have a bit too much to drink, come home, sit on the porch, and cry loudly for several hours, wailing something like "Mother, get those God-damned boys out of my house!" He never got physical in this, only vocal. Considering him no threat, I decided not to facilitate his weekend wishes. Besides, I had a window that opened on a gently sloping roof, which was ideal for sunbathing, and the house was convenient to the Presbyterian Church lounge and the campus. I decided to stay.

The several other boys rooming there were compatible; and my room, in addition to the roof access window, had a small door that yielded access to an attic area. This permitted me to apply skills learned at Kimesville Lake in the manufacture of homebrew, which I made in large crocks inside the warm environs of the attic. This became a lucrative business, for I supplied a number of fraternity parties. I stopped when one day I found several mice that had obviously feasted on homebrew that had bubbled over from the crocks, and had died on the spot. I never heard of any fatalities at the frat houses, and years later I realized that I had missed my calling by not manufacturing my product as rat poison.

It is an interesting aside that the major fraternity house enjoying my wares was the Kappa Alpha house, to which I had entry through my friend Alex Feild, who was a KA. This was clearly one of the better houses on campus. One member was Ike Belk, who is now head of a major department store chain that has given substantial sums of money to UNC Charlotte and to Campbell College. Ike had a white souped-up Ford convertible that was used to make weekly trips to South Carolina to purchase gin (there were no liquor stores in North Carolina then), which when mixed with grape juice, formed a concoction known as "Purple Jesus." Another member was David Masengill, the son of a pharmaceutical manufacturer in Tennessee, who had been at UNC for a number of years beyond those usually required to graduate. We thought he would never amount to anything, but his father died, leaving him the company, which he diverted to the manufacture of feminine douche products. Thus, he became a millionaire by the time I was looking for work following release from the Navy after WWII., with the Massengill name prominently displayed on douche products in every drug store in the country.

The Purple Jesus parties at the KA House were lively affairs. I partook of this beverage only once, finding myself awakening on a couch in the lounge area of the fraternity at 5 AM, dressed only in my boxer shorts, and literally covered with lipstick, some of which was planted in a most embarrassing place. Apparently some fraternity member had a willing ally in his date for the evening, and had had some fun at my expense. I know not what happened while I was out, but the experience was sufficient to make me a teetotaler for the rest of my time in college.

The Purple Jesus concoction had a remarkable after-effect: one could recover the buzz when it had disappeared by simply drinking a glass of water, which would somehow reactivate the impact of the alcohol. I discovered this by having a copious drink of water the morning after my first and only KA party, on the way to teach my Sunday School class of 6-9 year olds. I don't remember what I said to them that morning, but I suspect I gave convincing reasons for abstinence. I do recall telling the little girls that there were far worse things for them to be than prudes.

Alongside the campus radio station, association with Alex Feild and John Fesperman, the reading of my essays by Dr. Harper, the Snuffbuckets, and my various activities working my way through, was activity with the Carolina Playmakers, a product of the Department of Dramatic Arts. This department under Professor Frederick Koch, and later Dr. Samuel Seldon, held a rightful high status among its counterparts on other campuses, having produced a number of illustrious graduates including Frank Brink, notable in the Williamsburg dramas, and (later after I left) Andy Griffith. The department also profited from the presence on the faculty of Professor Paul Green of the Department of Journalism, who later became a Hollywood script writer of note and the author of the Lost Colony drama at Manteo and several other historical plays that are offered in North Carolina and Virginia, and for whom the Playmaker's new theater in the round has been named. I had no talent nor penchant for acting, but found work with the stage crews to be particularly rewarding. Thus, for the Pirates of Penzance, and Yeoman of the Guard, I joined the costume designer (Irene) in her work, and among other things making and shining the boots of the pirates and the yeomen in the Gilbert and Sullivan Operettas. And I never missed a Green Room party after a performance. It was this experience that prompted me to write a parody of the Pirates of Penzance which was a full-length takeoff called the Amazons of Penzance, and which I used to try to win the affections of the blonde who had caught my eye in the stage production of Pirates, Shroy Lange. Fortunately, all copies of this mss. have long since disappeared. It was in actuality a thinly disguised parody of events in the process of my unfulfilled love with Shroy, which she, to her great credit, refused to recognize until I revealed this to her. I think she was both a little flattered and a little scared.

Because of the need for young officers, my class was called to active duty in February, 1944, when most of the cadets in my class had completed the first half of their Junior year. I found later after discharge from service that I only needed about six more credit hours if I changed my declared major from Physics to mathematics, the latter subject one in which I had taken sufficient credits toward the Physics major to serve as a major in Mathematics . . . Thus my initial stay in undergraduate work was quite short; I entered active duty as a college senior with major in Physics; and, I knew that I would end up with a major in mathematics only about two weeks before completing degree requirements in a summer session after return from service.

Chapter 8

Initial Tour in the Navy

My Navy career actually began with an incident that I have already reported. This was when I was handling the controls in the campus radio station Sunday afternoon, December 7, 1941, and the program, focusing on whether or not we would go to war with Japan, was interrupted by the news that Pearl Harbor was under attack. That prompted me to get involved.

I had applied, with about 400 others, for the NROTC when I had enrolled in September, 1941, but apparently did not make the cut. With the new events, the ROTC extended invitations to an additional contingent of applicants, I among them. There was a physical, of course, and fortunately I sat by the eye chart while waiting to be examined, and had memorized it when my turn came. Getting in the Navy was about the most important thing I could think of. I fudged the eye exam, failed to disclose my childhood asthma, and thanked the good Lord that my age (16) and low weight for my height (112 pounds; six feet) had not disqualified me. I was accepted into the NROTC about two weeks before my 17th birthday.

My college grades ran the gamut from A to F, but the NROTC grades, as were my grades in English and most of my mathematics courses, were always in the A bracket. My biggest problem was in marching drills, where for the life of me I could not make my arms swing in the proper cadence. The more I was barked at for this infraction, the more aberrant my arm swings became. But I found I could mimic our NROTC Commanding Officer, a crusty old four-striper who was called back in from a retirement years before. He was either senile or sufficiently out of touch with people of college age that most of his speeches to us were considered strange or humorous, and I had much fun repeating things he had said (I could imitate his voice) to informal gatherings of fellow cadets. (A favorite speech that I repeated many times was one where he called the entire NROTC battalion together and lambasted us for charging "like a herd of cattle" into the university cafeteria after being released from a late-running drill.)

In the summer of 1943, we had a training cruise on the Chesapeake Bay. This affair involved two old gunboats, the Dubuque and the Paducah, salvaged from duty in the China rivers and brought to Annapolis for use in training. I was assigned to the Dubuque with several dozen of my classmates. I remember three things vividly from that experience.

The first was an event one evening after we had retired. Our sleeping quarters in the old Dubuque was a large open compartment used, with folding tables and benches, as a dining room at mealtimes, but the compartment had many pillars from floor to ceiling, spaced about 8 feet apart with rings on which hammocks could be hung, and was used as sleeping quarters at night. Thus, with layering, some 40 individuals could be accommodated overnight in a space of about 400 square feet. When lights were out, the game was some clown speaking out in the darkness to the others, and eliciting a retort.

Following some revelry of this sort on the first night, a grizzoned career Navy Bo'sun entered the compartment and ordered all to be quiet, or face dire consequences. A hush fell over the group, and after a few minutes, the Bo'sun left. The silence that followed was broken by someone expelling flatulence quite loudly, to which another replied "Stop that friggin' in the riggin'!" The compartment erupted in laughter, and we were rousted out and cleaned the heads for the next several hours.

The second instance that is burned into my memory occurred while several of us were stationed as lookouts on the bridge as the old Dubuque steamed toward Norfolk. A classmate from a very affluent family, and who was known for always overdoing a keen sense of propriety, had the starboard wing post on the bridge, and at one point cried out "Sail ho!" The officer of the deck, picked for that position, I am sure, because he was a stickler for observing Navy customs precisely, responded "Where away?" expecting to be instructed as to how many points off the starboard bow the sail was spotted. My classmate replied: "Far, far away, sir!"

The third event was more ordinary. At the end of the cruise, we docked at Annapolis, and were given liberty to go out on the town. I found a bingo game in progress somewhere in the center of Crabtown as Annapolis was called, and at a quarter a game, decided to try my luck. Of probably a hundred players, I won the first Bingo, where the prize was a five dollar bill. In 1943, that was a lot of money. It remained significant in my memory, because now for more than 60 years I have never won anything else, and, in fact, before quitting in disgust, lost the three nickels I put in a slot machine in Reno almost 20 years later.

With the war in the Pacific continuing, my class was called to active duty in February, 1944. Although most of us were a year and a term short of graduation, we were given commissions and orders. I remember leaving home from the train station in Burlington, with my mother in tears, and with orders to report to the Commandant, Sixth Naval District, in Charleston, SC. There, I was further ordered to report to the Commandant, Naval Section Base, Southport, NC, for temporary duty pending further orders. The next bus that would take me from Charleston to Southport was the following morning, and becoming aware that I was developing a fine case of mumps, I spent the night on a couch in an isolated corner at the Charleston YMCA, and reported to the gate sentry as I entered the Section Base at Southport that I suspected I was highly contagious. The sentry, backing off smartly, arranged for special transport to the base Sick Bay, where I languished until the swelling had disappeared.

I was assigned to one of several YP (Yard Patrol) vessels that went out each day to patrol a sector for any German Uboat activity. These vessels were converted shrimpers, with depth charges and racks installed on the stern, and a 20 MM machine gun added to the bow to make them formidable. I found the captains of these vessels left Southport each day and collected at a secluded anchorage some miles north, tied up alongside each other, and played poker. It was not surprising that no Uboats were ever discovered, and the officers thoroughly enjoyed their sentry duty. But I was shortly ordered to the ASW (Antisubmarine Warfare) Training Center in Miami.

At the ASW school in Miami, we were quartered at the Columbus Hotel, a downtown hotel on Biscayne Bay. Two officers were assigned to a room; and my roommate was a reclusive skinny fellow with a mustache and an English accent, named Richard Ney, who was widely known to be messing around with a lady old enough to be his mother—someone he had worked with named Greer Garson. He would sneak out of the room each evening, and I found that he was going to the lobby and closing himself in a phone booth. I could not resist sneaking into the booth alongside one evening, and listening as he professed such things as inability to live without the person to whom he was talking. He was exceeding quiet as a roommate until one day he spotted what he thought was lipstick on my jockey shorts, whereupon he lost his customary aloofness and exposed his very active imagination. I did not tell him that I had acquired the stains by using a pair of jockey shorts to rub off the price, which was entered in red, on the glass of a picture frame I had purchased for the picture of a college girlfriend. But I have to credit Ensign Ney for helping me to lose my awe for people with his basis for notoriety.

It was Miami where I had my first encounter with a homosexual. I had had a drink or two at the hotel bar after classes one day, and had been brought into a conversation with a young man who seemed pleasant enough. When the bar announced closing, he said he knew a place where we could get drinks and continue our conversation. I went along, and remember becoming exceedingly curious as he led me up an alley. He said he had to take a leak, and when I decided to do the same, he grabbed me without regard to the hazard of getting wet. Startled, I swung very hard with my free left hand, smashing his head against the brick wall of the building we were decorating. He was not a very big fellow, and fell to the ground. I zipped up and returned to the hotel, a somewhat more sober and wiser person. I checked the papers the next morning to try to see if any bodies had been found in the Miami alleys, but there was no such news. So, I assumed that somewhere in Miami there was a gay with a bad headache, chalked the episode up to experience, and went on with learning how to deal with enemy submarines.

One of the officer students was an agent for a popular music publishing house. There was a piano in the lobby of the Columbus Hotel, and one morning when the place was empty I played a song I had written just before I left college—a ballad of unrequited love for Shroy. He proved to be quite adept in saying, diplomatically, that it stunk. That was when I reaffirmed confining my interest in music to aural experience.

I remember full well the graduation address given by the ASW school commandant, who, in a speech vigorously delivered with much hand waving, urged us to proceed to our assigned ships, to capture all the Japanese we could find, to line them up on the fantail of our crafts, and then to machine gun them slowly, starting with their toes and working up. It was a rousing speech, but it did not have the effect he intended on me. I guess I was partial to the assistant commandant, one Lieutenant Commander Myers of Jamaica, who probably believed that any such vigorous activity should be confined to hacking sugar cane which would form the basis for his dark rum.

After a crash course in sonar detection and attack, I was ordered to report to the PC 1598 for duty, which was believed to be in Miami in transit to the Pacific from duty in the North Atlantic. I quickly found that my PC had already left for the Pacific, with a fueling stop scheduled at the Naval Section Base at the mouth of the Mississippi River. I was given air transportation to New Orleans, where I started the some 90 mile trip down the Mississippi River to the Navy Section Base. The first sixty miles were by bus, to a bar/general store on the river in the swamps where the road ran out. I waited here, was served bourbon and coke by a barefooted 13 year old bar maid, and boarded a water taxi that came to take me the final 30 or so miles down the river to the Naval Section Base. The PC arrived the next day, and, after replenishing fuel, embarked for the Panama Canal and the war in the Pacific with me on board.

I was happy to be finally on the way to the war. But I began to get suspicious when my Captain, whose aura suggested that he used bourbon for an after-shave lotion (whether he shaved or not), insisted on handling the navigation himself. He plotted our course between the western tip of Cuba and the Mexican coast, and insisted as we moved south that we were in the middle of that expanse. He ignored the lookout who suddenly asked what the trees were doing in the middle of the channel ahead, until we could see clearly the coral formations in the sea under our boat.—meaning very shallow water. We backed out until the ocean bottom was no longer visible, went about twenty miles due west, and then south again—very slowly. Another PC boat was shortly encountered enroute south, and our captain asked the skipper of that vessel if we could follow them. Thus, our captain's navigational skill led us miraculously to the entrance to the Panama Canal.

The Canal Zone was an adventure. We stayed several days at the Naval Yard on the Pacific end of the Canal, and had liberty each evening in Panama City, then a very primitive version of what it is now. I was much impressed by two things in this little city: the men's rooms in the bars were void of any fixtures, having only a trough around the edges with drain outlets at the corners; and, the streets had many store fronts with large plate glass windows, exposing a screen inside concealing all but the foot of a bed. These were brothels, of course, and one could have a fine evening simply strolling and observing the idle women sitting in the doorways inviting all passing males, mostly Navy personnel, to enter, or, where business had picked up, observing the two pairs of feet exposed at the end of the beds showing around the screens and through the plate glass windows.

Most of the bars were also brothels, with a row of chairs on the other side of the room from the bar and its stools, and with prospects for the evening sitting on the chairs waiting to be selected. It was in such a bar that a small boy, probably 9 or 10 years of age, came in as I was nursing a beer and asked to shine my shoes for a quarter. I told him that my shoes did not need shining, but that I would like for him to give me some Panamanian money in exchange for U.S. money. He eagerly agreed, saying he would have to go out and find it, and I gave him a couple of dollars. My companion from the ship said that that was the last I would see of those two bucks, but shortly the boy returned and dumped a fist full of coins in my hands. I felt vindicated, but did not tell my companion later that the boy had shortchanged me considerably.

From the Canal Zone we went up the coast to San Diego, where we again had a wait of a few days before we were ordered to Pearl Harbor. We were there long enough for me to be thrown out of several bars (I had just turned 19, and carding in San Diego then was quite strict), I did secure entry into one where a man I recognized as a former UNC student we called "Tiny" because of his weight (somewhere around 400 pounds) sang a paraphrased song "Benny's from Heaven." It continued "Every time I asked, she'd say—'Benny's from heaven." and concluded with a loud "Little Benny is from heaven and not from me!" The stay in San Diego also permitted me to visit Tijuana where I found the merchants lived not to sell but to bargain.

On the trip to Pearl Harbor, we learned that the weather in the Pacific in the late spring was anything but peaceful. It was bitter cold, and the seas were extremely rough—and PC boats are not noted for their stability. I figured that that Italian guy who gave the Pacific its name must have drained his compass of alcohol. By the time we reached Pearl Harbor, the weather had cleared, and we were quickly assigned to a convoy of munition barges headed to Eniwetok in the South Pacific. It was on this trip that my life changed.

Ens. Junius A. Davis, USNR, Honolulu, T.H., 1944

It was not that Eniwetok's uninhabited and tiny OO Island—spelled OO, and pronounced "Oh-Oh"—became my private paradise, which it did—but an event en route. Our Captain was a chronic alcoholic, and stayed in a state of feeling no pain most of the time. Somewhere off Truk, which had been bypassed but which was still a Japanese stronghold at that time, our sonar detected a submarine that could not identify itself as friendly. I was Officer of the Deck and sounded General Quarters, and started trying desperately to track the sub and drop a few depth charges. The Captain came barreling up to the bridge, I presumed to take over with the General Quarters call, but instead he began haranguing me about taking a cook off report for Captain's Mast, when he knew the cook had threatened another mess hall attendant with a butcher knife. (As the officer responsible for the crew's mess, I had met with the two who had patched up their differences, which turned out to be something like how much garlic salt should be added to bean soup.) But the Captain continued to yell and sweat a lot. I finally had to tell him either to take the conn, or to get the hell off the bridge. He took the latter course of action, but retired to his quarters where I later learned that he got catharsis by drafting a highly negative fitness report on me. The submarine must have dived deep, for we lost contact with it; it was probably delivering supplies to the Japanese isolated and bypassed on Truk, and anxious not to risk combat.

We got our barges to Eniwetok. The waters there were warm. The island inhabitants had been moved to one of the several islands forming the atoll ring, and we could go ashore to another one designated for recreation, beer drinking, and softball. I did a lot of swimming with scuba gear, because the coral reefs just under the surface of the waters were beautiful, and the tropical fish were colorful marvels to behold. It was here that I took a boat to watch over me, and swam around the circle, a distance probably of about 16 miles, in a 20 hour period.

Thus we had a lovely couple of weeks in the lagoon formed by the atoll, until we were ordered back to Pearl to pick up another convoy. Our Captain was several sheets to the wind, as usual, when we started out, and backed the PC over our anchor chain, damaging the starboard engine screw to the point that it could not be used because of intense vibration. We proceeded back to Pearl on the port engine, where the Captain received a commendation for bringing the damaged PC boat some 3000 miles with one screw inoperative, and where I was put off the boat for my gross incompetence. I was beginning to understand the Navy—or, more precisely, the Naval Reserve in wartime.

It was long after I had asked the Captain to take the conn because of the submarine contact that I learned that he had retired to his quarters to write the negative fitness report. Naval regulations required that such a report be given to the officer involved, and that he be given an opportunity to respond, before it was submitted. But it was some six months after leaving the PC that I received a copy from the Bureau of Naval Personnel and was asked to respond. I remember the Captain saying in it that having just turned 19, I was "most gauche and naive" and needed a billet with less responsibility than officers on a small craft had to assume, and that I had been told about my shortcomings and requested to respond (which I had not). Knowing that the Captain had been given his commission because of contact between his father and a source in the Senate, I decided to respond simply that I had now read the report and had no comment. I felt that sooner or later the Captain would be found out for his problems. Nevertheless, it was this report that made me decide not to persevere with a career in the U. S. Navy, a choice I had been considering, and thus I began to think of other career opportunities if ever I got home again.

I took up residence in the Ford Island BOQ and for several weeks worked as a message decoder for the Commander in Chief—Pacific. I even saw the CIC-Pacific—then one Admiral Nimitz—as he tooled around the yard in an open jeep. I volunteered for duty for an underwater demolition team but was assigned to the USS Marmora, IX 189—a tanker built in 1918 as the J.S. Fitzsimmons and given to the Russians for lend-lease (and named the Valeriun Kuibyshev), and given back to us in 1944. It was considered expendable but sufficient to carry 70.000 barrels of aviation gas to the active war zone, and there serving as a reserve or emergency supply. Learning later that the underwater demolition team I had volunteered for was responsible for going into Okinawa several weeks before the landing of US forces and rigging the coral reefs with explosives that would clear them when set off so that our landing craft could enter, I became grateful that my assignment was the Marmora. That old bucket of rust (we could not chip paint because of the danger of a spark igniting our cargo) became my home for the rest of the war. Our exploits are best summarized by the keynote speech I gave at the first reunion of its crew in 1983. That speech follows. I referred to it as "Comments made, on the occasion of the first reunion of the men of the USS Marmora, at Fair View Heights, Illinois, on May 28, 1983, by J. A. Davis (LTJG-USNR; then AH2c)" and entitled it "What Were We in 1944-45?"

"We know too well what the USS Marmora was—a bucket of rust; too slow to sail with convoy protection; unable to turn away from the wind if its force exceeded 28 knots; built in Seattle in 1918 as the James S. Fitzsimmons, and variously named and flagged until we [decommissioned her and] put her on the mud north of Mobile [at the end of the war]. Those of us with prior service on ships of the line—like Ezra Lang here [Lang was then the 20 year old assistant Engineering Officer] know the Marmora was not a glamorous assignment. But what were we, that would have caused us to seek each other out after 38 years? Let me attempt to define us, as we were in that period when we all came of age.

"First: *we were men with a prior history of spectacular accomplishment.* The Marmora was recognized as challenging duty, and only 'deserving' individuals were assigned. I won my billet by reporting to a former skipper my suspicion that his father and mother were unmarried, a conclusion well borne out by his behavior, but largely unappreciated; still another of us backed a minesweeper into a gate at the Panama Canal; still another was rumored to have drunk up the profits of the Officers' Club at Espirito Santo. I'll leave it to each of you to recall your own reason for the deliberate assignment. We generally deserved the distinction.

"*We were men of particular enterprise.* For example, we learned that we could get anything we needed from the 11 story supply warehouse at Pearl Harbor by faking sailing orders for dawn, and sending three or four of us over at midnight with a requisition that would take the one man on night duty to the 11th floor, while the rest of us shopped uninhibited on floors 1 to 10. Our captain was unreasonable when he made Jochmann [a fast-talking enlisted man for whom ethics was no problem] take back the jeep; but, even with that setback, we were among the best supplied ships in ComServPac.

"*In spite of our affluence of equipment, we were pragmatic men who could make do nicely with what we had.* Remember electrician mate Rich, for example, who tested for current by putting his thumb in open sockets? The fact that he isn't here tonight may mean that someone slipped him a 220 volt line!

All of us remember the long waits; and, all of us remember that *we were men who were hungry for action.* I recall vividly the midnight to 0400 watch I had enroute to Ulithi from Saipan when the bow lookout kept reporting neon-lighted, all-night hot dog stands at various locations off the starboard bow. Those stands, by God, were as symbolic of our hunger then as they were real for the lookout, who had probably been in the sauce prior to the watch, and needed a little food.

"*We were men who faced danger with casual nonchalance.* Remember Scanland's [a signalman who had worked as a cartoonist at the Walt Disney Studios] cartoon showing one of us chopping up the General Quarters bell with a fire axe, and saying 'You #!x%s, that will teach you to sound off when I'm asleep!' And indeed, most of us slept through the nightly air raids at Okinawa, after the first week or so. We didn't let the war get in the way of our physical needs; we were 'cool,' as we say today.

"*We were men who respected and backed up our superior officers.* How vividly I remember the steward's mate assigned to close the aft watertight doors at General Quarters, who clung in such situations closely behind Lt. Bono, and stayed lockstep with him until we had the Condition Green signal. I also note that the officers appreciated the rule you adopted: 'Do not fire at officers during air raids.' We returned this well-deserved respect, as you know, in our uniquely individual ways. (Who will forget the enthusiasm of Rudolph John Smith [the sadistic gunnery officer who could only talk about his many bedroom conquests], as he languished his love on us? Rest in peace, Rudy, but recognize you didn't give us much peace.)

"*We were men who thought big.* Remember Scanland's flag bags? He was tired of shallow bags and crumpled flags, and drew up specs for those we sailed with from Pearl; the two, if salvaged today, could each be rented out at $550 per month as two bedroom apartments.

"*We were colorful men of macho*—if not when we came on board, we were by the time we left. We started, of course, with such images as Chief Marshall, whose red mustache was 12 inches tip to tip, and whose whisper could be heard 7.5 nautical miles away; everyone looked up to Tex Hilcher [a 6' 9" well muscled petty officer]. The USOs had Caesar Romero and Carmen Miranda, but we had Milt Holznogel [a very handsome seaman] and Lucas [an effeminate seaman second class]. Sooner or later, all took on that macho image, each and every one of us, though in our own ways. The last one of us to come of age in this regard did so on the trip home, by having a 38 inch battleship tattooed on his 28 inch chest while briefly ashore at Pearl [this was our 100 pound yeoman, who was not present at the reunion].

"*We were men of real athletic prowess.* Jockmann, for example, was really the first person in history to break the four-minute mile. In fact, considering the meat cleaver that served as his starting gun, he would have made eight miles in six and a half minutes if Tex Hilscher had not called a halt (Jochmann had teased a cook while he was chopping meat for dinner). But Tex was always a spoilsport. [Jockman was present, and enjoyed the notoriety.]

"*We were men of unusual courage in battle*—though it didn't always pay off. I remember vividly how so many of you turned to, without regard to personal safety, when the Liberty ship alongside us was hit in the Number Four hold by Kamikazi, and Hank Hoener [a radioman] reported the rumor that to prevent sinking it was dumping its cargo of beer for the rec areas over the side. Sammy Nussbaum's [the machinist mate responsible for the small boats] motors never hummed so sweetly as most of us abandoned ship and sailed off through the smoke [laid out to prevent detection by enemy aircraft] in search of our quarry with boat hooks. And, although the forty cases that were retrieved turned out to be powdered eggs, not beer, it gave us the incentive to build our own still, and thus our courage bred self-sufficiency.

"Speaking of battle: I should note that *your officers stood (as best they could) with you.* Remember the time at Okinawa when the air raids had kept us up all night, and Captain Olsen ordered two cans of beer per man at dawn? For those of you who consequently missed it, three big air raids hit just after; and we had no one sober enough, except Garber [a very straight seaman] and Davis [I didn't drink then, of course!] to man a smoke boat or a gun. We probably survived (1) because we were so quiet and still in the dim light of dawn, when dead drunk looks like just dead, and (2) because the old Marmora always looked like it had already sunk anyway.

"*We were human, loving men.* Jorgenson (one of the cooks) started the trend by writing his wife to send him a pair of her panties. The rest of us, except one who was single and who already had a pair he wore at happy hours, followed suit [a reference to Lucas, whom all remembered showing up in a skit as a femme fatale in lacy underwear]. To the wives here: your generosity in this regard helped to keep all of you vividly in our minds; and, we had the distinction of having more fancy underwear aboard than that contained in the bargain basement at Gimbel's. But God, how we missed you!

"We took over the ship from the Russians, but *we didn't let the Russians out-do us.* Their doctor, a paymaster, and a fireman 2nd class, were female. But Bupers gave us Fay Gaither, Muriel Jackson, and Beverly Jordan [actual names of three of the crew] as shipmates. Go suck an egg, Moscow!

"*We were men of particular ingenuity and creativity.* I won't go into details of how the ship's cat got pregnant after 12 months at sea [I was ribbed about this, for the cat slept in my cabin]; but I do recall Chief Marshall and Guns Holznogel coming back from ashore at Okinawa with the live goat. Though the chief swore he loved animals, and felt such would add a touch of class to the fantail, we all knew he used the goat to pretest the saki he had found ashore, to assure that it had not been booby trapped with arsenic: the goat got the first drink from each bottle. But sadly, the goat, named McArthur as I recall [our ship was under the command of General McArthur while serving as avgas supply at Okinawa], deposited something other than a touch of class on the fantail, and was sent back to its terrestrial environs. The Chief survived, as we knew he would, arsenic or not.

"*We were very good at what we did.* Knickerbocker [our always deadly serious quartermaster] kept us on course when the navigator couldn't decide which end of the sextant to look through. Hoener [our radioman] could copy anything following -./.-/.- --/ .- [Morse code for NAJA, our radio code name] in his sleep, a posture he frequently assumed. Who will ever forget Jorgenson's cakes, pies, or bread? Or Messersmith's [a sheep shearer from Utah] skill at cutting hair? Or our systematic demolition of all the rental cars in Mobile [where we returned for decommissioning]? And, of course, there were the many ingenious ways of converting alcohol for salinity tests for the boilers to a potable state. We survived, when our sister ships didn't: The USS Chotauk (IX188) never got steam up (sunk by typhoon at Okinawa), and the USS Vandalia (IX191) still rusts on the reef (where it ran aground) at Naha Bay. And, McKinney's (our engineering officer) skill at poker got us (and himself) home early.

"That story may not be generally known. Let me tell you what happened. We weren't copying CINCPAC messages in the later days at Okinawa (Hank Hoener said he was fed up with the radio shack, and had a headache, besides)—our command (the Sub-Area Petroleum Officer, Ryukus—under McArthur's command) was doing it for us. An Army lieutenant there had a $2,000 IOU from Lt. McKinney, a result of a night at poker—while his colonel, liking our company, was canceling our orders they had received to transfer us back to Navy command and to send us home, the Army lieutenant came over to collect his debt in case the colonel failed. Captain Olson, in a typical show of protective concern for McKinney, decided to sail without the formal orders in hand, and we were 174 nautical miles west of Naha when the counter-orders came. We kept our course, and by the time we got to Pearl Harbor, someone in charge said what the hell—send that rusty old tub to Mobile for decommissioning. So, the Captain got us (and himself) home early.

"Most of all: I remember how much we missed home. I would have killed for a fresh green salad, or one properly-based scent of Chanel # 5; I know the engine room gang shared those emotions, for they got us the more than 9,000 nautical miles home in 58 days with only one breakdown. I think it was Massey [one of the engine room crew] who said we had five forward speeds: ahead one-third, ahead two-thirds, ahead full, flank, and home.

"But now: as the some 20 of us old salts reassemble here many miles from salt water, many with our lovely ladies: I realize that what brings us back together is not certainly love for the officers (actually, we officers were mostly ass holes, present company excepted, of course), or our love of country and pride in protecting it (we didn't pump much gas, and what we did pump got John Kennedy's PT 109 out far enough to get clobbered), or those other things fancy speakers tell about on Memorial Day [the speech was given on Memorial Day].

"We're here, I suspect, because whatever we were when we went aboard, we all grew up together—we came of age at Magiciene Bay in Saipan; at Bloody Ulithi; in those lonely nights at sea, wallowing in those rotten onion smells of aviation gasoline that our leaky pumps kept around us; in the typhoons when we went backwards with two anchors out and engines ahead full; in the sweet ambiance of the smoke generators at Naha Bay and Ie Shima. Those were good days, not because of our physical environment, but because we were together, and because we added something important to what we were from our experience with one another. That made the Marmora a damn good ship; that places each of us in the highest mutual love and respect for one another. As we grow older, that is what really counts in our lives. God has blessed us, each and every one, by giving us each other's company for a brief time 40 years ago. He's blessed us by letting us, with Gaither's, Hilcher's, and particularly Helen Gaither's help [these were the principal organizers of the reunion], rediscover our own Summer of 1945."

There were, of course, some things that I did not include in the talk. I should make clear that our basic mission was not to deliver aviation gasoline for the planes, but to serve as a back-up supply that could be tapped in an emergency. As such, we arrived at Okinawa six days after the invasion, when fighting on the beaches was visible from where we were anchored, and when Kamikaze air raids were continuous from dusk to dawn. It was interesting that after a week of responding to the air raids with all-night General Quarters, we began to ignore the hazards and sleep through, with a watch crew on duty to assure that we were concealed by boats with smoke generators. Once we heard that suicide swimmers with explosives taped to their bodies were swimming in the anchorage, and several times ships anchored within a few hundred yards were hit by Kamikazi planes, but our crew maintained their malaise, griping about the food and the lousy movies we were given to watch. (I remember coming home and my high school girl friend, anxious to be a good citizen, asked me hesitantly "How was it—over there?" I responded "It was hell," and she cried. I felt guilty for doing this, for her tears were sincere; nevertheless, I was also turned off, and had no further dating with her.)

One of the most vivid experiences was when young Ensign Lang and I decided to go ashore at Okinawa and find some souvenirs. We found one of the many caves that the natives used for burials, and that the Japanese had used for protective cover. It was in an area that had long been secured, and we felt it safe to venture in. About 30 feet inside, the tunnel rose and turned sharply to the right, and as we proceeded, darkness descended upon us. Suddenly, ahead of us something white came charging at us at several hundred miles an hour. It was long past us by the time we unholstered our .45 automatics and emptied our clips into the darkness. Our adversary was not a Japanese holdout, but one of the many goats that ran wild over Okinawa.

Another signal event that I omitted was the day that while our gunnery officer—Rudolph John Smith, who could not be restrained from regaling us with the report of his many female conquests—was sunning himself on an upper deck, I and a colleague sneaked into his cabin and sewed a dead fish inside his pillow. We were delighted that he did not find it for a full 48 hours.

Our captain was a quiet sheep rancher from Utah, who stayed in his quarters except when we were casting off, coming into port, or at General Quarters. He had all his meals brought to him, and talking with anyone was an extremely rare event. Each night around midnight he would come down the ladder from his quarters to the ship's office on a lower level, and poke around among the papers. The senior yeoman became quite incensed at this, and one night put an 8 ½ by 11 piece of paper under the 24" X 36" blotter on his desk with the simple message: "Find anything tonight, snooper?"

Although it was midnight, the captain broke from his usual stoic silence, called the officers together in the wardroom, and said that never in his life had anything angered him so much. There were only two yeoman on the ship—a senior career navy man, seen generally as an extrovert who talked a lot, and a Yeoman 2nd Class, a timid bespeckled man of about 100 pounds—so there was no doubt as to which of the two was summarily put off the ship at the next port. It was the Yeoman 2nd Class who took over the typing and paperwork, and who got his chest—or more precisely, the part of his anatomy between his navel and his Adam's apple—decorated by a tattoo artist on the way back, and who asked to go ashore in the Canal Zone to find a priest who would hear his confession (we wondered about what!) so that he would not have to face his home church padre with the account of his sins.

The old Marmora was caught in several typhoons. Unlike the one described in my reunion address where we were unable to turn into the wind and get out to sea (the large funnel and after section made the ship respond to wind like a weathervane), we were successful in one instance in leaving Okinawa. But our slow speed and the fast approaching storm caused the accompanying ships to desert us, and about a hundred miles east of Naha we were caught in the very eye of the storm—a brief period of complete quiet, and the lowest barometer reading ever recorded that we knew of -26.4, I believe. It was this storm where the winds—probably blowing in excess of 100 knots—got under my slicker as I tried to descend from the bridge, lifted me up, and carried me aft about 40 feet, setting me down on the catwalk. I was happy that the only way the old Marmora could sail in strong winds was into the wind. But the winds were sufficiently strong that water came in between the welded seams in the hull, and we were kept too busy with electrical fires from electrical short circuits to worry much about the winds and swells. I recall five of these in various locations over the span of about 12 hours.

One of the typhoons was the end of our sistership—the USS Vandalia, IX 191. The Vandalia had been commissioned with us at Pearl Harbor, and appeared at Okinawa one day not far from where we were anchored. But it failed to escape the typhoon, and sank in Buckner Bay, with the bridge still above water. Our engineering officer and I went over with our diving equipment to retrieve the safe in the ship's office, but the hulk lay in the bay, a reminder of ordinary dangers in extra-ordinary times.

The Marmora had sailed from Pearl Harbor to Saipan, and then to Ulithi, the staging area for the invasion of Okinawa. Ulithi was known to all Navy men as "Bloody Ulithi" because General MacArthur had set up an invasion there as a photo op. For that invasion, the atoll was bombarded mercilessly for five days, and most vegetation was so cleared. With cameras rolling, MacArthur had waded ashore from a landing craft, fearlessly leading the assault forces—but found no Japanese (a very small earlier contingent had abandoned the atoll), only some two dozen badly bruised and frightened natives. There was one casualty in this operation, we learned—a man was caught in the closing of a ramp in one of the LCVPs that brought men and equipment ashore. But a lot of film was expended, with the photographs never reaching the U.S

One event that attested the very best in the typical American spirit that infested our Naval servicemen occurred when we were sailing from Saipan to Ulithi. One of the crew got his right leg caught in heavy steerage machinery, which badly mangled it. At our flank speed, we were several days from the nearest Naval installation, and the captain authorized the radioman to break radio silence and ask that a physician be flown to the ship to deal with "a man with a badly mangled leg." In 20 hours, a destroyer from Ulithi came steaming up, and signaled that it was coming alongside to pick up the injured man. Its captain apologized that it took them an hour to get steam up and get underway, but we later calculated that they had moved at something around 30 knots, a most uneconomical speed for a tin can. The respect for the Navy held by each and every man on the ship grew tremendously that day.

I have mentioned that the command for our ship, inasmuch as it was carrying aviation gas as a reserve for the landing fields quickly erected on Okinawa, was transferred from ComServPac (the Navy's Pacific Service Force) to SAPOR (the Army's Sub Area Petroleum Officer—Ryukus). The Marmora was about 500 feet long, carried 70,000 barrels of aviation gas, and drew about 20 feet of water when fully loaded. We had gone to Okinawa six days after the invasion, and, upon the immediate formal transfer of command to the Army, some creative colonel sent us orders to proceed up a stream that emptied into Naha Bay and discharge gas to tanker trucks on a bridge overhead. The stream had a maximum depth of about 6 feet, so our captain invited the colonel to come out and help us carry out his orders. Somebody must have gotten to the colonel, for he never showed, and we did not lift anchor. And unlike Saipan, where marine pipelines for discharge of liquid cargo were available, Okinawa did not have such a luxury. Thus, we gassed PT boats and occasionally unloaded to a fuel barge, but by and large, very little of the gasoline we carried was put to use. Sitting on top of it, however, that cargo and the nightly Kamikazi raids gave us the hero status we all enjoyed writing home about.

But Okinawa was the scene where I became qualified for the Purple Heart. We were moored there when the armistice was signed, and when word came that the war was over, every ship and shore installation began to fire automatic weapons with tracer bullets into the night sky. There were probably at least a thousand celebrants, and it was quite a show. Later, we swept up two bushels of lead that had fallen on the deck of the Marmora. My purple heart? One sliver of lead from this barrage lodged in my left arm, and left a small hole that persists to this day. However, I somehow did not have the stomach to apply for the Purple Heart medal.

After decommissioning the old Marmora and depositing her on the mud banks north of Mobile, I needed about two months more of active duty to become eligible for discharge. I was assigned to the Naval Adjutant's office at the Charleston, SC Naval District. I found that my assignment was in most cases attempting to find out what had happened to a succession of sailors whose bodies had floated to the surface in the Cooper River. Tracing one by interviewing last known contacts, I quickly found that there was a thriving drug operation, with merchant seamen bringing in drugs as their ships once again began visiting oriental ports—and that sailors who had stumbled on this were quickly disposed of by strangling them and dumping them into the bay. The assignment involved two kinds of activity: taking court stenographers to witnesses for getting recorded statements, and sleuthing individuals who became suspected of involvement.

There were moments of great excitement—like the night when I was riding with Shore Patrol personnel and we got an emergency call to an address on downtown King Street. When we arrived, there were several dozen burly policemen assembling at the foot of stairs to an apartment over a store, from which loud wails could be heard penetrating the late night air. We waited until the police chief himself arrived to lead the charge up the stairs. There we found a completely nude woman—I recall vividly two patches of red hair—lying on a bed and crying her eyes out. She had, she sobbed, just lost her innocence, and was terribly upset as it was the only innocence she had. Several service personnel were standing thoughtfully around the bed, glasses in hand, listening, and since one was a Navy Chief Petty Officer, the Shore Patrol had been called in. The woman was swathed in a blanket and put in a patrol car, and we took the CPO to the Shore Patrol headquarters, got a statement, and gave him a ride to his ship.

But the greater excitement came from playing detective in trying to find the individuals responsible for putting the sailors in the river. In several days, and with the help of several prostitutes who had a remarkable knowledge of the people and places of concern, I located an individual with blood stains on the back seat of his car, and who was the last person seen with one of the sailors before his bloated body floated to the surface. I set out to interview him one evening, with the precaution of taking a Shore Patrol wagon and several burley SPs with me. At his home, on the edge of the Charleston City dump, his wife told me that he was expecting me (I had alerted him that I wanted to talk with him), and that he was down in the dump yard teaching his little cousin how to drive. The yard was expansive, with many alleys between the mountains of garbage, and we went up and down until a car in the darkness turned its lights on and pulled out to the road we were traversing. It was, of course, the man I was seeking, who had discovered that I was not alone. I did get a quick interview with him, and he did admit giving the sailor a ride, but stated that the blood in the back seat came from a cut the sailor had when he picked him up.

This episode was sufficient to get me transferred immediately to a secret destination, which turned out to be the Naval Ammunition Depot in Earle, New Jersey. There I was to wait out the two weeks before I would be eligible for release.

My roommate at the Naval Ammunition Depot BOQ was a nice enough chap—a swarthy fellow with a Greek name. He had a girl friend in a nearby town with prudish and Victorian parents, and asked me if I would double date with him, so he could get his girl out of the house. Being adventurous and single, I agreed. We went to the home of my date, where his girl was waiting, and my date was shortly expected. In a few minutes, in she came—all 400 pounds of her. Without stroking her mustache, she began sharing handbills for her brother's new business venture—Bill's Restaurant, which he had just opened that evening. My friend and his girl quickly split for parts unknown, leaving me with my Athenian queen.

I have repressed what we did for the next hour or so—I think we went to a movie. When I took her home, she grabbed me and gave me a kiss that would belittle an industrial model vacuum cleaner, and began breathing heavy. I broke away, and left her panting, and decided that never again would I be tricked into a blind date, and that I would forever more beware of Greeks, whether or not they were bearing gifts—and most particularly, if they were distributing restaurant handbills. Shortly after that, I was sent to Little Creek, Virginia, where I was properly discharged. It was now that I could return to the University, where I needed half a summer session (six weeks) to get enough credits to graduate with an A.B. Degree in mathematics, a subject I had almost completely forgotten, but in which I already had enough credits to serve as an academic major.

Chapter 9

The Mating Game

I recall vividly receiving a clipping from my mother when our ship was sitting at Okinawa as a reserve supply of aviation gas. The clipping was a newspaper photo and an item describing hometown girl Pegge Jill Morris of Graham as having been elected "Miss Pin-Up" at Elon College.

Little did I realize then that Pegge, a beautiful woman whose high intelligence is exceeded only by her grace and common sense, would within two years become my wife.

My first memories of Pegge were of her in her preteens wearing a short perky skirt and roller skates seemingly bigger than she was, skating on the sidewalk in front of Ms. Montgomery's house on North Main Street in Graham where her parents rented an appartment, and which was five blocks closer to the town shops than our house. I was getting bored on the old station tanker when I received the clipping from the Burlington *Times* showing the beautiful young lady in an evening gown that had just been voted "Miss Pin-Up" at Elon College. I thought to myself "My, how she has grown!" and wrote her a fan letter, but never received an answer.

But came my return to the US after the war, and in the process of being returned to civilian life, I had a "PROREP" or "proceed and report" set of orders to move from Charleston to the Naval Ammunition Depot in New Jersey. The PROREP meant I could take a couple of days to get to the new station. I went home to Graham, got in the family's 1937 Chevvy, and drove down town to see my good friend Tom Coble, who had just been released from Army duty, and who had obtained a job at the ticket window of the local cinema. It was just before 9 PM and the last show was about to start, but also the drug store across the street was about to close. Tom asked me to man the ticket booth for him while he went across the street for a Coke.

As the last showing was about to begin, a vision of loveliness came out of the theater and started walking south. It took me about 30 seconds to recognize her as the Miss Pin-Up whose picture I had salivated over at Okinawa, and another 10 seconds to close the booth and get in the Chevvy at the curb. I caught up with her about a block away, and stopped, told her who I was, and said as convincingly as I could that I would love to drive her home. (I was happy that my home town, Graham, was small enough—population about 5,000—that everyone knew everyone else, so I quickly and fortunately became no stranger!) After some hesitation, she got in the car, but held tightly to the door handle so that she could escape if necessary. I don't remember the small talk during the four block drive to her house, except that I did get a date for a later time when I would shortly be discharged from the Naval Reserve.

On that first date, we were going to the Plantation Supper Club in Greensboro for dinner, and it was late afternoon when I arrived at her house. A young man whom I assumed was the yard boy was mowing the lawn, and we exchanged pleasantries before I went to the door. My beautiful date was ready to go, and as we departed, she said to the person I had assumed to be the yard boy, "Bye, Dad." He was in his late 30s, but looked at least 10 years younger. I had the sinking feeling that it was curtains for me, but it turned out that her father enjoyed the mistake, though he never let me forget it.

The first date at the Plantation Supper Club in Greensboro, 25 miles away, was prim and proper, with both of us on our best behavior. The "club" offered a dance floor and live music, and a varied menu. I think I had a steak for dinner; I remember vividly that Pegge ordered shrimp. (Incidentally, we found a copy of the menu tucked away in an old yearbook, and noted that the dinner menu listed "Fried Shrimp Deluxe" for $1.25, and a club steak for $1.50. Drinks and deserts were extra, of course, and prices ranged from $0.10 to $0.30.) I was horrified the next day to learn that upon her return home, Pegge had had severe nausea. I got in the old Chevvy, tooled to Greensboro to the office of a Mr. S. W. Fowler, Public Health Engineer, Guilford County Board of Health, and with him went to the Plantation Supper Club where the owner took us into the kitchen and refrigerated area and let us inspect and sample the shrimp. No problems were found, although I knew somehow that I had blown any future welcome at the Plantation Supper Club.

Once out of the Navy, I had reentered UNC-Chapel Hill to finish the six quarter hours I needed to obtain my degree. This was possible in the upcoming summer session, and with the University only 20 miles away, it was easy to keep contact with Pegge.

It was during this period when I introduced a friend, Dan Reeves, to the daughter of our family grocer, Julia Bowman. Dan was not an attractive person: he had a wart on his nose, was stooped, and had a permanent sneer on his face. But Julia fell hard for Dan, and he for her, and they were married. I ran into him some ten years later, to find the wart gone, the stature erect, and no evidence of the sneer. "You look great, Dan!" I exclaimed. Dan replied: "It's Julia. Every morning she tells me how handsome I am, and I am beginning to believe her!"

Pegge and I had several dates—for local events or for activities at the university. I do not recall the occasion, but we attended some party at UNC where at one point the men were asked to compete in making a hat for their dates, from things that could be found where we were. I made a hat for Pegge with a paper plate, and with a large spoon glued across it. It was a lousy hat, but she modeled it to perfection, and Pegge was sufficiently beautiful in this posture that her hat won first prize.

Another memorable experience was taking her to a big band college dance weekend. Charlie Spivak's group came to the Woolen Gym for the two-night stand, and Friday night we gave several members of the band a ride back to the Carolina Inn where they were staying. On another occasion, we went swimming at my old summer job location, Kimesville Lake, where I got a photograph of Pegge in her bathing suit that verified that her election at Elon as Miss Pin-Up was quite valid. An enlargement of it has hung somewhere on our walls for over 60 years now.

It was during my return residence at the university that we were driving around on the campus in the early evening, and came upon the outdoor pool that had been built behind the indoor pool in the gym. The car radio was tuned to a music station. Leaving the radio on, we got out and sat down by the pool, and dangled our hands in the water. In the rush of emotion, two significant things then happened: (1) I proposed; and (2) the radio began to play "I'll be loving you—always." Showing she had more sense than I, she did not immediately accept, but said she would consider it. Thus began the most apprehensive 48 hours of my life.

I recall confiding my anxiety the next day to my adopted mother at the University, Mrs. Gustave Harrer who manned the University info booth. Mrs. Harrer was the widow of the former head of the Classics Department, and was stationed at an information desk in the lobby of the General Administration Building in the center of the campus. She was a most gracious lady, and was the adopted mother of many a student. I recall telling her that I had popped the question, but that Pegge had put me on hold. Then, a day later, I ran up to her, and said, breathlessly, "She said yes." Mom Harrier simply smiled a knowing smile, and said "I told you a girl needs a bit of time to make up her mind." Some years later when Mom Harrier retired, she was interviewed by the local papers, and recounted among other experiences attempting to console a young man who had proposed but had been put on hold.

Pegge was only 18 when she accepted my proposal, and her 19th birthday would occur some five months away, on November 8, 1946. Perhaps because of her tender age, and perhaps because our courtship had been somewhat whirlwind, Pegge set November 9 as the date for the wedding. I had completed my academic work for the A.B. degree, and had obtained a job as a buyer of men's furnishings for a new mail order plant of Sears Roebuck to be built in Greensboro; this involved an extended period of training at the Sears mail order plant in Atlanta. I moved to a bedroom apartment in Atlanta, commuting the some 250 miles to Graham every weekend until the date for the wedding.

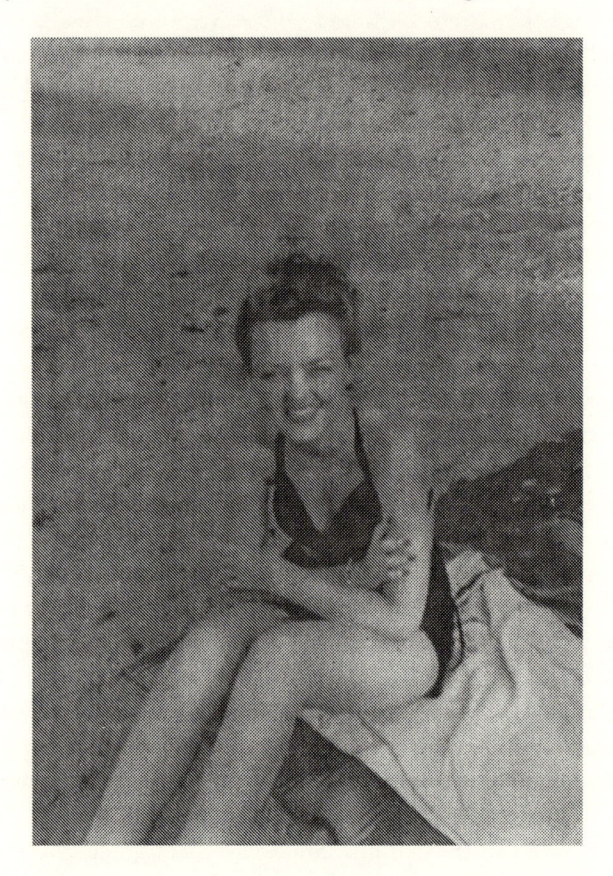

Pegge Jill Morris: Kimesville Lake, NC August 1946

    Pegge and I had dates during our engagement that were relatively simple. We would go to a movie or simply cruise around, usually stopping at a drive-in for snacks at the close of the evening together. Neither of us will ever forget the evening that Pegge ordered a large tomato juice to go with her hamburger, and I accidentally bumped her, spilling the entire contents on her pretty little yellow cotton dress that her mother had laundered, starched, and ironed so nicely. But we survived that, and very soon the appointed day came. I had a one week leave of absence from Sears for the wedding and honeymoon, and excitedly faced the wonderful new life that I knew we would have.

Chapter 10

Wedding

We had the usual fun and games associated with our wedding. The first problem that confronted us was the naming of a minister. I was uncomfortable with the pastor of Pegge's church, who was a bit too far-right and fundamentalist for me, and who had vigorously objected to my father's establishment of a hospitality center in town for servicemen trapped overnight in trying to hitchhike through town (the pastor felt the servicemen would corrupt the morals of all the young girls in town). Yet, there was no doubt that the wedding would take place anywhere but in Pegge's church. It turned out that the date Pegge selected—the day after her 19th birthday—was a day that her minister was scheduled to be out of town. We solved the problem by asking Charles Jones to officiate. Jones was the Chapel Hill Presbyterian minister later put out of the church for putting brotherhood of man over fatherhood of God (translation; he actually allowed Negroes at Sunday services!). Thus, we got Pegge's church and the minister for whom I had taught Sunday School while in college. We wanted to have a small, intimate wedding, and with great difficulty succeeded in scaling the guest list down to about 200

My next door neighbor, a Mrs. Ivy, took in sewing, and was commissioned to make me a pair of pajamas with the same cloth suitable for a first night that she would use to make a gown for Pegge. She did, but she put the buttons of my pajamas on the left side of the opening, as customary for women's clothing, instead of on the right side as is customary for men. This made the pajamas difficult for me to get into or out of, and I shortly gave them away . . .

The wedding rehearsal was a gala affair. Pegge had many friends who were involved in the wedding—Nancy Wilkinson, Jean Terrell, Betty Walker Robertson, Betty Horner, Theo and Drucilla Braxton, and Betty Lou Sharpe. Pegge's uncle Earle Garrett, recently retired from a high post in state government, came, leaving his suitcase in the room occupied at Pegge's home by her and her grandmother who lived with them. At some point the girls sneaked into the bedroom, found the suitcase, assumed it was mine packed for our honeymoon getaway, opened it and sewed the pajama bottoms together so that they could not be put on. We suspected Drucilla to be the ringleader of this escapade, but are sure that Grandma Morris aided and abetted the group, in spite of her knowledge as to the rightful owner of the suitcase. We understand that Uncle Earle used some choice language to punctuate his attempt at retiring for the evening a little later.

My best man, John Fesperman, and groomsmen were friends from the University. John came a day early, and we spent the night following rehearsal in the front bedroom of my parent's house, which was heated by a fireplace that we kept going all evening and into the early hours of the wedding day. Daylight for that day came quickly, and I used the first part to hide the car with a cousin several miles outside of town in the hopes that this would prevent its getting decorated.

John Fesperman and the minister, Charles Jones, and I got to Pegge's church about fifteen minutes before the formal ceremony was to start. Fesperman and Jones had not seen each other since before the war, and they had a good time waiting, exchanging dirty stories while I sweated out the possibility that Pegge might get cold feet. But she did not; our organist, friend Charles Dellinger, made only a few mistakes in the music, and we were hitched and after a round of picture taking and furtive goodbyes (Pegge said she had not realized she was leaving home!), we were chauffeured to the 1937 Chevy that we believed we had hidden and that we hoped would take us to Miami for our honeymoon.

As indicated, I had left the car with a cousin in the belief that this would prevent its decoration. But my cousin was unfaithful. After the wedding, when we tried frantically to escape the friends who seemed so loathe to see us go, we found that the car had indeed been variously adorned. When I say "adorned," I do so with awe and admiration that lasts until the present day. The hubcaps were filled with stones, as might have been expected, but we had not counted on the tin cans to be wired with very strong multi-filament wire, and secured to a part of the car far underneath. And the words describing our new status were written not with the usual soap, but with a mixture, I believe, of flour and water which had gone on as a paste, but which had quickly hardened as it dried, becoming an integral part of the car itself. Although I attempted to have the car cleaned the next morning, the outline of the words that had been written would not come off, and were still visible a year later.

I had reserved a room for the first night at the Carolina Inn in Chapel Hill. We kept this very much a secret, for the groomsmen were principally from Chapel Hill, and we knew that they would have no respect for our privacy if they found out. We therefore, in our decorated 1937 Chevy, attempted to reach Chapel Hill by country back roads, ending up hopelessly lost for what seemed like hours. When we finally reached the Inn, I drove up to the covered entrance, hitting one of the brick supporting posts for the roof of the entranceway. But I backed off, got Pegge inside, got the car parked, and said a thank-you prayer that no one in the wedding party had discovered where we were. The scar where I hit the supporting post was still visible years later.

We had planned to spend a week in Miami, and set out the next morning. It was 1946, and the tires on the old Chevy were multiple retreads. The first one gave way near Sanford, only 30 miles south; two more gave way in South Carolina, and the fourth required replacement by the time we reached Atlanta.

Replacements were at black-market prices, and the only ones available were retreads, not new tires. By the time we reached Atlanta, we had spent most of the money we had planned to use in Miami, and, with an apartment in Atlanta paid for, and the replacement tires retreads like their predecessors, we said that we would just draw the blinds and have our honeymoon there. The bedroom apartment was in a residence on Orme Circle, the home of two spinster sisters who were teachers in the Atlanta City Schools. We had a private entrance, and the sisters were great sports. They left us alone, except for one occasion when one of them chided me for smoking a pipe. "Pipes are for old men," she said. "A young man like you should smoke a cigar!"

But the week passed quickly; we ferried the car back to Graham, with only one mishap: the transmission fell out on the highway as we were passing through Clemson, South Carolina about midnight. Clemson, we do recall, was a tiny little town in spite of the university there, and the options for repair would not have been good in normal business hours. Now, more that 60 years later, we find that we have repressed how we solved this problem, but we did get the car back to my father, and returned to Atlanta and my job at the Sears mail order plant My colleagues in training for the new Greensboro plant were selected mostly from the University in Chapel Hill, so we were not among strangers. Sears had agreed to take Pegge on as a secretary, so we commuted to work and had lunch together. And Atlanta was a fun city, where we found much to enjoy.

Thus, in spite of investing a small fortune in junk tires and never consummating our honeymoon in Miami, we were off to a start of a relationship that would extend over more than the next six decades. For the years to come, I felt about her very much as my childhood friend Dan Reeves did about his wife Julia: "I think she likes me!" Little did she (nor I, for that matter) realize that marriage for her would involve putting up with a rat infested apartment in Greensboro over a beer joint; the uncertainty of life as a wife of a Naval officer in the peacetime Navy; apartment hunting and job seeking in New York City; supporting me through graduate school by working; three-time producer of our children. But she was endowed with excellence of taste in all things; avid reader, and later source of our several thousand books; graceful in movement and a talented dancer, and upon reaching 40, always looking at least 20 years younger than she was. But principally, she accepted without question the decisions I made as to our place and way of life, and joined without reservation in whatever challenges we were encountering at any point in time. In spite of our whirlwind courtship, engagement, and marriage, I have always felt that I did very well for myself.

Chapter 11

Our Life in Atlanta

Following our abortive honeymoon spent searching for replacement tires for the borrowed 1937 Chevy that we had hoped to take us to Miami, and our struggles with the transmission in getting it back to North Carolina, we returned and settled in late November, 1946, in our bedroom apartment on Orme Circle in Atlanta. Pegge joined me in employment at the Mail Order plant of Sears, Roebuck, and Co. This operation involved a large number of clerical type workers, who handled the records and merchandise transactions for those who ordered from the catalog.

Pegge, still fresh from her "Miss PinUp" days at Elon College, decided to use silk scarfs as headbands, folded and tied on one side. She was most attractive anyway, but this set her off in the finest style.

In the space of a week, however, several hundred girls at the plant began to appear with a similar scarf headband—and Pegge paid the price of being a trend-setter, by placing her scarfs in storage—to be used only when we went out to some major establishment as the dining rooms of the Biltmore Hotel or the New Hotel Ansley, where for the paltry sum of two bucks one could add a slice of bread to the order.

I shortly learned that there were no left-handed people among the some 400 employees of the Atlanta Sears Mail Order plant. A casual inquiry brought the answer that Standard Operating Procedure in filling an order involving merchandise from several departments was to create a "ticket" listing the merchandise, and to certify that an item had been added to the package by adding a label that was secured to the ticket with a straight pin. The reasoning was that left-handed order pickers would be stabbed by the pins when they removed them to add an item. But I found that the question as to handedness was on the general personnel application form, and that the rule applied to staff above the rank of order handlers. Pursuing this with the director of personnel, I learned that all left handed people are really brain-damaged klutzes, and, of course, none could be tolerated in this mail order plant. I was happy to learn that being right-handed, I was not a brain-damaged klutz.

I have forgotten why we had to move from the apartment at Orme Circle, but remember we were there during the period that young Herman Talmadge commandeered the Georgia State Highway Patrol to move the elected governor out of the Governor's Mansion, and move himself in. Our opinion of the Talmadge clan was predicated largely on the campaign tactic of Herman's father, old Gene Talmadge, who campaigned in a chauffeured Cadillac and who, when surrounded by voters in the red dirt areas of Georgia, would spit tobacco juice on the carpet of the car. Our two landladies were among the few Georgians we knew who took a positive view of Herman's acquisition of the office of governor, but we began to understand when we learned that young Herman had been a star pupil of one of them. But when we left Orme Circle, we moved to an upstairs one-room space in a private residence on North Highland Avenue, which was on the bus route that would take us to Sears Mail Order.

I had figured before job seeking that as a married man I would require a salary of $200 a month to make ends meet (no pun intended). My salary at Sears was a husky $50.00 per week, and with Pegge working too, we were in fat city. Accordingly, we treated ourselves from time to time to dinners in the best hotels or restaurants, and enjoyed the movies at the Fox Theater—which had a traditional presentation of an opera each summer that attracted the elite of Atlanta, with the men coming in tuxedos and the women in evening gowns and—believe it or not—fur wraps, in spite of the summer heat. This taught us that people who are very rich and that are leaders of society are hardy souls who can endure discomfort without protest.

We made several trips home to Graham, NC, during our training period in Atlanta, being careful to stay with one set of parents one time, and the other the next. Initially, we shared rides with other trainees who were going home to North Carolina for the weekends. I remember one trip where, as usual, we had stayed in North Carolina as long as possible, and were in a Studebaker driving back starting quite late Sunday evening. It was about 3 AM Monday morning, and we were somewhere en route near Greenville, SC, when I found that I was the only one awake. The driver, the wife of our host, was indeed sound asleep but the speedometer was sitting on 95 MPH. Knowing that a rude awakening would startle her, I began to sing, getting louder and louder, until she shook her head and slowed to a more reasonable 60 MPH. We made it safely back to Atlanta, but that was the last time we rode with that couple, in spite of the fact that they spent each weekend in Greensboro.

Other new-hires in training for Greensboro included several young couples just married, and we had a rich social life, going out together, or playing bridge in our living quarters. Particular friends were Ruth and Bob Lutfy, Orrell and Carl Clark, Ida Ann and Jim Currant, and Frances and Wayne Farrell, who remained close friends when we got back to Greensboro.

We did break away one weekend for a jaunt to Savannah. Pegge had contracted the mumps from her little brother on a trip back to North Carolina, and her recovery, we felt, deserved celebration. We flew down in an old DC3, with the windows rattling, and got a room at the Hotel DeSoto (although the desk clerk gave us a hard time because he could not believe Pegge was more than 15). We had a glorious weekend, spending time at the hotel's beach hotel as well, but when Sunday night came, we realized we were short of cash to pay our way back to Atlanta by any way but bus. We spent Sunday night on buses and in bus stations,. I recall a three hour layover in Augusta starting at about 1 AM, while we were waiting for the next bus to Atlanta. But, we made it back just in time to go to work at 8:30 am Monday morning. We must have looked like hell, but being newlyweds, this was not unexpected.

All too soon (in early 1947), construction of the new mail order plant in Greensboro, and our training, were completed, and we packed our belongings in a couple of suitcases, and returned to North Carolina.

Chapter 12

Our First Residence in Greensboro

In returning to Greensboro and our employment in the new Sears Mail Order plant there, we had limited time to search for housing, and settled for one of two three room apartments at 307 1/2 Paisley Street. It was over a beer joint run by the owner of the building, one Mr. Lanier.

This was fun at first, for we could do anything we wanted to with the apartment. First, we decorated—chartreuse walls in the living room, and a red floor in the bath with black footprints (from stepping in a pan of black paint) going to the tub, and white footprints emerging and going out the door.

My Aunt Cleo in Burlington had a surplus piano, which we thought would be nice to have. The problem, once we got it to Greensboro and the top of the narrow stairs to the apartment, was that we did not have the space required to turn it so we could get it in the door. There was nothing to do except simply take it apart and move it in piece by piece. But we soon had our own musical instrument, albeit with a somewhat tinny tone, a casualty of the disassembly/reassembly.

The rather cramped landing outside our entrance also was the scene of a frequent problem. The other apartment was inhabited by a couple of foreign heritage, and the woman, an overweight person of about 50, was a chronic alcoholic. Almost every evening, she would get herself soused, go out her front door, collapse on the landing (consequently blocking our front door), and cry for help until she had sobered up enough to get up and go back inside and join her rather stoic husband, who was either hard of hearing, inured to the situation, or soused himself. We were warned about this by our landlord, Mr. Lanier, and soon grew as capable of ignoring her cries as we later became when we moved to New York City of ignoring the Third Avenue El screeching to a halt at the stop about twenty feet from our second story bedroom window.

When our front entrance was blocked, we could use a back stairway to the alley behind the beer parlor. A larger problem was the beer parlor itself. There was a juke box which included a favorite of the time, a ditty that started with the line "There's just one place for me—near you." The phrase "near you" would then be repeated many times in the course of the song a kind of constant refrain. This record would be played several dozen times each evening, and the particular recording had a strong bass beat that rattled the panes in our windows and the dishes in our cabinet with each "near you."

We soon found that we were not alone in the apartment. It was heated by a water-jacketed coal-fired stove in the kitchen, with pipes behind it going into the wall and to old-fashioned cast iron radiators in the other two rooms. The holes behind the stove for the pipes were rather large, sufficiently so for wharf rats to enter with impunity as soon as lights were out. We were made aware of the seriousness of the problem when one morning we found a five pound sack of flour that had been dragged from a high shelf in the pantry to the middle of the kitchen floor, broken open, and strewn about the floor. The size of our intruder was nicely documented by the paw prints in the flour, coming and going from the hole in the wall behind the heater.

The experience was sufficiently unnerving that one night as Pegge and I were asleep, I apparently moved my hand from my side to my shoulder area, raking Pegge along the way. In her uneasy sleep, she was immediately convinced that we had a rat in bed with us, and woke the neighborhood. It did not take me long after that to seal the hole with wire mesh and plaster.

Buying for the Sears mail order plant in Greensboro was tolerable, and we were happy with the 10% discount employees received on any purchase from Sears. Pegge worked in the payroll department, so we could come and go to work together, and my supervisor had only one usually tolerable piccadillo: he could somehow never move his bottom off his chair except to go to lunch or to the bathroom, or home at quitting time, and would frequently yell from his office to the dozen or so buyers in an open space outside when he wanted to see someone: "Davis (or Bell or Simpson or whoever)—come in here!" He was the second person (after Grandma Davis) that I never knew to smile, and never had a nice word for anyone. But he was my first boss in civilian life, and I assumed that his behavior was par for the course in business elsewhere.

I generally managed to stay out of trouble with him, until our first buying trip to the parent office in Chicago. We went by train, and stayed at the old Hotel Sherman with its bullet-proof doors for several days, attending meetings at the mail order plant there during the day, and visiting the restaurants and burlesque houses during the evening. I kept a very careful record of my expenses, and entered them on the appropriate form upon return and handed them in to the supervisor for his approval. When he got to mine, there was a particularly explosive "DAVIS COME IN HERE!" and in I went, wondering what he thought I must have padded on the expense account. Instead, he loudly made a strong case that I had to have spent much more than I reported, and that if such an account as mine were approved, no one else would ever be able to afford the frequently required trips to Chicago. I tried to assure him that my report was accurate, and that in fact I felt I had been lavish in some regard, but he took his pen, slashed through the figures given, entered amounts generally double what I had reported, and shoved it across the desk with a scowl and a pen, saying "SIGN THIS."

But that first trip to Chicago had other fascinations for me. I had been favorably biased by Carl Sandburg's odes to the Windy City, and I found it to be truly a cozy working class city, where the blue collar riders in the loop were in the majority. And I recall my first trip, where I arrived about noon on a bitter cold Sunday, after an all-night train ride from Greensboro. As I entered the elevator of the Sherman Hotel after checking in, I asked the elevator girl if the bars in Chicago were open on Sunday. "Mister," she said, "If the bars here were closed on Sunday, the people would all move away, or just die." I felt that I could feel at home in this big city.

On later trips to the parent office, I used a non-stop flight that was offered by Piedmont Airlines. This company, based in Winston-Salem, NC, had a fleet of old DC 3s at that time. I recall taking a night flight back from Chicago one time when the plane hit an updraft over the mountains, and turned upside down, spilling the contents of the bathroom holding tanks on the floor of the plane, and leaving cherry cobbler, just served with the meal, deposited artistically on the ceiling. Apparently there was also some structural damage that concerned the pilot, for he made an emergency landing at the Hickory, NC airport. It was late at night, and although the runway was lighted, the only other light was in a phone booth alongside a closed hangar. The pilot got out, went to the phone booth, and (I assume) called his wife or girl friend that he would be delayed (I assume he had radioed Winston-Salem for a substitute plane). The substitute plane was about two hours in coming, and we had to stay in our seats, trying to breathe, to hold our feet off the floor, and to dodge dripping cherry cobbler from the ceiling until the relief plane came in.

In the work at the Greensboro Mail Order plant, I recall two particularly significant contacts with provider representatives. These involved a Mr. Stedman, the owner of Stedman Manufacturing Company in Asheboro, N.C., and a Mr. Liebovitz, the CEO for Fruit of the Loom.

Both of these men, though CEOs, took a personal interest in sales and their clients. Stedman manufactured inexpensive cotton underwear, but had been in business only a few years. I recall asking him how he had achieved the substantial fortune his large manufacturing enterprise signaled, and he revealed a modern secret of life that I will never forget. He said: "Ten years ago, I had twenty-two cents to my name. Today I owe four million dollars."

Mr Liebovitz was probably the kindest, most genuinely caring man I have ever known. It was he that got me in trouble years later in the Adult Sunday School class ("Applied Christianity") I taught at Amity Methodist Church in Chapel

Hill when I referred to him, a Jew, as "the most Christ-like man I ever knew." He was more like a loving father than a corporation VIP or a salesman, and his genuine concern for people extended to the ladies in his sewing or knitting lofts and to those who purchased their products. Overbought jockey shorts? "Send them back—I am canceling the invoice and will cover the shipping costs." Or, to my great surprise: "Happy birthday—how wonderful it must be to be 23 years old today!" And in spite of his responsibilities as head of a major cotton clothing company, he always had time to talk about his day and people and about my day and people.

But my tenure at Sears was dogged by one pervasive irritant beyond the vocal prowess of my supervisor. The new Greensboro plant was scheduled to take parts of territory previously covered by Philadelphia and Atlanta, and company records were used to project what the sales for all catalog items in our area would be as the percentage of sales in the last several years in the Atlanta mail order plant. I proceeded to buy the items for which I was responsible according to this formula, purchasing what would seem to be a two month supply. My purchases included cowboy hats, a hot item from a several page spread in the Atlanta mail order catalog. They were listed in the Greensboro catalog as they were in the Atlanta catalog, and I believe that in the first year we sold about five such hats, leaving the other thousand or so taking up space and budget for new acquisitions. It turned out that the Atlanta cowboy hat business was generated by citrus pickers in Florida, and were decidedly unpopular in our sales territory—in fact, I had a 10 year supply! After two years, I was finally able to job them to a wholesaler at 10% of their original cost. But what a relief to get rid of them.

I have forgotten what the idea was, but I came upon one matter where a particular investment that would lose money the first year was bound to become a money maker in time. I presented this idea to top management, and the promise was recognized. But I was told that what we had to deal with—the ultimate criterion, as it were, of success or failure—was the bottom line at the end of the current fiscal year. That was the way business had to be. My proposal was rejected. I thought of this years later, when the catalog sales plants of Sears were closed and the catalog sales discontinued. Thinking now of some of the commercial giants of that day that have since disappeared brings to mind Pogo's "We have met the enemy, and he is us."

I began, however, to tire of the routine of getting weekly sales reports for each item, projecting demand fo the remainder of the sales season, and placing orders for a portion to assure that the item would be in stock. The coup de grace came one Christmas season where sales were very brisk. To keep the stock bins loaded so that orders could be filled and no sales lost required extra effort. I had been working 12 hour days to keep up, staying at my desk as Mr. GETINHERE brushed past at 5 P.M on the way home. After two weeks of this, the dreaded "DAVIS COME

IN HERE!" was heard one afternoon, and I was told, loudly, of course, that if I were truly responsible I would just have to start working overtime for the season to be sure the bins were not empty and that orders could be filled.

I did not protest this, for prior experience suggested that my supervisor was quite deaf. But that evening I made arrangements to go to the office of the Commandant, Sixth Naval District, in Charleston, SC, and see if I could not be taken back into active duty in the Naval Reserve. I made the trip; I found that there was a staffing need for a mathematics instructor at the Naval Academy Preparatory School in Bainbridge, Maryland, and that my credentials well qualified me for this billet. I accepted, and returned to Greensboro, where, when my orders for return to active duty shortly came in, I was granted a leave-of-absence from my buying job to permit my return to service in the armed forces. I had no intent of ever using this, but considered it insurance in case of unexpected problems in the near future. I found I could still fit into my uniforms, and so we gave the piano to a fellow buyer who would move it to his house without realizing the problems of moving it out of the appartment, transferred the few items of furniture we had to our parents in Graham, got in the Ford we had purchased upon return to North Carolina, and set out for Bainbridge, Maryland, where the Naval Academy Preparatory School occupied the old Tome Academy on the bluff overlooking the little village of Port Deposit and the Susquehanna River, with the old wartime Bainbridge boot camp now an adjacent set of deserted buildings.

Chapter 13

Second Tour of Duty in the Navy

Dusting off my old uniforms, I reported for duty in the late summer of 1948 to the Naval Academy Prep School ("NAPS"). NAPS was on the grounds and in the building of the old Tome Academy which was on a promontory overlooking the Susquehenna River at one end of the now vacant Naval Training Station, one of the wartime boot camps for inductees. We were assigned quarters in an old four story house just inside the base fence, that had been split into two four story apartments. It was about 20 feet from the main road into Port Deposit as it took a sharp dive toward the river and town, but separated from that road by a high chain link fence that enclosed the Navy property. This was quite a change from our little apartment that we shared in Greensboro with the wharf rats. The other half of the house was occupied by a chief warrant officer and his bride, a welcome change from the alcoholic lady who blocked our front entrance in Greensboro. The wife of the chief warrant officer had been employed by one of the Mafia families to transport large sums of money to foreign banks. Her accounts of her activities helped introduce us to the real world neither of us had ever known.

Shortly after we arrived, one officer's wife's cat, a white long-hair Persian, escaped for a night out, and shortly had kittens We were offered a pair, both long-haired males—one solid white, and the other solid black. We named them Pomp and Circumstance, and marveled at their habits. Although the chain-link fence separated our house from the road outside to Port Deposit, the cats would chase cars as they passed, running along the inside of the fence. Another strange activity was that the two would fight over grapefruit rinds as if they were tuna. But otherwise, they had all the endearing and non-endearing characteristics of cats.

But alas, we shortly lost Pomp. We took the pair to a veterinarian for routine shots when they were six months old, and shortly thereafter both cats came down with distemper. Circumstance survived, living later to a ripe old age of 19, but Pomp did not. With Pomp gone, the name "Circumstance" seemed no longer applicable as well as triggered sad thoughts, so we renamed him Spooky after Smoky Stover's black cat in the comics. Spooky stayed with us until our later move to New York City, when he was adopted by my mother and father in Graham, NC.

NAPS, it turned out, had as its main purpose the recruitment of good athletic prospects for the Naval Academy who might be enrolled as the 10% of the entering class each year that were "fleet appointees," rather than Congressional appointees. We had two missions. One was to give them a review of high school work to bring them up to snuff for the Academy; the other was to provide a mechanism where the most promising athletes in the fleet could join the teams at the Naval Academy. All of the students had been out of school for some time, and many had more athletic prowess than academic ability.

Accordingly, the other teaching staff included Academy graduates who had distinguished themselves in sports while at the Academy, and who were assigned to coaching positions in addition to their teaching duties. This included Jake Welsh and Bobby Jenkins, football; John Fletcher, wrestling; Walter Grechanic, swimming. I have forgotten who was responsible for the other sports, but recall a very lively basketball program.

The mornings were spent in review of high school subjects. Although I had been assigned to NAPS as a math instructor and had no significant athletic experience, I was allowed to teach English, my first love, and appointed as an associate swimming coach, an area in which I had some proficiency. The afternoons were consumed with athletic drills. In the evenings, the students studied, and the officers congregated at the Officer's Club, an integral part of the old Bainbridge boot camp, and now a well-established fixture on the NAPS grounds.

The school involved twice as many as could be accommodated in the 10% allotment at the Academy, and even if the student had some very unusual athletic skill, the final selection of those who would get four years of cost-free training was determined at the end of the year by a competitive academic exam, where the top half would be admitted to the Academy. There was no deviation from the authority of the test: there was much grief when an all-American class basketball prospect had to go back to the fleet. We had no problem with student motivation, for ending the year in the winning half meant not only an expense paid college education, but also an early release from active duty as an enlisted person.

Life was really pretty easy. We had a retired Navy commander named McGhee as our superintendent of instruction, and he provided good practice opportunity and monitoring as we assumed our instructional duties. Each new instructor was required to prepare a lesson and deliver it to the other officers for critique, and we had a crash but very good course in teaching methods. I recall worrying as to whether I would fill the time for my first pilot test lesson, but found Commander McGhee calling a halt as I entered the third hour of the one hour test class. But I was hooked on teaching, and shortly gained the experience I needed to fill the time exactly.

We shopped at the commissary at nearby Aberdeen Proving Ground, and although the NAPS staff included a medical doctor and a dentist, we could use the medical facilities at this post, still a very active enclave for the Army. The well stocked commissary saved us much money in grocery shopping. NAPS had a nine hole golf course professionally designed, as well as tennis courts and indoor and outdoor swimming pools, which had been provided for the several hundred officers back in boot camp days, but which were now available to the some thirty of us on the teaching staff. We had a well equipped hobby shop, with equipment ranging from jewelry making to photo processing and enlargement. A focal point for evening activities was the Officers' Club, which not only provided booze for ten cents a shot, but had a TV set, then a rarity, whose 6 inch screen showed such fare as the Ed Sullivan Show. Whatever hell war may have been, we found peacetime service to be a complete opposite.

But the truly exciting part of this tour of active duty for me was the teaching. The students were, as indicated earlier, highly motivated, and took to the subject matter with vigor. I recall one rough and tough Bo'sun Mate 2nd Class from Brooklyn whom I asked to summarize the plot in Shakespeare's *As You Like It*, and his five minute account beginning, in fine Brooklyn accent: "Deese guys were going to rassle, and . . ." But I felt comfortable preparing my lectures, and found fulfillment from the student interest in my lectures and assignments. My father had said that of all the things he ever did, teaching was the most fulfilling, and that a piece of him died when he left that profession. I knew from my experience at Bainbridge that this was what I wanted to do.

The quaint little village of Port Deposit, perched on the narrow banks of the Susquehenna, was a treasure. The head of the local bank, the Cecil National Bank, was an amicable gentleman named Pierre LeBruin, who had an honorary membership in the Officers' Club, and who treated the officers as if they were his own children. It was also in Port Deposit's lone eatery that we were introduced to a delicacy known as submarine sandwiches, then non-existent in the South. It was at the nearby town of Havre de Grace that we discovered Crab Imperial. We also enjoyed frequent trips up and across the river to Lancaster, Pennsylvania, for shopping and observing the Amish in their horse-drawn carriages.

The base hospital at the Aberdeen Proving Grounds turned out to be most useful. The Academy graduates assigned to teaching/coaching roles had all been at sea for at least two years, and nine months after they were united with their wives, most became fathers. We recall in May, 1949, the base ambulance taking off several times each day for the Aberdeen Proving Grounds hospital with a prospective mother in beginning labor.

We had time and room for guests. My mother and sisters came up for a week, the highlight of which was traveling to a nearby marker for the Mason-Dixon Line and taking photographs of one or another of us trying to pull my mother over, but not succeeding. Another momentous visit was that of Pegge's parents and her younger brother, then about 9, who had acquired a fear of water and who had never learned to swim. Daily trips to the outdoor pool on the base permitted me to take his development seriously, and by golly in a week's time he had gained confidence and was swimming like a porpoise. Another set of guests were my old shipmate from the USS Marmora, Ezra Lang and his bride, who had settled nearby in Levitown. Pennsylvania. We usually ended up playing bridge when they visited, finding that they each took it seriously and that the other could only make stupid plays. She had a degree in Law, and both were very bright. They were quite vocal in the course of the sets, and each seemed to enjoy the very lively critique of the play the other had just made—winning or losing the rubber was of little consequence in comparison to the spirited exchanges after each play. But we did not get involved in bridge again until some years later at Emory University, where the controller was a master at the game, but truly enjoyed playing (and showed it) with people of limited skill—which made it fun again for us, duffers that we were.

Several of the instructors at NAPS were not Academy graduates, but were, like me, Naval Reservists returning to active duty for one reason or another. One was our dentist, a Lieutenant Commander Gorenberg, who left his practice in Baltimore and returned to active duty because the boxing commissioners were closing in on him for giving prizefighters Novocaine shots in the jaws before fights. He said that the boxers felt this would insulate them, but in fact, of course, it would not. The practice, however, had been highly lucrative. I used his free availability to rid myself of three wisdom teeth that were bothersome, which he removed, one at a time, after loosening them substantially with a little hammer. He left a fourth one in place, as it was so impacted that he could not get at it with his little hammer, and reasoned that it seemed to promise no problems. He played a mean piano at the Officers' Club in the evenings, and we rewarded him with the nickname "Paddy" O'Gorenberg, which seemed to please him very much.

We also had a young doctor on the base, who was convinced that he could fatten me up (I then weighed about 130 pounds) by increasing my calorie intake, but who gave up when I reached the point of stuffing myself for several weeks to the extent of 7,000 calories daily without gaining an ounce.

Close friends with no Academy history were LTJG Leslie Price and his wife., Leslie's father ran a funeral parlor and ambulance service in North Dakota, and Leslie had spent his time between tours of duty driving for the parlor. He was at complete ease driving at 90 MPH, a carryover from his civilian role. Leslie and his wife were delightfully laid-back people. Neither Pegge nor I will ever forget Leslie saying that they had "learned about love the hard way."

Our friendships were not confined to the non-academy graduates. There were a number of other young couples that we found most enjoyable to socialize with, the males of which were Academy graduates. This included the Bill Cooks, the Jortbergs, the Keepins, and the Oglivies. Betty Oglivie had been a ballerina in major stage productions in Chicago, the most recent being *The Song of Norway*. The officers also included their share of odd balls—we remember Lt. Casey, who had little to do with the rest of us, but bred Great Danes which he favored in appearance, and Lieutenant Fallon, a Marine Corps Naval Academy graduate who headed the English Department and was very warm and friendly the first few months. An adjustment at the Bureau of Naval Personnel in dates from which seniority in rank could be calculated switched our positions in the pecking order (I had outranked him by a few days, but now he outranked me by a few days), and he immediately became rather formal and aloof. This never bothered us, but it gave us insight into the fact that the armed services harbored a strong class system even among officers of equal rank, which I found objectionable.

At the end of the academic year, the decision was made in Washington to close the NAPS function at Bainbridge, and move it to the grounds of the Naval War College in Newport, RI. We were not affected by this, for I had felt from the experience that teaching was what I wanted to do, and had been assured in a trip to the Pentagon of a teaching spot at the Air Force Academy if I transferred to this branch of service, and if I acquired a Master's degree. I had therefore applied for a transfer from the Naval Reserve to the Air Force upon attainment of the Master's degree, and made plans to enter graduate study. My costs in graduate school would be covered by the GI Bill, and we would count on income from Pegge getting a job.

I was interested in the the field of guidance and counseling, and was advised by a knowledgeable friend that the best programs were with John Darley at the University of Minnesota, Frank Fletcher at Ohio State University, and Donald Super at Columbia University in New York City, Both Pegge and I felt residence in the Big Apple would be an adventure, and Minneapolis, Minnesota, and Columbus, Ohio, seemed far away and dull in comparison to New York City. So, I applied for admission to the graduate program at Columbia University. Because I had gone to a public university, and because of some low grades on my undergraduate transcript, I was required to take the Graduate Record Examination as an admission credential. I recall making a perfect 800 on the Math portion, but a much lower score on the Verbal portion. I was admitted, however, on the basis of my scores on this examination. The need for this extra justification to establish eligibility gave me the resolve to show the people at Columbia University that this requirement in their admissions procedures might have problems of validity.

But in closing out NAPS-Bainbridge, many items were slated for disposal, and among them was a bountiful supply of liquor at the Officer's Club. Everything had to go, of course, and the officers who had belonged to this establishment were given the opportunity of purchasing it for a dollar a fifth.

I had maintained contacts with my colleagues at Sears Mail Order in Greensboro, and I called one to ask if good booze at half price would be attractive to our friends there. He called me back shortly with an order for some 7 cases, which I purchased and put in the trunk of our car. I have forgotten why Pegge did not make the trip with me, but I left the night of July 3 with the precious cargo, giving our 1946 Ford a decided cant to the rear from the weight in the trunk. I was motivated not so much by interest in sharing the wealth with friends at Sears as I was by the money from the sales, which I felt could be put to good use in our NYC residence. I was tooling along late at night at about 70 MPH just inside the NC line when a flashing red light signaled a State Trooper in hot pursuit. Knowing that my goose was cooked, I came to a stop. The trooper pulled up behind me, got out, came to my window, and asked for driver's license and registration. This I produced. He then pulled out of his pocket what appeared to be a ticket pad, wrote something on it, and, handing it to me, returned to his patrol car. It was a minute before I could stop shaking enough to examine the ticket he had handed me. When I did, I found on it the following words: "The North Carolina Highway Patrol wishes you a safe driving holiday, and wants you to live through many more Independence Days."

Thus, I drove more slowly the rest of the way. But the booze was delivered to my contact in Greensboro, and profits from my bootlegging served to help support my graduate study, as my homebrew sales had helped support my undergraduate study.

Chapter 14

Our Life in New York City

Having been admitted to graduate study in the Department of Vocational Guidance, Teachers College, Columbia University, it behooved us to find a place in the city to live. I recall with horror the first "apartment" we looked at—it was a single room, in Hoboken (but only a couple of blocks from the ferry to Manhattan), and the "kitchen" consisted of a single gas hotplate protruding from a wall in one corner of the room. Fortunately, we found another one-room deal at 89th Street and Third Avenue—one flight up and just even with the elevated Third Avenue El stop, with tracks about 20 feet away from our two windows. The room was without air conditioning, so we slept with our windows and blinds open. Our bed was across the room from the kitchen area, by the windows. It was sobering each morning, as the El screeched to a stop just outside the window, to awaken and see the riders looking in on us while the train had stopped at the 89th Street station.

One other fascinating aspect of our little apartment was the one room apartment just over us on the third floor. This was occupied by two young men who spent the days and nights recording popular music, obviously using equipment involving a microphone and a speaker. They must have been rerecording on vinyl, for the hallways frequently accumulated large balls of the fluff from the grooves. One of them had an apparently unwelcome girl friend who late one evening rang their bell down at the downstairs entry for the automatic release of the lock, and when they ignored her rings, she apparently rang every other apartment bell until some naive soul unlocked the door for her. Being new to the building, I was that soul, for that night after answering the page to unlock the door, I peeked out from the peekhole in the door to see this frazzled hair blonde with a very angry expression dashing past and up the stairs to the third floor. Just after that, the noise of the music being recorded ceased, and the night air was laced with a shrill feminine voice making a strong case for something.

We wanted to keep our car, and usually parked it on Third Avenue just below our apartment. But the neighborhood kids would break into it, play the radio until the battery was run down, then abandon it. We also had trouble because of a new law, enacted a month or so after our arrival, that required cars to be parked on alternate sides of the street from the day before, leaving the other side vacant for street cleaning purposes. While we appreciated this concern for sanitation, finding a space on the opposite side of the street each day was a considerable nuisance, for with the new regulation there were about twice as many cars as parking spaces. Even before, parking generally was such a problem that we used the buses and subways anyway.

Finding our car to be more of a liability than an asset, never having time to get out of the city, and with public transportation more useful anyway, we decided to sell the car. We placed an ad in the *New York Times*, after producing the title, as required by the *Times*, to prove the car was ours, but the ad did not produce any prospects. Accordingly, I decided to head South, planning to stop at each Ford dealership for an offer, and disposing of it with the first dealer that offered to purchase it at a reasonable price. I was unsuccessful until I reached Graham, where our friend and the original dealer, Charlie Ivey, said he would take the car off our hands. Thus, the transaction was consummated, and I caught a bus back to NYC where I had left Pegge because of her need to stay with her job.

I had been gone only one night, but what a night that was for Pegge! Sometime during the wee hours, she said two large black limousines raced up Third Avenue between the pylons supporting the El, with each firing machine guns at the other. That, and the fact that our closed entryway provided a haven for drunks to pass out in, requiring us to step over them to gain access to the stairs that would take us up to our apartment, made the availability of a University-owned apartment on 121st Street and Amsterdam Avenue for our second year in the city like getting title to a little piece of heaven.

But back to year one in the city. There were dramatic experiences in our life on Third Avenue. One that we can never forget involved the apartment building directly across the street from us. There was a bar on the ground level, and the next several levels were apartments. Each day, precisely at noon, two men would emerge from the bar. One was tall and skinny, and the other rather plump; the skinny one wielded a saxophone while the portly fellow had a trumpet. Once on the sidewalk, they would turn toward the building, and play (rather badly) one chorus of "Cruising Down the River" while an aging and somewhat overweight and decidedly frumpy lady on the third floor would open her window, place a dingy pillow on the ledge upon which to rest her elbows, and would disappear inside once the chorus of the tune was completed and the two gentlemen had returned to the bar. We had much fun speculating on the circumstances which might have precipitated this daily event.

The street level was lined with little stores or shops. One was a deli, that received a bag of bagels each morning. These would be delivered in a wide mesh string bag, tossed upon the sidewalk in front of the deli, an hour or so before it opened for business. I remember seeing a scrawny cat trying to make a bathroom call by clawing the sidewalk beside the bag one day, and not succeeding in digging a hole, using the sidewalk anyway. We decided we could survive without bagels from that deli.

But the neighborhood—called "Germantown"—turned out to be a friendly place. Paddy Rafferty, the greengrocer at the 88th Street Corner of 3rd Avenue and a true son of the auld sod, became a close friend, and we partied in our one room apartment several times when he moved his stands from the sidewalk back into his little shop and before he caught the El for his home in Brooklyn. The butcher directly below us never let us buy meat from the glass display case, but would go back into his refrigerated room and select the choicest cuts for us. And although we never partook of the benevolence of Jacob Rupert's brewery a block up Third Avenue where the daily tours always ended in a tap room with free samples of their product, it gave a nice malt and hops ambiance to our little neighborhood, particularly in warm weather.

Although our apartment on Third Avenue was an adventure in itself, the city offered even greater experiences. There were many aspects of life in the Big Apple for which we were totally unprepared. For example: shortly after arrival, we caught a subway at the peak of the morning rush hour, when people were packed inside more tightly than sardines in a tin. We had cashed a check for $40, and decided for safekeeping that each of us would keep $20 on our person. Somewhere before Grand Central Station and transfer to the Broadway IRT line, a pickpocket managed to sneak an arm across the crowded subway, open Pegge's purse (despite the fact that she had a hand on the flap to keep it secure, and stole the twenty dollar bill. That was a lot of money in 1949.

At the same time, there were advantages that seem unbelievable today. As previously indicated, our apartment did not have cross ventilation, and air conditioning was a luxury unheard of on Third Avenue. Some times when the weather was sweltering, we would leave the apartment at midnight and walk the two blocks west to Central Park, where we could doze more comfortably on a park bench. That was the period from fall, 1949, to August, 1950, when the Park was as safe as Sunday School.

We also had a taste of the contrasting realities of the city when Pegge started job hunting. One of the first ads she answered took us to a 42nd Street address where she interviewed for a receptionist job with a fourth floor organization. She was offered the job at a fantastic salary after a very short interview, but could not find out what the business was about. I had waited for her in the lobby of the building, and when she came down in the elevator and said that the interviewer had not revealed the nature of the business when she asked, I tried the question on the building's elevator boy. "That's a bookie outfit," he replied. We left quickly and never returned.

Shortly thereafter she was offered a job in personnel management at the Plaza Hotel, but at the same time an opening at the American Mathematical Society for a secretary became available. This would place her only a stone's throw from where I would be going to class, and so she accepted this position. The offices were in Columbia University's Low Library, where the university president's office was also housed. The president then was Dwight Eisenhower, and we once encountered him as we entered the building after lunch. He greeted us and asked if he could help us locate anyone in the building. This very non-presidential behavior endeared us to the institution, and damn near made Republicans out of us (but we reverted by the time we got out of the building).

We shortly found opportunities to enjoy the cultural activities of the city. Dizzy Gillespie was playing at Birdland, and we went one hot evening in the summer of 1950 when a packed crowd rocked to his rhythms. Pegge, wearing a pink cotton off the shoulder dress and looking the picture of innocence, fainted after a short time in the stuffy smoke-filled basement hall, and I carried her upstairs to find a taxi. As luck would have it, there was a Salvation Army band at the curb at the head of the stairs. The good soldiers turned hostile at the sight of us, and I got past them with some difficulty.

I hailed a cab, but had only a couple of dollars. That got us about half way back to our apartment, and we walked the rest of the way. But it was a memorable evening, nevertheless.

We never made the Metropolitan Opera, but got to the top of the Empire State Building, the Museum of Natural History, the Metropolitan Museum of Art, Carnegie Hall, and the Modern Museum of Art. We rode the Staten Island Ferry. We did get to a ballet by one of the major companies, and also saw a number of plays on Broadway, including Kiss Me Kate, Charley's Aunt, The Most Happy Fella, and several others. We went to Radio City Music Hall until it began to seem rather small, and to some of the little arts theaters; and, we got in to watch radio broadcasts of a play starring Ruth Hussey. We found the little bakeries on 9th Avenue in Greenwich Village, where bakery shops lined the street, the bakers came before dawn, baked until 8 AM, opened their doors for sales, and, when finished, moved to a chair on the sidewalk outside their store, where early placement signaled success over the competition. The little bar at the Chelsea Hotel in the Village, now a fleabag but where in more glamorous times Thomas Wolf and some other notables had lived, was a favorite haunt, as were several restaurants on the top floors of skyscrapers. And, of course, somehow we made it to the department stores from one end of Fifth Avenue to the other, with Blumendale's thrown in as a side trip. Although we seldom purchased anything of value, we thoroughly enjoyed our shopping excursions.

And, as some of the prior accounts of our experiences in New York City indicate, the city was full of people who, while characters in their own right, had instructive qualities. The bus we caught to get to Columbia University involved a transfer at the corner occupied by the Waldorf-Astoria Hotel, and I frequently got a quick cup of coffee between buses at the drug store/soda shop opening on the street at the base of the hotel. I found a regular there was an older lady who obviously lived at the hotel, but who came down each morning for a cup of coffee and advice on the stock market from the man behind the counter. She apparently made buy and sell decisions each day based on his advice. But somehow I figured she got to the position in life where she could afford to live at the Waldorf by some mechanism other than profits from the stock market.

We marveled at the mix of people the city accommodated. At one extreme was the fat woman just in front of us who squatted and relieved herself on the concrete floor of the subway station at Grand Central Station one morning at rush hour, and the other extreme was Pegge's boss and her husband, Lindsey Boyle, who were the epitome of taste and discernment, yet openly friendly and responsive. And there was the head of the American Mathematical Society at that time, an eminent mathematician, and a bachelor who proudly "saved money" by shopping for groceries at a supermarket in the village, but then catching a cab back to his upper Manhattan apartment for several times what he had saved in his grocery shopping.

We had a one year lease on the one room apartment on Third Avenue. I got my master's degree in that time, but decided to go on for the doctorate and withdraw my application for transfer to the Air Force. The one year wait enabled us to acquire a University apartment adjacent to the campus on 121st Street. Thus, we left our digs on Third Avenue, and learned that the one month rent deposit we had been required to make to obtain the lease was suddenly non-refundable. But on 121st Street life was duller but more reasonable, and the apartments had separate rooms for cooking and eating, sleeping, and relaxing. Instead of a locked door with a bell and remote latch device, there was a receptionist in the lobby who controlled entry. (and who turned out, incidentally, to be a close friend of the Mrs. Galbreath whose husband had written *Cheaper by the Dozen*). It was right across the street from a back entrance to the Columbia University's Teachers College, and we found we could dash across the street and descend to underground tunnels for the steam pipes that would take us to Pegge's office in Low Library two blocks away. We thus did not have problems with the weather.

We continued to enjoy the copious advantages of the city. There were other close calls with danger, though more mundane that the machine guns on Third Avenue. Pegge was taking Saturday sewing lessons, offered by Singer Sewing Machine Company, somewhere on Fifth Avenue near the Empire State Building, when a hurricane passed over the city. She was on the sidewalk when winds collapsed windows in a tall building just across the street, raining glass on the pedestrians underneath. She was fortunate in getting a cab to bring her safely back to the apartment. I had stayed at the apartment that day, and had found the radio reports of what was going on down town to be sufficiently unsettling that her return was a considerable relief.

The new apartment, while more sedate than our residence on Third Avenue, was nevertheless entrenched in the unique ambiance of the City. We recall a lady in her 70's who stood motionless each day on the corner of 121st Street and Amsterdam Avenue, gazing expressionless in a south-southeast direction from dawn to dusk. And there was a Chinese restaurant around the corner on Amsterdam Avenue where we were served one evening by a Chinese waiter who was full of ginger, but who, after bringing our order and returning to the kitchen, emerged at flank speed through the restaurant and out the door, with a grizzened little old Chinese man in an apron and chef's hat in hot pursuit, swinging a meat cleaver. They never returned while we were there, which saved us the tip.

We also had a visit from old friends from Sears, Jim and Ida Ann Currant, who were in the city for reasons I have forgotten. But we decided to assure that they had a good supper with us, and I went down to the little butcher shop around the corner, where, as in the shop on Third Avenue, the butcher always went back in the refrigerated section to select something special for us. I told him the occasion, and he produced some very choice fillet mignons and told me how to prepare them. Before that we had, as Max Schulman recognized in *Barefoot Boy with Cheek*, cooked our steaks southern style (Shulman, from Minnesota, had defined the South as the place where "they actually *fry* steaks"), and the four of us gained a bit of cultural sophistication at dinner that evening, for Jim and Ida Ann had always fried their steaks, too.

But our residence came to an end as I finished my course work for the doctorate. We purchased a new 1951 Ford from our friendly dealer in North Carolina, and set out for Middletown, NY, to seek housing for ourselves and others who would work on Professor Super's Career Pattern Study.

But my graduate study experience in itself was the principal reason for our residence in New York City, and deserves separate treatment. An account of some of the particular highlights follows.

Chapter 15

Graduate Study at Columbia University

The graduate study department I had entered was the Department of Vocational Guidance at Columbia University's Teachers College. It was a master's degree program, where classes largely consisted of lectures, but required some courses elsewhere in the College. In addition to Professors Donald Super and Harry Kitson, I thus had Statistics with Helen Walker, some measurement courses with Robert Thorndike and Irving Lorge, some clinical psychology courses from Joe Shoben, Child and Family Development with Arthur Jersild, and Social Psychology with Goodwin Watson, the brother of J.B. Watson of behavioral science fame. These faculty members were internationally known for their contributions in their fields.

I even had a couple of courses in the Department of Psychology of Columbia University proper—one with the well known social psychologist, Wayne Dennis, a visiting professor, who surprised me by reporting, in a discussion of white collar crime, that if he found a book he wanted in another professor's office and the professor was not there, he would take it and keep it—and that his colleagues did the same to him. I also had a class with a Professor Woodworth, a psychologist who became famous in that discipline in the early 1900s by developing, among other things and before Binet's work, a test of intelligence which consisted of having the subject hold his arms outstretched for as long as he could, with the score being the total time of endurance. This gentleman was in his 80s, suffered from COPD, and always creaked in to class supported by his secretary who would read any announcements or assignments before our professor lectured in sentences punctuated by wheezing and some 30 seconds of silence between phrases.

At the master's level, most of the courses at Teachers College had from 100 to 500 students—I recall sitting in the amphitheater balcony for Goodwin Watson's Social Psychology, making faces at him, and although he was 100 feet away, obviously discombobulating him. Nevertheless, I made straight As, and, with no thesis required, obtained my Master's Degree in Vocational Guidance in two semesters.

That first year was relatively uneventful. As noted elsewhere, we were then living on Third Avenue at 89th Street, and commuting; Pegge worked during the day while I did assigned reading and required papers, and my classes, as previously noted, were mostly in the evening. The reason for this was that the city afforded large numbers of teachers going for their master's degrees at Teachers College while working full time during the day. They really gave me little competition, for they were both tired from their day's work, usually at school, and suffered from the usual academic handicaps that most public school teachers possess. The shock was the large classes: in my undergraduate work at the University of North Carolina, I don't think I ever had more than 20 classmates in any given class.

Teachers College was that part of the Graduate School of Columbia University that offered courses for people involved in one or another aspect of education. My department, focusing on Vocational Guidance at the master's level, became the Department of Counseling Psychology at the doctoral level, still closely associated with other Teachers College departments focusing on school psychology, clinical psychology, and early childhood. There were many shared courses among these areas. Although this could seem to be a set of graduate programs fortuitously depending on each other to provide a core of courses, it actually added considerable strength to each program, for the instructional staff were quite frequently leaders in their fields. This was particularly manifest in the year-long counseling practicum required of doctoral students in each of the clinical fields—counseling psychology, clinical psychology, and school psychology. The students worked with live clients and recorded their sessions. Each counseling session was recorded and presented by the student in a seminar setting, and rigorously reviewed by a team of faculty and NYC practitioners of various specializations which included psychoanalysts, child psychologists, behaviorists, gestalt psychologists, psychiatrists, and the like These people did not hesitate to attack one another in the discussions when theories clashed. And clashing was frequent. Neither they nor the graduate students could afford to bruise easily, but this experience was far more intense and instructive than any clinical internship elsewhere could have been.

Those students interested in continuing after the master's degree were required to take a comprehensive examination covering all the courses in their master's program, and attain a score considered satisfactory. Actually, this was a way of simply sorting out the top 12 or 15 percent of the master's degree recipients for the more limited doctoral study. The hurdle was frightening, for it seemed the halls in the block on 120th street between Broadway and Amsterdam Avenue, which was Teachers College, were littered with the bones of prior unsuccessful applicants. I burned the midnight oil in prepping for it. But, it turned out that I and one other student, a fellow named Marty Hamburger, made perfect scores on it, answering correctly all 100 questions. This was apparently an unprecedented performance, for the two of us were not only admitted to the doctoral program, but awarded the two teaching assistantships allocated to the department—meaning that we graded papers and tests for the professors we were serving, and taught their classes when other duties took them away. I was a teaching assistant for Donald Super, the head of the Department, who traveled internationally, with it not being unusual for his wife to meet him at Idlewild International Airport with clean shirts, as he deplaned from a trip to Oxford, and caught another plane to a South American or Asian university. I also frequently received calls from his mother, who would ask me such things as to remind Don (Dr. Super) to be sure to wear his rubbers when he left to go home to Montclair, New Jersey, for it was raining. The stipend was pretty meager, amounting to about 30 cents an hour, we figured, but the experience was enjoyable and instructive in itself.

The incidents that were sufficiently memorable that I recall them with clarity almost 6 decades later were of two kinds. First were the personal associations with faculty and students; and second were some significant experiences in the course work itself.

First, the students. One that impressed me greatly was a beautiful flaming red haired Russian Jew named Florence Moskowitz. When I say "beautiful," I refer both to her physical appearance and her inner personality, for she was one who someone like me viewing her luscious proportions would immediately forget any sexual fantasies when she spoke, substituting a deep interest in how her association with me would improve me as a person—no small accomplishment for a beautiful woman.

Florence contributed immensely to my graduate study. She lived in the Bronx, and reported one day that the previous evening she had stopped on the way home at a neighborhood delicatessen for a quart of milk. The sole proprietor was occupied with two elderly Jewish ladies who were having trouble deciding on their purchases, so the proprietor excused himself and turned to Florence, whom he knew from previous encounters like this, and said "May I help you?" Florence reported that one of the old Jewish ladies turned to the other and voiced a rather vulgar term in Yiddish roughly translated as "dirty Irish Catholic." Florence said she turned to the two, and in her very best Yiddish said "And what's wrong with the 'dirty Irish Catholics'?" She said she would treasure the expressions on their faces for the rest of her life.

Most unfortunately, that "rest of her life" was much too short. Several years later I heard she had been hit by a cab crossing the street on Amsterdam Avenue near the University, and had died instantly.

Another student that I recall particularly was Bob Rossberg, a nephew of the Weschler who created, in 1939, the Weschler-Bellevue Intelligence test, then and now a kind of gold standard for individual assessment of intelligence. When Bob finished his course work for the doctorate and started his thesis, he not surprisingly obtained a job as a counseling psychologist at Bellevue Hospital, where his illustrious uncle still apparently had some pull. As he was unpacking his books the first day, a nurse came in with the news that the emergency room had just admitted a teen age boy who had a fountain pen cap lodged in his anus, and needed to get Bob to do an intake interview. Bob said that he stopped unpacking his books, washed his hands, and was seated behind his desk as the boy was brought in. I recall being caught up in this account, and said to Bob as he got this far in describing his first day on the job: "Bob, what did you do then?" Bob answered quickly: "I said,'don't sit down!'" Bob spent the rest of the day notifying and counseling the boy's parents, obtaining releases, and other routine matters, and the situation was ultimately resolved by surgical removal of the fountain pen cap.

I recall meeting several years after completing my course work Mort Rabin, a fellow I had liked very much during the masters' year, and who had wanted to escape from the restaurant business his father ran on Long Island, and his father's ambitions for him therein, by obtaining the doctorate. But alas, he had failed to make the cut on the doctoral qualifying exam, and had gone back to run one of the two restaurants his father owned. I remember running into him later and asking him what he really wanted to do now, and his answer always brings tears to my eyes when I recall it. He said "my wife and I would like to go somewhere in season." I had always had the feeling that he would have become a most sensitive and capable counseling or clinical psychologist, far superior to some of the egoistic fellow students seeking the degree primarily for personal status. He was in sharp contrast to another who failed to make the cut, and who was caustic, arrogant, and not very bright. I ran into him 30 years later, learning that he had become a project officer for one of the Federal offices in Washington, and was making considerably more money managing Federal contracts that I was in carrying them out.

But it was Martin Hamburger, the other student who did so well on the doctoral qualifying exam, and who worked with me as a graduate teaching assistant, that became my closest colleague and dearest friend. Marty was single and in his early thirties, five years my senior, and one of a large number of boys—seven, I believe—whose father was a Jewish immigrant from Hamburg, Germany, who worked making trousers in a loft in the village. His brothers had all attained substantial professional positions, and Marty was on his way to join them. He was probably the brightest person I have ever known. He had reached doctoral study via scholarships in the CCNY system, was extremely well-read, and could talk on any subject. He had a keen sense of humor as well. He and I, and one of the junior professors, Chuck Morris, frequently burned the midnight oil in the department offices grading papers, or finding and discussing the humor in the daily experiences. Chuck had obtained his doctorate 8 or 9 years earlier, and had been appointed to the faculty. He had gone though a nine year period of having a child a year, and the 11 of them—Chuck, his wife, and the nine children—lived in a three room apartment on the fifth floor in the University apartment building to which we moved from Third Avenue. Chuck's apartment was clearly visible from the street, for it was the only one with bars installed on all windows to prevent his little ones from falling out. I think I know why he spent most of his days and evenings in the departmental office. But he was an excellent teacher, both in the classroom and in conversation, and Marty and I profited greatly from our association with him. In spite of the fact that as a trio we represented Catholic, Protestant, and Jewish faiths, we got along famously. And Marty was the one contact that we will encounter many times over the next decades in this account.

I have mentioned my class experience of bugging Dr. Goodwin Watson by making faces at him as he lectured. I think what prompted me to behave in this way was the ludicrous nature of the some 500 students in the amphitheater that served as our classroom, and Dr. Watson speaking in a less than sonorous voice into a microphone in the 7PM to 9PM class until precisely 8:50 PM, when he would turn the lecture over to a teaching assistant, and dash for the subway and the last train out of Grand Central Station to the northern suburb where he lived. And this was a course I encountered in the first semester of my initial year, and thus seemed to serve as an introduction of things to come in graduate study at that institution.

The strangest experience, though, was a second semester course in Educational Economics, taught by a Dr. Clark who had been an educational advisor to Franklin D. Roosevelt. This again was a large class, probably of about 200 people. As I recall, we did not have a text, but depended on the lectures and assignments that Dr. Clark gave. The problem with this was that try as hard as I could, I could never understand anything Dr. Clark said in class, nor see any relationship between successive sentences—and recourse to fellow students revealed I was not alone. Dr. Clark assigned a term paper to be turned in a week before the last class, and stated that our grade would be based on this paper.

I had taken notes—copying down many sentences verbatim, hoping to make some sense out of them later, but never succeeding. For the term paper, I decided to take my notes, cut slips each containing one sentence of his, then sorting them into some order where there was at least a continuity of thought from sentence to sentence. I pasted the sentences together, I recall, on a roll of paper 8 and ½ inches by about 12 feet, typed it in essay form, and, although it still made no sense whatsoever to me, handed it in. Came the last class meeting, and Dr. Clark said something like: "This is a large class, and I do not get to know students personally. But there is one among you that I would like to identify." He then called my name, and asked me to stand up. I did, trembling and bracing myself for being reprimanded for my abject foolishness and plagiarism, for each sentence in that paper was a *verbatim* quote of Dr. Clark's. But instead, Dr. Clark said something like "I have been teaching this class for many years, and finally, I have found a student who understands perfectly what I have been trying to impart. I want to be able to recognize him, and I want the class to do the same. Thank you, Mr. Davis!" He did not return the paper, for if he had, I would have reread it and tried once more to make some sense out of it. But prior efforts toward this objective had failed, Dr. Clark was finally fulfilled, and I got the A that I needed to have a perfect record.

One other experience that had a strong effect on me occurred during the final exam in a course on the nature of human intelligence taught by Dr. Irving Lorge. Dr. Lorge was an individual who had risen to fame on the coattails of Robert Thorndike, the association resulting in the Lorge-Thorndike Test of Intelligence. Dr. Lorge was a person that would make Simon Cowell of American Idols seem like a pussy cat. He delighted in being tough, rough, and nasty in all relationships with both his students and the other faculty, and had the remarkable facility of making every comment, even in his lectures, supremely sarcastic. A large man, he blithely punctuated his comments in class with expulsions of flattus.

His final exam for that class was as tough as he was. As I sweated over my answers to the questions, I noticed two middle-aged Black ladies, both considerably overweight, with an open textbook on the desk seat between them, with one turning pages to find the answers to the questions. Dr. Lorge had left the room, and exams were conducted under a student honor system. I became so upset with this that I got up, went out to Dr. Lorge's office, and reported the infractions. Dr. Lorge returned to the room, confirmed what was going on, snatched up the two exam booklets, and stalked out. I later shared this evidence of my integrity with my friend Florence Moskovitz. She reminded me that students at Teachers College cheat all the time, that Dr. Lorge's course was required for many different teacher education programs and was known as a tough one, and that I had frequently seen other students cheating as she had. She then asked me why this was the time I was angered enough to take action. When I could find no ready answer, she added: "But of course, even though you are from the South, you aren't prejudiced, are you," she said. The only time I remember such pain and growing so fast from the experience was when I was twelve, and had sneaked out into the swamp at my grandfather's house with his 12 gauge shotgun, and had shot a little yellow bird a few feet away just to see if I could do it. But I have been grateful for that experience every time in later life when I have encountered a white person who says about people of other races or religions: "But of course, I'm not prejudiced . . ."—or when some occasion prompts me to feel that I am without sin in this regard.

Through all of this, Pegge worked as the secretary for "Miss Hull" (Mrs. Lindsay Boyle), the office manager for the American Mathematical Society office, which was housed in the Low Library building at the University. My assistantship served to supplement her salary's contribution to our expenses, and GI Bill benefits lasted right up through the last semester. But I found one other lucrative venture, which was administering a battery of tests to pilot applicants for the major airlines in classroom space at LaGuardia Airport.

This work was done under contract between the airlines and Dr. John Flanagan, whom we called "Smiling Jack" from a comic strip about a pilot popular at that time because Flanagan usually maintained a serious countenance. Dr. Flanagan was then in Palo Alto heading the American Institute for Research, a consulting firm, but had developed, with my major professor, Donald Super, the testing program used by the Air Force to select pilots in World War II. I, and usually a colleague, would take the tests to the testing site at La Guardia Airport where the pilot applicants were assembled, administer the tests, and return to the department office and score and report them. This always involved at least a 14 hour day, but the pay was good—$100 for the day, which was a hefty amount at that time. And the applicants were fun to deal with. Most of the applicants had more than 3,000 hours of multi-engine flight experience in the armed services, and were convinced at the beginning of the day that their skills could not be captured by paper and pencil tests. But the tests had sufficient face validity that the pilots would end the day saying that they were impressed with how well the tests captured the challenges they faced in flying multi-engine aircraft.

I completed the course work for the doctorate in a summer session and two more semesters, and Pegge and I embarked with our friend Marty Hamburger and my department chair to Middletown, New York, to assist in the first year of the Career Pattern Study, a planned 20 year longitudinal study of vocational development designed by Dr. Super, and from which Marty and I, and other doctoral candidates involved, would draw the data for our doctoral dissertations.

Chapter 16

Our Year in Middletown, N.Y.

In the late summer of 1951, Pegge and I went some 60 miles up the Hudson River to Middletown, NY, to help Professor Donald Super with the first year of his 20 year longitudinal study of vocational development—Pegge as his secretary, and I as a research assistant hoping to use some of the data for my doctoral thesis.

Pegge and I went in as an advance team, to find housing for ourselves and a multi-bedroom home that could be rented for the year to house the other study staff—Dr. Super, and graduate students spending the week in Middletown. We got a room in the New Hotel Waldo, a decaying businessman's hotel razed shortly after we left the area, until we found an apartment for ourselves—the upstairs portion of a private residence, but with a heated garage that would accommodate our car. We also found and leased a nice little house on the edge of town for study staff.

Dr. Super had negotiated study offices in the main building of the nation's first community college, Orange County Community College, and then in its second year of operation—occupying a mansion donated by a wealthy local family (Morrisons) We were given office space in exchange for providing cost-free faculty for the college. I contributed several hours a week teaching a class in introductory sociology, while Pegge, and two local secretarial types who were comfortable only when the thermostat was set at 80 degrees, labored in the donated offices trying to type up our recorded interviews with the research subjects, eighth and ninth grade boys—no trivial task, considering the "Ampro" brand tape recorders available to us.

The year in Middletown produced many strange and wondrous adventures for us, not the least of which was a six week period where the warmest temperature was minus 20 degrees, a condition that made us value the heated garage. But despite the cold, we have warm memories of the year—and one of the warmest memories was our clandestine activity each weekend regarding the college.

The Morrison mansion that was the community college and our headquarters was locked for the weekend, but we had a key. And there was a student lounge in one of the former second floor drawing rooms with a rarity of that era, a TV set. We would make ourselves a bag of popcorn, drive through the gates of the site with headlights out, and sneak into the Morrison mansion and grope our way to the lounge on the second floor. There, once we had drawn the draperies to prevent being detected by the light of the tube, we were able to watch such performers as Sid Caesar and Imogene Coco. There was no watchman on the premises, and we were never caught, although I suspect there was a janitor who wondered about the popcorn under the couch.

The research project involved giving a battery of vocational interest and aptitude tests to all eighth and ninth grade boys, and interviewing them and their parents. This was the base year of a 20 year study of vocational development contrived by Dr. Donald Super, my department head at Teacher's College, and subsequent followups did indeed take place. It was quite an adventure. The scope of the study, and its plan to track each of the subjects for twenty years into the time when their adult life style would be established, was epic for social research at that time and Dr. Super was a clearly established leader in the area of vocational development.

But putting the unique promise of the research aside: the culture of the community was an experience in itself. This was a section of New York State known as the "black dirt" area, and as such was noted for growing certain crops (onions was a prominent one). The population was heavily Polish, which permeated the school culture where the school song was a polka; and the best restaurant in town was the Middletown Diner, where the house specialty was sauerbraten. (We had tried to develop a taste for scrapple when we were in Bainbridge, but never made it; we had absolutely no similar problem with the sauerbraten.)

The in-depth interviews with the kids were enlightening, for there were wide differences in backgrounds and family situations of our interviewees, and our subjects had virtually no inhibitions in responding to our questions. A significant discovery for me was learning something about the extremes in home and background situations when one looks at a complete cross-section of humanity. I recall one boy describing his home life—he lived in a chicken coop with his impoverished mother, who had been abandoned by his father. And one little fellow, after describing some of the ever-present conflicts between his father and his mother, told me: "*There's not going to be a marriage in the next five generations of (his surname)!*"

Another thing I will never forget is the response one boy gave to the Incomplete Sentences Test, a measure of personality. The test involves the start of sentences, and the testee is to complete each sentence with the first thoughts that come to mind. The stem for one item was "I hate _____" and the student had written in "basil spats." If "basil spats" was a person, that item would be given a negative score; if it were an object that was perfectly reasonable to hate, it would be given a positive score. Therefore, after being unable to determine what the boy had meant, we called him in and asked him to read his answer and explain it. He read "I hate Brussel sprouts." We decided that he was an O.K. kid.

As the only married couple on the site, we had our own apartment. But the house we had leased for those who came in for the week, but returned to their homes in the New York city area on the weekends, was the scene of adventure as well. Our project director, Don Super, spent the week there, returning to his home in Upper Montclair, NJ, on the weekends. He was the only child of an internationally known professor of sociology at the University of Missouri who had held many important positions in England and the European nations, and who, during WWII, was the head of the Free Polish Relief Fund in London. Don had grown up in the drawing rooms of Europe and spoke many languages fluently. His living in the house with the other graduate students working on the project during the week was a learning experience in itself for both sides. Don, who sang operatic arias in the shower, and who had impeccable table manners, resided with such as my best friend in the doctoral program, Marty Hamburger, who had grown up in an ethnic neighborhood on the lower East Side. Don tried hard to be "one of the boys," and made considerable progress, but never quite attained that goal.

I began to refer to him outside his presence as "Jolly Don," drawing on his given name and his M.A. Oxon degree, a credential he always made public in the textbooks he had authored. One day we were walking from the study office in the Morrison mansion to the cafeteria which had been installed in the former stable behind the mansion, and I turned to Hamburger and, knowing that Dr Super had planned to eat with us, said: "Where's Jolly Don?" Just behind me came a familiar voice in a somewhat higher pitch than usual: "Here I am!" He had been right behind us, and I had not seen him. Nothing more was ever said about it, but I had the feeling that he enjoyed it, for he interpreted it as meaning that he had finally become one of the boys. But we all abandoned this moniker for him from that time on.

That cafeteria turned out to be the scene of another experience I can never forget: Pegge, Marty Hamburger, I, and some of the others were in the cafeteria line when I had something I wanted to say to Marty. I called out "Hey, Hamburger!" and promptly got one on my tray from the server.

Some of the other graduate students involved provided an unusual menagerie. There was Charles Warnath, who stayed at the study residence, and although a very nice fellow, was totally devoid of humor and imagination. There was Harry Beilin, then a bachelor from the Bronx in his early thirties, who had the strongest sense of self I have ever encountered. He was very bright, but without ready empathy for others, which proved to be a handicap when I tried to teach him to drive a car so that he could get licensed. After many near misses with telephone poles when he turned a corner, I discovered that the problem was that he simply would not start the turn when the front of the car was in position for the maneuver, but would wait until *HE* was in position, forcing him to overshoot.

There was Chuck Nicholas, a swarthy middle-aged man of Russian extraction who sweated a lot, and whose mustache made him sinister rather than dapper. He was on the project team in a conditional status, and his eagerness to make good got him and the project in trouble. It was during the stage of the work where we were interviewing parents, and Chuck knocked on a door repeatedly without anyone responding. Knowing that there was someone inside, and anxious not to get away without the interview, he went around to the back door and pounded on it. The lady of the house, it turned out, was taking a shower, and had stepped out to see who was so insistent on calling, and saw Chuck's mustached vision peering at her through the curtains in the glass panel of her kitchen door. This led the lady to threaten to take action to have us thrown out of town, but Jolly Don, ever the perfect gentleman, smoothed this over, and the project continued.

Another student helping us with the interviews was a lovely but tall lady of uneasy virtue, one Phoebe Overstreet, a graduate of Smith College in her thirties. Again, like Don Super, she tried to be one of the boys, but hardly made it. The project staff was surprised a year later to find that Phoebe and Chuck Nicholas had gotten married, for they seemed to have little in common or to do with each other on the project.

Our experience in Middletown further endeared us to Marty Hamburger. As previously noted, we had competed vigorously in graduate school for top grades, and no one else had ever come close to achieving the scores we made on the comprehensive exam given to Masters' Degree recipients who apply for doctoral studies. And, both of us, as previously noted, had been appointed teaching assistants to Don Super. Working with Marty was an education in itself, for I have never found anyone as bright and verbally quick on his feet as Marty. It was strange, for in spite of Marty's exemplary verbal ability, he had difficulty putting words on paper. Once in later years I worked from a recording of a speech by Marty to turn it into a journal article, for it was difficult for him to write for publication. But his reputation as a lecturer gave him a rich litany of visiting professorships in U.S. and foreign universities, and he took each of several sabbaticals working his way around the world from university to university.

I am sure he has forgotten this, but one of the nicest things that happened to me in the rough and tumble life we led in Middletown, NY, in 1951-52 was his part in a surprise engineered by Pegge. She asked me to keep a particular weekend free, for she said she had something she wanted us to do. Very shortly she produced two tickets to a stage presentation of Booth Tarkenton's "Seventeen" in New York City. Marty Hamburger had helped her procure the tickets, and had maintained the surprise.

We had a lovely evening, with dinner as I recall at Adano's restaurant on 44th Street. And the play was delightful, despite the one instance where the stage father had to utter emphatically the word "Damn!" on the porch of the seventeen year old's home as she sat in the swing. It was pretty obvious that this was not in Tarkenton's original script, but was a bone tossed hopefully to the NYC critics who were felt to demand something risque. But Pegge's surprise was one that I would relish.

We decided to drive to North Carolina for the Christmas season in 1951. We left Middletown the afternoon of December 24 in a blinding snow storm, heading down through Pennsylvania and staying west of the larger cities—New York, Trenton, Philadelphia, Washington, Richmond.

As we entered Pennsylvania, the snow storm was so blinding we could not see the road, and darkness was descending. We would catch a tail light and try to follow it, hoping to stay on the hard surface. By 10 PM we had reached Bethlehem, PA, and the snow storm had abated, but the roads were packed with snow that had turned to ice. As luck would have it for idiots like us trying to move under such conditions, we reached a hill that was simply too slick to get up. But lo and behold, the townspeople were out en masse, and for each car passing through, they got behind it and literally pushed it up the hill. We never saw any public recognition of this remarkable Christmas gift from that community, but it strengthened our faith in our fellow man.

We reached Warrenton, Virginia about midnight, and the rough weather was continuing. We decided to hole up until morning. We got a room in a decaying hotel, near a clock with a loud gong that loudly rattled our windows each hour as the early morning progressed, and the double bed in our room had a mattress that sagged noticeably in the middle, throwing us on top of one another if we relaxed our guard and hold on the side of the bed. I had trouble sleeping, and went down to the lobby about 6 am to see if I could find some coffee and a newspaper.

There, on a well-worn sofa in the small lobby, were a relatively nondescript man and woman, both overweight, and in blue-collar casual clothing. They were obviously waiting nervously for something or someone. Before I could move on in my search for coffee and news, a rather plain lady of about 30 came down the stairs (the hotel had no elevator), dress and hair disheveled, and one shoe missing. The two waiting, obviously parents of a spinster daughter, began immediately with such comments as "How could you? Do you realize what you have done? Who is he? Where is your other shoe?"

The plain lady with one shoe seemed unperturbed by this interrogation, simply responding to the questions without speaking but with a kind of smirking, satisfied smile that seemed to further confabulate her parents. They packed her into a car and left. I speculated that the lost shoe ended up in a trophy room somewhere. And remembering Rudolph John Smith, the fellow officer on my tanker during

WWII who said he always collected an intimate garment as a souvenir of his tryst, I suspected the lady with the smirk was missing more than a shoe.

Thus, within a twenty-four hour period, and on a path that normally involved a drive of about 17 hours, we had a taste of how the Christmas spirit touched the people of a little town in Pennsylvania, and how a lonely spinster in the Warrenton, Virginia area got an early Christmas present.

But back to Middletown: I don't know what happened to Chuck and Phoebe Nicholas, but Charles Warnath, Harry Beilin, and Marty Hamburger went on to distinguished careers in graduate departments of major universities—Warnath at the University of Oregon, and Beilin at the City College of New York. According to Google, Warnath became "the gadfly of professional counseling" at the University of Oregon, and in his later years suffered from retinis pigmentosa. Beilin died in January, 2007, at the age of 85, after 40 years at CCNY Marty, who had grown up in New York City and had never learned (or wanted) to drive, remained a close professional friend. He went from the study project to a faculty appointment at New Haven State Teachers College, and shortly thereafter, to New York University where he spent the rest of his career. Marty used his sabbaticals for foreign travel, with a favorite apartment in a village in Italy that he used several times, and one year in which he literally lectured his way around the world. A first marriage, at the end of the year in Middletown when Marty was in his early 30s, did not work out, but when he retired some three decades later he married the widow of a good friend and they moved to the Miami area in retirement. They visited us once some years ago in Chapel Hill, and seemed truly happy.

Our year in Middletown came to an end, and Don Super had helped me gain an appointment at Princeton University. The Career Pattern Study had provided me with data for my doctoral thesis, and with this bundled with our books and clothing, we set out for our new life in Princeton, N.J.

Chapter 17

Life on the Faculty of Princeton University

Our year in Middletown had come to an end. I had the data I planned to use for my doctoral thesis, begrudgingly approved by Donald Super, my major professor who said that although he tried very hard, and was aware of my mental ability, he simply could not understand what I planned to do or why, but that it was probably all right. (I planned to look at some hypothesized correlates of empathy as manifest by agreement between self-perceptions and the perceptions of individuals by their peers in early adolescence). Dr, Super was internationally known both for his own research and as the only son of his famous father, who had left a professorship at the University of Missouri to head the Free Polish Relief Fund in London during WWII (and while Super collected a master's degree from Oxford). He repaid our assistance on his proposed 20 year study of vocational development by helping us land a choice faculty and administrative appointment at Princeton University.

This appointment was as Instructor in Psychology, and Assistant Director of the (University) Counseling Service. It would keep me near Columbia University as I worked on my thesis, and pay a meager but living wage (an aspect of the fact that people would work for free in exchange for the recognition of being on the Princeton faculty!). We moved into one of a group of apartments built by the University for housing graduate students and junior staff during the war, which consisted of units of three apartments, each with a kitchen, living/dining area, bath, three closets, and two bedrooms.

Pegge also shortly became part of the University, accepting a job as secretary for the Director of the Alumni Office, a George Cooke, one of the many well-heeled Princeton alumni who had returned to the scene of their college experience for the salary of a dollar a year. His recollections turned out to give us an unusual perspective into the University history and its traditions.

The university itself was an eye-opener. Nothing had prepared me, in my prior experience, for the group of students that included such individuals as Harvey Firestone, Jr., Juan Batista, Jr., or Thomas Dewey, Jr.

Learning how this segment of the population lived was a series of continuing revelations. I recall monitoring a test in one of the large lecture halls, and looking down on the test-takers and marveling at how varied and odd their head shapes were (crew cuts were common then). Yet, the all male student body, and the fact that most had been maid-raised at home briefly before being packed off to boarding schools like Exeter or Lawrenceville, had left them with rather poor habits of personal hygiene, meaning that the odor of unwashed feet was nigh overpowering if one was confined in a classroom with a dozen or more of them. I recall vividly a cartoon in the campus humor magazine. It showed a student peering into a large closet in a palatial home, with the caption "God, Mother, who cleaned my white bucks?" I was reminded of the title of the first chapter in a favorite book: Aubrey Menen's autobiography, *Dead Man in the Silver Market:* the title was "How I was Initiated into the Best Tribe."

I quickly found that the University catered to the very rich in other ways. The dormitory rooms were unfurnished, and the students provided their own furniture. I recall one who hired a NYC decorator for a fee of $10,000 to decorate and furnish his room. In 1951, that was a lot of money—enough to purchase a small house. Yet, this aspect of student housing yielded a bonanza for Princeton residents at graduation time, when the departing seniors put their furnishings up for sale at truly bargain prices.

It was also a discovery to learn that no one flunked out. Failing grades were simply not given. The reason soon became apparent: I was called in to the Dean's office one day and told to do what I could to help a particular student cope with his academic assignments. "His father is going to give us the money for a new gym—if we can keep him in long enough to award him a degree." And I recall the freshman who went to the Bank of Princeton to withdraw $15,000 from his account. The bank manager felt this was a lot of money for a 17 year old not yet shaving, and told the student it would require some time to assemble that amount, but to come back in a couple of hours. He then called the University dean and asked for advice. After conference with several of us, the dean phoned the boy's parents to explain the situation and get instructions. The mother came to the phone, and was obviously irritated with the dean for the intrusion, for she said "Well, it is HIS money," and hung up the phone on the dean. So, the dean called the bank, and the young man retrieved that amount of cash from his bank account.

Another student was expelled for two weeks for violating the ruling that only seniors could have cars on campus. He went up US 1 a few miles to New Brunswick where he kept his airplane, and flew back low over Nassau Hall, the

Administration Building, and bombed it with beer cans. I am not sure what the price was for this transgression, but he was back in class shortly.

In my role as a counselor in the Counseling Service, it turned out that the major task was finding and approving tutors for students needing assistance with their academic pursuits. There was also a heavy emphasis on helping students improve their reading skills. I could not help but assume that the powers that were at Princeton University believed that any Princeton student was beyond the commonplace malady of personal problems with which he could not cope, and that needs were related only to helping students survive the academic rigors and prevent scalping by tutors. This view was also reflected in the fact that there was less than a 5 percent attrition rate: once in class, failure was most difficult.

Approving tutors for students needing help with coursework was routine, but the reading improvement and counseling functions were real. I recall a young Bill Bradley wanting help with improving his reading speed. And there were a few instances of students needing counsel for personal problems. One of the counseling cases that I remember was a shy young man who came a number of times before getting up the courage to tell me his real problem. It was that he was 19 years of age, and had never kissed a girl, having spent most of his life at private boarding schools for boys. I remember that I advised him to join a young people's group at one of the local churches, and find a girl that would let him walk her home after the meetings. This must have worked, for he did not return to counseling, and I recall seeing him later on campus where he greeted me with a sheepish smile that said "Thank you," and that attested the success of my counsel.

I spent a substantial amount of time with the son of an internationally known urologist at the Mayo Clinic. This physician had spent a year in residence in Cairo, Egypt, attending to King Farouk in the days before ED had become a household word, with remedies prolifically advertised on TV. This doctor wanted more than anything else for his only son to graduate from Princeton, enter medical school, and become a physician like him. The only son, however, wanted anything but a career as a physician, and felt, I believe, that flunking out at Princeton was a fail-safe way to achieve this. His reason was simple but poignant: he felt that he could never exceed—nor for that matter, equal—his father's attainment as a physician.

The father flew in every other week to talk with me about his son, to ventilate (as he did when he found the son had charged several thousand dollars for ski equipment at Abercrombie and Fitch for one weekend in the Poconos), and to follow his progress in the remedial activity with me. (Incidentally, I learned long after leaving Princeton that the young man had graduated with a mediocre average, but had been accepted by a medical school, and had become a physician. A Google search revealed that he is specializing in psychiatry in California.)

There were many manifestations that some routine developmental experiences I had taken for granted were missing in the young people who attended Princeton University. For example, it was a weekly occurrence for a student, gasping for breath, to be taken from the university dining hall to the emergency room at Princeton Hospital, where a hunk of steak that had not been chewed was removed from his gullet. That one must chew his food before swallowing it was something I thought most parents considered important, but this was simply one of the many consequences of absentee parents that predominated for the students who came to Princeton University.

It was at Princeton University where I came within a hair's breadth of achieving international notoriety. I had an hour at noon one day free of responsibilities, and had to go the 9 miles into Trenton for some urgent reason. I was dashing down the back road (the old Princeton Pike) when out from behind a parked car strode a glowering figure. It was Albert Einstein, leaving his house for a walk to the Institute for Advanced Studies. I brushed his clothing, and had he started across the street a split second earlier, I would surely have done him in.

In addition to the Institute for Advanced Studies in Princeton was Princeton Seminary, which was not related to the University. It was there that a noted theologian had addressed the student body that had been assembled to dedicate a now building on the campus. The speaker started his oration with the words: "Today is a most auspicious occasion, for it marks the first erection on this campus in over 100 years." To the credit of the students, they roared approval after a few seconds of silence.

For my teaching assignment, I shared with Professor Sylvan Tompkins responsibility for "precepting" his course in the Psychology of Personality. "Precepting" was a Princeton tradition initiated by Woodrow Wilson when he was president, and consisted of required discussion groups of from ten to twenty students after each lecture to discuss the points made therein. This proved to be a most remarkable innovation, and I believe it added much to the formal coursework. My only problem was that I had four one-hour "preceptorials" one after the other, making it difficult to remember whether some comment had been made in the present or an earlier group of students.

The University had its stock of significant events in its history. One dated back to the early 1800s when the toilets were outhouses strategically placed about the campus. With students even then acting like the traditional students of today, some event that involved a professor not being given proper respect had prompted an administrator to rule that any student encountering a faculty member walking on campus would stop, remove his cap, and stand at attention until the faculty member was 200 feet away. The students rebelled by waiting until one after another professor had entered an outhouse, whereupon they descended and nailed the door shut. This process continued until all the outhouses had been so immobilized, and most of the faculty were contained.

The fact that a hundred and fifty years had not eroded this characteristic spirit was demonstrated while we were there by an election of student officers by the student body. Someone as a joke proposed a write-in candidate for president of the senior class on the basis that the student named had been completely and utterly undistinguished throughout his prior prep school career, and deserved this last chance to get some accomplishment attesting leadership ability on his personal record. The students responded with enthusiasm, and, although a write-in candidate, he was elected by the largest margin in Princeton University history. (Everyone was amazed, however, that in his tenure he was clearly the most effective class president that anyone at Princeton University could recall.)

Colorful characters abounded on the campus. Howie Stepp, the swimming coach and registrar, kept a violin on his desk, and he would pick it up and begin playing it if a student came in with some sad excuse or a complaint. The chair of one of the science departments was a daily coffee drinking buddy at a restaurant just across the street from Nassau Hall, and was convinced that such phenomena as ESP and clairvoyance were real. He got very excited when I told him that Pegge had had a premonition that something terrible had happened to her father when the wind from an open bedroom window blew his portrait off the bedside table, and then she found he had been hospitalized with a bleeding ulcer. He did not accept my later explanation that the real signal to Pegge was probably not the wind-blown picture, but the fact that her father had not written her for several weeks, a fact that had escaped Pegge's conscious recognition, but had probably triggered her unease.

My department chairman the first year was a tall man named Carroll Pratt. He was generally to be found each afternoon strolling along the path beside Lake Carnegie at the edge of the campus, with his wife dutifully following about 10 paces behind. He was a lovable figure nevertheless, for he knew the birthdays of each member of the Psychology Department, and never failed to surprise us with a telephone call to wish us a happy birthday. He was followed the second year I was there by Hadley Cantril, whose main claim to fame lay largely in the analysis he made of reactions of the citizens of nearby Grover's Mill in West Windsor Township, NJ, to Orson Welles' broadcast of "The Invasion from Mars." Grover's Mill was the scene of the fictitious invasion that had prompted a national panic, and many of the its inhabitants had been spooked like the rest of the nation.

But life outside the University was exciting in its own right. In the apartment unit across from ours was a career air force sergeant, Jay, assigned to the Air Force ROTC, and who with his wife Hazel became close friends. It was at his apartment that we got sufficiently addicted to TV that we purchased one of our own, cutting a hole in the wall of our living room with a closet on the other side of the wall, so that the TV could fit flush with the wall rather than consume precious space by protruding into the room.

Another apartment across from ours housed a stock clerk in the physics department, his wife, and more children than I can remember counting. One was a little two year old boy named Jeffrey, who wandered about the area between the apartments in the ill-fitting shorts handed down from an older sibling. I recall one summer day little Jeffrey coming to our screen door, and anguishing about wanting to be let in. We ignored him. But after a few pleas, he muttered, quite clearly: "Hey, you, it's hot as hell out here!"

The group of apartments had a baby sitting pool that one could join, and which offered a sitter for the number of hours that you, as a member, sat for someone in the pool. After our son Michael was born, we joined the pool. I remember going to the apartment of a graduate student in English, who had posted instructions that started:

1. In case of fire, remove my thesis notes from the file cabinet by my desk.
2. Return to the apartment if possible, and retrieve my child.

Our apartment was in the middle of the unit of three apartments. Our kitchen faced a bedroom of the apartment on one side, and our bedroom faced a bedroom and bath of the apartment on the other side. The walls were paper thin, for we could hear when the occupants on our bedroom side were playing drop the soap in the shower. But the apartment on our kitchen side, the one with the bedroom adjacent to our kitchen, was occupied by an Army ROTC officer who went on training duty in the summer, and who sublet the apartment to a young lady who worked somewhere at the University. The problem was that she had numerous boyfriends, and the bed in the room adjacent to our kitchen bumped against the wall when vigorous action was being taken upon it. Since our normal dining table was against that wall in the kitchen, we not infrequently did not need to stir our Wheaties and milk each morning because of the vibrations emanating from that bedroom. That the activity therein was too important to be disturbed was attested to by its continuance even though I would whistle loudly "Love, oh love, oh careless love" each time the "thump-thump-thump" started.

We had some excitement when a number of the apartment dwellers discovered a peeper prowling the area. One night the peeper made the mistake of peering into our Air Force sergeant's apartment, and Jay, barefoot and clad only in his boxer shorts, chased him for three blocks before losing him. I recall that I suggested we have all the wives undress with blinds open, and have all the men stationed just outside in the darkness to pounce on the peeper when he appeared, but somehow this suggestion, while popular with the men, was not warmly received by the wives. I think we ultimately discouraged the peeper by hanging a pair of bodacious panties on a clothes line just outside our back entrance, with a tin garbage can rigged on the roof to come crashing down if the panties were touched. The last we heard of the peeper was a night when the can came clattering down on the concrete below.

One of the apartments connecting to ours was occupied for one year by Christopher ("Kitt") and Buff Blake. Kitt was a graduate student from Scotland, and the couple and a little one were delightful people. Kitt was on a one-year stay in Princeton as an exchange scholar. Their child, a boy named Duncan, was about the age of our son Mike. When their year was over, we drove them to Idlewild International Airport for their return to Scotland, and found when we were back in Princeton that they had left little Duncan's supply of diapers on the back seat of our car. Discretion prompted us not to ask how they coped on the flight home, but we assumed that the airline had a solution, and a later letter reported a safe flight home with an unexpected 24 hour layover in Newfoundland without reference to the diaper problem.

The second year, that apartment was occupied by a mathematician and his wife. They were noted for constant loud arguments. Each morning he would pick up the paper delivered to his door, walk to his car, sit at the wheel and read the paper, and, when finished, toss it into the back seat before driving off. I remember when we left Princeton, his car was at the curb with the back seat area completely engulfed with discarded newspapers, making the interior rear view mirror useless.

In general, however, we avoided social contacts with most of the fellow junior faculty. The University profited by its ability to attract the brightest new Ph.D.s, but had the infamous "Five Year Rule" that prescribed an automatic termination for any instructor who was not promoted to the rank of Assistant Professor in that time span. Such promotions were extremely rare, for the University could easily replace such staff with individuals of like kind. The result was cut-throat competition among the instructors, with their wives particularly vulnerable to attempts to undercut the others. That rule, and the prevailing reaction to it, only served to speed our interest in getting out of that situation and moving on elsewhere. The romance of Princeton University was beginning to fade.

An exception was one Prof. Bill Smith, a fellow faculty member in the Department of Psychology. He appeared genetically unable to utter a sentence without some outrageous expletive in it, and his wife was what women in Mississippi would call "a mess," for she could talk enthusiastically for hours on end about absolutely nothing. They had just had a Fulbright for an academic year in Norway, and had decided to spend the summer in Paris before returning home. The mattress in their apartment was such that her husband had trouble sleeping, and so Mrs. Smith, mustering her best French, told the concierge that her husband's "maitresse" was lumpy and must be replaced. She later learned that the concierge was aghast because "maitresse" is French for *mistress,* not *mattress.*

The unease in social situations involving fellow faculty peers that existed for us had a parallel among members of the senior or tenured faculty. It was apparent, from contacts with the few such as the chair of the science department consumed with ESP, that interaction among them, or by them with their graduate students, was nil. A very notable exception to this was Dr. Carlos Baker, the chair of the English Department and noted Hemingway scholar, who was known for hosting frequent social gatherings of his faculty and graduate students.

None of our three children were "accidents"—all three were planned. Our first, Michael, was born the second year we were in Princeton. Pegge became toxic in her seventh month, and the obstetrician felt the fetus was sufficiently developed that labor could be induced. Thus began 45 hours of hard labor, with pains every 3 to 5 minutes and my feeding Pegge crushed ice by the spoonful between pains. About the time I was ready to go get the obstetrician, Dr. Summers, with a gun, he came to the hospital and delivered Pegge by section. That turned out to be the only way Mike could have come into this world in one piece.

It was 6 AM and my 46th hour in the hospital; I was at the nurses' station and duty nurses were scrubbing up the newborn in a room just down the hall Suddenly one called out "Hey—there is something wrong with this baby!" I tried every possible strategy to get an explanation, but was unsuccessful. The nurses quieted down, and I assumed there was no major problem requiring special attention—and anyway, it was clear that I would get no elaboration from them. Dr. Summers had left, and I decided simply to go home and get some sleep—there was simply nothing else I could do. Later in the day I found that the "something wrong" was a very minor, though rare and surprising anatomical aberration of no real consequence. A larger problem was a huge hemangioma in the middle of his back, that our pediatrician, a young fellow whose practice with Princeton mothers had prompted him to put a sign over his examining table "Babies are hard to kill." recommended be surgically removed. We delivered Mikie, as we had begun calling him, to a hospital in Philadelphia where a highly recommended surgeon had agreed to remove the offending birthmark. I will never forget the apprehensions that Pegge and I shared as we left our new young son in a hospital ward with two other children, ages probably 2 and 3, in adjoining beds. Their parents were with them as they wailed and wailed; a few minutes before visiting hours were up; the parents left, and their two took a long look at each other, and broke into gleeful giggles. Thus, we learned early that kids can be much smarter than their parents. Mikie, of course, later reinforced that insight.

The surgeon, a pudgy man with very thick glasses named Dr. Burbage, was the man recommended for the removal of the cyst. Special care had gone into his selection, for there was a risk that the hemangioma was entangled in Mikie's spine, and it gave us considerable pause when we found that Dr. Burbage had a marked tremor in his hands. We learned that his tremor persisted until the moment of incision, when somehow he became steady as a rock until the cut was made. The hemangioma turned out to be on the surface only, and the operation was a success. And our young pediatrician soon told us that babies, particularly first babies, were like new cars: you just had to get all the bugs out before you could breathe easy.

Mikie was a good baby. The most trouble I remember was a few occasions of getting soaked while fussing with a diaper change, a matter in which he became quite proficient, and one 3 AM feeding when he cried and cried until I found that I had the bottle inserted in his ear.

I remember waiting breathlessly for his first word, hoping it would be "Da da." But this was not to be. The first word he spoke, to our knowledge, was "car-car." He seemed to take an extraordinary interest in automobiles, and I recall once when later visiting a friend that he, then three, called the man of the house out to the street, to show him our old 1951 Ford. "It's old, but it's clean" he told the man.

Once talking, he was seldom at a loss for words. Later when he was three and Pegge was trying to administer a dose of medicine, he said "Thank you very much, but I don't care for any." He also proved to have an insatiable taste for beer as soon as he could walk. I recall visiting a man who was sitting at an outdoor table enjoying a beer, and who left it there while we went into the house for something. When we returned, the beer mug was empty and Mikie had a silly grin on his face.

Among our closest friends were Jack and Karla Bardon. Jack was the school psychologist for Princeton High School, and like me had a private psychological counseling practice aside from work. The Bardons also had a daughter who was born about the same time as Mikie, which added to the communality. Jack and I frequently discussed our clinical problems, and Pegge and Karla were close friends. After we left Princeton, Jack assumed a position on the faculty of nearby Rutgers University in New Brunswick.

When we first moved to Princeton, I had signed up as a blood donor at Princeton Hospital. Yet, two years passed before I was called to donate. I did so, and after yielding a pint of blood, I found out why they had not needed a donor for two years. I was asked if I preferred Scotch or Bourbon in return for my donation. And I learned that after dropping a pint of blood, a little alcohol goes a long way. Nevertheless, the blood bank had no problem getting donors.

I learned that the University saved money by using graduate students or, as previously noted, people like myself who were replaced after five years, as instructors to teach the majority of courses. Many students complained that in four years at Princeton, they had had a truly qualified professor for only one or two courses. This also helped me lose my delusions about higher education in the Ivy League, as I began to look elsewhere for employment. We had been at Princeton University for only two years when Dr. Super called to tell me of an opening at Emory University in the Counseling Center and the Department of Psychology. I jumped at the chance. With his recommendation, I was a shoo in, and I accepted the appointment. We packed up our books and belongings, put them on a rented trailer hitched to our 1951 Ford, and started out for Atlanta in August of 1954.

Chapter 18

Our Life at Emory University

In the late summer of 1954, we packed a trailer with our belongings and headed for Atlanta and my new job at Emory University. Our UHaul trailer was the largest we could get, and we packed our books on the bottom and furniture on top, and covered all with a tarp. We moved down in August, and soon found that the load was a little too much for our poor Ford, for it kept overheating and needing water. For the first day, we would pray for a service station in the next few miles so that we could replenish the radiator's contents. I recall one country station in Virginia that refused to give us any water unless we made a purchase of gasoline. That was easier to solve than the fire in the trailer that was caused when I foolishly tossed a lighted cigarette out the window, and it landed in some bedding on the trailer. Having gotten off to this kind of start, the experience of the first day convinced us to continue the trip at night the next day when it would be cooler and when any fire on the trailer could be spotted immediately. We arrived at the apartment complex on North Decatur Road that would be our home for the next year without further incident.

The apartment complex, owned by Emory University, housed many other young faculty, and there were many playmates for our son Mikie, then two. In his first trip out to the yard where his set played, he found the group threatened by a swarm of bees. To show his prowess, and though barefooted, he stamped them out on the ground, and smiled confidently at the group as he came inside. Once in, he burst into tears, and I removed a half dozen stingers from his bare feet. But he had shown his mettle.

Sometime later he told me he knew who God was. I pursued this, finding that he was referring to my immediate boss at Emory, one Sam Webb. And it appeared that Mikie was with me on campus when I spied Sam coming towards us, and said "My God, there he is!" Sam was a native of Oxford, NC, and held a Ph.D. from the Psychometric Laboratory at UNC. He and his wife Neva became dear friends. He was a pragmatist, and as I was trying to complete my thesis at Columbia for the doctorate, he told me of his experience. He had done a most significant study of the Strong Vocational Interest Inventory, and had filed a copy of his thesis, as required, in the University library. When he did this, however, he had placed a twenty dollar bill between certain pages. Ten years later, he said, he went back to the library, checked out his thesis, and retrieved the twenty dollar bill. (This prompted me to try the same thing at Columbia a couple of years later, with the same result!)

When I had interviewed for the job, I had met with the vice president, Dr. Ernest Caldwell, a scholar who had been one of the translators of the Dead Sea Scrolls, and who later became the president of Clairmont College in California. He was examining the budgets of the various departments at Emory when I entered his office, and he could not restrain himself from commenting on a department head that he had just found had returned several thousand dollars in his budgetary allotment for the year to the general fund. Dr. Caldwell said that this indicated to him that the department head simply wasn't ingenious enough to find something to spend the money on, and that this was a sign of great weakness.

My salary as an instructor was hardly adequate for a family of three, and when I learned that we had another on the way, I looked about for ways to supplement our income. I began to take in private clients for counseling, and this helped some. But then I realized that I had an expensive set of golf clubs that I had purchased when we were at the Naval Academy Preparatory School at Bainbridge, and I sold them to a graduate student in my department whose stipend was $9,000 per annum. My salary at that time was $5,000 per annum.

Emory proved to be a vigorous environment, in spite of (or perhaps because of) the tradition of no intercollegiate sports. Each fraternity house had a live-in housemother, a practice that struck me as odd, for this would have been unthinkable at the University of North Carolina when I was there, or at Princeton, where a tie on the door knob of a student's room meant he had a girl with him. But my concerns may have been misplaced, for it was a group of these ladies that during a semester break painted the lion statue in front of the Phi Delta Theta house a bright and bilious green.

The close affiliation of the University with the Methodist Church did not stop the male students from embarking one evening on a panty raid, in vogue at the time. They were stopped cold, however, when they descended on the girl's dorm: lights went on, and the stately dean of students was found to be sitting on the porch by the entry way lugubriously rocking back and forth in a rocking chair. Emory was also the province of Dr. Sam Shriver, a normally deadpan Professor of Modern Languages, who was known for two things: first, putting a Swiss yodeling record on the turntable for the recorded chimes in the University chapel, treating the community for miles around by playing it at full volume, then retrieving his record and continuing on his walk home. Second, he was noted for entering the University library one afternoon and, oppressed by the quiet, emitting an ear-shattering rebel yell. These activities were all the more significant because he was otherwise considered rather dull in demeanor, and was always expressionless.

These escapades built on a legacy left years earlier by a Professor Peed. Professor Peed had a T-Model Ford that he used to drive the three blocks from his home to the campus, but who frequently forgot whether he had driven the car one way when he had to traverse the other way. One night he left the car on the campus, whereupon a group of students seized it, disassembled it, and reconstructed it on the top of the University chapel, some fifty feet in the air. And it was Professor Peed whose wife was entertaining the Emory University Faculty Wives' Club for afternoon tea with the Professor in the bedroom taking his afternoon nap when his wife took the guests on a tour of the house. The bedroom had two doors to a hall outside, and as the group entered one, Mrs. Peed said "Cover up, Professor, the ladies are coming through." Professor Peed always napped in the raw, and he reached down to pull the sheet over him without realizing he was already covered. Thus, he picked up the bottom of the sheet, and raised it over his head, exposing his altogether nude body. We thought of this incident later when the *Atlanta Constitution* dutifully reported on a meeting of the "Faulty Wives Club at Emory University."

It was on North Decatur Road that ran by Emory University that I learned one of the more important lessons of my life. I was taking a TV set into Decatur for repair, and had it sitting on the passenger seat beside me. I was watching it more closely than the car in front of me, and collided with that car when it stopped unexpectedly for some reason, causing some minor damage to each car. We stopped and waited for a policeman to arrive. I was standing with the driver of the other car, a student whose jeans contrasted with my three piece suit, when the cop came up. He recognized me as a faculty member at the University, and, not realizing which of us was driving which car, said to me: "I am sorry this happened to you, sir, but we will take care of it in just a minute." Then, turning to the student, he said "And what the hell do you think you were doing?" A report of this incident came in very handy when some years later I was teaching police in New Jersey about how prejudices could affect their behavior, for the driver of any car involved in colliding with another in front is always at fault.

Emory University had been generously endowed by the Candler family, whose wealth came from Coca Cola. Because of the University's deep obligation to the Candler family, the soft drink machines about the campus dispensed only Coca Cola. And, in Emory University Hospital, the post-operative and pediatric diets consisted of Coca Cola. Tufts may have had its stuffed elephant as a tribute to the Barnham circus family that contributed so heavily to it, but Emory, by golly, never forgot the Candlers.

Our dentist, Roy Smith, who practiced at Emory University Hospital, was a neighbor and he and his wife were good friends. He verified all that I had learned in vocational psychology about the fine manual dexterity of successful dentists, and he relished his handiwork. He was also a perfectionist, and did the cleaning for his patients, rather than assign this to a dental technician, for he could never be satisfied with the work of others. But Smith also applied his manual dexterity skills to the building of a 35 foot sailboat in his 40 foot family room, and, upon finishing it, only then realized it was too large to be moved outside the house. Thus, a wall came down, the boat was extracted, and the wall replaced.

Another non-faculty friend was Minor Blackford, M.D., a physician with private means of support who took only one patient a day, and insisted on starting the visit with luncheon as his guest. I was referred to him because of the discovery, just before leaving Princeton, of a "red-hot" exothalmic goiter, and this had been his specialty at the Mayo Clinic. He was a most capable physician and a most endearing friend. I recall his way of dealing with the threat of smoking: he would ask for a cigarette, light it and take a couple of puffs, then take his pulse, and exclaim "O my goodness—110!" and frantically stamp the cigarette out. But Dr. Blackford found that the goiter could not be controlled, and he arranged for a sub-total thyroidectomy at Emory by a surgeon who divided his time between the operating room and the wild blue yonder as an Air Force reservist. (I recall when he made a post-op visit to me at the hospital, he was wearing his Air Force uniform.)

The Department of Psychology turned out to be a true hotbed of high quality scholarly work. There were eleven faculty members in the department, and the group usually assembled around the mail boxes in the departmental office when the daily mail was delivered, and delighted in informing each other how many requests for reprints of their journal articles they had received. The usual winner in this was William Bevan, a Ph.D. in experimental psychology from Duke University, who later became the Executive Officer of the American Association for the Advancement of Science, then Provost of Duke University, and then Executive Director of the John D. and Catherine MacArthur Foundation. An Emory University departmental record shows that Bevan published 46 papers between January 1, 1950, and September 30, 1957. Another experimental psychologist, Art Riopelle, who later accepted the prestigious directorship of the Yerkes Primate Laboratory then in Orange Park, Florida, came in second with 33 papers during that period. Paul Secord, later chair of the Department of Psychology of the University of Nevada came in third with 18. I'm afraid I came in sixth, squarely in the middle of the distribution, publishing only twelve papers during the period reported. Clearly, I was outclassed.

My duties involved teaching one course each quarter, and devoting the rest of the time to counseling students. I was responsible, as an Instructor in Psychology, to the department chair, Curtis Langhorne, and as a counselor in the University Counseling Service, to Sam Webb. Both these men were exemplary in their positions, and completely approachable and concerned for the welfare of those who reported to them. Curtis was effective in getting each of us to publish and to gain recognition beyond the department itself, and Sam was as much friend as boss.

Sam Webb and Neva, his wife, had an adopted son named Sandy, who became a friend and companion of our son Mike. Sam had no trouble with the birds and the bees bit when Sandy saw a woman in the last stage of pregnancy, and told his dad that Mrs. X was very, very fat. Sam said he took that opportunity to tell Sandy, then about 4 or 5, that the woman was carrying a baby that would soon be born, whereupon Sandy exclaimed: "Ugh. I am glad I was adopted!"

One of our instructors was a man named Oscar Adams, a bachelor who resigned and took a research position at Lockheed-Marietta when he got engaged. Sam's comment: "Oscar wanted to get married, and just didn't feel he could make ends meet on his Emory salary."

The counseling function was much more satisfying than at Princeton, for two reasons: first, the students were more normal or ordinary people, and their problems were the traditional ones I could readily understand; and second, I now had an excellent counseling psychologist working with me in Richard Goodling, who had a Ph.D. from Penn State as well as a Doctor of Divinity degree from a Lutheran seminary. Dick was an ardent Rogerian in his approach to counseling, but I felt he overdid it when, after reading the classic case that Carl Rogers presented of "Mrs. Oakes," he had the walls of his office painted pink and put up gingham curtains. But he was an excellent counselor, and it was good to have someone with whom to discuss particular challenges. He was a very solid clinician, and also had a lively sense of humor. For example, he once asked me following a session with a most attractive young coed: "Jay, if I told her she had a nice body, do you think she would hold it against me?" Dick later moved to a faculty position at the Duke University Divinity School His wife, Ruth, died an early death from cancer, and Dick married another "Ruth" who looked just like the first Ruth, and whom I hired as a secretary in my ETS office in Durham some years later. She moved on to other things, and Dick died in the early 1990s.

One tough counseling case at Emory was a graduate student who came in for help in getting ready for a qualifying test in the English language that the University required of all Ph.D. candidates. He told me that he had completed his course work and his dissertation, had successfully defended it, and in fact had only the required English language test between him and the degree. He said he was getting desperate, for he had failed the test on two occasions, and it was a three strikes and you are out proposition. Finding this hard to believe, I said to him: "Do you mean to tell me that the English test is your only remaining requirement for the degree?" To this he answered: "Dr. Davis, I have did everything but pass that gosh-darned English test!"

I remember all too well counseling a pretty but sad girl named Betsy, who was having trouble motivating herself for her course work. It turned out that her mother was a well-known member of the Georgia General Assembly, and this lady, reeking of Chanel Number Five, barged into my office one day to discuss Betsy. She said that her main purpose in seeing me was to thank me for trying to help Betsy. "Betsy," she said, "has always been an ugly child, and I have considered her hopeless from the day she was born. Anything you may be able to do with her will be a miracle, but don't expect much . . ." It was here that I began to believe that women in significant political leadership roles might be miserable failures in some more common roles.

In the summer, I had two different programs as a counselor. The first was an activity sponsored by the Methodist Church and the University to bring young people from the church groups to the campus for a week of attending classes and counseling as to academic major prospects. I recall one boy, who started the testing part of the program with an Otis IQ of 72. This low score was confirmed by several other tests of academic aptitude. I took great care in explaining the importance of the test in predicting academic performance, and graphing his position on a chart, together with the range of scores of Emory students on the same chart, so the discrepancy would be clearly apparent. When I finished, I leaned back, and said: "What do you think now about choosing Emory for pre-law work?" He replied: "Oh, sir, I am sure I will like it!" I fell back on what I had learned long before entering graduate study in counseling psychology: I said "You can't come to Emory—it would be too hard." This he not only understood, but accepted, for his response was "Well, then, I will just have to think of something else."

The other summer activity was intensive psychological testing and appraisal of Methodist missionary couples who were on furlough in the States from foreign duty before reassignment. This was an extremely instructive enterprise for me in at least two ways. The first was insight into what missionaries in developing countries do. For the most part, they were mostly educators, and relied on recruiting native ministers to handle the religious activities. I recall several saying that their biggest problem was keeping their native ministers from committing adultery with the female members of their congregations, or preventing them from stealing from the collection plate. And I learned that those who were successful did not achieve this by saving souls, but by teaching such things as hygiene and how to grow food crops.

The other thing I learned was more sobering. The testing and appraisal involved some 8 hours a day for a period of five days with each individual—the husband and the wife. Dick Goodling would take one, and I would take the other. Our probing was highly personal and we used the most advanced tests of personality and behavioral functioning. What I learned was that inevitably I would start with a charming, likable, apparently stable person, and by the time our probing was through he or she had been reduced to all the petty little deficiencies all of us have but hide in our normal contacts with others. This was a dramatic lesson in what I had been told at the beginning of graduate study: counseling and clinical psychology is not an activity for those who love people.

It was at Emory that I came to a firm decision to abandon practice as a counseling psychologist. The event that triggered this was a case in my private practice where the presenting problem of the client, a mother, was that her 13 year old son was hiding in the woods rather than attending school, and then lying about where he spent his day. With Dr. Goodling taking the boy and me his mother, we began an intensive series of counseling. We were careful, working by the book so to speak, meeting weekly for some six months. The mother, a classic domineering type who took firm control of everything about her, gained insight into her attraction to a milk-toast husband who let her control him and his portrait photography business, and she began to put the screws on him. He retaliated by having an affair with his secretary, and was caught by the wife. With this discovery, she put several bullets into his head, shot her son who managed to crawl outside before expiring, and turned the gun successfully on herself. Thus, we started with a child who was truant, did everything carefully, and ended with three dead bodies. I knew that one had to be tough for counseling, and indeed I was—but this episode served to make me lose faith in the efficacy of therapeutic procedures, and I decided to bolt and focus on teaching and research.

The students at Emory were bright and fun to teach—probably because we had relatively small class sizes, light teaching loads that gave us adequate time to prepare, and relatively bright students anyway. An exemplary graduate student was a young lady named Gail Bostelman who frequently assisted me in the Counseling Service, where remedial reading was a frequent need. Gail hit upon asking the individual to tell a story, recording what he or she said, then typing it up, and using it for reading drill. Although I have seen no reference to this technique in the literature in the 50 or so years since, it proved to be remarkably effective.

But it was the undergraduate students who were truly fun to teach. I started with a course in Industrial Psychology, and a coterie of about 15 students formed and proceeded to take each new course that I taught. Most I got to know personally. I recall particularly a young lady named Jo Beth, a tender, innocent, and frequently gullible type, who came to me one day in great distress. The night before, she said, she had dreamed that her little nephew, who lived with them at home in Decatur, was brutally murdered, and although she tried to help him, she was unable to get to him. She said "But I love my little nephew, and wouldn't hurt him for the world. Does my dream mean that secretly I hate him enough to kill him?" "Jo Beth," I responded, what did you have for supper last night?" Obviously confused by this, she wiped a tear away and said: "Why, I went to a covered dish supper at our Baptist Church last evening, and had several helpings of a delicious potato salad." "There's your problem!" I told her. That salad may have been delicious, but in this warm Georgia climate it can frequently spoil just enough to cause bad dreams." Jo Beth was much relieved, and both of us learned an important lesson.

I recall a very good student who came to me and said that he enjoyed the class with me so very much that he would like to become a professor, instead of a physician like his father. "But I don't think I could live on only $15,000 a year," he said. This sum was three times what I was making, and probably about what the President of the College was making at that time.

Two of my students decided to enter the doctoral program I had completed at Columbia. One, however, had a terminal illness (Hodgkin's Disease), and had been given 5 years at most to live. He felt this would prevent him from gaining admission to graduate study, for several graduate programs had turned him down in spite of an exemplary academic record. I called my major professor at Columbia, Don Super, with that inquiry. To his credit, Don said "Certainly—tell him to come on. His physical prognosis is simply irrelevant, for it is not under our control. Why just last week, we lost our best departmental doctoral candidate to a traffic accident on Amsterdam Avenue."

I had gone to Emory with my data collection for my doctoral dissertation complete, but had had trouble starting writing the dissertation. Some four years had gone by since completing my research, and I was confined to the instructor status until I had the doctorate in hand. Pegge started taking in typing. Her first job was typing a doctoral dissertation on a topic very similar to mine for a candidate for the Ph.D. degree at George Peabody College. This man was a part-time faculty member for whom I had little respect. She asked me for help with some of the technical terms, which pricked my interest in the thesis. I read it, and believed it to be pure junk. I thus advised Pegge to collect her money when she finished and before he turned this monstrosity in, for I felt he would never get his doctorate on that effort. But, he returned from Nashville a week or so after she finished typing it, with his Ph.D. confirmed.

I immediately took a week off from counseling and started writing. After the first 79 pages, I made copies and mailed them to Don Super, who was my thesis chairman at Columbia University, to get his reactions. While awaiting his reactions, I had driven to a professional meeting in Asheville, NC, where I was to present a paper. When I arrived, Pegge called from Atlanta to tell me that Don Super had called to tell me that my last chance that year to complete the language requirement for the Ph.D. was a testing session to be held at Columbia University in five days. Columbia required proficiency in two foreign languages, and I had qualified in French while in residence, and had let the second language requirement slip up on me. If I failed that opportunity, the doctorate was inevitably another year away. I went to a bookstore in downtown Asheville and bought a first year Spanish text and dictionary. I crammed for the next 72 hours and on the way back to Atlanta, letting someone else drive. On the morning of day 5,

I caught a plane to New York City, text and dictionary still in hand. The test turned out to involve translating a passage from the Spanish language edition of *Life Magazine*, and the outcome was certification in a second foreign language. I had become a five day Spanish language scholar!

Back in Atlanta, I was called shortly by Don Super who had completed reading the 79 pages I had sent him. He advised me to stop writing, put a closing paragraph on what I had, and come back to New York City for the orals. By this time I had another some 70 pages, but I brought everything to a close and mailed the required copies to Don. A date for the orals was then set, and I flew back up for this final hurdle.

For some reason, I remember boarding an old Constellation with three tail fins at the Atlanta Airport. The pilot, a huge hunk of a man, then came aboard, walked up the aisle, and as he was about to enter the cockpit cabin, turned and said to a stewardess "Let's go a whizzing!" That we did, all the way to NYC's Idelwild Airport.

The required extra-departmental member of the orals examining committee at Teachers College turned out to be Irving Lorge. The reader may remember my description of him from my account of taking his course in the Nature of Intelligence—his reputation was two-fold: one, he was the protégé of the great Robert Thorndike, and two, he was the meanest man in the institution, with a reputation for delaying the degrees of all who came before him. As a member of an orals examining committee, he had held up one friend (Harry Beilin, later on the faculty at the City College of New York) for several years on a minor technicality. My thesis chair, Don Super, apologized for Lorge's membership on my orals committee, but said the choice had been out of his hands. At the orals, Dr. Lorge opened with a suicide kind of question—i.e., "How can you claim X when you admit Y was present?" I responded: "Please, sir, tell me what part of my specific explanation of this on page 97 you do not understand." He obviously had not really read that far in the dissertation (actually, I had no idea what was on page 97), for he shut up. The others asked reasonable questions, and I responded; I was asked to leave the room while the committee members discussed my defense and voted; I was called back in, and Don Super said something I will never forget: "Congratulations, Dr. Davis!"

I was given a 21 step checklist describing what I had to do to be formally certified as having a Ph.D. degree from Columbia University. These steps involved getting various signatures certifying that this or that was in order, paying required records fees, turning in any library books and keys to lockers, and the like, and finally depositing the required copy of the thesis in the library. I shortly found that Step 16 sent me back to Step 13, and thus began a circular path. With a scheduled flight return to Atlanta, I decided to skip Step 16 and go on to Step 17, forged some initials in the blank provided, and shortly finished the other checks and certifications needed. My diploma would be mailed, come the next commencement, if I was so little moved as not to show for the formal ceremonies on the steps of Low Memorial Library. With the thesis placed with the librarian, I spat on the statue in front of Low, and caught a cab to the airport.

Somewhere in the city I had found a printer who made up a copy of a page resembling page A1 of the *New York Times*, with the headline "Davis Finally Gets Ph.D." and mailed this to my mother in North Carolina with a note saying I was on the way home. She responded in a letter saying "Son, if you have a Ph.D., you ought to know that the word "coming" in "coming home" is spelled with one 'm,' not two."

Returning to Emory I now began to feel that we had found a permanent home. We contracted one Fred Dempsey from a village near Stone Mountain, Ga., to build us a house to our design on a sharply sloping lot on Luckie Lane, a scant two blocks from the Emory University campus, and we moved in from the University apartment in our second year at Emory.

Pegge soon found herself pregnant, and we were happy to have the University hospital right next door so to speak. When Pegge's time came, she was scheduled for a Caesarian Section the same time that I had to teach a class, and I remember hurrying to get through that and to the hospital to see what had transpired.

Pegge had been surprised to find the delivery made in an OR with a glassed in balcony area for medical students to observe the proceedings below. She was felt to be emotionally stable to be kept conscious for the delivery, and the obstetrician was interested in pioneering this method. She was given an epidural as a local anesthetic which would permit her to stay awake for the delivery, not a a normal practice for a Caesarean, and she recalled students behind the glass above laughing and drinking cokes as they watched before she defied this bold experiment by the surgeons and passed out. The delivery went with only one small hitch: Chris was nicked in the hip by a scalpel, yielding a scar that he still carries today. But as he was removed from utero, Pegge awakened enough to hear one of the nurses exclaim "Look—he has his thumb in his mouth!" He weighed in at a husky nine pounds and three ounces, and was nineteen inches long. We proudly took him to our new home, where he vied for attention with our son Mike, and demonstrated a remarkable inability to distinguish night from day. Pegge's mother came to help, and we settled in comfortably as a family with two fine sons.

During the period I was on the faculty at Emory University, I was also active in the Naval Reserve. There was a point incentive for inactive duty officers to take courses in one or another basic skill. I was initially a student in these courses, but with a faculty appointment in civilian life I was fortunate enough to be asked shortly to serve as an instructor. These courses were offered at the Georgia Institute of Technology. Over a period of several terms, I taught, as a volunteer, several courses each of 12 weeks duration: Basic Seamanship, Navigation, and the Uniform Code of Military Justice. Navigation was my real love, for I had served this role on the old USS Marmora, from Pearl Harbor to Okinawa to Mobile, Alabama., and because it utilized many of the mathematical skills from my university major. I had also developed some special forms—computational guides—for calculating lines of position from sights on celestial objects that were unquestionably a considerable improvement over those provided by standard texts or procedures.

The course in the Uniform Code of Military Justice was something I had to learn as we proceeded through the text. I found this a most useful acquisition, for the basis of the course was essentially the rules of law. I also had considerable help from several reserve officers in the class who were lawyers in civilian life. And the students were adults, mostly well seasoned naval reserve officers, including a most personable Rear Admiral in the inactive Naval Reserve, which made the teaching experience quite different and even more rewarding than that involving college age students. I was in my early 30s, and as most of the "students" were considerably older, I found their attention flattering and the camaraderie rewarding.

During this period I also twice accepted two weeks of active duty in the Naval Reserve, again an option promoted by the Navy for reserve officers on inactive duty. I was assigned to a group of about two dozen educators—public school principals and college professors—that met each summer for two weeks at the 6th Naval District Navy Yard in Charleston, SC, with the mission of planning the conversion of a particular institution of higher education into a Naval Training Center in the event of a national emergency.

For an eight hour period each day, we met in space provided by the Commandant, Sixth Naval District, but were free to seek out whatever leisure activity we desired in the evenings. One of the officers made a contact with a female employee of the local telephone company switchboard office in Charleston, and this young lady had a number of associates who enjoyed going out on the town at night with my colleagues. I did not get involved in this, and I suspect that no serious hanky-panky ever occurred—but the men who did participate—particularly the public school administrators who lived under intense public scrutiny at home—enjoyed their evenings of freedom with the young ladies eager to be taken out.

I remember one officer who was an elementary school principal in North Carolina. He confessed that the freedom we experienced at Charleston was extremely precious to him. As an example of what he had to put up with on the job, he recalled a telephone call from an anxious mother who told him that she thought her little daughter had gone to school that morning without wearing panties, and asked if he would please check and find out.

In the first year, we completed the plans and prepared the specifications for the changes needed to convert the specified institution into a training center in

30 days—walls to be moved or erected, dormitories to be converted for increased occupancy, and every thing else, right down to the number of paper clips needed for each instructor and administrator. We were reassembled in a second year to continue the task, which had been completed in the first year, so after reviewing and affirming the work of the prior year, we had to find ways to amuse ourselves during the day. We found that each of us had a rich store of off-color jokes, and after several days of listening and then saying "That reminds me of . . ." we decided to record them in a book that could be published. We agreed on a title—*The Thrifty Tomcat, and Other Stories*—which referred to the story on page 39 of our draft—and ran mimeographed copies of the collection that numbered something over a hundred jokes. I lost touch with the officer who had agreed to try to find a publisher, and my own copy disappeared over the years. But the individual stories, I find, are recalled by other stories now in sessions where men get together and amuse each other with dirty jokes.

I provide, with some reluctance, the story about the thrifty tomcat, for I am sure that mention of this may have most unfortunately whetted the appetite of the reader. I say "with some reluctance" because the story was probably one of the more mediocre ones in the collection. It was a simple two liner: "Did you hear the one about the thrifty tom cat? He put all he had in the kitty!."

Unfortunately, my later move from Atlanta to the graduate deanship at UNC-Greensboro in 1959 did not leave leisure for the Naval Reserve activities, and I declined continuing involvement in the instructional or summer active duty for training programs. In 1965, having accumulated 24 years of active and inactive duty and reaching the ripe old age of 40, I retired formally from the Naval Reserve. But I have to recognize that some of the happiest days of my life were in the Navy—from the ROTC cadet experience on the old USS Dubuque in the Chesapeake Bay in 1943, to the alcoholic skipper on the PC boat, to the Bucket of Rust that carried Aviation Gas to the Air Force at Okinawa, to playing detective in the back allies of Charleston, to the teaching at the Naval Academy Preparatory School at Bainbridge, to the inactive duty experiences at Georgia Tech and at the Charleston Navy Yard. And, I knew that I had achieved a distinguished record in the service: I was probably the officer promoted from Ensign to Lieutenant Junior Grade in the shortest time, and the officer with the longest tenure in the rank of Lieutenant Junior Grade that the Navy knew before or since.

But back to Atlanta. At this point in our young married life, it seemed that we were always hard up for cash. I had borrowed $3.000 from Pegge's father, with the understanding that I would repay him by supporting the college education of her younger brother, Marty. Since Marty was not particularly scholarly, I felt I had a safe deal.

We recalled a high school guidance counselor who wrote Pegge's parents that she could not understand how anyone as bright as Marty could make the lousy grades he achieved in high school. Perhaps it was because he ran with a group of friends who were always getting stopped by "Scholtz," the state highway patrolman stationed in that area. Marty reported that he had always been in the back seat, but that Scholtz, who was anathema to the high school crowd, began to recognize him, and cheer him up with the admonition as he arrested the driver: "You, son, are next!" Scholtz surely felt that this would be a deterrent, but Marty said that it had quite the opposite effect on him. And Marty was probably brighter than Scholtz.

But it so happened that Marty graduated from high school and was ready to enter college when we were at Emory, and had moved into our new house there, which had an extra bedroom. The admissions officer, with whom I had a special relationship because I did the admissions research to guide admission decisions, had admitted a Candler (from the Coca Cola family) who had flunked out of several private schools, on the grounds that his father had "purchased the right for the son to fail at Emory" by underwriting several of the pink Georgia marble buildings. He had violated the admissions formulas I had given him for the Candler lad, and he said that for me it was only fair that he would admit my brother-in-law who had high SAT scores but a lousy high school average grade. Thus, Marty came to live with us just before the fall semester in 1956, which gave him time to discover a number of local fishing holes from which be brought copious supplies of fresh bass. If Marty had one best aptitude, it was for catching fish.

Although we were not addicts of fresh bass, we tried to provide the kind of diet that Marty wanted. We recall that he said his favorite breakfast was waffles, and for six weeks Pegge prepared a stack of waffles each day for his initial meal—until he begged her to stop and try something—anything—else. He nevertheless revealed a remarkable capacity for milk, and upon getting out of bed each early afternoon would consume a quart or more directly from the bottle.

But when Marty started classes, he had some trouble with attending, principally because he needed to sleep until two or three in the afternoon, when he would get out of bed, go to the refrigerator, and use milk as an eye-opener. He soon became involved in the extra-curricular life at Georgia Tech, where the fraternity parties started each evening about dusk. I recall him being particularly impressed with a party one evening at a fraternity house where the piano was rolled out on the terrace, soaked with gasoline, and set afire while the party goers toasted the flames with their mugs of beer. I assumed that this episode was just another manifestation of the Georgia values system that prompted old Gene Talmidge to get votes from the red dirt farmers by spitting tobacco juice on the carpet of his Cadillac limousine.

Unfortunately, the end of the first quarter came, and Marty's report showed four F's and one D (he obviously had one crip course!). Marty concluded that

Emory was simply too hard, and returned to North Carolina. Although I was left with the larger portion of the $3,000 debt unpaid, I later learned that my contact with him was not without having significant impact on him. For, at some point I had told him the joke about the king who was shipwrecked and thrown up on a desert island with his court jester, the only other survivor—and in a month's time, so the story goes, the king was at his wit's end. I know this had an impact on Marty, for he returned to Wilmington, and, his home being only a few miles from the Wrightsville beach area, he was attracted to work in a bar for college students vacationing there which was named "The Wit's End." The place was unique and endearing to the college crowd by such little touches as a large chicken snake placed in an aquarium on the bar with a sign that read "To whom it may concern: you left your snake on the bar. Please come and retrieve it."

Marty's response to Emory turned out to be his last hurrah to adolescence. He has written an excellent autobiography (entitled *Memoirs of a Morris Man—the Journey to Character*) which explains his early years. He writes: "My character was cast in my youth much to my liking. I did fairly well in most things that I attempted and I was generally well-pleased with myself. I didn't give a continental about much and this laissez-faire attitude served me well for a number of years until it was impressed upon me from several fronts that good enough was not good enough, that I must meet a higher standard. As you will see, this transformed me from a trusting, fun-loving lackadaisical youth into the cynical, anxious, control obsessed man that you all know and love today—even if I do shake frequently now like a puppy pooping peach pits."

As testing hurdles later in the Air Force confirmed, he was exceptionally bright, and he succeeded brilliantly on matters he considered important. He enrolled in the University of North Carolina in Chapel Hill, where he met a lovely dark-eyed girl whom he married shortly before graduation. Resisting the stigma of being drafted, he joined the Air Force, and after Officer Training School became a military attache for the U. S. Embassy in Tel Aviv. Here, according to his autobiography, he met such people as Joe and Michael Douglass, who were in Israel with their father, Kirk Douglass, who was making a film at that location. After release from the Air Force, Marty took an executive position with a national packaging company headquartered in Charlotte, NC, where he was eminently successful. He and his wife Sue have two daughters: Ashley, a Mensa, now a housewife in Glasgow, Scotland, and Susannah, the wife of the head of a highly successful overseas evangelical enterprise in Burlington, NC. Marty and Sue have now retired to a palatial home they built on the Outer Banks of North Carolina, where with a couple of four-wheel drive Jeeps Marty continues his lifetime love of and devotion to fishing.

But back to Atlanta. In 1957, Dr. Joe Moore, a friend and head of the Psychology Department at Georgia Institute of Technology, contacted me to tell me that he had convinced the Board of Regents for the University System of Georgia to initiate a minimum admissions test standard for the 15 institutions in the University System, and needed a research-oriented person to assume a new position as Director of Testing and Guidance for the System to help the admissions officers to cope with the new requirement. Although I was getting more comfortable at Emory, I decided to explore it. I learned that the chair of the Board, a Mr. Arnold, had read Audrey Shuey's book *The Testing of Negro Intelligence*, and was convinced that the way to keep blacks out of the traditionally white university system institutions was to require an admissions test. Knowing that such a regulation would guarantee, not prevent, blacks entering the system, and seeing this as a chance to improve the admissions process at public institutions (none of which then had an admissions test requirement), and getting a husky increase in salary as well as a private statement of support from regent Howard (Bo) Callaway, I accepted the job. (Callaway later was appointed Secretary of the Army, and got a reputation for tooling around the District in an old Ford Mustang.)

As a first order of business, and with two bright young ladies as research assistants (one, Delores Garcia, from my classes at Emory, and the other, Gretchen Franz, the daughter of a prominent west coast psychologist), we collected data from each institution to establish admission formulas based on the College Board's Scholastic Aptitude Test (SAT) scores (which Dr. Moore had advised be used) and High School Rank in Class. Early one afternoon in desperation to convince the admissions people that High School Performance added significantly to the prediction of academic performance from SAT scores, I spent a few minutes drawing up a graph which would permit the easy translation of high school rank in class of graduation to a standard score scale comparable to the 200-800 scale on the SAT,. This permitted the admissions officers, who frequently had been oversold on the test, to look at the measures side by side. This table somehow was later adopted over the country by admissions officers anxious to consider high school performance in addition to test scores. I know that it was my work of a few minutes that created this practice, for I had made a small typographical error in one of the several hundred entries in the table, and the conversion charts I saw later in institutions about the country duplicated this error. Of all the professional work I ever did, this was probably the most positively influential, for its impact was keeping the college gatekeepers from putting too much emphasis on test scores, and paying attention to past academic performance as well.

A major part of my responsibilities involved traveling around the state and meeting the presidents, admissions officers, and faculty of the 15 institutions in the University System. I was always greeted warmly and treated as royalty, because I came from the Regent's office. I was frequently asked to address the faculties, and a favorite game was reading a set of institutional goals for an institution of higher learning. Some faculty member was usually quick to point out the abject absurdity of some or all of the goals statements, and when there was general agreement expressed I took great delight in revealing that the statement of institutional goals that I had just read had come from the catalog of that institution.

It was during this period that I attended a conference held at Warren Wilson College in Swannanoa, North Carolina. The conference involved overnight stays, and those attending were assigned two to a room in a college dormitory. When time for bed came, whoever was my roommate had not arrived, so I went to sleep. I awakened the next morning with the smell of cigarette smoke quite strong, and with the bathroom door in the room slightly ajar exposing that the light inside was on. I got up to investigate, and found Cliff Wing, then Director of Admissions at Tulane University and a member of the governing board of the College Entrance Examination Board, attired only in a pair of boxer shorts with figures on them, sitting on the john alongside a bathtub littered with several dozen cigarette butts. I will never forget his red eyes and dour expression as he looked up at me, and said "Jesus—you snore!"

The year with the Board of Regents passed without any problems, and permitted Pegge and me to get a taste of the way of life of the old South elite. The Board of Regents decided to have their monthly meetings at one after another of the homes of the members of the Board, and to bring their wives along. Pegge and I went to one of these meetings. The men met in a drawing room of the regent's mansion, while his wife entertained the ladies. Pegge recalls vividly being led to a large upstairs bedroom area after a morning of visiting local gardens, where Black maids helped each lady loosen and remove her outer clothing and lay down for an hour's rest or nap, or girl talk with the other wives. We felt from this experience that the South that Scarlett O'Hara knew before the Civil War had been fully restored.

We had continued to live in the house we built on Luckie Lane when I moved to the job with the University System of Georgia, and I recall a trip to several of the institutions that I had to make in 1958. Mike was 5, and I decided to take him with me to relieve the burden on Pegge who was consumed with the care of Christopher.

It was on that trip that we arrived in Savannah one evening, with appointments the next day at Savannah State College, one of the traditionally black institutions in the System. We got a room at the old Hotel DeSoto, then a very fine hotel. I recall waking up at 3 am with Mikie on the phone ordering himself a sumptuous meal from room service. He succeeded in getting a hamburger with all the trimmings and a gallon of milk, which settled him down for the next day at the college.

Our visit at Savannah State College started with the President's office, and his secretary offered to keep Mikie amused while I met with other faculty and administrative staff. Upon return to the office a couple of hours later, the secretary directed me to the circle in front of the Administration Building, where Mikie was stopping each car that came by, giving them a "ticket" for some infraction (the secretary had helped him make a number of these with an office mimeograph machine). I confess that I was too proud of the initiative that Mike showed on this trip that I could not resent his early morning expenditure at the hotel, nor his policing the traffic around Savannah State College.

Toward the end of the year, the Southern Regional Education Board hosted a meeting of college administrators from across the South, and I was asked to make a speech describing the conversion of the Georgia public institutions to the admissions test requirement. In the audience was one Dr. William Whyburn, Vice President for Research at the University of North Carolina at Chapel Hill, former professor of mathematics, and recognized for getting, through a grant, the magnificent (then) IBM computer facilities at the University when he had difficulty getting approval for a desk calculator under state purchasing requirements. The Woman's College of the University in Greensboro had an opening for a Graduate Dean, and Dr. Whyburn needed someone to chair an All University Admissions Advisory Committee. He apparently liked what I said, for he shortly had an invitation extended to me to apply for the deanship. This was not only a heady opportunity, it would take us back to our home state. I interviewed for the job, and was made an offer which I accepted. I learned later that the selection committee decided to make the offer to me when I said to several of them "I must confess that I don't know what it takes to be a good dean—for I have never known one!" But in September, 1958, we moved to Greensboro and I assumed the role of Dean of the Graduate School and Professor of Psychology and Education. Curtis Langhorne, the chair of the Department of Psychology at Emory, bought the house we had designed and built on Luckie Lane, about five blocks from the campus. We were thus on our way home to North Carolina.

Chapter 19

Graduate Deaning at UNC-G

My father found it incredible that I had been appointed Graduate Dean at UNC-G. He knew my predecessor, Franklin McNutt, and wrote me a simple postcard saying *"They don't make feet to fill them shoes . . ."* I consoled him with the reply that Mike, now six, was telling his friends that his father was going to be a "gradual dean."

UNC-G was also at that time strictly a woman's college, and there were only Caucasian women involved as students. I wondered if our marriage had matured too far, for when we first started out in academia, Pegge had said that she never wanted to see me in a girl's school, but now she did not seem to mind. I was, at 34, an old man, and my first impression of the girls in the classes I taught was that they were very much like male adolescents—having the same hangups and problems of immaturity that were present in boys of the same age. They were simply adolescents first and foremost, females second.

My duties at the college were challenging and enjoyable. The graduate program that I inherited consisted of master's degree programs, with a strong emphasis on teacher preparation, although a doctoral program in Home Economics had just been established. I was to guide the institution through this first doctoral program, and work toward the development of others. Institutional politics, however, had created a ban on "duplication of function," and graduate programs at the University in Chapel Hill or at NC State University in Raleigh could not be threatened by duplication. That left us very little options beyond Home Economics, for there were already strong graduate programs in most of the academic disciplines.

Although I wondered why one faculty member in the Home Economics Department with a brand new doctorate had a salary in the $15,000 range while another seasoned veteran in the English Department with substantial publications and a couple of Fulbrights could only get a salary in the $7,000 range. I took the responsibility seriously of creating a legitimate graduate program. The first year was spent writing a set of regulations and guidelines, and getting these accepted by a Graduate Administrative Board consisting of senior faculty.

An early incident was when I placed a phone call to a junior member of the psychology department, and when he answered the phone, I said "Is this mister _____? I was still hung up on the trend at Princeton University to use the term "Mister" instead of "Doctor." He responded with considerable anger in his voice: "No, this is **DOCTOR** _____." I could not resist saying: "O.K., Doctor. This is Dean Davis. Would you get your ass over to my office ASAP?"

He came quickly, although he never apologized for his initial response.

I recall the day when my first two doctoral theses came to my desk for final approval. One was entitled *A History of Women's Underwear from the 1890s to the Present*, and had used Sears Roebuck catalogs from the institution's library over that period as the source of data. The other was entitled *Storage Requirements of Bathrooms*. This one intrigued me particularly, and I read it carefully. The introductory chapter explained that the population used in the survey involved: some 40 homes in the immediate area of the university because the author felt she should not wander too far from campus, given that she was, in fact, knocking on the doors of strangers and asking rather sensitive questions.

A subsequent chapter described the survey instrument, Part I. This consisted, first, of open—ended questions such as "What do you keep in your bathroom?' but moved then to a more direct set of questions such as "Do you keep mascara pencils in your bathroom?" This chapter was followed by one describing the survey instrument, Part II. This consisted entirely of the same question about each item identified by the Part I instrument and was "How big is the (name of item) that you keep in your bathroom?"

The excitement was held for the results chapter, which consisted of a set of fold-out tables of space requirements for bathrooms: e.g, a space 1" x 1" x 3" for the mascara pencils, and so on.

Putting this thesis under my arms, I walked over to the next building and barged into the office of the Dean of the School of Home Economics. She was a fiery little lady of Italian extraction, with dark eyes that could burn holes in asbestos. She was also tremendously perceptive, and somehow detected the nature of the response I was about to make, for she stood up, dark eyes flashing, and striding back and forth behind her desk and pounding her fists in the air at an imaginary attacker, stated that this "poor girl" who had done the study was one of their best students, and had worked hard on the thesis, that it had been duly accepted by the orals examining committee, and that if I had any reservations I could put them in a place where the sun didn't shine. "You misread me," I said as calmly as I could. I continued with something like: "This is an impressive document. I am just concerned that the ideal bathroom the author comes up with does not have storage space for toilet tissue or for contraceptive equipment, both of which I keep in my bathroom." The good dean became truly furious: "You can't expect one of my girls to ask such questions of strangers!" she said angrily. We were thus off to a running start on crafting and managing the doctoral program for which I had ultimate responsibility.

It was then that I knew there was much work ahead. This was also apparent from the graduate course for elementary school mathematics teachers that was using a third grade math textbook as text for the course. When I asked the instructor why he was using this particular text, he answered that it was because the teachers didn't understand it, and had to be led through it page by page. The challenge was enormous. My mentor in the University President's office in Chapel Hill, Dr. Whyburn, who was always available for sound guidance, said something in response that I had trouble understanding. It was "Remember, you have a lot of power until you start using it." But I stuck to my guns, with the result that I gathered the respect, I believe, of the capable faculty in such areas as English, History, Mathematics, Philosophy, Art, Music, Psychology, and the Physical Sciences. I blew it with the head of the Sociology Department when I gave a paper at some departmental occasion where, as a psychologist, I defined sociologists, in jest, of course, as "psychologists who study rats in their natural habitats." Although my paper was laudatory and noted the many contributions of sociology to social and clinical psychology, my relationship with that department from then on was somewhat cool.

As graduate dean, I attended and frequently made presentations to the institution's Board of Trustees. I recall making the best case I could for the elimination of the requirement that only females could be admitted to graduate study, and will never forget the dressing down I received from one august member of the board, a successful lawyer in Greensboro. "Young man," he said, with the sneer in his face somehow appearing as well in his voice, "Do you realize that we are going to be forced to admit colored students shortly? And do you realize that it would only be a matter of time before one of our white girls danced with or otherwise got herself involved with a colored boy? And do you realize what that would do to this institution when her parents found out? You are supposed to be bright, but you surely haven't shown it today!" It was clear that the matter of male enrollment would have to wait for a new generation of trustees.

I had instituted a requirement that the outline and plan for any proposed new course for graduate credit be presented to the Graduate Administrative Board for approval. I lost friendship with the Dean of the School of Education who excitedly came to a meeting of the Board with the news that they had a new course planned which was entitled "Introducing Children to the World," and that he has secured the consent of Ms. Frances Horowitz, of the nationally shown TV show "Ding Dong School" to teach it as a visiting professor for its first offering. With some strong allies on the Board that shared my concerns—such as Vic Cutter, Chair of the Biology Department, Helen Barton, chair of the Mathematics Department, Warren Ashby, chair of the Philosophy Department,and Greg Ivy, Chair of the

Department of Art, we failed to approve this course, and Ms. Francis never got to Greensboro. And the Dean of the School of Education became a staunch ally of the Dean of the School of Home Economics.

Another innovation I required was admission standards for graduate study, which consisted of a letter of application with no more than two grammatical or spelling errors, together with a better than chance score on the Miller Analogies Test which could be administered in the office (there were 100 items with four choices for answers to each, thus making 25 a chance score). I held to this despite some flak from the Schools of Education and Home Economics, and being told by the chancellor that he feared I was trying to turn the graduate school into a "Little Harvard." Throughout these travails, however, Vice President Bill Whyburn from the Consolidated University Office in Chapel Hill remained a staunch friend and constant comforter.

In spite of these kinds of problems, there were enough advocates on the faculty that I constantly felt I was acquiring strength. The departments of English, Modern Languages, History, Psychology, Sociology, Mathematics, and similar traditional liberal arts and sciences programs, contained many truly outstanding faculty—the poet Randall Jarrell and Bob Watson in English, or Richard Current and Robinson Blackwell in History, Greg Ivey in Art, etc. I gained tremendous respect for the Academic Dean, Ms. Mereb Mossman, a stern but gracious lady who was very bright, had a liberal supply of common sense, who could listen, and who could be forceful and gentile at the same time. Never was the "iron fist in a velvet glove" description more appropriate.

But I found that taking a stand for matters in which I had strong beliefs brought out the opposition. The Dean of Students was one such, and the fact that she had been a frequent hurdle some fifteen years earlier when I was dating Woman's College girls as an undergraduate at the University in Chapel Hill did not help us see each other in the most favorable light. Although she had been instrumental in divesting UNC-G of an earlier chancellor by spending much time at his house and consequently scandalizing him, she had stayed on, seeing herself as the guardian of the morals of the young ladies and their protectors from evil men who would take advantage of them. (Years later I learned that she had left the college and had married the ex-chancellor who had taken a job in New York City.)

But she was convinced that I was evil when I took my classes out on the lawn. But I was not alone on her black list. She was also the bane of the business manager whose attempts to conserve costs always crossed with some objective of hers. For example, the business manager wanted to serve milk in the student dining halls in their cartons rather than glasses to save costs of glassware and dishwashing, while the Dean refused, demanding glassware, on the argument "Would you serve milk in cartons at your dinner table at home?" In addition to her belief that girls had to be protected from men who were all inherently evil, she represented that side of the institution that believed the mission of the institution was to take young girls from plain backgrounds and provide a kind of "finishing" education. But in spite of her self-styled role as a vigilante of morals, she missed entirely a small group of girls who worked the annual furniture exposition in nearby High Point, NC, as prostitutes. Although this upset me, I was not about to rat on them to the Dean of Students.

This Dean of Students was also the administrative official responsible for planning and overseeing social functions on the campus, such as prepping the most attractive students to visit the North Carolina General Assembly the day they were considering academic budgets, or the annual reception the institution had for parents of the students. This involved most of the faculty and all of the administrators and their spouses, and took place in a large ballroom area of one of the campus buildings. The dean insisted on a formal rehearsal for this function, and we found that everything was planned by the numbers, so to speak. We were to stand at position 23, an imaginary but well-defined spot on the floor, for exactly 12 minutes, whereupon we were to move to position 17 for exactly 12 minutes, whereupon . . . et cetera. We felt the orchestration showed in the result, and quickly abandoned the schedule laid out for us. We don't believe that anyone but the dean noticed, but for her the insult was unforgivable.

There was another side to the institution. Nowhere was the schizophrenic nature of the institution more apparent than in the admissions research I conducted. My test validity studies found, amazingly, that the lower the admissions test score and high school grade average of the student, the higher the performance at the institution during the senior year, and, of course, the higher the admissions test score and high school grade average, the lower the performance at the institution during the senior year. There was a rather simple answer to this strange phenomenon: the brightest students majored in such areas as history or English, where it was tough to earn an A, and where grades of D or F were not infrequent, while the poorest students gravitated to the School of Education, where not infrequently all members in a class received an A as their final grade for that course.

Although I felt I was successful in bringing some needed changes to the overall institution, the most pleasant and rewarding part of my tenure was teaching an occasional class in the Department of Psychology. As at Emory, the students were responsive and motivated, and classes were pure fun for all of us. I usually taught wearing a button front cardigan sweater and loafers, which I could kick off when lecturing as I sat on the desk in the front of the room, a practice which further scandalized me with the Dean of Students. I began to see myself as a truly talented teacher, a conviction that lasted for the next two decades—until I ran into a young lady who said she had been in one of my courses at UNC-G, and that it was the best experience of her college life. Intrigued by this confirmation of what my ego had been telling me, I pressed her for the name of the course. She could not remember this, or the name of the text, or the particular content. "But what was it that made this course so special for you?" I asked. She replied: "It was those truly funny stories you always started your lectures with." Thus, I acquired insight into what contributes to excellence in teaching, and what critically important residue from course work remains in the consciousness of students in later life.

One of the prized graduate students was a young lady from South Carolina, Lou Anne Smith, who was an accomplished painter and sculptor, and a graduate student in the Department of Art. Lou Anne was most instrumental in helping me free the graduate students from the over-protectiveness that the Dean of Women imposed on the undergraduate girls. She was also one of the white students who achieved national fame by sitting in at the lunch counter in downtown Woolworth's with some black students from A & T State University, demanding that they be served.

Lou Anne frequently came by my office at night when she was tending a pottery kiln in an adjacent building, and we would plan strategies for one or another change that both of us would like to see. One night we abandoned any serious talk, and after clocking the campus police car patrol to be sure of its schedule, we proceeded to the statue of the founder, Duncan McIver, on the lawn in front of the Library, and planted pole beans close enough around the base to ensure that the mower would not destroy the young sprouts when they germinated.

A note on the institution founder, old Duncan McIver. He was widely quoted as the author of the saying "Educate a woman, and you educate a family," which had become a treasured logo for the institution. His personal library had been donated to the UNC-G library when he died, and in one of his books by another author, he had underlined the sentence: *Educate a woman and you educate a family*. Although this was of little consequence, it became a carefully guarded secret. Ol' Duncan had said it, and by golly, it must have been original with him!

There were some other fun things that happened beyond our agricultural effort. Pegge and I used college students as baby sitters, and one night I was returning a young lady to her dorm on campus about 1 AM when a new campus guard jumped out in the middle of the access road to the dorm area, drew his weapon, and shaking mightily, declared "***You can't go in here!***" I responded as gently and carefully as I could "It's all right—I am Dean Davis." The response: "I don't care if you are Dean Martin, you still can't go in here!" A little more persuasion, and saying I would report him for preventing a student from returning to her dorm room and requiring her to spend the rest of the night outside, coaxed him into the car to assure that indeed I was not pulling his leg. Even so, I noticed that he kept a firm grip on his now holstered pistol.

Our life in Greensboro involved many things not directly associated with my duties as Graduate Dean. Coming back to Greensboro meant reuniting with old friends from Sears Mail Order. In fact, the apartment we found when we first came back to Greensboro was a duplex unit with Sears friends Doug and Polly Welfare in the adjoining unit. Some friends like Carl and Orrell Clark had moved to other Sears locations, and some had left Sears employ, but we came into a community where we felt we had a substantial foot in the door. From old friends at Sears, I learned that my old boss, Mr. GET-IN-HERE, had retired, and was devoted to the care of his wife who was in advanced stages of Parkinson's. I was moved to call on them, and found him gentle and loving in regard to his wheel chair bound wife, and gracious, tender, and a receptive listener to me. It was hard to believe this was the same man who in his supervisor role for Sears had shown such disdain for his staff.

I had said to the Chancellor during the job interview that I was loathe to leave the dream house we had just built in Atlanta, and he had replied that we could rebuild in Greensboro, and that there were surely some mistakes that we could rectify by so doing. We purchased a nice wooded lot in Hamilton Lakes, drew up our own house plans, and found a builder who would convert our sketch into blueprints, provide the used brick that we wanted, and let us deduct tasks we could do ourselves (like interior painting) from his estimate. With a growing family and the expectation that we would need to entertain, we constructed what seemed to be a palace. The floors were white tile throughout (a mistake, we later learned, for they picked up heel marks); a large kitchen with an island for food preparation in the center; fireplaces in both the living room and the family room which was adjacent to the kitchen; copious built-in bookcases and speaker system; a number of lighting fixtures in the living/dining room that afforded a hundred different combinations of lighting; and every room accessible from a long L-shaped hall. The contractor completed his part in only 9 weeks, using a slab construction method that got the walls and roof up in the first two weeks. This was in time for Pegge's homecoming with our third child—finally, a girl! And unlike the addition of Christopher to the family in Atlanta, there seemed to be no sibling rivalry this time around. The boys took their new sister seriously, and although we had expected that they would consider her a rival, they seemed to share our pride in her.

Chris, who was three years old before he started talking, began talking now, and in whole sentences. But some of his labels were hilarious. We recall particularly his account of the "bummy habits" that populated the woods around our house. Another favorite expression was "Bank Boo," which translated meant "Thank you." Although he talked in sentences, there were some sounds he could not handle.

At one point when Chris was about three years old we went to an amusement park in Burlington where a number of rides were offered for little children. One consisted of small boats in a shallow container of water, with the boats secured by spoke-like appendages to an axle to produce a ride of several turns around the artificial pool. But it was a hot day, and the water was inviting—so out of the boat and into the water went Chris. He was apparently spotted by a reporter for the Burlington *Daily News*, for the episode was written up the next day in that paper.

The School of Education ran an experimental school (the "Curry School") that was truly first rate. It was here our first-born son, Michael, went to kindergarten. At the end of the school day, he would walk across the street to the Administration Building where my office was located, and come home with me at the end of the day. One day the Chancellor was having an important meeting in his office with the executive committee of the Board of Trustees on some matter, when in through his window came a small boy with a backpack who stepped from the window onto the table, jumped down, said "Hi, Folks!" and went out the door. It was, of course, my Mike on his way down the hall to my office. Fortunately, the Chancellor was most amused, having a couple of sons of his own. Mike's teacher at the experimental school was a Professor Nancy White. Although Mike had developed occasional petit mal seizures from a playground accident when we first came back to Greensboro, Nancy was simply superb. She liked Mike (as she did her other pupils), and Mike liked her (as did the other pupils). Mike had few inhibitions, and Nancy seemed to relish this. We recall a singing part he had in a class play, and although we were very nervous about this, he did us proud. Shyness was simply not a part of his behavioral repertoire, and he belted out "I, Said the Cow . . ." in perfect pitch in a manner needing no amplification.

It was after we had moved into our new house that the Academic Dean, Mereb Mossman, came to visit. She was sitting on the couch in the living room, and little Mike was entertaining her. He had just received a play doctor kit, and was happily showing this to Mereb. From the kitchen where I was preparing drinks, I heard him ask "Would you like for me to take your temperature?" Mereb, ever the gracious lady, said "Of course." Before I could get there, Mike responded with "Well, lay down!" Mereb helped him to find quickly another game to play.

But of all the events in the three year period that I was being the "Gradual Dean," the most significant was the birth of our daughter, Jill. I had somehow wanted a girl before, but had twice had to accept boys. As this was Pegge's third Casearean Section, this had to be it. And Jill was both a good baby and was quickly accepted by her two big brothers, who became careful about such habits as burping at the dinner table, and seemed as proud as we were.

Jill was the causal agent both for our hiring a helper one day a week, and for dismissing her shortly. We left Jill one day with the helper while we did some shopping, and on return found that the maid had cut Jill's beautiful blond hair. Although the helper was quite pleased with her handiwork, we were devastated, and let her go.

There were other events that hang in my memory. At one point, Pegge decided to take a course in English Composition, taught by Professor Bob Watson. She did an excellent job on the stories she wrote for this class, and enjoyed the experience immensely. And I was very proud of her, even though she wrote much better than I did.

And I recall flying back to the Greensboro/High Point Airport from New York City where I had gone on some mission, and finding our poet in residence, the great Randell Jarrell, on the same plane. He had gone to New York City to give a lecture on his poetry to some distinguished group, and was returning from that event. We deplaned, retrieved our luggage, and together started out the airport entrance. He obviously expected his wife to pick him up and take him home, but she was delayed for some reason. Her absence precipitated great distress, and I offered to drive him home. This solution did not appeal to him, and to assure that he was not stranded, I waited with him. In a few minutes, this great man broke down in tears, sobbing heavily until his wife appeared to take him home.

As a teacher and on University committees, Jarrell was a very awe-inspiring and powerful teacher. He had written a novel, *Pictures of an Institution,* which exhibited remarkable insights into the forces extant in a fictitious college for women. There was no outward sign of his child-like dependence on his wife. But some time after we left UNC-G, his wife had to attend to her father in another state for a six week period, and placed Randall in the psychiatric ward at the UNC Hospital where she felt he would be safe. He walked out one night, and stepped in front of a car and was killed. The acquaintance with this man who wrote poetry of such power, the secrets behind his facade, and his tragic demise, touched me deeply.

There were other amazing adventures peculiar to the woman's college. I remember going into a liquor store and coming upon a shy spinster lady professor of physics who was trying to get out with her bottle of plum brandy without being seen by me.

And perhaps the closest I got to notoriety came when the *Greensboro Daily News* reported one morning that the evening before one Junius Davis was arrested for urinating on the window of Blumenthal's Department Store. The article referred to another Junius Davis, a black vagrant, who had had a little too much to drink. But the chancellor called me into his office to find out if I was out on bail. There was a third Junius Davis in Greensboro at the time, a pharmacist, who was frequently late in paying his bills, and inevitably the strong arm collectors would stop in the phone book at "Junius A." and descend on me. But I had become accustomed to this, from the Junius S. Davis in my class at UNC, now a pediatrician in New Bern, NC, or a Junius Davis who worked the swing shift at the Hapeville, Georgia Ford Assembly plant, and for whom our phone in Atlanta frequently rang at 2 AM. None of these people came close to the first Junius Davis I heard of, who was a prominent lawyer and civic leader in Wilmington, NC, in the 1862s. Although the Davis name is common, the first name "Junius" is not, and therein lay the root of my trouble. Somehow, no one could believe that there were more than one of us.

And there was a very minor incident that taught me a great deal. One day about noon I was leaving the campus to drive home for lunch when passing an ice cream store on the edge of the campus a little girl, 5 or 6 years old, dashed out in front of me. I was not moving very fast, and by stopping quickly I only bumped her to the pavement. She did not seem hurt, but I felt that she should be examined by a physician—but her mother would have nothing of this. The problem was that if the child saw a doctor, her husband would surely find out that the mother had left the little girl, who was feeble-minded, unattended in the car while she went across the street to get ice cream for her, and her husband would raise holy hell with her for this lapse of responsibility in leaving the child alone in the car.

Our second residence in Greensboro came to an end when Norman Frederiksen, my boss at Princeton University when I was there and now the Director of the Research Division at ETS, recommended me to Henry Chauncey, the President of Educational Testing Service, to be Chauncey's special assistant. It was very difficult to think of abandoning our dream house, but I met with Henry; we "clicked" and the salary offer was one I could not refuse—and I went North with new duties that involved—well that is another story in itself. After three years of Graduate Deaning and our second residence in Greensboro, and following our two residences in Atlanta, I was on the way back to our second residence in the Princeton, NJ area.

Chapter 20

Entrance Bigtime into the Testing Movement

My title upon joining ETS was "Assistant to the President." This role involved three distinct activities. First, and most important, was conducting a research project of personal interest to the president; second, was writing his speeches; and third; was hosting the president's VIP guests that for one reason or another might stay on the ETS campus for more than a day or two.

The principal research interest of the president had to do with his search for personal traits that might augment intellectual ability (as measured by the Scholastic Aptitude Test) or scholastic achievement (as measured by the College Board subject matter achievement tests). In the simplest terms: he wanted to be able to improve the prediction of performance in college by measuring personality traits that moderated intelligence and past achievement. Initially, I took over a study involving ratings of students on a number of personality factors by college faculty, in a study group of eight elite institutions of higher education. This study attempted to identify non-cognitive characteristics of students that teaching faculty valued, and utilize factor analytic methods to determine the structure—or identifiable, separate dimensions—that might be related to achievement. Although the research identified some reasonable personal traits that faculty valued, and although we were able to group these in reasonable dimensions, attempts to relate these to the variance in academic performance not accounted for by past achievement and intellectual ability were not successful.

Providing data for this study were eight elite institutions, and I made visits to each. One was the California Institute of Technology in Pasadena, California, and a friend from the west coast advised me to stay in the Hotel General Greene, a "posh" but reasonably priced hotel. I had just visited Amherst College, staying at the Lord Jeffrey Inn on the advice of another friend, and had found it truly superb. I reached the General Greene a little after midnight, and found a lone college student type manning the desk.

I checked in, and the desk manager became the bellhop who took my bag and ushered me to my room. It turned out to be sparsely furnished, and lit by a single unadorned light bulb dangling from the ceiling. As I looked around the room in amazement, he said "Goodnight," and turned off the light as he went out the door—leaving me standing in total darkness. My insight then was confirmed by the faculty people I met the next day at CalTech: the old General Greene had seen better days, and would shortly be demolished.

All the work on the president's personal research projects was remarkable in that ETS had a very substantial research group, with many of the best psychometric and statistical research minds in the country. These scientists, however, had clear cut perceptions of their own, and felt that the president was dabbling in Reader's Digest kinds of issues—popular but fallacious notions to explain human performance. My job was to facilitate the president's research in such a way that it might be acceptable to the body of research specialists employed by ETS whose work had to do mainly with issues involving the traditional measurement activities that were the bread and butter of ETS.

This particular job demand—somehow sanctifying work dealing with popular notions to make it acceptable to the rigorous research methodologists—came nicely to a head when the president encountered a most unusual lady named Isabel Briggs Myers. Mrs. Myers was the daughter of a physicist who had been head of several Federal bureaus, and was a graduate of Swarthmore. She, with her mother, Katherine Briggs, had visited Jung in Vienna, and had developed a personality test based on Jungian typology that according to some fragmentary research by Mrs. Myers was a powerful non-cognitive indicator of performance in particular professional positions. Mrs. Myers was not trained in psychometrics—she was simply a very bright lady with a lot of enthusiasm and the belief, validated by her experience, that she could do absolutely anything she wanted to do. At one point in 1929 and prior to getting deeply involved with her mother in Jungian psychology, she had entered a contest for authors of detective murder mysteries, and had sat down and in the five months available composed a book-length novel entitled *Murder Yet to Come* which won over other entrants, including a young Ellery Queen. This book is still available from Amazon.com or Barnes and Noble.

The president asked the research division to explore her test, and a study of its validity was assigned to a capable young researcher who was to develop a manual, and get the instrument ready for marketing. The researcher succeeded in taking a year to trash the device completely as without psychometric merit, completing his report in draft form in March, 1962. Mrs. Myers, of course, hit the proverbial ceiling. The researcher had been given a task that he felt consisted of proving the preconceived and popular but naive notions of non-researchers, and some of his "findings" could indeed be challenged as more emotional than rigorous. But

Mrs. Myers was not a person to be taken lightly, and the ETS president was not a person to be quieted by a 27 year old junior researcher. The graybeards in the research division, however, stood by their young man. I suggested as a possible solution that the offending research report be held for later release, with such release to be at a date that Mrs. Myers, having been allowed to do her own work to validate the instrument and prepare a test manual, would have that manual ready for release. To assure the acceptability of the manual that Mrs. Myers would produce, I suggested that she be assisted so that the techniques she used would pass muster with the career researchers. Thus, as a result of my big mouth, Mrs. Myers moved to ETS for a period of many weeks to develop the test manual and have it completed by July, 1962, with me assigned to her to ensure that what she did met acceptable research standards.

Before Mrs. Myers would accept me as her mentor, however, she insisted that I take her test. She scored it with secret scales that she said she could never release, for if the Russians got hold of them the United States and civilization itself would be lost. But after completing the scoring, she came skipping into my office and said that she was extremely pleased that I would be assisting her. And yes, she actually skipped—and to see a woman in her mid-sixties with gray hair in a bun skip with long, magnificent leaps, into one's office was like discovering the eighth wonder of the world.

A full and fascinating account of what happened is provided by Frances Saunders in her book *Katharine and Isabel: Mother's Light, Daughter's Journey*, published in 1991 by Consulting Psychologists Press, Inc., of Palo Alto, California. But for present purposes, suffice it to say that the next weeks up to the July deadline for completion of the manual were the most unbelievable of my life.

Isabel was not only frightfully bright, she was also supremely confident of the integrity and power of her theories and her instrument and fiercely determined to utilize the status of ETS to get it into the public domain. She moved into my office, bringing a foul-smelling concoction in a thermos that she called "Tiger's Milk," consisting of brewers' yeast blended with milk and Hershey bars. This she considered the ideal high energy food. That it must have been, for she did not leave the building for the next six weeks, working day and night. We would consider what needed to be said next; she would write for a couple of hours, then submit it to me for critique. I remember saying at 3 am one morning "Isabel, I simply have to go home and get two or three hours sleep," and Isabel replying "Can't you nap on a table in the seminar room across the hall, for I will have some material for you to review in just a few minutes."

Her husband, whom she called "Chief," would come in every few days with a fresh supply of brewers yeast, milk, and Hershey bars. Without a blender, the concoction was not as easy to swallow, but for Isabel this was a minor irritation. I remember overhearing Chief tell her one day that someone visiting their home that month (it was April) expressed surprise that their Christmas tree was still up. They had a chuckle in recognizing that neither of them had noticed this before the guest pointed it out.

The manual was finished; the test prepared for sale through a somewhat obscure country store kind of outlet maintained by ETS for tests outside the scholastic mainstream, and her manual and the original report released in September, 1962. Although her manual was clean so far as its methodology and conclusions, the climate at ETS had become dichotomous, with the Cooperative Test Division, that part of ETS which marketed educational achievement tests in significant sales volumes, joining the powerful Research Division lobby against the president, holding that the test was something more appropriate for the *National Inquirer* than for the sacred halls of ETS. Thus, after much effort, the matter ended as the poet stated the way the world ends—"Not with a bang, but a whimper." The test—known then and now by the title "Myers-Brigs Type Indicator," or "MBTI," was placed at ETS on the internal chute to obscurity.

In regard to the name: Isabel wanted to call her test the Briggs-Myers Type Indicator, in recognition of the earlier contributions of her mother, Mrs. Briggs. It fell to the able Executive Vice President of ETS, William Turnbull, to call her in and advise her of the custom of test users to abbreviate test titles, and tell her that her choice would surely lead to her test becoming known as the "BM Type Indicator." She reluctantly switched the order of the names of the authors.

Incidentally, the contract between Mrs. Myers and ETS was terminated in 1975, almost a decade after I had left ETS-Princeton, and Isabel placed the MBTI with Consulting Psychologists Press in Palo Alto. The president of this firm succeeded because, as Saunders wrote in the volume cited, "(The CPP president's) marketing the MBTI was made easier because of the already widespread knowledge and use of the instrument. (His) decision to publish the MBTI, unlike Henry Chauncey's, was not influenced by the opinions of a group of psychometricians with impeccable credentials who objected to the unorthodox statistical logic behind the structure of the MBTI." Under that management, the instrument has become one of the most widely used selection devices by business and industry, and has attracted as well many academic users involved in counseling individuals.

Writing speeches for the ETS president was a labor of love, even though he frequently deviated from the text, and was not a particularly accomplished public speaker. We would meet for ten or 15 minutes and he would outline what he wanted to say; then, he would say "Give me about twice as much as I can use." I was then and am now happy that only he knew who had given him the material he spouted, for inevitably he would add his own touch, butchering, I felt, the fine points I had made for him to impart to his audiences.

The facilitation of the president's visitors, usually professors who had developed some prestigious test, was a joy. My function was to make available to them any facilitation that ETS might provide during the day, and to see them appropriately wined and dined in the evening. One particularly well-known professor with a widely used test came to ETS for several days as the president's guest, and he was my charge after the first evening when he was the guest of the president at his house for dinner.

Like many professors, life on his campus had been somewhat grubby, and he was impressed with the attention lavished upon him. The second evening he pressed me to "get me a girl." One of the secretaries was a most attractive divorcee, named Allison Munn. with a magnificent spirit and sense of humor, and she agreed to help me out with this. We went to dinner at the Nassau Tavern, and my guest could not keep his hands off her. She tolerated this tactile show of interest nicely. He visibly salivated when she offered to drive him back to his hotel room at the Princeton Inn, relieving me of that function. I then left them, and retreated back to the parking lot at ETS where Allison was to meet me and report. She drove up only a few minutes after I arrived, struggling to keep her laughing from interrupting her report. "What happened?" I asked. "When we pulled up to his hotel, I said 'It's been a nice evening, and give my regards to my good friend, Beatrice (name of his wife).'" It turned out to be a perfect scam, for the next day he could say nothing about it to anyone, including me. And we doubt that he gave her regards to Beatrice when he returned home.

There were many other events in the relationship between the president and his assistant, but one stands out in my memory. His VIP guests were always treated to dinner at his house on the grounds of ETS, where Laurie, his wife, his two little girls who were brought down stairs in their pajamas to say goodnight to the guests, and I would join the visitor. These meetings happened several times a month, and Chauncey had a heavy hand with his pre-dinner martinis. One night I fell asleep in an easy chair after dinner as the president and the visitor chatted, and awakened several hours later in a dark house with doors locked. Considering all options, I decided to try the windows, and found one that would let me out. I sneaked home, and came in early the next morning to Chauncey's office to tender my resignation. But he laughed and laughed, saying that they had tried to awaken me but were unable to do so, and he hoped I had not been too uncomfortable. I had a new admiration for this man who was a descendant of an early president of Harvard, at which institution he had been Director of Admissions before taking the helm of ETS, and who tooled around the countryside at excessive speeds in a well-worn VW Beetle.

ETS had its share of critics, of course, but it also had more than its share of VIP visitors. John Goodlad came and gave a lecture that was pure eloquence squared. He had been chair of the Department of Education at Emory when I was there and was now in a prestigious position at a West Coast institution; he had written a number of books that were well received and influential. Another visitor was a man whose name I can't positively recall, newly appointed by President Kennedy to a high post in the Department of Health, Education, and Welfare. He came to ETS in the course of making introductory rounds to think tanks to share and receive ideas about education. This man indicated that he was going to emphasize basic reading skills in his administration, and I said something like "So reading is going to be your man on the moon.!" He seemed to like this, and it did not diminish my ego a bit when I found that he adopted the phrase and used it frequently, until his untimely death several years later in a small charted airplane crash in Arizona.

It was ETS that provided my two trips abroad in the 1960s. The first was to Grasmere, England, the site of the Wordsworth cottage (found to be still surrounded by daffodils), with Earl McGrath (whom I called "Curley" because of his bald pate), the former Secretary of Education and then Professor at Teachers College, Columbia University, and W. H. Crowley, of the School of Education at Stanford University. Our meeting was called by Vice Chancellor Charles Carter, of the University of Lancaster (the queen is the chancellor of all British higher education institutions), and involved, in addition to the three of us from the United States, five from the British Isles. We met at the Prince of Wales Hotel in Grasmere in April. The conference involved an examination of the prospects and problems in selective admissions to higher education institutions, and my principal paper was a history of selective admissions in the U.S. It had been dashed off the week before departure, and I had finally been able to start it when in my Sunday School Class at the Hopewell, NJ Presbyterian Church I encountered the first chapter of the Book of John. I began my paper "In the beginning was Harvard . . ." I was familiar with the main events in the selective admissions test movement which actually started at Harvard, and the paper flowed quickly after I got the five word start, and was very well received by the conference participants.

The highlight of the conference for me, though, began on a Sunday morning when a Scottish participant came down to breakfast in a complete Scottish outfit, including plaid kilts, a shawl, and even a large knife in his left stocking. For some unknown reason, I had packed a red gym sweat shirt emblazoned with the Superman "S" emblem on the chest. The Scotsman's attore emboldened me to go up to my room and don the Superman shirt for the morning session. This was well received by all but the gentleman in the kilts, who reappeared shortly in mufti.

The second trip abroad was to a meeting in Geneva, Switzerland, which was to organize an international association on scholastic testing. Although I had moved to RTI, the meeting had been arranged by Bill Turnbull, Vice President of ETS, and surely was suggested to him by my tenure there. He and I were the only U.S. citizens involved, but there were some two dozen delegates from other European, African, and Middle Eastern countries. The meeting was successful in organizing the international association, with Bill Turnbull as the first president, but I never heard anything about it after we left Geneva.

It was here, however, that I learned how super-sensitive international relations could become. The group hotly but transparently debated whether to seat the two man delegation from South Africa, because of the apartheid nature of their government, and agreed unanimously on the second day of the meeting to eject them. They angrily stalked out and presumably caught a plane home. I also learned that the concept of democracy by the foreigners involved having a vote on a single nominee, rather than for one of several nominees, and this caused all manner of trouble, for the individuals nominated after the first nominee would get angry and decline the nomination.

Other memories of this trip had to do with attempts to choose something exotic in the restaurants of Geneva by ordering the most expensive thing on the menu, and ending up always with pig's feet in one form or another—a fate I escaped on the last night there by purchasing a bottle of wine, a loaf of bread, and a chunk of sharp cheese. And although I was quartered at a posh hotel, the toilet was unisex and down the hall, and I found use of it difficult because of the bideau. One other significant memory of this trip was walking across the bridge over Lake Geneva to the church door where Martin Luther posted his document

On the flight back to New York City was a most attractive young lady of about 20, traveling alone, and clad only in sandals, very short shorts, and a flimsy halter—all clothing probably weighing a total of 6 ounces. On my return from England earlier, my seat mates were a middle-aged couple who had argued all the way back about some experience abroad. But this time my seatmate for the return flight from Geneva to New York City was the barely clad young lady. Her conversation was as scanty as her costume, and I assumed, of course, that I had shared the flight with one of the Jet Set who would soon marry a Princeton graduate and grow fat gracefully.

At ETS we had a spell of hostility toward any test development activity by the president, probably reflecting scars from the MBTI escapades, and he was increasingly not invited to speak anywhere. I became, in succession, the head of several groups in the new Developmental Research Division—a group established to do practical research as opposed to the highly theoretical and statistical work of the existing Research Division. I served first as the head of the Guidance Research Group, then the Educational Sociology Group, and finally the Higher Education Research Group. We did a number of rather significant studies and instrument development activity that would be dull reading, so I will focus on only two products produced in this tenure that at the time had no pay-off.

The first was the use of spare time to design, with the bright young researchers I had brought into the higher education research group, a dream project we called

"Project X." This involved the notion, probably suggested by Don Super's 20 year study of vocational development, of taking a national sample of high school students and following them through later education and into establishment in adult life. It was a "pie in the sky" kind of thing, and although we shared various drafts of the idea with education officials in Washington and the foundations, it was too sweeping in scope, too expensive, and too tardy in pay-off, to attract the needed funds.

The second was the decision to write a book about higher education. I came up with the title "The Onion Patch," and completed several chapters. But then, the University of California's president Sanford's classic, *The American College*, was published, filling the void nicely. I got involved in other things, and the draft went to the back of a file cabinet.

But the file has been preserved. Let me share two quotes from the first chapter.

First, my introduction read as follows:

> "Few among us have any patience for a definition or description of the American College. It is common in our folklore and in our physical surroundings; its doors and its products are open to inspection. It is accepted as philanthropic; its purposes would seem to be the enhancement of the individuals, faculty and students, that constitute its population, and the enrichment of the society which it serves. It is infinite and eternal; it has existed in the same form for centuries, with its pattern of bringing learned into contact with learners, and its content the ideas, expressions, and assorted accumulata which has been relatively enduring for a time among the best if not the happiest people. What true believer would demand an empirically provable definition of God? What boy, with one in his pocket, would ask what a frog is?"

The next excerpt captures the tenor of what I had hoped to say:

> "Our greatest dilemma is probably our difficulty in providing any proof in what the college does to and for its students. Faculty teach and students learn; we tend to overlook the fact that unless the later societal role of the individual requires specific and continuous practice, little factual or attitudinal stuff in retained or resought. The college trained person must be better equipped to handle and enjoy life, we assume, because he is exercised with the good and exorcised from the maudlin. Few college educated could pass (or for that matter, value passing) any final examination from their freshman year at any point three months or more distant."

Getting freed from the apron strings of the president, and having the ability to add some capable people to help, brought a considerable change in daily life. I was back into more honest research, and I and the group dealt with studies of the American college and university trustee, of organized student protest, of measurement of institutional climate, and the like. I also had opportunities to teach in area universities, and at one time or another taught graduate courses at Rutgers, New York University, Brooklyn College, and Teachers College-Columbia.

My work involved a considerable amount of travel, and this almost always resulted in an instructive or otherwise memorable event—like the plane losing a flap when landing in Richmond, VA, or a taxi running over a large package of flour tortillas I had purchased in Denver but dropped as I exited the cab at the airport on my return leg. One of the most interesting (and instructive) events occurred in Evanston, Illinois.

I have forgotten why I was there, but remember vividly staying at the Hotel Ormiston and being unable to sleep because of raucous people of high school age congregating noisily in the halls all night long. At one point I went out and asked a couple of acne-infested kids why the party, and one told me I was simply too old to understand. This piqued my curiosity, and I persisted with another, who told me that the group, high school athletes the local university was trying to recruit, had been housed two to a room but provided girls as companions for the evening. Thus, one of the two males was displaced to the halls for a period. The mystery was further unclothed and validated the next morning, when I found a coach from the university and his wife waiting for the girls to come down for transport back to downtown Chicago. A bus would pick up the boys later. I suspect that that institution had a very good percentage of recruits accepting that institution.

In 1964, I chaired a symposium at the annual meeting of the American Psychological Association in Los Angeles. The concern was with what psychologists should know about changes that the future would bring. I invited several individuals I thought would have provocative and sound ideas, including Bob Roelofs, Chair of the Department of Philosophy at the University of Nevada, and my old friend from graduate study days, Marty Hamburger, now at New York University. Two memorable things happened. First, since the participants did not know each other, I arranged an informal get-acquainted session for them in my hotel room. Bob Roelofs said, in introducing what he planned to say: "Remember that I am a post—Christian." Marty Hamburger, of Jewish heritage, came quickly with the rejoinder: "That's all right. I am a pre-Christian!"

The second memorable thing was a comment that Roelofs made in his presentation. He said that if everything ever written was typed, double spaced, elite type, on 16 pound paper, in the year 2040 the mass would exactly equal the mass of the earth—and that technology would have to find a way to deal with this. At that time, of course, what I have stored on my hard drive would have filled a small library.

And one summer I took leave to teach a graduate course in the School of Education at my alma mater, the University of North Carolina. For this teaching appointment, I took son Christopher, then 10, with me. To pass an afternoon one day after class, I took him to see a Woody Allen movie that turned out to have all kinds of sexual innuendo. Frightened at this discovery, I asked him if he had any questions about what we had seen. "Yes," he answered. "Why did that man say at the wedding ceremony 'I take this woman to be my awful wedded wife'?" Explaining this to him was easier than explaining to Pegge why I had let him see a movie that today would be X-rated.

We frequently had VIP visitors of one sort or another to one of the research groups, and I recall Joyce Brothers coming to see Dick Peterson, one of the researchers in my group. Dick, a completely self-contained and self-satisfied kind of person, was not impressed with this visitor, and left her languishing in his office while he took his time down the hall in the coffee lounge. I think Dick may have recalled my report of Bob Hope's visit to Cornell when he tried to call on Chancellor Tolley, who didn't know any "Bob Hope" and finally retreated by way of his window at the end of the day when Hope refused to leave the reception area until he was seen.

I recall Dr. Brothers sitting uncomfortably on a hard chair in his office, short skirt tightly around her clenched legs, literally fuming at the reception she was being given.

While I had full reign in choosing and hiring professional staff in my group, the ETS personnel office persisted in choosing our secretarial support. I was given a motherly widow in her late 50s, who fussed over me as if I were her son. I think she needed to make me dependent on her, for she reorganized my files so that only she could find anything therein.

She became proficient in reminding me of scheduled events, and one day put an airline ticket in my hand to Dallas, Texas, where I was to give a speech to some professional group meeting at a motel. I dashed to the Newark airport, where I found my ticket was for the next day. Feeling that my secretary had slipped on the flight date, I exchanged the ticket for the current day, and a couple of hours later landed in Dallas. I rushed to get a cab and asked the driver to take me to the motel where the group was meeting, and he said "Mac, I have been driving a cab in Dallas for 20 years, and there ain't no motel of that name in Dallas." I dug into my brief case, and found that the meeting was in Austin, not Dallas, but I did have the right day. I lucked into a ticket to Austin, and arrived at the correct motel a few minutes before I was scheduled to speak.

At another professional meeting, I recall running into Gretchen Franz. Gretchen was the young daughter of the West Coast psychologist who had worked with me in the Georgia Board of Regents' office. I learned that she had gone from there to the University of Colorado, picked up a Master's degree, bought an old car, and driven to San Francisco to find work. In the first week just past, she had offers for two jobs—one as director of admissions for a San Francisco institution, and the other as a go-go dancer—and was torn between them. "I could use what you taught me in Georgia in the admissions job," she said. "But in the other, I would have the cutest little costume, and would get to slide down a pole and do a little dance on the bar!" I learned later that she had accepted the college position.

Elsewhere in this account I have referred, without elaboration, to the "popular revolt against Kay Sharp." Kay was Secretary of the (ETS) Corporation, a very bright but very firm woman with her own opinions about how things should be done. She was pleased with everything she did, all of which was remarkable, but I can't say that the men on the research staff agreed with this perception. For example, when a new Research Building was built in a wooded area on the ETS campus, we quickly wore a path through the woods from the parking lot, using this instead of the much longer concrete walk. Her response was to have a barbed wire fence erected across the path.

She had a heavy hand in designing our new research building, and we were horrified to find that there were no urinals in the Men's Rooms. For her, these were as inappropriate for the office as they would be at home. The Men's Room did have a large plastic waste receptacle for paper towels that stood about four feet high. I placed a sign on one that proclaimed "This urinal is too tall!" and sent her (anonymously, of course) a photo. But it was too late for change, and Kay had prevailed. And ETS probably has the only office building in the State of New Jersey inhabited primarily by males that has absolutely no urinals.

The men in my ETS research group frequently were associated with one another in their research, and got along together famously both on and off the job. They established a tradition of a weekly poker game at one or another of their homes. Having had a disastrous experience with poker in the BOQ on Ford Island in Oahu, Hawaii, a decade earlier, as well as having little interest in socializing, I did not join them for some time. They kept the pressure on me to join in, and one night I relented.

The game that evening was at Bob Linn's house in Lawrenceville. It turned out to be a significant occasion for me. First, Bob accidentally spilled a full pitcher of beer on me. Then, his dog, hiding under the large table we were using for the game, bit me a number of times in the ankles. Finally, I ended the evening with a financial loss of something over forty dollars. Needless to say, I did not go back, and the men were hesitant to invite me, getting the impression from somewhere that I was a sore loser.

My professional staff were not only extremely competent, they were a great deal of fun to work with. I can never forget inviting a candidate for a professional position that was recommended by Rod Hartnett. I decided against making him an offer, and sent him the kindest "Dear John" letter that I could muster. He replied with an emotional and angry statement making assumptions about letting personal factors intrude on professional judgment in turning him down. Rod, of course, was fully aware of the several events. It was several weeks later that I received in the mail, on the letterhead of the august American Association of University Professors, a letter stating that formal charges of bias had been filed against me by the candidate I had rejected, and that a full investigation was beginning. I responded, of course, to find that the professional association had no record of the alleged charges, and most certainly had not written the letter. It then dawned on me that the culprit was Rod Hartnett in the office next door, enjoying my distress as the events unfolded. This triggered an exchange on borrowed letterhead that went on for several years between the two of us. Although I don't think either of us won, it kept life lively for some time.

After I left Princeton, Bob Linn became head of the Developmental Research Division, and later distinguished professor at the University of Colorado at Boulder and president of the American Educational Research Association. Rod Hartnick became Academic Vice President for Academic Affairs at Rutgers University. John Centra, who had joined the staff with his friend Rod Hartnett and constituted the "Mutt" to Hartnett's "Jeff," became the head of the Department of Higher Education at Syracuse University. Rod Skager went back to his beloved UCLA where he had done his graduate study, and became a frequent figure on national television as a specialist on the psychology of drug addiction. Dick Peterson returned to ETS-Berkeley, where many of his research projects served to improve life in California and beyond, and where, I assume, he was safe from Joyce Brothers.

Chapter 21

Life in Hopewell, New Jersey

My move to ETS required our second residence in the Princeton area. This time we avoided Princeton proper, and took a house in a smaller and lower rent part of Mercer County: the little village of Hopewell, NJ. The ETS campus was only about 7 miles away, and the community seemed to be a comfortable one.

Hopewell itself had a population a little under 2000; had no public sewage system (each house had its own septic tank). I recall a hardware store, a soda shop, a restaurant, a drug store, a bar with an upstairs full of willing ladies; and two gas stations, but no grocery store or bank. Two signers of the Declaration of Independence were buried there, and the former home of Charles Lindberg, from which his infant son was kidnapped, and the woods where the body was found, were just outside the town limits. Unlike several other New Jersey communities of this size, it had not a one room school house but an elementary school with grades 1 through 5; a Presbyterian and a Methodist church, and so far as we could tell, an all-white population. Our house was rented from an ETS professional staff member who had transferred to the San Francisco office. It was here that we settled on a corner at the edge of town, with a single tree about 10 feet high and an inch and a half in diameter in the front yard. Neighbors included the principal of Princeton High School and his wife and family, and a basement full of Alaskan Malamutes which provided supplementary income from sale of the pups; Helen and Chuman Chun, an American/Korean couple with three children; and, some other people who were easy-going in social contacts. And just across the street was an Amoco station, whose proprietor, Andy, was most friendly and helpful in any need.

Hopewell had a single policeman to maintain law and order. He was a genial fellow, though somewhat timorous. Our house was on the main drag through the little village and just within the formal town limits, and became a favorite spot for him to pull over any vehicle that had exceeded the speed limit through town. A large part of the attractiveness of the spot was that he could usually count on me to hear his siren, come to the window with a loaded rifle, and provide backup for him as he got out of his patrol car and walked to the offending car's driver.

There was never any problem, of course, but our policeman became a staunch ally, and gave us special treatment.

Mike had some initial problems with his academic work. When we explored this with his teachers, we were told that we had to accept the fact that he was brain damaged (the transfer record from the Greensboro schools reported the pre-school head injury followed by brief petit mal seizures), but we fought this by commissioning a Weschler-Bellevue Intelligence Test which suggested an IQ in the high 140s. He did substantially better after this was communicated to his teachers. But he was, after all, in a school where a teacher reported a tremendous letdown at a state training workshop where she had elected to attend a session on "Exceptional Children," and had found it to be concerned not with very bright children such as the Hopewell school's population, but children with mental handicaps, of which there were virtually none. This we learned from her sad report after the workshop to the PTA. But Mike did not really blossom until his sixth grade when he moved to a Pennington township school,. Here he developed a love of history from an exceptional teacher of that subject. He also achieved special recognition at this school as "the most improved student" in his initial year there.

It was in the sixth grade that Mike learned that New Jersey was known in the capitol city of Trenton as the "Garden State," and that the state motto was "People, Purpose, and Progress." With an eye to the slums of Newark and the pig sties of Secaucus, I suggested to Mike that it was more appropriately the "Garbage State," and that a more valid motto should be "Pigs, Pestilence, and Poverty." He delighted in communicating this view to others.

Mike had always been a special travel buddy, and having flown by himself to his grandparents in Wilmington, NC from the Philadelphia airport and back without incident the year before, went with me to the annual meeting of the American Psychological Association which was held in Philadelphia one year while we were in the area. He was about 12 years old at this time, and given his resourcefulness I felt he could be given carte blanc to tour Philadelphia while I was in meetings. We had met an old friend from Columbia University, Dr. Leo Goldman, when we arrived, and had chatted with him for a few minutes in the lobby of the host hotel. At the end of the day I met Mike at the prearranged spot, and found that he had tired of the tour quickly, and had returned to the hotel, talked the clerk into giving him the key to Leo's room, and had settled for an afternoon of television there, where Leo, who later confessed amazement, found him. Thus, although we were commuting from Hopewell to Philadelphia, Mike had made himself completely at home in Philadelphia while we were in the city.

Pegge found housewifery to be insufficient to keep her intellectually stimulated with the three children now in school, and followed Jill to school where she took a volunteer job at the school library. Her boss, a Mrs. Parker, later told everyone that she was doing a "prodigious job." This involvement gave her contact with many children and their mothers, and was a happy activity for her.

Chris did well in school, but more importantly, seemed to enjoy an immense popularity with his peers—and particularly with his female peers. I remember asking him the secret of his success with the girls, and he responded: "Well, I make a face or call them a name they don't like, and then I run and they chase me, and then I fall down and they catch me." I somehow knew then that Chris would never have problems with the opposite sex.

Mike recalls a schoolyard bully named Mike Gilmore, whose father's seat on the town council seemed to guarantee his son carte blanc on the school playground. One day Mike was sitting on a large tractor tire when young Gilmore and a pre-teen henchman named Irving Hare came by. Gilmore, swaggering, indicated an intent to knock Mike off the tire, and climbed up to do just that, but Mike held his position and it was Gilmore who tumbled to the ground. Gilmore called for his henchman to take care of the matter, but Mike unseated him as well. He had no more problems from this young bully. It was about this time that I learned that Mike could throw a football a good forty yards.

It was during this period that we visited Pegge's parents, and her father loaned Mike a .410 guage shotgun and promised to take him hunting. When Pegge expressed concern, Mike assured her that all he was doing was going out "To shoot something for a little snack."

In Hopewell, Jill quickly developed a coterie of friends, took ballet and piano lessons, and became quite adept at skiing. She amazed me by picking up a slide rule one day when she was about 4, playing with it for a minute or two, and then exclaiming "Hey—this thing can multiply and divide!" She had a natural fondness for animals, and was instrumental in our adopting a long-haired rabbit which we found we could quickly housebreak to a paper in the garage which was an integral part of the house, and which we kept until it reached pubescence and became ornery, eating holes in a plastic wastebasket and generally exhibiting a a high-strung and uneasy temperament. And when it ultimately came time to move, Jill was panicked because she realized that her mother would discover the frog she had kept hidden in her closet and had not told any of us about.

One of Jill's special friends was Julie Batten, the daughter of an English immigrant who was a skilled carpenter and who had found employment with a large building contractor. He was a man of considerable intelligence, but confined to his craft by limited education in England. As an Englishman working in a blue collar job with immigrants such as the less prestigious Irish or Polish, it was interesting to hear his accounts of how the other minorities deflected the prejudices they felt upon him. And I recall him inspecting some carpentry job that I had done at the house, and exclaiming that I drove nails just like he would expect of any Welshman. But I found him to be intellectually a provocative companion. He told me, for example, how he felt war with Russia could be prevented with certainty. The trick, he said, would be to set up an exchange program where 10,000 U.S. children would each spend a year in Russia with a Russian family, while 10,000 Russian children would be placed in exchange with U.S. families. "Neither country would ever drop a bomb on the other if this were so," he said. I felt that if somehow he had graduated from Oxford, and had secured a high level job in the State Department, we would have been less fearful at the time.

Our neighborhood had many children whose ages paralleled the ages of ours, and I had great sport collecting a half dozen or so of them and stuffing them in my car, taking them to the soda shop and lining them up on the stools at the counter, and telling the proprietor to "Fill 'em up" The mothers were kinder to me than to the lady in town who had several sexually active cats, and who got rid of the kittens quickly by putting a bow around their necks, putting them in a basket, and standing on the corner by the school as the lower grades released their children, saying "Would you like a kitten? They are free!"

In Hopewell, we were active in the Hopewell Presbyterian Church, where I was named an Elder. I taught a Sunday School Class of pre-teen boys, and Pegge worked with Barbara Epps Deering, the daughter of a Greek professor at UNC Chapel Hill, teaching in the church kindergarten class. The church had many activities other than the usual Sunday services, and I recall some magnificent model-building contests for the church sponsored Cub Scout groups that I served as Cubmaster. The minister, a Reverend Barringer, was a most personable individual, and helped keep us happily active. And it was here that we learned all about pasties, the preparation and sale of which was an annual event for the women of the church, who vied with the men of the church who were adept at preparing fried chicken, also an annual fund-raising event following the pasties sale by six months. Given the pasties and the fried chicken, the church remained financially viable.

I particularly remember volunteering one Halloween to take a dozen little children (age 6 to 9) from our church on a Unicef Trick-or-Treat visit to town houses. After several instances where a knock on the door brought lights on down stairs, yielded an old lady at the door who returned upstairs and came back several; minutes later with a few pennies, we came upon the bar with the bawdy upstairs. One of the little ones said "There's a lot of guys in there—let's go in." Getting assured that they would stay on the first floor, I led them in, and as they walked down the length of the bar, the men sitting there emptied their pockets of much folding money which they placed in the Unicef containers. Not only did the children emerge with a considerable feeling of triumph, our team won the prize hands down for the largest collection. Unfortunately, some of the mothers did not share the appreciation our prize reflected.

Our social life was satisfying. Beyond the parents and other friends we accumulated in Hopewell were the ETS staff themselves, and nice parties were not uncommon. I recall one where in a rather crowded den I found a bowl of cream cheese on a tray with various items on which to spread it, and seeing what I thought was a slice of pumpernikel bread, I spread it liberally with the cream cheese and, with some unexpected difficulty, took a bite. The "bread" turned out to be a dark brown, square, cork coaster. Our hostess was most gracious about this, but I suspect that with one of the set of coasters missing a bite-shaped piece, she was somewhat restricted in how she served drinks.

Once when Pegge and the children had gone to Wilmington, NC, to visit her parents, I decided to have a small party at the house. One of the researchers at ETS, a bachelor who had reached the end of his interest in freedom, came over the day before to help with the arrangements. I recall him looking out the kitchen window with a plastic red geranium on the sill, where our treeless lawn and an errant septic tank came between the viewer and the line of mass produced houses, and saying that this was indeed an idyllic sight. I knew that his time was coming, and added a bright but quiet spinster lady who was a statistical assistant at ETS to the party. Although I found her asleep behind the couch the next morning long after the other guests had left, she had made the crucial contact with my bachelor friend, and they were happily married shortly after.

Hopewell was just a stone's throw from Buck's County, where we had a favorite restaurant, the Lambertville House, on the river, and another over in Pennsylvania where one could move to soft seats in front of a fireplace for after-dinner desert or a glass of port. The Lambertville House had a female chef who had a marvelous knack for baking fresh bread as well as other delights, and the House was popular with the celebrities who came to Bucks County for roles in the plays at the Bucks County Playhouse just across the river. We recall dining one evening, with Julie Harris at the next table. We spent considerable leisure time in Lambertville, and across the river in New Hope, where we enjoyed the shops and the Playhouse. It was there that we saw "The Moon is Blue," and another play, name now forgotten, with Veronica Lake.

Being in close proximity to New York City meant that Pegge and I could go into the city for dinner and a play with ease, except for the cost (parking in the city, meal at a good restaurant, tickets for a play, and baby sitter fees could easily exceed a hundred dollars, which was a lot of money in the 1960s). Nevertheless, this was a special treat for us several times, and we saw such plays as The Most Happy Fella, Luv, Cactus Flower (with Lauren Bacall), and How to Succeed in Business.

On a couple of these occasions, we were hosted by Hopewell neighbor Chuman Chun and his wife, Helen. Chuman was a corporate entertainer for a large firm doing business in the Orient, and had an unlimited expense account for entertaining, which he employed when we went into the city together. But the most exciting trip was one I took with Mike and Chris to see the Yankees play the Baltimore Orioles in Yankee Stadium.

We planned to take a bachelor friend from ETS, Fred Fritzski, who had grown up in the city and who was no stranger to professional baseball, to ease our way to the stadium. Fred's mother was a talking cosmetic salesperson, and Fred, a doctoral candidate at Princton University and research assistant at ETS, was the first in his family to go to college.

We went to his apartment to pick him up. When Fred did not answer our knock, we entered the unlocked door, and wandered about inside looking for him. His mother had given him a 36 piece place setting of china, each plate of which he deposited in the sink after he had used it until some girl friend took pity on him, ignored the green things growing from the stack of dishes, and washed them for him. We found his sink loaded and sprouting green. His bedroom was similar, for there were mountains of discarded clothing on his bed. Not finding him, and suspecting that he might have forgotten and gone to his office at ETS, we picked up the phone on a table by the bedside, and as I sat down to make the call, something stirred under the pile of clothes on the bed. Yes, it was Fred, who was taking the occasion of a day off to sleep late. He got up, looked at himself in the mirror for a time, and decided to go back to bed, leaving us to go it alone as we left for the bus station for the trip into the city.

We took a bus from Princeton to the Port Authority Bus Terminal, and then found our way uptown to the stadium by subway. I marveled that Mike and Chris had no trouble finding what they needed to know about how to get there from the milling and usually unforgiving crowds, and were not traumatized by the hordes of people packed on the subways—until I realized that this was similar to what they experienced in school each day at the change of classes. We got to our seats in the stadium and the boys spent most of the game going to a hot dog vender somewhere above our seats. This continued until at one point in the game with the Orioles at bat, Mike suddenly straightened up, and said as a Baltimore player approached the home plate to bat *"Look—that's Tom Tresh! Right there! Tom Tresh!"*:

Hopewell was close enough to Rutgers, New York University, Columbia University, and Brooklyn College that I could moonlight. My most pleasant experience was teaching a graduate course in Principles of Guidance at Brooklyn College, where I had a class of 23 Jewish ladies who were teachers or guidance counselors in the city school system. Shortly into the course, I had a lecture on prejudice, and I told the story of my grandfather being ejected from the Baptist church (as reported in the first chapter), with the result that I had grown up believing that Baptists were inferior, and that what we Catholics, Jews, and Protestants other than Baptists had to do was stamp out Baptists. The result was an immediate bonding, and one of the ladies invited us to her home for the next session, and of course the others followed suit. They were a most attentive and eager class, and the food they served was exceptional—each tried (and succeeded!) in outdoing the previous hostess. I came away from this experience several pounds heavier and with a new appreciation for Jewish mothers.

Brooklyn College was otherwise an experience in itself. All the female students at that time had a tendency to use entirely too much eye makeup, and they always seemed to me to be ready to go out trick-or-treating on a Halloween evening. I recall seeing one young lady at the student union one day who, unlike the others, was stunningly beautiful. But in a minute, she removed her dark glasses, and exposed that she was really no different from the other girls.

Another event beyond the class with the Jewish ladies also endeared me to the New York City area and its ethnic mix. I taught an evening class at Columbia University one summer, and had to park several blocks away in an area populated primarily by Puerto Ricans. When I got back to the car about 11 PM, it would not start. A Puerto Rican gentleman sitting on the steps of his apartment building came up and offered to take me in his car to a mechanic he knew. The mechanic was roused, and came to my rescue. I tried to reimburse both for their time and trouble, but they would hear nothing of it.

A personal encounter with "New York's Finest," the city cops, left me with the conviction that the sobriquet was accurate. I was driving down Broadway on the way to the Lincoln Tunnel when a woman stepped out from behind a parked car, and I hit her, knocking her to the pavement where she lay motionless. The police quickly arrived and took charge. But the drivers of cars passing were diverted by the several police cars with flashing lights, and after two fender benders I was told to get in my car and drive to the nearest police station and wait while they cleared the scene and took care of the woman. "That woman you hit is not hurt badly, we believe," one cop said—"she's just dead drunk!" I followed their directions; they came shortly and took a statement, and I went on my way back to Hopewell. My insurance took care of a later lawsuit filed by the woman, with whom I had no further contact. But in a city where no one is supposed to trust anyone else, my contact with the city police was most comforting.

When I had business travel within a couple hundred miles of driving distance, I frequently took the family along. There was a seminar on some topic that I have forgotten at Harvard University where I was invited to give a paper, and having several days required for the meetings and it being summer when the kids were not in school, I got hotel reservations in Cambridge and packed the family into the car for the drive from Hopewell to Boston.

After getting through New York City, we decided to pass the transit time by singing songs, and did this with high energy and each of us trying to sing a bit louder than the others. It was early the next day that I had to read my paper, before a group of some 200 scholars. But lo and behold, I found that the vocal activity the day before had weakened my voice so that I could only cough and squeak, and people in the audience began to put their hands to their ears and make faces. A kind gentleman from the audience got up and gave me a cough drop, which made it possible for me to complete the presentation.

A little later some participant took some three minutes in a discussion period to say that any respondents should keep their questions or comments brief. When it seemed that he would run on and on with this comment, the man who had given me the cough drop stood up and interrupted him, saying angrily "You made your point a few minutes ago, now follow it. I mean, *SHUT UP!*" The verbal participant turned beet red and sat down in a nanosecond. Afterward, I asked who the man with the cough drops and patience problems was, and the response was "Why, that is David Reisman!" I felt like the man that Bennett Cerf reported in a Men's Room at the Waldorf-Astoria, who was told by the man beside him at the urinal "Gee—right on top of Cary Grant's!" Reisman, for those who may not know, was at that time one of the brightest luminaries and well-published legends of Harvard University, and the author of the American classic, *The Lonely Crowd.*

Before leaving the Cambridge area, the kids asked us to come with them to the exciting stores they had found roaming Cambridge while I was involved in the seminar. Although we prided ourselves that we never refused to let them purchase any book that they wanted, they did not abuse this license, and frequently asked our advice about purchases. The "exciting stores" that they had found turned out to be book stores. I remember finding an 1850 book of five funeral sermons for the man for whom the Choate School was named. The sermons, constantly laudatory in an obviously strained way, could not conceal the belief that the man was important but a notorious scoundrel. The children had found a book or two at each store that they wanted to ask us about, probably to get a blessing for its purchase. And, at each of the stores we entered, the clerks invariably would say "Hello, Mike—Hello, Chris—Hello, Jill." We believed our kids when they said that they had been in the store the day before.

I don't remember the trip back, but I don't think we sang.

In Hopewell, I sometimes came home from ETS via the Pennington traffic circle on Route 66 where there was a supermarket and a very nice little working class bar. One evening as I stopped for a quick beer at the bar, the man sitting next to me, clad in overalls, was nursing a boiler maker. After a few minutes of silence, he said, to no one in particular, "I raise pigs." There followed a minute or two of silence, and after ordering a refill, he said, again to no one in particular, "I like pigs." A minute later he had disposed of his shot of bourbon, followed it with the beer chaser, and getting up to leave, exclaimed "In fact, I like pigs better than people!" Somehow I treasure that experience more than I would have treasured a meeting with Einstein.

My pig-farmer friend was a stark reminder of the gulf between the town of Princeton and where we were, only some dozen miles away. The experience with the pig farmer was somehow in sharp contrast with an incident when I first returned to Princeton that had a substantial effect on where we chose to live this time in the area. Before I found housing and Pegge and the children joined me, I had taken up temporary residence in a rooming house in Princeton just across from the Nassau Presbyterian Church parking lot, and one day drove in to check mail at noon. There were no parking places on the street, but the church's 40 car lot just across the street was empty. So, I pulled in there, leaving my motor running, and dashed across the street to check my mail. Returning a minute later, I found a large black limousine at the entrance to the lot, with a portly gentleman in a clerical collar in the back seat. Obviously irritated, he called me to the window, and said something like "Can't you read? This is a no parking area!" On an impulse, I asked "What church is this?" He responded: "The Nassau Presbyterian Church!" I replied, "Well, I guess that is why I belong to the Princeton National Bank," got back to my car, and moved toward the exit with sufficient speed to cause the chauffeur to move out of the way.

One particularly delightful weekend was when we had a visit from Marty Hamburger, then on the faculty at New York University. Marty surprised us by coming the some 40 plus mile distance in a New York City cab. When I expressed concern about what the trip must have cost him, he said that the cost was but a very small fraction of what I paid for cost of car and depreciation, license and tax, insurance, and gas, oil, and wear and tear. I had to concede to myself once again that Marty was just plain smarter than I was.

Before returning to warmer climes, our area of New Jersey experienced a tremendous snow fall, with drifts up to 16 feet over the highways, with all traffic at a standstill for the two weeks required to assemble earthmoving equipment to deal with it. Our three were delighted, for not only did they get a holiday from school, they were able to build a snow fort, which they spray-painted with gold paint and dubbed "Fort Gold." This structure was built in the front yard at the curb, and was big enough to contain all three of them inside. The depth of the snow around our house was probably about 5 feet, which was sufficient to relieve us of a local ordinance that sidewalks on our property be kept clear of snow—no minor requirement for a corner house on a large lot, with sidewalks on two perimeters!

But though the snow fort was a magnificent hideaway, and though Jill enjoyed her skiing and the boys their sledding, we were all happy to return to North Carolina in 1967, where more than an inch or two of snow at any time during the winter months was a rarity.

Chapter 22

Return to North Carolina

John Caldwell, Chancellor at NC State University, was Chairman of the ETS Board of Trustees in 1967, and convinced Henry Chauncey that the establishment of a field research office in the then new Research Triangle Park in North Carolina would be a good idea. I had been assisting Everett Hopkins, then Vice President for Development at Duke University, with the establishment of a Regional Educational Laboratory in Durham, which with Federal funding became the Regional Educational Laboratory for the Carolinas and Virginia (RELCV), with Hopkins as its director.

I was offered the directorship of the new field research office, and with some longing to return to our home state, I accepted. RELCV would pick up half my salary for the first year in exchange for my continued assistance, and with the other half time I could establish the field research office for ETS. ETS had purchased land in the Research Triangle on Davis Drive, and the plan was for an office to be built on that land as the field research office got established. I took up offices in space rented from North Carolina Mutual Life Insurance Company, where the Regional Lab was also housed.

Short shift can be made, unfortunately, of the RELCV. Under Hopkins, the major press of activity throughout the year was the preparation of a proposal for continued funding the following year, and there was much wheel-spinning. There were some few programs of merit: probably the best was one run by Anne Borders-Patterson, Coretta King's former baby sitter, which took doctoral candidates from the major universities in the area who had completed all requirements except the thesis, and placed them as faculty in struggling institutions while they completed their dissertations. There was also a major accomplishment by Professor Joe Straley, of the Department of Physics at the University of North Carolina at Chapel Hill, in providing further training for high school teachers of physics.

It was when I was helping organize the Regional Education Laboratory in Durham that I first met Harold "Doc" Howe. He was heading the Learning Institute of North Carolina at that time, and it was housed at Quail Roost, the former mansion of George Watts Hill, Sr., who had given it to the University. The mansion had a swimming pool, and Howe spend most of his time floating on a rubber raft in the pool when the weather would permit this. He proved to be an interesting conversationalist, although he would frequently let things said absorb him in thought and remove him from further exchange. He later was named the head of the Center for Advanced Study in the Humanities, the Research Triangle Park's think tank for humanists, and I was his luncheon guest there several times. He was not an easy person to get to know, A bachelor into midlife, he married following his appointment as Commissioner of Education by President Johnson, occasionally returning to the area to renew contacts with old acquaintances.

My higher education group at ETS had been interested in encouraging institutions of higher education to establish an office of institutional research, to provide a resource for addressing problems amenable to formal study. One activity of the RELCV that I attempted to carry out was the encouragement of such a function, and the provision of training for the persons appointed to head it up, who were more frequently people that supported the president than individuals with any research background or skills. Accordingly, we set up a two-week workshop at Montreat-Anderson Junior College, in Montreat near Black Mountain, NC, the home, incidentally, of Billy Graham. The workshop was attended by a dozen or so institutional staff newly appointed to this responsibility in North Carolina institutions. I had brought two researchers, Rod Hartnett and John Centra, from my old group at ETS-Princeton to act as instructional staff, and at one point went to Montreat for a couple of days to check on how things were going. Son Mike, then 14, came with me, and roamed about the college campus during the day when I was with the workshop.

Montreat-Anderson Jr. College operated as a resort hotel during the summer, and Mike and I were housed in a hotel like room that doubled as a dormitory in the winter. I came back from the workshop the first day, expecting to find Mike back in the room and ready to go to dinner, but the room was empty. I did some writing while waiting for him to show up, and when he had not and an hour and a half had passed, I decided to go on to dinner by myself, and opened the closet door to get a jacket. As I opened the door, Mike, stiff as a board, fell forward and into me. I got a considerable start, and he had a considerable laugh. This was his idea of a prank. I had to marvel that he had been patient and quiet for so long.

Somewhere in the late1960s I attended a conference on higher education in Raleigh that lasted for several days, and provided rooms in the Velvet Cloak Inn for attendees. My roommate turned out to be Senator Byrd from West Virginia, then and now a hero figure. I have to confess, however, that the essential thing I learned from this association was that the Senator snored most substantially. I don't remember what went on at the conference.

But by and large, the RELCV activity turned out to be more sound than fury. I was instrumental in attracting several outstanding staff—including Howard Boozer, later Director of the Higher Education System in South Carolina, and Bob Glover, one of the fair haired boys of the College Board,. Their efforts were stymied, however, by the mediocrity that infested RELCV: Hopkins, though thoroughly affable, had a complete inability to accept good ideas from other people, and both Boozer and Glover left having had absolutely nothing in their in-baskets for months, and having been repulsed when any ideas were offered. I returned full time to ETS after the initial year, and the Laboratory died a quiet death a few years later. Allen Fine, its financial officer, started a title insurance business that quickly made him and those who invested in the company he created quite wealthy.

Bob Glover was an impressive figure—probably six or eight inches over six feet in height, who walked as if his shoes were too tight, and who could conceal inner laughter by an expressionless face. I have forgotten why we were in Minneapolis, but I recall the bar at the old Hotel Lemmington where we were staying that had a piano. The night we were there, Bob and I went down to the bar for a nightcap, and the piano was too much of a temptation to ignore. Inspired by our libations, I played and we sang for an hour or so, not surprisingly well after most of the others at the bar had left. Suddenly, two women entered the bar, both smelling of cheap perfume, one middle aged and the other in her late teens. They bustled up to us at the piano, and the older one offered to help us relax. Bob turned to her, and, without changing his constant deadpan expression, began reciting the Gettysburg Address—"Four score and seven years ago, our forefathers . . . . etc." The younger woman turned to the older and said: "Mama, these guys are crazy—let's get out of here!" They left very quickly, but they had broken the spell we were under. So, we had a final sip of our beer, and retired.

For the ETS field research office, the idea that I attempted to sell was that of cooperative research where the ETS researcher would be close to and participate in the action of concern, rather than be isolated as in the Princeton research offices. We would work hand in hand with other researchers in the institutions, and be concerned with highly practical problems. But we were transferred to a different vice president, and it shortly became apparent that the office was expected to generate its own support. The individual institutions were delighted to have free advice and support in their research endeavors, but were not about to pay ETS for helping them with problems. We had some limited successes getting small grants that could be split with an institution or group of institutions, or that could be used to explore a problem of interest to them, but this was hardly enough to sustain us at our overhead and cost rates.

I soon found a nice solution. With freedom to bid on whatever might be of interest, and the greater flexibility in responding that was possible in the relatively autonomous field research office, I rather quickly was fortunate in getting several lucrative and sustaining Federal contracts—one to assist the University of Puerto Rico Medical School establish a retraining program—or a "Curso de Perfeccionamiento" for physicians from foreign medical schools who had failed licensing, but if passing after retraining would commit to a year in a rural area of acute health need in Puerto Rico. The second major contract was an evaluation of the impact of the federally supported developmental studies program, which research was modeled on an earlier study I had done of Black students in traditionally white colleges in North Carolina. The North Carolina study was one where we hired and trained black students from a number of campuses to interview their peers, and then had them come back and tell each other what they had learned. Their discussions proved to be most enjoyable for them, and our tape recorders listened. It was in that initial study of Black Students in Traditionally White Colleges, which was supported by a grant from the College Entrance Examination Board, that one of the black students hired was Ike Hill from Catawba College. Ike later played professional football, starting with the New England Patriots, and later with the Oakland Raiders, and married the most attractive roommate of a law student at Yale named Hillary Clinton. The Hills later had a son, Grant Hill, who became a Duke University All American basketball player, and then went pro with the Detroit Pistons. I will never forget Ike and his beautiful wife later coming to visit us in Chapel Hill the first off-season period he had with the pros, to see if we had any research that he could help us with. He said that the experience he had interviewing black students on his campus for us was one of the most exciting periods of his life.

The larger study of the Federal Developmental Studies Program was national in scope, and involved not only black students but other minorities, particularly American Indian and Chicano students. We assembled a team of multiracial researchers: Anne Borders Patterson was hired away from the Regional Education Lab; some consultants, such as Grayson Noley, a Choctaw and head of Native American Studies at the University of Oklahoma, and Sam Rigsby (female), a Chiricahua-Apache, in Durham. We utilized a number of staff from other offices of ETS as well. Notable in the latter category were Roberta Eldred, a sharp and beautiful Chicano in the Princeton office: Jajai Hsi, Chinese from the ETS Evanston office; and Chuck Stone, then of the ETS Princeton Office, the former assistant to Adam Clayton Powell and later syndicated columnist for the *Philadelphia Daily News*.

I cannot resist commenting further on Anne Borders Patterson, who had been hired away from the Regional Education Laboratory. Anne, who as previously reported had baby-sat for Coretta Scott King, and who as a 6 year old had danced for pennies at Mammy's Shanty restaurant on North Peachtree Street in Atlanta, was the daughter of a Mr. Borders, a well-known mechanic and deacon in MLK Jr.'s church in Atlanta. In the course of various Federal contracts involving minorities, we traveled over the country together. I can never recall coming into an airport—Chicago, San Francisco, Denver, Dallas, and, of course, Atlanta—that someone did not come up to her and say "Why Anne—what are you doing here!" Anne was 95 pounds of pure dynamite, and I grew enormously from working with her.

I recall a contract we had for evaluating the impact of Sesame Street on children in poverty families, and where we had given a TV set in exchange for being permitted later to interview the children. Anne entered a home in a housing project in Durham to find the mother had been stabbed in the eye by a boyfriend, and the eyeball was dangling from its socket. Anne first called the police to go tell the husband and contain him, and only *then* called an ambulance to take the mother to emergency medical care. I asked her why she did this in this order, and she said that if the husband had found out before he was controlled by the police, he would find and kill the man who stabbed his wife.

But of all the studies I have been involved in, the study of the impact of the Developmental Studies Program in Higher Education was clearly one of the most exciting. We had ample funding, and our Federal project officer, Robert Berls, held a Ph.D. From Yale and was a superb person with whom to work. We assembled minority students from across the country in regional training groups. I recall, particularly, the challenges of working with the Native American students, for unlike the black students, I knew little about them and there was not much to go on in the literature. And while the Chicano students were generally willing, trusting, and eager, the Native American students were hesitant to trust us unless and until a tribal elder had heard their report of our activity and agreed that it was in their interest to participate. We also found that any structured information gathering technique sent the Native American students to a tribal elder, for instructions as to how they all should respond—and thus there was frequently no variance in the answers for a particular college group.

In the national study, we assembled groups of students in various locations for training, sending them flight tickets and cash advances to enable them to travel to the training sites. I remember one young Native American girl, Faith Spotted Eagle, who flew into O'Hare Airport for training sessions at a downtown Chicago hotel, and who hiked into center-city from O'Hare. The large knife in her stocking, as well as something in the way she carried herself, explained completely why she was quite safe from molestation on the way into the city.

The most poignant moment of many for me was at dinner at a table in a Santa Fe motel with a young Indian girl who was being trained as an interviewer. (The other staff had gone off on an excursion with Eldridge Cleaver's cousin, one of our student interviewers, to visit with some of her relatives.) After a long pause, my dinner companion said "I just want to go home." I assumed she meant back to her campus, but she quickly corrected me. "I always did very well in school," she said, "and the tribal elders decided that I must go to college and learn how to be of greatest service to my tribe. But I just want to go back to my mother and father, my tepee, and do my woman things."

The Native American contingent was not only the most illuminating and poignant, but also the most troublesome. We assembled a group of Indian students from a dozen or so west coast institutions at the Holiday Inn at Fisherman's Wharf in San Francisco. Most had never traveled farther than the distance from their reservation to their college, and I recall one young student who became deathly ill. She told me that she had never experienced such a variety of foods as her travel expense account and the city of San Francisco permitted, and had finished a dinner of raw oysters with fried bananas for dessert the night before.

But the San Francisco training session would prove to be more dramatic than we had figured it would be. I recall speaking to a group of some 15 Native American students in a conference room at the motel, turning to the blackboard to write something, and turning back to find some 20 Native Americans seated in the room. With each time I turned to put something on the board, I found still another addition to the group when I turned back to face the participants. When the group had reached about 30 individuals, an older individual stood up, announced that he was the director of the Native American Rights Fund in Denver, and that he believed that the Federal Government was using the guise of the research project to punish further Native Americans. This, of course, threw a considerable bombshell into the study, and we had to terminate the sessions, although we were later able to recoup most of the individuals and proceed in good faith, relying on mature Native American consultants who knew that the intent of the study, its sponsors, and those conducting it was one of honest concern and search for improvements.

The activity was rewarding not only in terms of the students and what they taught us, but what I learned from association with members of the research team. I remember walking from the Brown Palace in Denver with Chuck Stone when a (Caucasian) lady of the evening approached us and said "Would either of you boys like to have a little fun tonight?" Chuck Stone, his brown skin gleaming and with a smile that would have seduced the Queen of England, said immediately: "Gee, that is so awfully nice of you to ask. Unfortunately, we are fixed up for tonight, but could we meet right here tomorrow about this time?" The lady of the evening was snowed, of course, and thanked us and backed away, and of course the following evening we were airborne en route to our next meeting.

The Puerto Rico project was exciting as well. We worked closely with Dr. Jose Sifontes, Dean of the UPR Medical School, and Dr. Edijio Colon-Rivera, a Professor of Pediatrics who had run for mayor of San Juan. Dr. Colon-Rivera directed the Curso de Perfeccionamiento, and supervised the UPR Medical

School faculty who served as instructors. The doctors were charming people and delightful associates, who also delighted in sharing their country and culture with us. It was fun to go to some native restaurant with them, such as a diner/gas station combo in Caguas south of Hato Rey, where the waiters also changed oil for the customers coming for this rather than food. It was here that I had the most delicious turtle dish that I could imagine—and where the hosts always drank popular American brands of beer such as Michelob, while I and anyone with me from the States decided between Carta Blanca or Corona, the other generally available Puerto Rican beer. I also recall warmly dinner at Dr. Colon-Rivera's house, where the women did not join the men at the table but waited on them, a local custom when guests were involved for a meal. I was also impressed by the huge avocado tree in Dr. Colon-Rivera's back yard.

An event I was told about spoke volumes as to the kind of men these two doctors—Sifontes and Colon-Rivera—were. They were on a flight together from Seattle to Dallas and then home to Puerto Rico when a flight attendant came on the speaker system to ask if there were any physicians on board. A passenger had virtually stopped breathing, and the responding doctors found heart medication in his pocket and assumed heart failure. Thus, as the plane dashed for an emergency landing in Denver, they began treatment for this condition. Thereupon, a public health nursing student came up, hit the man a sharp blow on his shoulder blades, and he ejected a piece of steak that was stuck in his windpipe. They used the story to describe their very human weaknesses when I had made some comment as to their professional skill and concern.

We held a faculty workshop at the Hotel Barranquitos in central Puerto Rico, and I started a presentation telling the story, in my best Spanish, of the young man with an emotional attachment to "El Pato," or his duck. According to the story, the young man was unable to part with El Pato even for a minute. So, when he decided to see a movie, he stuffed El Pato down inside his trousers so that he could sneak him into the theater. The doctors started roaring with laughter, and assuming my Spanish was the source of their amusement, I continued, telling them that the young man, recognizing the dark in the theater, opened his fly and let the duck's head out to see the movie. Shortly the woman sitting next to him punched her husband, saying "Hermano, the hombre sitting next to me is exposing himself!" The husband looked over, then said "Just ignore it." The woman replied "I can't ignore it—it is eating my popcorn!" Dr. Colon-Rivera explained to me later that in Puerto Rico, "El Pato" is a popular slang expression for a male homosexual, and that this explained the untimely laughter.

Probably few Federal investments paid off so handsomely as the support to the University of Puerto Rico for the Curso. Many small villages on the Island had either no physician or a single physician, some of whom suffered a daily case load of over a hundred patients. And, I recall a local 16 bed hospital with all toilets inoperative (clogged up), sterilization equipment unpacked in a hallway, and flies in the kitchen from a faulty screen door. The proportion of physicians attaining licensure after the Curso was high, and there were several iterations of the Curso. And we also had a contract for a follow-up study to examine, with the help of physician cohorts, the quality of practice of the Curso graduates—an activity carried out once before in North Carolina by Oslar Peterson, M.D., then a faculty member of the UNC School of Medicine, who was made unwelcome because of his effrontery in conducting such a daring study. We had no political problems whatsoever in Puerto Rico, a tribute to the sincerity, integrity, and professional competence of the faculty physicians of the UPR Medical School.

The frequent trips to the Island provided opportunities to take one or another of the family with me. Pegge was the first to go. The highlight of that trip was a tour of the island in a rented car after I had completed my work at the Medical School. We had heard of a native restaurant in the middle of the island called "Todo del Monde" which, though native was supposedly equal to the best five star restaurants in Paris. We located it at the end of a long one-lane dirt road in the central part of Puerto Rico, and found ourselves the only diners the evening we were there. We ordered a pork dish, and recall hearing a pig squeal, followed by a long wait, before being served. We assumed that the pork was fresh, and indeed the fare was delicious. Continuing our tour, we had driven down to Ponce on the south side of the island, and were returning to Hato Rey on the highway that runs directly over the mountain that forms the center of the island. At one place along the highway there was a fruit stand, manned by a single man, but displaying a variety of native tropical fruits. We purchased a pineapple, from which the man removed the skin with a large machete which he first dipped in a barrel of water, and sliced the meat deftly in convenient chunks. This was, without exception, the best fruit we had ever tasted.

Jill, then 9 years old, was the second to go. We flew out of Baltimore for San Juan, where we were upgraded to first class, and dined on lobster en route; Jill found quickly that most menus in Puerto Rico had, as the most expensive item, a local lobster, and consumed many pounds of the crustacean before our return four days later. But the significant events were more than dietary. We went to a night club in downtown San Juan where the main attraction was flamingo dancers, and one of the dancers took Jill from the table back into their dressing room where she showed her all their costumes. And I recall renting a car for a tour of the island, and spending a night with her in a native hotel in Fajardo, and being awakened at three in the morning by unearthly screams on a lower level. It turned out that the hotel owner was breeding fighting cocks in the basement of the hotel, and they began to greet the world very early each morning. But if Hitchcock had ever experienced screeches like those we heard, he would have abandoned *The Birds*, and built several additional movies around the Puerto Rican fowls.

Our return flight provided some drama. After we boarded our plane, a fuel truck pulled away without detaching the hose, rupturing the hose and connecting fitting, and spilling several hundred gallons of kerosene beneath the plane. After a considerable time in the stuffy cabin of the plane, men in asbestos suits, talking excitedly in Spanish, ushered us off, and we were told that there would be a four hour delay before another plane could take us back to the states. Other passengers were most distraught, but Jill was ecstatic: "Dad," she said, "Now we can go to that club you mentioned that has a good Mariachi band, but we did not have time for!" The look on the flight attendant's face when she heard this response was angelic and grateful, for the other passengers had vented their frustrations on her. We caught a cab to El Sombero on the outskirts of San Juan; the band was loud and colorful, and we returned to the airport in time to catch our replacement flight home.

Chris was the next to go with me. We also rented a car and toured the island, coming upon a huge mountain of earth on an isolated highway in the western central portion of the island, which completely blocked the road and required us to turn and go back a number of miles before we could continue our trip. This was apparently a mud slide that had not surprisingly gone unnoticed by the Puerto Rico highway department.

Not all activity at ETS Durham during this period was exciting. A former student from moonlighting at UNC, now a faculty member at Auburn University, telephoned me to ask if I would serve as a consultant for a workshop the University had contracted for public school guidance counselors. I agreed, and reported to his office the morning designated. He then took me to a stuffy classroom (it was July) where about 40 sweating people sat at the student desks. There, he said "This is Dr. Davis from ETS, who will lead our workshop on Title I." He then very quickly left the room. Having no idea at that time what Title I was, I once again recalled Moses praying for 40 days and nights, and for two days simply talked about a variety of things. It turned out that the attendees really didn't care, anyway. The purpose of the workshop was to absorb a great deal of Federal money, and in that we succeeded.

It was this period that I spent many hours flying somewhere, and there was frequently some excitement involved. The most sensational experience was when I was the only passenger on a commuting flight in a small plane from Santa Barbara to San Francisco. All went well until we approached San Francisco International Airport. The pilot asked me to come sit in the vacant co-pilot's seat and help him with the instructions from a flight manual. He admitted that this was his first flight for the little commuter airline, and his first landing at SFO. The instructions from the tower on the loudspeaker had a sense of urgency about them—"Turn!" "Climb!" "Descend!" until finally at touchdown the tower said: "Keep moving—you have a 747 right on top of you!" Suffice it to say that we made it to the far end of that long runway in record time.

Another commuter flight that had me concerned from the start was a flight from Jackson, Alabama, to Hartsfield Airport in Atlanta. Several of us had boarded the plane before the pilot came aboard, and our pilot turned out to be a young female, who might weigh as much as 100 pounds if dripping wet. The four stripes on her uniform seemed to take up most of her arm. I rationalized that she must be pretty good to have this job, and relaxed to the degree permitted by my self-serving conviction that I was not prejudiced. But the kicker came when we approached the Atlanta airport. Traffic was extremely heavy, and many planes were circling in holding patterns. But with the speaker system on, we heard a controller respond to the female voice of our pilot: "You all just come right on in, honey."

Not all fun was on the road. One year during this period, the (national) Psychometric Society met at the University in Chapel Hill, and Bob Linn, from ETS-Princeton, and Sam Webb, still at Emory University, were attending. Knowing that Bob, a native of Wyoming, was curious in a leery way about the South, I invited him and Sam to the house for a southern breakfast of eggs, country ham, biscuits, and grits—but dumped some green food coloring into the grits, winking at Sam as I did so. Sam, always one to abet in such a situation, smacked his lips and said something like "Goody—GREEN grits! They are the very best kind!" Sam and I finished ours with gusto, while Bob tried valiantly, but unsuccessfully, to take a taste. We never enlightened him.

But fortunes of the ETS office changed when John Caldwell left the ETS Board, and we were assigned to Sam Messick, Vice President for Research. Although I had been instrumental in getting the office of Vice President for Research established, and had nominated Sam for this position, he was loyal to his research values from his Princeton University Ph.D., and felt that the only true research had to be in pristine laboratories such as that at ETS-Princeton. Contract research was considered, by him and other purists at ETS, to be tainted by the nature of the source requesting it, and only topics of concern selected by the researcher himself were considered pure. He could only interpret the work we were doing as stuff for *Readers Digest*, and most certainly not appropriate for the think tank role he perceived the research function at ETS-Princeton to serve. I suspect that there may also have been some jealousy over our success in getting large Federal support, which the red tape procedures at the Princeton office made difficult.

In the third year, we were asked to become a "representational office" like the ones in Evanston and Atlanta, where the principal job was selling the ETS testing products to institutions, and servicing any concerns that developed by test takers or their parents. I steadfastly refused to accept this mission, and we began to be squeezed in many ways that served to make life uncomfortable. I received an offer from the Research Triangle Institute (RTI), a not for profit contract research affiliate of the University of North Carolina, N C State University, and

Duke University, to head their new education research center, and when I accepted and reported it to Sam Messick, he joyously said on the phone to me "That's it. We are closing the office!" And so it was. The two senior researchers were shortly additions to the research staff at the RTI Center for Educational Research and Evaluation, while Anne Borders Patterson returned to her role as wife of one of IBMs bright young technicians, and to graduate study at UNC.

As a final gesture, I amused myself with a little paper that I entitled "How to Succeed at ETS." I shared it first only with Charlotte Farley, the head of our contracts office and a dear friend (now deceased), and she advised burning it quickly before anyone else could see it. This prompted me to share it, in strict confidence, with Executive Vice President Bill Turnbull, who I believed was intelligent and self-assured enough not to be threatened by it, and whom I felt would both understand and appreciate it. He never acknowledged it, but later invited me (when I was at RTI) as the only other United States representative to a meeting in Geneva, Switzerland, to establish an international testing organization. I am placing this paper in the appendix, for it characterized ETS at that time in a facetious way but close enough to some painful truths, and explains very well how I was cured of any romantic ideas about ETS as an institution.

Chapter 23

Duke University, On the Side

Although my permanent position from 1967 to 1973 was with the Southeastern Office of Educational Testing Service, I moonlighted occasionally at Duke University as a Visiting Professor, teaching graduate courses in the Department of Education, but more frequently undergraduate courses in the Department of Psychology. I also served on doctoral committees at both Duke and UNC.

And Duke was an institution known locally as "the Stanford of the East." This I had confirmed by observing graffiti in the men's room in the University Library. One inscription on the wall proclaimed that "Moby Dick is not a social disease." Another was an inscription over a urinal that said: "Please flush after using—Chapel Hill needs the water." This was particularly appropriate, for at that time a water shortage in Chapel Hill had been alleviated by digging a pipe line from Durham to Chapel Hill nine miles away, and by the Town of Chapel Hill purchasing water from Durham.

But it was not only the institutional prestige and presumed intellectual acumen of the students that attracted me. Teaching served for me in about the same way that I imagine confession would serve for a devout Catholic. I found time to do a reasonable job of preparation. There were only three major problems that I can recall at this time.

The first was parking. Clark Kerr, of the University of California, had said that a college president had only three major problems: sex for the students, athletics for the alumni, and parking for the faculty. Duke, in all its opulence, had parking spaces for probably 20 percent of those who drove to work there. Faculty coming in during the day to teach a class generally allowed a couple of hours to find a place—a luxury I could not afford given my responsibilities at ETS. As a result, I collected a parking ticket for each class session I taught on the main campus—enough to paper a bathroom wall, but Pegge protested.

The second problem was athletics. I had a faculty pass for the football games, with a seat in a special section with other faculty members. The only game I recall attending was when Duke played my alma mater, UNC, and of course I had no problem in deciding whom to support. I recall Pegge tugging at my sleeve, saying something like "Shut up and sit down, or Dr. Beaumeyer is going to slug you!"

The third problem became apparent at a social function at the home of one of the tenured professors that I had known for many years, and involving a number of faculty invited for an "open house." We were asked to preside at the punch bowl from exactly 4:30 to 5:00 P.M., and did so routinely. It turned out that in the Duke social regimen, this was a signal honor that sent messages to all present, and we had treated it in cavalier fashion. That was the last formal social function we attended at Duke.

Duke University owned several large tracts of land, and an important fringe benefit for regular faculty was the provision of a cost-free loan, payments to be deducted from salary, to purchase a lot at a price well below market value, and, with favorable interest rates, to finance the building of a house on this property, with the only restriction that if it were ever sold, it must be to a faculty member of the University. This was the basis for Duke Forest, an enclave on the southwest corner of Durham that became an exclusive faculty community. It also permitted Duke to retain faculty without raising their salaries very much, for the loan became due in full if the faculty member left. Virtually no faculty member rejected the opportunity to live in Duke Forest: it was an offer they couldn't refuse.

We did attend a little party at the home of Cliff Wing, the former Director of Admissions at Tulane who had moved to a faculty position in the Department of Psychology, in which Duke President Douglas and Mrs. Knight were guests. Lee Wing, Cliff's wife, was a lady of tremendous and wide-ranging talent, with such achievements as composing words and music for songs that Pearl Bailey sang and an off-Broadway play, and at the other extreme, assisting former Duke President Terry Sanford in his political activities, as North Carolina governor and as candidate for the U.S. presidency. She also bristled nicely when I called her by her full first names: in fine southern fashion, she was Lucy Lee.

But suffice it to say that the Wings were an uninhibited fun couple. At the party we attended at their house, we found that Charlie Byrd, the famous guitarist, a friend of Lee's, was there to provide music. Someone got into a discussion with President Knight's wife about standing on one's head. "No problem," she said, and promptly inverted herself in the middle of the room. The informality was more our style than the pouring of punch incident, and we marveled at the range of social life represented by the activities we sampled.

Our involvement with Duke was during the era of the Kent State riots, and racial agitation was rampant in Durham. A local downtown hot dog stand run by a man called "Shorty" was a popular place for lunch or snack, and the hot dogs were true Coney Island style. But over the period of racial unease, Shorty placed a large Colt revolver on top of his cash register by the door, as an accompaniment to the signs on the register and in the window stating in bold lettering "Niggers Not Welcome." Needless to say, the clientele was all white at that time.

I taught a large class in adolescent psychology at Duke (though I recall when we could not meet in our usual room in the Allen Building because of the residue of tear gas that had been used to break up a student occupation of the Registrar's Office). This was the time when the Duke students protested President Knight's membership in an all-white private club, by assembling by the statue of James B. Duke in front of the Chapel, and appointing student monitors for such responsibilities as the prevention of paper or other waste being left on the lawn or leading protest songs (scripts provided as handouts). It was also during the period when students assembled on the lawn of President Knight's house one rainy evening in continuing protest, when kindly Dr. Knight came to the door, said that he was ill with a cold, but if they would come inside and make themselves at home he would talk with them in the morning. The students accepted this offer, and his large house had many guest bedrooms in which they could camp. But of course their first order of business was establishing a set of rules (e.g., "Absolutely No Smoking") to govern their behavior while they were guests of the University president. It was at this time that I decided to use some class time to see if more effective forms of protest could be contrived and put into operation by these obviously culturally impacted and, in my opinion, culturally disadvantaged students. First, the students were asked to identify evidences of problems needing correction. The huge pistol on Shorty's cash register came immediately to mind, and this was voted a priority for action. I had told them how women in Chapel Hill had closed a downtown massage parlor in less than two weeks by having one of them stationed on the sidewalk by the entrance with a camera, and pretending to take a picture of any male entering. The first suggestion was, of course, that they call for picketing the place until Shorty relented. But all I needed to do was wrinkle my eyebrows and scowl a bit, and they quickly realized that this would only salve their egos, not solve the problem.

Then, with much debate, and given some supervised "freedom," they soon came up with an ingenious plan. They would get fifty or so Duke students together with fifty of so Black students from neighboring North Carolina Central University, and descend on Shorty's with each ordering a couple of hot dogs and professing that they were the best they had ever experienced. This plan was accepted, and put into action the next Saturday. More than a hundred students, including both black and white, descended on Shorty's emporium. Shorty, of course, could not resist the huge profit this promised, and went to work until his refrigerated storeroom was barren. Somehow, the pistol and offensive sign disappeared, and Blacks were able to rejoin whites at Shorty's.

But there is more about Shorty: He also had a hot dog stand on Highway 54 between Highway 55 and Chapel Hill. A year of so later the local newspaper carried an item reporting Shorty's death in an automobile accident somewhere enroute to the beach, but stated that at the hospital where he was taken a recent bullet wound in his stomach area was discovered, and that there was no explanation for this.

I stopped one day a month or so after Shorty's death for a hot dog at the No. 2 stand, which was now run by Shorty's energetic wife. I expressed my sympathy, of course, as I munched on my hot dog, and commented on the "mysterious" bullet wound. "That's no mystery," she responded. "I shot the son of a bitch!"

Suspecting she had good reason, and finding the quality of the hot dogs unabated, I decided to finish my hot dog, wipe the chili from my chin, and go on about my business.

I am unaware of whatever events may have followed, but Shorty's No. 2 closed about a year later. Sometime before this, there was an unexpected snowfall, and I was caught on the highway (I was returning to Chapel Hill from RTI) for several hours just past Shorty's No. 2. At one point, Shorty's wife and a young lady came walking by toward the hot dog stand, and we exchanged pleasantries. They came slogging back by an hour later, finding me precisely where they had left me, for the icy roads had completely stalled traffic. I will always remember and treasure the comment made by the young lady as she passed: "You should have went with us—we would have had us a good time!"

The class in Adolescent Psychology gave me as much fun as any class I ever taught. It was a required course for psychology majors, and was apparently usually given by someone who had a reputation for being either extremely dull or extremely rigorous, for some 325 students registered for it when it was announced that I, an unknown, would teach it. This required the large amphitheater in the Administration Building, and I was provided with three graduate student assistants to help with roll taking and grading papers. The course was apparently required for School of Nursing students as well, for there were also a substantial number of these present.

I recall one student who always came to class in a moth-eaten floor length cheap fur coat, and for the life of me I could not tell whether the coat concealed a male or a female. The name on the course registration gave no clue, for it consisted of two initials and a surname. I was surprised at the end of the course when this person, now well-washed and smelling of Ivory soap, and decently attired, came to me to thank me for the insights she (for it was female) had been able to attain. She said that she was living in a communal house off campus at the start of the course, and about three-fourths of the way through it she watched cockroaches going up and down the wall beside her bed, decided that there was more to adolescence than she had achieved, and that how she had chosen to live her life up to now had to go.

This was a class where I devoted considerable time to adolescent sex, presenting it as an immature and inadequate way to play being an adult. I think most of the students got the message, although some had some surprising interpretations. One young lady thanked me for what I had said, and proudly reported that as a consequence she had decided to restrict herself to one partner. But the strangest consequence was a late night telephone call from a female married student in the class to come to her off-campus apartment and provide some badly needed counsel regarding her troubled marriage. This sounded suspicious, although I felt the need to respond. As a safety precaution, I asked daughter Jill, then 10, to come with me. When we got to the apartment, Jill was sleepy, and the young lady showed her a bedroom where she could sack out. She and I talked for a time about some squabble she and her husband had had, and the result was that he had stalked out and she was afraid that he would never return.

After about 30 minutes of conversation, the front door opened, and in strutted the husband. "Oho!" he said—"So this is what you are up to!" At that point, I called out "Jill, come in here!" and a sleepy little girl emerged from the bedroom. Although the husband had gone bowling and had been drinking, he sobered up rather quickly, and we had a productive three-way conversation. The two decided they liked each other, after all, and Jill and I went back home to Chapel Hill.

That Adolescent Psychology course had one other benefit. One of the best students, Susan Kerner, whose grandfather founded the North Carolina town of Kernersville, came to work as a research assistant in my ETS office. She moved to Washington when the ETS office closed, married, and as Susan Kerner-Hoeg became a project officer for the Department of Defense at a salary well above mine, and later a vice president for a research organization in the DC area.

At grading time, a characteristic of the Duke student body came crystal clear. The top of the grade distribution contained all females; the middle portion of the distribution contained all males; and the bottom part of the distribution again included only females. The top group could be explained by the more stringent admissions procedures used for females majoring in the arts and sciences; and, the bottom group were all students in the School of Nursing, which was trying to keep afloat by accepting any applicant that could spell her name (it was later terminated). The boys were a cross section of mostly affluent families who had kept their sons at home and in the public schools, unlike the private school crowd I had found at Princeton.

Another class that was a genuine fun experience was an undergraduate course, offered by the Department of Psychology, on Methods of Social Research. This was a class where I abandoned any texts, and had the students, singly or in small groups, design and carry out a research project. The choices were unusual but good. One young man decided to hitch-hike from Durham to Chapel Hill and back for several hours a day, for a week as a hippie—with beads, beard, long hair, and outlandish garb—then, clean shaven and neatly coffered, and in a three piece suit, repeat the hitch-hiking experiment. He kept meticulous records of the time and number of cars passing before pickup, and the characteristics of the drivers who accommodated him. His findings were subjected to appropriate statistical analyses, and he found decidedly for the hippie image as significantly more conducive to success in getting a ride. And some of the conversations with the drivers were of interest: e.g., a couple of high school girls skipping school, and interested in finding a source of marijuana; or, a minister who felt the nine mile ride between Durham and Chapel Hill was sufficient to save the soul of his hitchhiking passenger. This young man, Bryan McNally, was later hired by me as a research assistant in the ETS office, where his creativity persisted, for when time came for a raise, he told me in mock seriousness that he had been unable to purchase a pair of shoes on his salary, and that he had to sleep with his sneakers on, for if he took them off the odor kept him awake.

One day shortly after the close of the semester in which I taught this course, I found several young men, neatly dressed in royal blue Duke blazers, pressing their way into my ETS office to gasp at what I had unknowingly done: I had flunked the basketball center, thereby destroying his eligibility! I asked who this might be, and the name they gave me, containing more consonants than vowels, brought to mind a name of a person that had appeared on the class list from the registrar's office at the beginning of the semester but who had never appeared for class, nor had he canceled his registration. Following the prescribed rules for such, I entered a "WD-F" for "Withdraw Failure" on the final report to the registrar.

I explained that I had followed Duke policy and procedures, and that the fellow simply had never shown up for any of the 30 class sessions. The young men in blazers protested vigorously, and finally asked if I would let the young man take a final test and report his grade from that as a correction. I explained that I had used no text or tests, and had based the final grade on the research reports. I told them that I could draw up an exam from my lectures and the class discussions, although I saw no way the young man could be successful, given the nature of the content. The Blue Blazers persisted, for a research project would delay a grade well into the basketball season. I accepted a date two weeks later when the young man could come to my office and be administered a final exam.

Two weeks later, a young man notable for the way he had to stoop to enter my office appeared and identified himself as the person with the name with more consonants than vowels. I seated him in the tallest chair available and gave him the test and a blue book in which to record his answers. He labored for a hour or so, turned in his blue book, and took leave. I carefully went over what he had written, and filed a corrected grade with the registrar—F. Somehow, I was never asked again to teach an undergraduate course at Duke.

Chapter 24

Tenure at the Research Triangle Institute

In 1973, I moved to what would be my professional home until retirement, the Research Triangle Institute (now, RTI International). This organization is a non-profit contract research organization created by forces at Duke University, N.C. State University, and the University of North Carolina at Chapel Hill; officers at these three institutions constitute the majority of the board of governors for the Institute. It has a group of specialists in a number of disciplines, such as chemistry, the life sciences, engineering, and a social sciences component, which was strong in sampling and survey research.

The social sciences component was the result of the original researcher in this area being a sampling statistician who had become the senior vice president by the time I joined the staff, and the social sciences division grew largely from the work of sampling statisticians, whose values permeated the other social science groups. I was interviewed for the role of the head of the Center for Educational Research and Evaluation, one of five social science groups, containing four doctoral level researchers and their secretarial and research assistant support staff. After meeting with the staff, I was called by the president of RTI to offer me the job, but to advise me that all four senior staff members had said that although they would welcome me as a research colleague, they advised against appointing me as their director. I immediately stated that I was withdrawing my application, but the president persisted. Since rejecting the change of the ETS office from a research to a representational role, life at ETS had become increasingly uncomfortable, and the move would involve a nice increase in salary. Ergo, I accepted.

The four doctoral level researchers were at work on a proposal responding to a request for a major national longitudinal study that would trace a large sample of individuals from high school into adulthood, to be managed by the (Federal) National Center for Educational Statistics. This study was highly similar to the pipe dream we had created, as "Project X," in the higher education research group at ETS-Princeton back in the 1960s, and RTI proposed me as project director. I have forgotten the dollar amount of the contract which we won, but the overhead was sufficient to provide for the erection of a new high rise office building that housed RTI administration and several of the social science groups. This win, and the fact that in the next several years the Center for Educational Research and Evaluation won 90% of the dollar value of contract proposals submitted, provided a nice reception for us. The Center shortly expanded from 7 to a total staff of some 45 individuals. In the period from 1973 when I assumed the directorship through 1980 when I stepped down, the Center had won approximately $17,000,000 from Federal, state, and private sources.

The first year of the study that was known as "The National Longitudinal Study of the High School Class of 1972" was a busy one. It involved a rather extensive questionnaire administered to a national sample of 23,000 high school seniors. Its purpose was the identification of factors affecting later career and life styles, through continued periodic followups. Our project officer, a career federal employee, was overwhelmed by the responsibility of overseeing our work which involved literally billions of bits of data, and made many visits to our offices and engaged in substantial nit-picking. I soon found that responsibility for a large-scale Federal contract called for more than simple management or research skills.

This necessary attempt to ease the Federal Project Officer's anxieties that we considered unreasonable had its drawbacks. When he visited, I frequently took him home for cocktails. This developed, for him, into a warm personal friendship, with such gestures as frequently being urged to join a Toastmaster's Club, because he had found that he grew so much from it. A shy and uneasy man, the responsibility of the major study weighed heavily upon him At one point, he stopped payments on the contract for completely unreasonable demands, and, being unable to resolve these with him, we appealed to his supervisor. This included taking myself and several RTI officers to his supervisors in Washington, where we laid out our explanation of the problem. At one point in the proceedings, he was called in, and we found him to be a pitiable figure—smelling of alcohol, and in the beginning stages of growing a beard. But our problems were resolved; he was replaced; the study was successful, and led to repeated follow-up contracts. But the affair left me with the sad feeling that our initial project officer was a victim of the system in which he operated, where heavy responsibilities were assigned not to the most capable but to the most senior. And, in the Federal government as is so frequently the case in education, it is the mediocre who persist in their area of incompetence.

His demands, while trivial and not really detrimental until he stopped payment on the contract, had been a constant bother. I had some occasion to comment on our constant problems in keeping him pleased with our successes with my female friend Sam. Sam was the Native American whom I had employed as a research associate when I was with the Regional Education Laboratory and who I later found was in her regular role the madam of Durham's most elite prostitute ring.

Sam was quick to offer support: she said *"Send him to me. I have a girl that will give him something he can never get rid of!"*

(While I am on Sam and her regular profession, I need to fill the reader in on what attracted me to her in the first place. We needed ethnic representation on a project I was conducting several years earlier when I was on the staff of the Regional Education Laboratory, and Sam was a Chiricahua-Apache, who was obviously very bright and effective in personal contacts. In working with her, I learned that her childhood was scarred by the fact that she had grown up without normal contact with parents—she principally remembered her father from visits, when she was a little girl, with him in prison in Tennessee, where he had been incarcerated, and later executed, she told me, on a false charge by racist whites. She was a very bright and sensitive person, and when with people she knew she was the epitome of uninhibitedness. I must report one other colorful thing I experienced with her. A year beyond the point of her offer to take care of my project officer, she was found to have cancer and was told it would be terminal. She proceeded to have one of her clients, a well-known attorney in Durham, draw up a will, donating her body to the Duke School of Medicine, with the wish that "The medical students have as much fun playing with it now as they did when I was alive!" She went to Arizona to die, but miraculously reappeared several years later, apparently completely cured (she attributed this to yoga), married a former client who was a hippie several years her junior, and disappeared. But I had learned many things from my contact with her over the span of a dozen years.)

In spite of having an anile project officer in this initial phase, the longitudinal study was exciting and filled with many discoveries beyond those reported in the voluminous statistical summaries of survey responses. One that I recall and have kept where I could find it was a letter from a Native American girl who was caught up in the national sample of 23,000 high school seniors. A copy of her letter, responding to a questionnaire, and which was neatly printed on plain paper, follows.

"Dear People:

I am writing to tell you that for several reasons I can not participate in your survey any longer. One reason being that I feel a lot of your questions are an invasion of privacy and I can't feel that I want to have many people other than myself knowing the answers. Reason number two is even more relevant however—I never did graduate—I was 2 credits or a credit and a half from graduating and I left school.

"I also find it hard to fit my life into your questions—I live in a Sioux tipi and plan on doing so throughout the winter. I am not legally married—per se—but I am married all the same. I don't even have electricity or running water never mind a color tv. and I don't feel a desire for a (word unintelligible)—life style electric dishwasher or many other things—I do read about 10-20 books a week but I have since 5th grade.

"I didn't really learn much of anything of use in high school—as a result of an I.Q. test I was coerced into a college Prep course—I think I dropped out of school mentally in the fifth grade.—(physically too—my hatred of school developed into hypochondria which had made me feel the after effects for a long time—I thought it was wrong to hate school as much as I did—I see now there are alternatives too late for me however.)

"I have starred (*) the questions I found ambiguous or irrelevant and I'll tell you klow (sic) why.

"I like my job. I get to cook, clean, serve, talk, eat, and generally just be a human being. My high school training didn't teach me any of those things. I'm even allowed to make mistakes—wow!

"Ques # 107 (about husband's occupation) is one that I object to because of the invasion of privacy thing—that is his business, and he doesn't feel you need to know.

> "Now # 132 ((self regard) depends on how early I got up—the weather, what I did yesterday, what I have to do today.—I feel good today.
> d. I try—it depends—I don't tune cars very well but I make great chili

h, Some days yes—some no—I think it evens out

"#134 (political activity) I don't think politics—or politicians help—you can just fix your own life and pray no one does anything final.

"135A (Adequacy of money for food and shelter) I guess our idea of what is enough however varys (sic) greatly from the norm.

k. I still don't know if my idea of what educated me and what you want to hear are the same.

We basically want to buy some land and farm. Having helped numeous (sic) friends build up theirs we hope we have a realistic veiw (sic) of what it takes. #143—I could circle about ½ or ¾ of all these things—they all go with farm manager.

"#149 (Teacher's expectations of the individual)—I could circle all of these.

"#153 This varies too.

"I'm sorry that I cant (sic) do anymore than this. Please try not to hassle my parents.

Sincerely, Lorraine E. Lee"

As noted earlier, RTI was a contract research organization, with the majority of contracts with the Federal government. Life there consisted of starting the day by scanning the *Commerce Business Daily,* a Federal publication in which requests for proposals, or "RFPs." were advertised. These ads would describe the work to be done, suggest the level of effort (dollar value) of that work, and ask for competitive bids by a certain deadline, usually in the relatively near future. If requested jobs seemed feasible, work on the bids, or competitive proposals, would need to proceed immediately, and there was seldom enough time for a thoroughly adequate response. On many occasions, this involved writing around the clock for several days, and many times I—and Graham Burkheimer, a competent associate I had brought over from the ETS office I directed—would work around the clock for as much as six or seven days—without sleep or showers, and with food brought in (other staff members would usually poop out after a couple of days!). It was a rough life, but the results generally justified this effort.

RTI was also a place where I spent many weeks working over 100 hours, and where in 15 years I was there, I took no vacation and only limited sick leave when hospitalized for surgery. I also traveled extensively over the U.S., with the most frequent destination Washington, D.C.

The plane schedule for Washington from the Raleigh-Durham airport had the first flight to DC leaving around 7 AM. I can recall dressing in the dark so as not to awaken anyone at 5 AM one morning for a 7 AM airplane departure to DC, and, dropping something in the closet as I groped for shoes, having three little children bounding out of bed saying "Daddy, you aren't leaving us again, are you?"

But the Washington trips had their bonuses: our notorious Senator Jesse Helms always caught the late afternoon flight back to Raleigh-Durham each Friday, and the first time I was on the same flight I was accompanied by my research colleague, Rod Hartnett. I said to Rod: "That's Jesse Helms over there—I think I will go over and sit with the sonofabitch!" In person, Jesse was most pleasant and affable, and I think he and I began to enjoy our conversations on the weekend homecoming trips. Despite the rabble rousing he was famous for, we never got into political matters. I could never see him politically as anything but a much too far right blind despot, but I had to admire the effectiveness of his Congressional office, his responsiveness to problems of his constituents, and the energy he put into his daily work.

But winning work in the highly competitive environment of contract research with Federal clients was not just a matter of long hours, but also of knowing something of the underlying reasons for the RFPs. I found a variety of sources of good information, from the sponsoring office staff members to congressional aides, and spent many hours in information gathering.

One reliable source of information was Robert Berls, a respected project officer in the Office of Planning, Budgeting, and Evaluation of the U.S. Office of Education. Berls was a career federal employee with a Ph.D. from Yale, whose wife was employed in an executive position with the Library of Congress. They were a childless couple, in their late middle ages, and both intense in their work. I recall when they moved into an apartment with two bathrooms, and further celebrated this rise in status with *two* subscriptions to the *New York Times*. They had both worked hard, and richly appreciated their deserved success as attested by these two simple luxuries, for them the gold key to the executive washroom.

At this point, some 19 years after retirement, I find I do not recognize some of the studies on my vita, much less recall the major findings. Toward the end of my tenure, I had several studies of the impact of federal funding on education and training of primary care physicians, and got to visit a number of the then 127 allopathic medical schools and 15 osteopathic schools. This experience was an eye opener, for the content and apparent quality of training varied tremendously from one medical school to another. I recall visiting one that had an unusually high proportion of students electing family medicine as their specialty. To discover why I made a careful investigation on campus, observing, and interviewing students, faculty, and administrators. I found their secret rather quickly: after the first year, consumed as usual with such basic subjects as gross anatomy, students declaring their academic interest in family medicine were sent, in groups of 30, to "practice" in the free public health clinics of the large city in which the school was located—with a single medical doctor as a supervisor. This "hands on" experience for second year medical students was most effective in convincing them to declare that department their major, and it was argued that scores of the very poor in the city had enhanced contact with a health professional.

I also found the medical schools even more infested with academic politics than colleges and universities in general. At one major medical school, I found the family medicine department in temporary and makeshift quarters, while the other medical specialties were in rather plush environments. I asked the dean, an internist by specialization, if the many hundred thousands of Federal dollars the family medicine department had brought in were not important; he snorted, and retorted *"That money did not come to the Medical School—it came to the Family Medicine Department!"* This was in marked contrast to another major medical school where the chairperson of the Family Medicine Department was the personal physician for the majority of the teaching faculty across all departmental areas, and the teaching faculty and students across all areas not only held that department in respect, but saw it as fully equal in the business of producing highly competent physicians.

One member of the advisory panel for this study became a close friend and valuable adviser. This was Dr. Barbara Ross-Deering, chair of the Family Medicine Department at the Michigan State University School of Osteopathic Medicine. Who was she? She was the sister of Diana Ross, and for my money the true Supreme. A meeting with her was like a reunion with a long lost and loved relative, and I gained a new respect for osteopathic medicine from talking with her and the ladies on her faculty. And again, like Anne Borders-Patterson, she had experience as a baby sitter—for her sister Diana when she married the man from Denmark.

One of the most significant encounters I had in the series of studies of schools of medicine was with Dr. Oslar Peterson, at the Harvard Medical School. Dr. Peterson had done a landmark study in the quality of medical practice of physicians in North Carolina when he was on the faculty of the UNC medical school (as previously reported), but had found the reception of the study less than enthusiastic—not for any question about the integrity of his findings, but for the simple impropriety of conducting such a study in the first place. I asked him about his perceptions of the Harvard program, where some rather unusual and costly teaching practices took place—e.g., ten or a dozen specialists in a particular area dividing the lectures for a given class. Dr. Peterson snorted, and said that it probably made little difference. "With the academic quality of students we admit, we could turn them loose in the library for a couple of years, and they would emerge as well or better prepared than when we subject them to these elaborate procedures."

I had always looked down on chiropractors and osteopaths, but found a new respect for the people and programs in the osteopathic institutions. Dr. Barbara Ross-Deering at Michigan State University surely played a part in this, but I developed the feeling that the academic programs at the schools of Osteopathic Medicine were more substantial and rigorous that those of their counterpart Schools of Medicine. I wondered then and now if this was not a function of the fact that the osteopathic schools felt they had to prove their validity, while many of the medical schools could not believe there could ever be any valid criticism of anything they did or did not do.

One other doctor among those we studied or on the study team stood out then, and still does, in my mind as a truly exemplary person. An event in which he was involved is indicative of the man. This was Dr. Harvey Estes. He was chair of the family medicine department at the Duke University School of Medicine and was assisting us in the inquiry as a consultant. We were in Philadelphia walking from our hotel to appointments at Jefferson Medical College when a disheveled derelict, apparently with too much to drink, tried to cross a busy street but fell down in the middle and could not quickly get up. My associate did not hesitate, but dashed through the traffic to the man, helped him to his feet, and saw him safely to the sidewalk. When assured that he was not injured, we continued to our appointments.

At RTI, 95 % of the Institute activity was contract rather than grant research. While in most grant work the researcher creates the responses to the problem, in contract work the sponsor generally controls the parameters. Management officials outside of the physical sciences seldom see research as a way to discover unknown but useful information as in the physical sciences, but to support prospective decisions that have already been made. In a study of remedial courses in a large university system, the findings were favorable but not what the project officer for the university system wanted (it turned out that he was looking for a way to cancel the funding of the remedial activity). I had pressure to change the results to suit his preconceptions, and, when I refused, he first required a conference with the institutional representatives who had provided the data for the study. Such a group were convened with the project officer attending and in spite of his forceful interrogation, the objective results as I had reported held. He then refused to accept the report, and we interceded with his superior, the president of the system. The president solved the problem quickly: he asked me to add a statement at the beginning that the results were the findings and interpretations of the research team and did not necessarily reflect the opinions of any officials of the university system. This was added to the report; the report was delivered; and we were paid for the contracted work.

One other example stands out. We were contracted to do a very expensive national survey of the impact of the Federal migrant education program. The funds available and our corporate capabilities made the prospect one on which we had to bid. The imposed design involved a before/after impact study, which could only produce non-significant gains, a fact well known from other research. But the purpose of the study was not to find out whether the federal investment was effective, nor to find ways to improve its impact, but to provide data that could be given to the Congress to get the funds diverted to other uses. The argument would be (and unfortunately was) that a huge effort and expenditure had found no significant improvement from the federal investment. That statistically significant findings of change associated with the program over the time span involved were simply not possible was not known by those who acted on the findings.

Not all contract research work was so structured, and there were some attempts to use it to learn or to improve practice. A notable example was a series of studies for the Bureau of Program Planning and Evaluation of the U.S. Department of Education that sought ways to identify when the seed money from grants had been used to generate other more regular means of support. But there were other projects for other Federal departments where this concept not only did not apply but was seen as dangerous, for it would obviate the grant program and the Federal employees and departments that fed upon it. My most important lesson from the RTI experience remained as previously cited: when people concerned with management and who have no background in the discipline of research commission it, it may not be an attempt at discovery, but a vehicle for affirming and selling decisions already made. This would not have been a hazard at ETS, for it would have been recognized and dealt with appropriately. But with the sampling discipline the heritage for RTI social science research, it was felt that our integrity in this regard overrode all possible criticisms: if the sampling procedures were without flaws, there could be no other problem with the methods or the findings. I believe the hazard of using research to affirm decisions already made, applicable not to physical science research but to social science research, has not been given sufficient recognition. To do so would cost research contractors like RTI big bucks.

The implicit need for RTI to give the government what it wanted is illustrated nicely by its contract work on coinage. This work produced recommendations that resulted in the creation of the Susan B. Anthony dollar, which is what the project sponsors wanted. The resulting fiasco was followed by the move of the project director to a job outside RTI selling mobile homes, but the only corporate lesson learned had to do with what projects to feature in the annual report.

And RTI was found to be, in many ways, what I consider the standard for both the best and the worst in current conventional business or organization practice. Industrial Psychology was the first university level course I taught, and was from then on a favorite. It gave a chance to examine conventional practices in business management for what they were: i.e, fringe benefits as a less expensive (than salary increases) strategy to maintain workers. A prime example of the real underbelly of RTI, an organization that purported to work to improve the condition of mankind, grew out of an instance when a secretary expressed concern to me about the fact that she had been unable, because of work schedule, to get screened for breast cancer. I wrote a memo to the Director of Personnel, suggesting that the County Mobile Xray Unit, a community service, be invited to the campus for a day or two so that female employees could get checked without missing much work time. His response, expressed in a tone that clearly signaled that he minded his own business and I should mind mine, was that this had been discussed in a recent meeting of area personnel directors, and none of them had encountered lawsuits from female employees for failure to facilitate breast cancer screening tests. Ergo, my suggestion was foolish, and no action would be taken on it. I never told him that I then made a practice, which other cost center directors emulated, to permit any female employee interested in such a test to take time off for that purpose without penalty. Thus, my concern was partially served, and the cost to RTI greatly increased. But that mentality made me grateful that I was away from it when I retired. For one thing, I no longer felt the need to take a shower at the end of each day that I went to the office.

As for the showers: when I was a pre-teen, my next door neighbor, a year older and thereby a hero, had a father who owned a store with magazines for sale. My friend would borrow a copy of such racy journals as *True Confessions*, and he and I would try to add to our maturity by hiding in a closet with the magazine and a flashlight.

I recall vividly an account of a young lady who worked until midnight as a waitress at a diner. She would walk home several blocks away when she got off work. One night on the way home she was set upon and raped in turn by each of 17 men.

After this terrible experience, she continued home, where, in shock, she could tell no one what had happened. Instead, she took 17 baths in an attempt to cleanse herself.

My days in Washington and at RTI had much the same impact on me. I took a lot of showers.

Chapter 25

Family Life in Chapel Hill

Given my employment at ETS-Durham, the Regional Education Laboratory for the Carolinas and Virginia, and the Research Triangle Institute—spanning the years from 1967 to 1988—we were able to live in one location, at 405 Holly Lane in Chapel Hill, NC. It was here that our three children largely grew up, and this was the home they left when they became independent. In our move from New Jersey, Mike entered high school in Chapel Hill; Chris started in the fifth grade; and Jill started in the third grade. All finished high school in Chapel Hill.

Victor Borge always replied when asked how many children he had—"Three—one of each!." So it was with us. If there was a trait shared among these three, I never discovered what it was. My friend Marty Hamburger had introduced me at some professional forum as "author of widely non-read publications; married, with three children who hate each other, and a distraught wife." It is only fair to say, however, that actually the three children got along beautifully when out of the family context. If they were together and any one of them was made uncomfortable in some way by an outsider, the maligned one received immediate substantial and vigorous support.

But they were different from each other. I recall returning to our split-level home one evening to find Jill in her upstairs bedroom with some little friends for a slumber party, playing Donnie Osborne records (she denies ever playing a Donnie Osborne record, but it sounded to me like someone with his distinctive nasal qualities). Chris was in the kitchen on the main level with several of his friends, happily engaged in discussions about such things as cars and girls. Mike was in the basement family room conducting a prayer session with a number of his friends.

That this characterization was not a temporary or chance phenomenon is attested by some New Year's Eve events one year when Mike was home from college for the Christmas holidays. He went to a friend's house, where they drank Cokes and played ping-pong until midnight, then sang "Auld Lang Syne." He was home a few minutes after midnight. At about 3 AM I had a call from Chris, then a High School junior, to come get him at a university sorority house, for he felt that having had something to drink he should not try to drive home. I went to the house, honked, and Chris emerged, a university coed on each arm, pleading "Chris, please don't go yet." I don't remember what Jill did that year, but whatever it was, it was not what Mike or Chris did.

But Mike was an exemplary citizen in school. We recall the Black director of athletics telling us that Mike was the most responsible student in his class, and that he always put him in charge when he had to leave the room for some reason. And although we were frequently called by someone at the school who reported that our son Michael was once again in considerable trouble, we were quick to point out that we had learned that there were TWO Mike Davises at that school, and that the one about which the caller was concerned was obviously the other Mike Davis.

Much of my research over this period involved minority groups, and Blacks were frequent visitors to our house. One was a remarkable man named James Coleman, then a graduate student at North Carolina Central University, but on his way to Meharry, who not only taught us some choice vocabulary but also did his share of educating our children to the real world. I remember one evening when he suddenly asked Mike how many black teachers he had in high school, and Mike answered "Two—no, three—(long thoughtful pause)—no, five." Jim was delighted to find that Mike had not compartmentalized his teachers by race and counted them before.

From early childhood through teenage, Mike maintained a substantial interest in Naval history, and became quite conversant on "firsts" in naval warfare. He also assembled a nice collection of military bayonets.

In his high school years, Mike made substantial money by contracting to mow lawns in the neighborhood. He was always frugal with his money, and I remember his apologizing for needing an allowance of $5.00 a week spending money while in college, but, he said, there were times that he got hungry for pop corn. He was indeed a popcorn addict, which prompted Jill one year to give him a ten pound package of it as a Christmas present.

We belonged to a neighborhood swim club, and in his senior year, Mike took a date to an evening pool party. I was pleased to discover that his bikini-clad date was stunningly beautiful in both face and figure. When he came home later that night, I asked him if he had kissed her goodnight. He replied "No—she had braces on her teeth, too, and I didn't think it would work."

When Mike graduated from high school, we attempted to help him choose a college by taking a summer tour of colleges about the state where he could talk with faculty and students, sit in on classes, and generally get the feel of the institution. He was planning to major in history, and was much impressed with that department and faculty at Appalachian State University in Boone, NC, but a few days later spent a day at St. Andrews Presbyterian College in Laurenburg, NC, and found a match that he felt could only have been made in heaven. Although this was a private school and more expensive than a public institution, we were still with ETS at that time, and a fringe benefit was college tuition for any child of an employee.

Chris made average grades in school, but was what I considered the model of all boy. He had many friends of both sexes throughout school, and enjoyed the many benefits of growing up in a university town without suffering any of the handicaps from the dangers thereof—at least to our knowledge, which is better to relie upon than on unwarranted suspicions.

By the time Chris turned 16, he got his driver's license, and his first car.—a Corvair, which he took to college with him. He picked up a second somewhat dilapidated car which he humorously called his drinking car. It was later when he was home from college that he purchased a souped up Camero with all the trimmings—a Hurst shifter, wire wheels, special carburetor, etc. This very hot car was sold to a family whose teen age son was just learning to drive, and we understand that he totaled it the first week he had it.

Chris was a very self-sufficient member of the household Once when Marty Hamburger had come up from his retirement location in Florida and we were talking in the basement family room, there was a "snip—snip—snip" sound from the kitchen just upstairs. I asked Marty if he could figure out what that was. He could not, and so I revealed the answer to the mystery—it was "small boy making himself a banana sandwich." Marty was incredulous, so we went upstairs to the kitchen where Chris sat at the table, a peeled banana on a plate in front of him beside a second plate with two slices of bread, adorned with mayonnaise, and being successively covered with round slices of banana which Chris was snipping with one hand from the peeled banana on the other plate.

Chris was handy with mechanical things and tools, he ground his own valves, and at one point bought a used Covair which was immobilized because of a fly wheel problem, simply to use for parts for his Corvair. Good and varied use was made of this car before it was sold to a scrap metal dealer—our grandson Joey, for example, now has one of the bucket seats.

Chris left for Western Carolina University in Cullowhee when he graduated from high school, and had a relatively uncomplicated stay to graduation there. That institution's academic advisors were a sandwich short of a picnic, however, so I took over this role. It was here that he phoned us from a phone booth that he had trouble breathing and could not move (this turned out to be a pneumothorax, which was treatable at the local hospital). A remarkable coincidence was that Jill in Chapel Hill had a pneumothorax the same day. At Cullowhee, Chris shortly moved out of university housing and went in with a friend to share a trailer.

We were impressed with Chris' studious habits when he was home from college during the summer and on holidays, for he frequently went out in the evening, telling us that he would be at the library. It was some time later that we discovered that the "library" was actually "The Library," a beer hall and fooze ball parlor in downtown Chapel Hill. It was principally here that Chris honed his fooze ball skills, reaching an advanced stage that permitted him to compete in a few tournaments. And the legend of "The Library" persisted, for in 2004 he sent me a Father's Day card that showed on the cover a father on the phone saying "Jail? Why no, officer, there must be some mistake. Our son's at the *library!*" Inside, it read "Just curious, Dad. Have we gotten to that 'Look back and laugh' stage yet? Happy Father's Day!"

After college, Chris came home to look for work. He wanted to use his sociology major in social research, but without graduate training could find no employment. He took a job with a phonograph record company with a substantial overseas business, and was responsible for their international shipping. He moved into a pad in nearby Carrboro with a high school friend and a recently divorced book store owner. It was from this base that he met Sherry, who would become his wife.

Chris had felt particularly the void when Sam Spade, our Beagle, was put to sleep, and although we had Gideon, the Siamese cat, he liked dogs as well. He found pedigreed Siberian Husky pups advertised in Cary, and he and I drove over to inspect them. There was one shy, sweet, cuddly puppy that we could not resist, so we brought him home cradled in Chris's lap. In Chapel Hill, this puppy quickly outgrew laps. Our exploits with this amazing dog, which he named "Tosha," are chronicled elsewhere, but Chris took him when he and Sherry established their own place in Cary., where they first rented a house, then bought another a mile or so away.

Jill started out in Chapel Hill as my special buddy, and I had great fun introducing her, at the age of 8 or 9, to escargots, and remember running into "Sweet Jim" Lalanne, the fabulous UNC quarterback when I was an undergraduate, at the Pines restaurant with Jill recommending the escargots to him. Both of us also had great fun, as chronicled elsewhere, in a trip I made to Puerto Rico with her, where she quickly developed a taste for the little lobsters always at the high price end of the local restaurant menus.

As she matured, she began to show a striking tendency for independence. Not infrequently, we were met with the sentence "Id just rather do it myself." And in this, she always did whatever it was very, very well.

She continued her ballet lessons which she had begun when we were in Hopewell, NJ, with one year in Chapel Hill giving her a total of four years of instruction. She had many friends, and I recall a happy weekend on our boat with a neighbor her age, Julie Hawkinson, and her father. She became an active horsewoman, favoring a horse named Redman that became very special for her.

Jill did very well in both elementary and high schools in Chapel Hill. Her mathematical skills had always been superlative. She worked very hard in her senior year on a theme chronicling the life and contributions of Martin Luther King, Jr., and her final product was, of course, excellent.

As she proceeded through adolescence, her concern with independence increased. Somewhere in her coming of age she became less of a buddy and even more of a self-contained and self-directing person, and Daddy simply had to face the fact that his little girl was growing up.

We had helped her purchase a car when she attained a driver's license, and this aided her in her quest for independence. For one or another reason, her cars shortly needed replacement, and she had owned several by the time she was 20.

Jill proved to be a remarkable manager of money. After a short period in a rented house while she was supporting herself with an 80 mile paper route for the *Chapel Hill Newspaper,* she purchased her own little house in Hillsborough.—which she later sold, after marriage, for more than twice what she had paid for it a few years before.

It was after she had purchased her little house in Hillsborough that she decided to enroll in "The University of North Carolina at Haw River"—or, Alamance Community College. Here she quickly earned an Associate Degree in Early Child Development. She particularly enjoyed one required activity which was working with a group of physically or mentally handicapped children in nearby Burlington. Her academic work led to work as a nanny for two professional couples in succession, to whom and to whose children she quickly endeared herself.

With the children having flown the coop, Pegge and I eased our remorse with a sense of freedom. We did some things that would not have been possible if encumbered with the children. Notable were two Elderhostels, one at Lake Junaluska, NC. in an aging hotel, and the other an Old Dominion University sponsored affair in Norfolk, VA. Each of these involved multiple classes, and the Old Dominion experience was particularly memorable. We had a excellent class on the American Indian following the English settlements, and Pegge took a course in folk dancing—which attracted a filming report by the local TV station, and, given Pegge's natural grace of movement, the resulting telecast featured her in very fine form.

Chapter 26

Medical History

It was over 75 years ago, but I remember it as if it were last week. I had reached the age of 4, and in 1929 that meant my tonsils and adenoids had to come out. I was bundled up and taken to McPherson's Eye, Ear, Nose, and Throat Hospital in Durham, and the superfluous glands were exorcised. It turned out to be a treat, because for several days I feasted on ice cream.

I don't recall when it started, but throughout the eleven years in public school I was plagued with bronchial asthma. Attacks were completely debilitating, and would last for from 24 to 48 hours. They were particularly troubling when I was in high school, and I recall that one year I missed 30 days of school because of asthmatic attacks. They were less frequent in college, and my last attack was an overnight episode at the Naval Section Base at the mouth of the Mississippi River as I awaited the arrival of the PC boat to which I had been assigned in WWII. I guess that evening was a kind of good bye to childhood, for in the more than 60 years since I have not been plagued with this malady.

Twice during public school I broke an arm. The first was when I was about ten and was dared by a playmate to jump from the roof of a building some twenty feet in the air, and the second, which was a nasty compound fracture, was the result of showing off on the bars supporting swings on the school playground. This occurred during the 11th grade, my senior year, just after I had enrolled in a class in typing. Not being able to do the exercises, I was given a D in this course—the only grade I had ever received in public school that was less than an A.

My first injury in service was when I was part of the gun crew on the three inch cannon mounted on the bow of the PC boat. We were target shooting in practice while underway in the Pacific, and I got too close to the muzzle. The ringing in my ears subsided in a few weeks, but I have not been able to hear very well since then with my left ear. And now, in my 80s, I have trouble hearing as did my mother and one of my two sisters.

I have been told that a war wound qualified me for the Purple Heart, but I never applied for it. It was the result of a small lead fragment about the size of a lentil hitting my left forearm and penetrating the skin slightly, and came from the wholesale firing of guns in the air at the Okinawa anchorage when news came that the armistice had been signed in Tokyo Bay. I doused it with alcohol and removed it with a toothpick, and have been none the worse for wear—with just a small hole in my forearm that is so small I have to hunt for it.

The next experience of any significance was during my second tour of duty in the Navy, when I decided to have impacted wisdom teeth removed. This has been reported elsewhere, but will be summarized here. The dentist assigned to the Naval Academy Preparatory School was a Baltimore dentist who traditionally loosened firmly planted teeth with a hammer before extracting them. He removed three wisdom teeth—one at a time, loosened before extraction by pounding for several minutes with his little hammer. The fourth was beneath the gum surface, so we left that one alone, to be removed some 50 years later by a remarkably competent dentist.

My next encounter was with a thyroid problem that developed at the end of my employment at Princeton University. I was placed on Lugall's solution and referred to a prominent physician in Atlanta where we were headed in my acceptance of the faculty position at Emory University. This man turned out to be none other than Dr. Minor Blackford—a former Mayo Clinic internist who was sufficiently affluent from family wealth and book sales to carry only one patient a day, and always to take him or her to lunch before getting down to business. He was a direct descendant of the Blackfords of Virginia, one of whom (his mother) had written a poignant defense of the South in Civil War times, called *Mine Eyes Have Seen the Glory*.

Meeting with Dr. Blackford always turned out to be great fun, though he was a practical joker for whom fun was a personal experience, rather than necessarily that of his target. He would bum a cigarette, light it and take two puffs, then take his pulse, and exclaim "My goodness—up 20 beats a minute!"—and then frantically snuff out the cigarette. And one time when I went to him with a bad cold, he instructed me to take off all my clothes (it was January), and run around the house three times. "That will give you pneumonia—and I can cure that," he said. "But I can't do anything about your cold." The thyroid problem did not go away, so he assigned me to surgery at Emory University Hospital by a physician friend who was first and foremost a pilot in the Air National Guard, and who met me for pre—and post-surgery visits in his Air Force uniform. The operation required an unexpected four hours ("tying off bleeders," he told me), but was successful except that I lost my ability to sing—apparently from scar tissue from the tracheotomy involved. And I learned that the post-operative diet at Emory University Hospital was Coca Cola, in grateful recognition of the contributions to the hospital from the Candler family.

I was able to avoid doctors and hospitals for the next three decades, until persistent bleeding where there should have been none signaled some problem. It was not taken seriously until I pressed my doctor to take some action when I hemorrhaged at the Washington National Airport on a business trip in 1978 and decided to catch the next plane home. This time I was sent to the University hospital for the indignity of a barium enema. I will never forget the little miniskirted nurse who at the beginning of the procedure approached the table on which I, clothed only in the farce they call a hospital gown, lay and said: "I am going to play around down here for a little while, so if you are embarrassed, you can just pull this gown up over your head." The finding, by a proctologist who died a couple of years later of colon cancer, was that I had colon cancer, and needed immediate surgery.

My surgeon, a man whom I find I have also outlived and who also died of colon cancer, removed several superfluous feet of my sigmoid colon, and placed me in a room with a simple man whose side was encased in bandages. I finally asked my hospital roommate what happened, and he said that he was in bed with a friend's wife in Hillsborough when the friend came home unexpectedly, and the friend got his shotgun and shot him! "I don't think that I'll be his friend no more," he sadly mused.

After release from the hospital I was called back in for the usual six weeks' check. A blood test called a CEA was administered, and I provided an abnormally high reading, which is sometimes associated with cancer. My surgeon insisted that he must not have gotten all the cancer, and that I must return immediately for follow-up surgery. Knowing from the Love Canal work at RTI that smoking could also cause an elevated CEA, and being a heavy smoker then, I asked to be allowed to stop smoking for a week or two and return for the test, but he was insistent—and my regular physician whom I asked for a second opinion advised me to go ahead.

I reentered the hospital reluctantly, in some part because I was behind in chores at work. I was sitting on the bed in my room shortly after admission, still attired in a three piece suit, and using a dictaphone to take care of correspondence, when a feisty little 5' 6" doctor, exhibiting all the characteristics of an over-sexed bantam rooster, barged into the room with a dozen medical students in tow. After all the students were inside and dutifully arraigned behind him, he said in a loud voice: "Do you know why you are in here?" I could not resist looking very hard and straight at him and saying: "Yes—it is because I have an ass hole of a knife-happy surgeon who doesn't know how to read a CEA." The little doctor turned beet red; many of the students behind him suppressed a chuckle by putting their hands to their mouth; and the little doctor spun around and left the room without further ado, and, in a moment or two, the students followed suit. Little did he know the important lesson that he had given in the teaching hospital that day!

Nothing was found in the second surgery, but I wheeled myself into a doctor's ready room while recuperating and found, on the bulletin board, an announcement by my surgeon of a forthcoming seminar on colon cancer that he was conducting. There were 24 cells, each with a different problem. Only one was still vacant—that of a patient for whom the first surgery did not get all the cancer. When I returned for the six weeks' review, my surgeon seemed depressed, but said "At least you know now that you don't have cancer!" I left him picking his nose and looking across the hall at a shapely nurse in a miniskirt bending over a table, effectively bringing the end into sight. And, I suspect he had to make do with 23 cells for his seminar.

Having survived more than three decades since this experience, and finding that my surgeon was later promoted to the headship of his department at the hospital, I guess physicians should never underestimate the power of conducting 23 cell seminars.

And I returned to the routine care of my internist, who had provided the "second opinion" that I should go ahead immediately with the second surgery. In the first meeting with him after this event and the negative findings, he snorted: *"That was a pretty drastic thing to do on the basis of an elevated CEA!"* At that point, I decided prudence demanded that I locate a new personal physician. A physician friend at the University, who had been a cohort in a number of my research studies, recommended a most capable woman in private practice, and I moved to her care until she decided to retire to give full time to her family.

I learned following the experience with my colon cancer that it was not the first in my family, having hit several cousins, and that there are hereditary links. I hope my children and grandchildren never forget that it is particularly important to have regular checkups after age 40, for it is not the kind of legacy I would like to leave them.

It was about the time of retirement in 1988 that I stopped smoking. I began this habit when I was 16, and for many years was a three pack a day smoker (which accounted, I told my friends, for my colon cancer). I had moved to a pipe supplement at middle age, and had moved from cigarettes and pipe to cigars the last several years, finding the latter deeply satisfying. But having read about the dangers of smoking, and swearing off reading as a result many times, I decided upon retirement to bite the bullet and quit. Cold turkey worked, although the smell of cigarette smoke was tantalizing for a time—like the next dozen years.

It was some time later—just after retirement—that I had moved to a physician operating a near-by Urgent Care walkin service. Although he had a penchant for outrageous charging, Medicare now took care of most of that, and he seemed to have a considerable amount of common sense. He convinced me to take a pneumonia shot following a bout with this problem, saying that if I did I would never have pneumonia again—although I took the shot, and have had several recurrences since then. I also found that his father had died unexpectedly of a heart attack—and he sprang into action when I noted one time that I had chest pains and insisted that he call an ambulance to transport me to a hospital. I was sure that the doctor was over-reacting, but given the stakes, decided to go along. I had seen a Durham physician earlier who specialized in heart problems and was much impressed by her, so I had asked for her before being transported to Durham General. My heart specialist was waiting, and stayed with me the hour and a half that I languished in ER I learned later that my short stay in the ER was because (1) there was the possibility that I had a serious and urgent problem, and because (2) the attending physician had greased the skids. But several days and countless tests later, the heart monitor was removed and I was discharged with instructions to watch my diet for gas—producing foods. It was at this point that I left the urgent care doctor and returned to the physician who had referred me for the two colonectomies. I figured that he was the lessor of the several evils, and that I had learned not to trust him explicitly.

The colon cancer event triggered a series of periodic invasions of privacy called "colonoscopy,." involving insertion of a flexible lighted tube that permitted visual inspection of the sigmoid colon. The first time I encountered this indignity was in a cluttered basement room at the University hospital, but my second experience was in a private physician's office. Just at the point that I had accommodated 40 centimeters of tube there was a power failure. Thus, I waited, tube in place, for some forty minutes until power was restored. But the result was the removal of five non-malignant polyps, and the installation at the physician's office of an emergency electricity generator.

This procedure (the colonoscopy, not the generator installation) has been repeated every two or three years, each time involving the removal of several non-malignant polyps. In only one instance has there been any problem. It was three days after a procedure and during a visit, as part of a research contract, to the Morehouse School of Medicine with a physician cohort that I awoke in the Atlanta motel with massive hemorrhaging. I phoned my cohort who was staying at the same motel and told him that I had to break a rule and seek his medical advice. It was to stay near a bathroom, ingest only liquids, and stay as inactive physically as possible. Thus, I lunched on Jello, and we completed a day of interviews with the medical school faculty, returning that night to the Raleigh-Durham airport. The problem turned out to be one that occurred rarely—polyps were usually exorcised in the process of the colonoscopy, and sometimes bleeding could occur following the polyp removal.

It was in 1995 when I had reached the age of 70 that I took some younger family to the North Carolina Zoo in Asheboro. It was after this that grandson Joey told a neighbor housewife about our visit. She said she had been, too, and her favorite place there was the birdhouse. Joey, then 6, confided that his favorite place was not that, but the aviary. The trip was significant for me, though, because at the end of the day when we caught a crowded Zoo bus back to the parking lot, a pregnant lady offered me her seat. It was at that moment that I began to feel old.

In 2001 I was returning from a trip to the Carrboro Post Office and waiting for the left turn from the Chapel Hill 15/501 by-pass to Elliot Road and the Harris Teeter grocery store when I had the sensation of the car spinning wildly. Attempts to move were futile, so I sat it out, and the feeling passed in a few moments. I then continued to the grocery store, but the spinning returned as I was checking out with a half-gallon of milk and some essentials. Anna the bag lady, who has since become a personal friend, saw that a chair was provided, and the man behind me in the checkout line turned out to be a physician who quickly called an ambulance and the hospital on his cell phone. The usual seven hour wait in the ER passed with only occasional nausea, and after many tests, including an MRI where I was told to remove my watch but where lack of other instructions resulted in 35 credit cards in my pocket being degaussed, I was sent to a patient's room for observation. I was put on an IV, which I found when I awakened the next morning had leaked and left me in a considerable puddle. A chatty nurse, whom I learned was the wife of a favored cook at a local five-star restaurant, said she would fix this immediately, and brought several towels and placed them over the puddle on the waterproof mattress. This was 5 A.M. I was discharged at 4 PM that day, leaving the bed still in its soggy state. No routine change of bed clothes had been made, and the towels, while absorbent, had exceeded their capacity. One of the many attending physicians speculated that I had had a small stroke, or Transient Ischemic Attack ("TIA"), prescribed daily aspirin, and took me off Vioxx which my internist had added a couple of years earlier for arthritis. It was about two years later that the Food and Drug Administration announced the finding that Vioxx was associated with stroke and heart attacks, and took the drug off the market. I accepted pressure from an ambulance-chasing law firm in Texas to join a class-action suit against the drug manufacturer, but dropped out when I received several dozen pages of medical history to fill out and doctor's signatures to get.

Although I did not recognize it immediately, a consequence of the TIA was, I believe, an inability to put words together smoothly when speaking to groups. I had never had any trouble in large or small classes, or in presentations to a handful of people or to a group of several thousand, as when I introduced Arthur Jensen at a forum of the American Educational Research Association in Boston. My ability to put words on paper after the TIA seemed less threatened, although I often have to come back later to find the right word. And where I had enjoyed simply winging it before an audience with an outline or an idea, I now found that if I address a group—as I did for Charles Edge's funeral, or in the several presentations I have made to the Triangle Stamp Club—I have to write down my speech and read it, or suffer unexpected and embarrassing inabilities to find the words I want to use. I am also finding increasingly an inability to remember familiar names of people and places, and many times in writing this account I have had to come back and fill in a name later when it suddenly reappeared in consciousness.

It was when I reached the age of 75 that I was diagnosed with type II diabetes. This was controlled by drugs, until a period where nausea from some other source kept me from eating for a week, and I stupidly continued the diabetes medication. I ended up with hypoglycemia, which put me out and required Pegge to have the 911 boys carry me to the hospital, where I languished for the usual seven and a half hours in the Emergency Room. My problem had been eased when I was given a glucose injection by the EMT people prior to their depositing me in the ER, and the hospital put me in a pricey room for observation and returned me to normal diet and medication. And this time there were no hospital problems except for a roommate, endowed with a voice that would easily carry several miles, who was being held because he would return to drinking if released. He would not agree to that stipulation, consequently and continually applying some choice invectives to the hospital staff. Medicare was once again soaked in my case, starting with a $525 charge for the ambulance ride to the hospital 4 miles away, and the hospital probably got sufficient finance for a new wing from their varied and creative charges.

The colonectomy in 1978 surely saved my life, but it led to my next serious hospitalization. Some 15 years later, I began to see one, then a second, operational hernia emerge in my tummy. For some ten years they were retractable, meaning that they could be pushed back in and were not serious or requiring attention. But in early 2006, the larger hernia of the two came out and could not be pressed back into place. Intense pain forced me to go to the emergency room where the UNC hospital's usual sequel to the Keystone Kops took place—the highlight being a 400 pound nurse catheterizing me with a tube several sizes too large. I was variously Xrayed and administered some other costly diagnostic devices to assure that my Medicare would make my visit profitable for the hospital, treated with an IV diet, and allowed to go home for a couple of weeks before surgical repair could be performed., and with an appointment for same with some flunkie at that hospital.

Having risked too much before at that hospital, I sought out my own surgeon—a most capable man who was a graduate of the US Naval Academy, and who operated at Durham Regional Hospital, now a property of the Duke University Medical empire. The ventral hernia repair was supposed to be an ambulatory procedure, but some problems—I suspect muscle damage from the two prior colon probes—required the insertion of a mesh and a stay of two nights in the hospital. The minor surgery turned out to have major complications, however, for after about 10 days instead of healing it began to hemorrhage considerably, requiring emptying the blood from my shoes and daily trips back to the surgeon for a couple of weeks, and leaving me with a second navel—proof, I told Mike, my minister son, that I have been born again! My surgeon and his assistant saw the humor in this observation, but I don't think Mike did.

It has subsequently come as no surprise that hospitals are frequently the scene of gross mistakes, and are hotbeds of infections of various kinds. I am quite sure that care for the sick is secondary, and that their primary purpose is to enhance themselves and provide an increasing financial base for their staffs. There were confirming revelations in the Raleigh *News and Observer* in October of 2006 that the CEO of the UNC Health Care System had his annual salary of $489,030 augmented with a bonus of $110,010, with the total bonuses for hospital executives and lower level managers also receiving bonuses. Outside investigation revealed the total bonuses paid in 2006 to UNC Hospital staff were at least $2,531,256. This prompted one of my published letters to the editor (provided in the appendix under the title "Well-Cared For Pay") that ended with the sentence "It is nice to know that our state hospital includes its own executives in its mission to care for the people of North Carolina." But this record was dwarfed when the *News and Observer* reported that the CEO of North Carolina's Blue Cross and Blue Shield was awarded a salary and bonus of $3.1 million in 2006. That resulted in another letter, which the old *N and O* also published, and which is also included in the appendix. The letter about the UNC bonuses may have had some effect (although I was not alone), for on May 24, 2007, the *News and Observer* reported, in an item on page 1 of the business section, that the board that oversees the UNC Health Care System "has decided to cut executive bonuses after harsh public criticism last summer about financial windfalls paid to leaders of the state-supported system." But this curable romantic has just learned that his raise this year considered the prior salary plus the bonus plus a mid-year adjustment increase as the base for his annual increase, reporting it as 7.2% when in actuality it was 41.1% more than his formal salary the year before. Some fights can't be won!

As I write this, I have reached the tender age of 82, and take 13 prescription drugs, and several over-the-counter drugs, each day. My hearing has deteriorated to the point that Pegge is constantly frustrated trying to speak to me, and that most of what goes on aurally on television is like the noise of the fighting cocks in Fajardo. I am told that I am in remarkable health for my age, although I get winded when I walk up the handicapped ramp to the rear door of our house, and find that the only thing I need to do when I want to live dangerously is to go out without my cane. And, although the oft-cited characteristic of old age applies to me ("everything I have either hurts or won't work"), I am most certainly doing much better than I deserve, given a lifetime of bad habits.

The reader can readily understand why I lost my awe of physicians long before getting several million dollars to study them. I have been fortunate in having had five that I totally respect and trust, the last one of which is my current personal physician. And although it pains me to acknowledge it, four of these five are female. Like the lesson I learned from the 90 pound pilot with her long blonde hair in curls who wrestled the big Fairchild turbojet from Jackson, Alabama, into Hartsfield Airport in Atlanta, I have to believe that our prejudices against women in professional work roles serve to screen out all but the very best when it comes to the professions that have long been male-dominated.

Chapter 27

Inlaws

Pegge's father and mother were, understandably of course, rather remarkable people as is she. Although ardent Republicans (her father had been Republican Mayor Pro Tem in Graham, NC, and her mother could never believe that Nixon did anything wrong), they were much younger than my parents, and filled with a youthful exuberance for life. In their home in Graham, they had organized a tennis club and provided land on a lot behind their house for a first-class lighted tennis court. The impetus for this was a physician at Duke who advised my father-in-law to find some diversion that would help him get his mind off his work, and tennis seemed a likely option. Pegge's parents were also ardent bridge players, and we spent many happy hours in the early years of our marriage playing bridge when we visited.

Pegge's mother, Nell, was one of those remarkable women who always looked a great deal younger than her age. Once when we went out together in Graham, we were mistaken for man and wife. Pegge had a resemblance to her, and people assumed that she was Pegge.

When we were married, Pegge's father, Herman, was an agent for Imperial Life Insurance Company of Asheville, NC, and worked out of nearby Burlington. The company was later acquired by Western & Southern Life Insurance Company in Ohio, and Herman was promoted to Training Manager, with responsibility for training new agents across the state. After a couple of years in this role, he was offered a position as manager of the district office in Wilmington, NC., which he accepted. Wilmington's most famous athlete, Michael Jordan, was merely a gleam in his father's eyes at that time, but Herman wrote policies on other sports notables from Wilmington such as Roman Gabriel, Sonny Jorgenson, and Chris Hamburger. Gabriel purchased a policy from Herman as a present for his mother, with her as beneficiary, but insisted on a border of black for the policy document. Herman complied by sending his secretary out for some India ink and a stylus, and delivered the amended policy personally to the purchaser, who was quite pleased with the result. And as for Michael Jordan: we all remembered the tall high school basketball hero who had to stoop to wash dishes at Shorty's Restaurant his senior year in high school.

After the move to Wilmington in 1955, Pegge's mother Nell became an inveterate fisherwoman, going out for hours on a pier in all kinds of weather and winning a handsome annual trophy from the New Hanover Fishing Club for several years for the largest king mackerel caught from a pier by a woman. Her father was an avid hunter, and generally kept a half-dozen or so hunting dogs which he meticulously trained, achieving a well-earned reputation for excellence in this art. I remember that he sold one small mixed breed dog with an excellent reputation to another hunter for $1,000.

Nell Morris with Prize King Mackerel, Wrightsville Beach, NC, 1965

Herman Morris, Returning from Sea on the Beachcomber, 1968

Herman loved his dogs. The dogs he worked with were seldom a particular breed, but were bred from other dogs that had been particularly proficient at hunting. Although most were hounds of one mix or another, they were a strange lot, and they were usually kept in a pen behind his house. Herman was a hard taskmaster in training and treating these dogs: discipline for a foolish mistake in hunting was accomplished by shooting the dog with bird shot, and if they barked at night, he could be particularly rough on them. But they seemed to love him as much as he loved them, and I can remember the obvious joyful excitement they exhibited when they were loaded into the back of the old car he used for hunting trips.

One dog I remember well was Blackie, a small longhaired black dog with a few white spots, whose ancestry defied any valid description, but who was extremely proficient when it came to finding rabbits and chasing them into shotgun range. At one time there was also Big Red, a large hound that had to be separated at feeding time to permit the other dogs to have a share, and two beagle type dogs from the same litter, whom he named Bugle and Bugle Ann from their sonorous bay when on a scent. The boys and I had many a happy hunt with him, and although we occasionally had to come in with a dog missing, it was usually found the next day by someone in the area who found the dog and called the number on its collar. And on a day's hunt, Herman would take a lunch of Vienna sausage, sardines, pork and beans, and crackers. I can remember sitting on a log with him about noon one day while the dogs worked the surrounding territory, sharing the lunch from the tins, with his comment "This food is better'n what you could get at the Waldorf-Astoria!" It was at moments like this that he was sublimely happy.

Herman was a good cook, and his dishes were true soul food. I recall, however, trying to get him to eat eggs Benedict which were a special talent of mine, and he could not get up the courage to try them. And one time when we went out to eat at a Mexican restaurant, his dish involved a flour tortilla, which incensed him greatly: he called the waiter and spent several minutes trying, in spite of the language barrier, to tell him that the bread served was uncooked dough, and being uncooked it was inedible. This was finally resolved by the waiter returning it to the kitchen and grilling the flour tortilla.

Herman was also an avid sports fan in addition to hunting and cooking gourmet Southern food, to the extent that on Saturday afternoons when a number of games would be broadcast or televised, he would have a second TV set tuned to another station, and several radios each following a different game. His wife Nell put up with this nicely, but began to feel that she should show a little interest of her own in sports, and decided to sit with him one Saturday and watch the sportscasts.

The main TV had a collegiate game on, and there was a spectacular play where the quarterback released a long pass, and the receiver artfully dodged several tackles and scored. This was a deciding touchdown, and the cameras showed the stadium gone wild as my father-in-law slapped his thighs and made loud happy sounds himself. But then, the telecast showed the customary replay, whereupon Nell exclaimed excitedly: "Look, Herman, he's doing it again!" Needless to say, she somehow got back to her fishing, leaving Herman with his multiple inputs on game days.

Their residence in Wilmington put us about five miles from the beach. Before we brought our cabin cruiser from New Jersey, many happy hours were spent fishing or exploring the islands along the coast in a small outboard motor boat named the "Miss Jill," after our daughter. Outings were usually exciting, but one time a metal detector being used signaled a find that we hoped was Blackbeard's buried treasure, but instead was a very rusty anchor, on which Jill cut her hand badly, requiring a quick trip for emergency stitches. But most of the expeditions resulted in gathering crabs and clams, or blow fish, groupers, salt water trout, or other fish that were plentiful in that area. On one occasion, one of us hooked a small sand shark, which pulled like a Mack truck before we finally landed it. And then there was the time that Sam, our beagle, snapped at a fishing lure dangling from a rod, embedding the hook firmly in her lips, and requiring a dash to a vet for its removal. Poor Sam, normally a happy little dog, was thoroughly subdued by this experience.

A family ritual that we particularly enjoyed was an oyster roast, local style. This involved getting a bed of hot coals, putting a piece of ½ inch thick sheet iron over it, shoveling several pecks of well washed oysters onto the sheet iron when it was almost glowing red, and covering the pile of oysters with wet burlap. The oysters were done when their shells cracked open a bit. As we all grew older, the oyster roast was replaced by the easier procedure of steaming them in a large pot, and I can remember easily downing a couple of pecks at one long sitting.

Herman was from a large family—in fact, he was the seventh son of a seventh son, a distinction which kept him in some kind of awe of himself. He was particularly attached to his older brother Claude, who was also our favorite uncle, and who shared Herman's love for hunting and hunting dogs. Claude purchased large tracts of land near his home in Troy, NC, and in the mountains south of Roanoke, Virginia (on which lay the spring that marked the start of the Dan River) and used these lands for special hunting expeditions. Both had century-old houses, which he kept in sufficient repair for himself and his hunting companions to camp out in overnight, and he, like his brother Herman, was a first class cook if one did not expand the boundaries beyond rural North Carolina. I recall going on a deer hunt at this North Carolina property, and sitting around a pot belly stove in the evening where a pot of squirrel head stew was bubbling, and which would shortly go over the hoe cakes he prepared in a cast iron griddle on the same stove. He was a versatile raconteur, and could regale us for hours with colorful stories about people he had known, or unusual situations he had experienced.

My last hunt with Claude was a three day affair at his Virginia property, with Claude, Herman, and a friend of Claude's. We were after both turkeys and deer, both being plentiful on that property, but had no luck. Claude was 98 at this time, and negotiated the hilly terrain with a rifle and a shotgun as if he were a teenager. Claude died in 2006 at the age of 103, and my preacher son Mike, who was then the minister of the church that Claude belonged to and who idolized Claude and his wife Villie as we did, preached one of the most sincere and finest funerals imaginable. The text of this sermon is included in the appendix, for it is an important family history document.

One other member of my in-laws' family became an important involvement in my retirement years. This was Nell's younger sister, Elizabeth (or "Libby"), for whom I assumed power of attorney in 1999 when she was 85. This involvement has been documented in Chapter 31, Retirement.

Pegge's mother had fallen and broken her hip in 1997, and although she had good surgical repair, suffered from other problems, most of which were probably associated with chemotherapy following a bout with cancer a number of years earlier. Following the broken hip, she was in considerable pain from a fractured disc in her spine, and entered into a terminal illness in 1999. She was placed in a nursing home, and died shortly after on June 17, 1999.

On the morning of Pegge's mother's funeral, her father fell and hit his head on the baseboard of the bedroom. This seemed inconsequential at the time. But on the day following Nell's funeral, which was Father's Day, we were unable to arouse Herman. He was taken to the local hospital and, never regaining consciousness, died a week later, on June 24, 1999. It turned out that he had a brain tumor that hemorrhaged from his fall when he got up the morning of the funeral. Pegge had always been very close to her family, and in spite of their politics, they had been best friends for me. The double loss in such a short time was hard on both of us, but particularly on Pegge, and on her brother Marty.

But Pegge's father left a rather remarkable document: he wrote, and self-published, an autobiography entitled *A Seventh Son of a Seventh Son*. This was the principal impetus for a similar effort by Pegge's brother, Marty, and for this account of some of the more curious or nicer things that I think I remember, or that I believe were instructive.

Chapter 28

Pets

A word of warning: many of the accounts in this chapter have been provided earlier when they were an integral part of our activity at the time described. But to assure proper treatment of this part of our life *en famille*, an attempt is made to cover the most memorable aspects of our pets. Although we did not go so far as my Aunt Stella and Uncle Eddards, who had variously such housepets as a duck (never successfully toilet trained) and a pig (quickly trained, and a bedfellow with the little ones), our pets were significant in their impact on me.

Shortly after I was born, my father returned to the University for a teaching credential, and we moved in with my maternal grandmother who had a large house in Graham, NC. My grandmother had two cats that immediately became a large part of my life.

One was a large white tom cat named the Papa Cat. This magnificent animal was proficient in utterly defeating any dog that dared to venture into its territory, to the extent that I remember dogs crossing over to the other side of the street when passing our house to avoid any possible contact with the Papa Cat. New neighbors moved in on several occasions, bringing with them fierce cat-hating dogs, and inevitably they would come over and warn my grandmother that her cats were not safe. She would thank the people for their concern, but chuckle quietly to herself. The papa cat never let her down, and I recall a neurotic Labrador with a badly torn ear next door.

The other cat was a gray calico cat with a white face that was named the Monkey Cat (that's him with the little guy on the cover). Although not endowed with the same combination of canine hatred and combative skills as the Papa Cat, he was a loyal companion.

Years later, my grandmother had died, and the cats had predeceased her. Some family acquaintance came through town with a one-eyed dog that their German Shephard bitch had produced after contact in Canada with a male wolf. The puppy seemed innocent enough, and the one eye made him an endearing companion. We adopted him, and named him Popeye.

My two sisters were below school age at the time, and played in the front yard. Our house was on North Main Street in Graham, a busy thoroughfare. Popeye would attend the two religiously when they were out front, keeping between them and the street. Should one wander in that direction, Popeye would grab them by their dress hems and pull them back toward the house.

In spite of his intelligence and gentle nature, Popeye was known by neighbors to be half wolf, and they were most uneasy about this. We reluctantly gave him to country cousins in Bladenboro, whose house was on the edge of Deep Swamp. After a few months, Popeye disappeared into the swamp, but could be heard baying occasionally. Apparently he succumbed to the call of the wild—either that or entanglement with a little female wolf.

But the pets that we had as adults were also important parts of our lives. In our later years we developed allergies to pets, and have not had to put up with cats that shed or produce hair balls on the carpet, or with dogs that protect us from the men who come to steal our garbage, but leave several generations of fleas in our carpets. But this was not always so.

After our apartments in Atlanta and Greensboro which were home when we were first married, our Navy tenure at Bainbridge afforded a house that could accommodate pets. A lieutenant commander's wife had a pedigreed Persian cat that had apparently not been too choosy in the cats with which it associated, and had produced a litter with one solid white and one solid black cat—both long hairs. They were offered to us, and we accepted them eagerly, naming them "Pomp" and "Circumstance." They grew quickly to be fine cats, though with some eccentricities.

The front of our house was about 20 feet from the main highway from Havre de Grace to Port Deposit, with a fence protecting us from the road. The cats would amuse themselves by chasing cars as they passed. A second characteristic that surprised us was that they would fight each other over grapefruit rinds, with the same zest that other cats would expend on a can of tuna.

When they were about six months old, we decided to take them to a vet for the necessary shots. This turned out to be most unfortunate, for they both contracted distemper from another cat that had been treated that day by the vet. Pomp died, but Circumstance had a slow but sure recovery. We renamed him "Spooky" after the black cat in the Smoky Stover comics, and he became a loyal friend.

When we moved from Bainbridge to New York City, there was no possibility for pets, so Spooky became part of my parent's household in North Carolina. Spooky adapted nicely to this new environment, but was always happy to see us. Spooky lived to the ripe old age of 19, when he developed some sores that would not heal, and had to be put to sleep.

It was not until we had moved to Hopewell, N.J. that we had another pet. Jill was still of kindergarten age, and Mike and Chris were in elementary school, when we acquired a gray male baby rabbit. We had been told they were easy to housebreak, and indeed found this to be so—"Tom" trained quickly to a newspaper on the floor of the garage which was enclosed as part of the house. We gave him the run of the house, and I delighted at seeing the expression on a visitor's face when old Tom once hopped into the living room and situated himself on his lap.

Unfortunately, as Tom matured, he also became as horny as only rabbits can become. He became testy when touched, and demonstrated acts of rebellion such as taking bites out of our shoes and digesting any shoe laces from footwear left in closets. We placed him with friends in the country who had a cage to keep him in when we went south for a week, and when we returned we learned the sad news that dogs had gotten to the cage and had chewed access to it and to Tom.

Another pet that was an important but brief part of our lives was a black kitten that for some reason that I have forgotten we named Yom Kipper, or "Kippie." We were still living in Hopewell, but I was commuting to North Carolina to help with the organization of the Regional Education Laboratory to be established in Durham by Everett Hopkins, then a Vice President of Duke University. Kippie was the runt of a litter from a cat of nondescript heritage owned by Hopkins' secretary. Kippie was not well when I went to the airport with her to fly back from Raleigh/Durham to Newark, and I recall putting her on the ticket counter while I put luggage on the scales. Kippie lay perfectly still, and so attracted the ticket agent that she let her fly sleeping in my lap, instead of encasing her in a pet container.

Kippie quickly grew into a healthy and affectionate cat. When we bought the boat at Barnegat, we frequently spent the weekend living and working on it, and on one occasion shortly before leaving for North Carolina, took Kippie with us. During the night, she apparently jumped ship, and, getting frightened in the strange surroundings, wandered off. The wife of the marina owner later reported hearing a cat under a pile of scrap lumber in the boatyard, but we never found her in spite of vigorous efforts.

When our children were little, we were generally pet free.—although I recall a gerbil that escaped from its cage in the apartment we first lived in when we moved from Atlanta to Greensboro, making any peaceful sleep difficult until a few months later when we found his body in the well of the floor furnace. But when Mike reached teen age, he expressed interest in owning a dog. From a breeder, we acquired a golden beagle puppy which Mike named Sam. Sam was a female, of course, but we kept the name, simply adding a second word: to make the name "Sam Spade."

Sam was a house dog, with all the tender affection qualities that mark the beagle breed. My father-in-law suspected that Sam might be made into a good hunting dog, and we took her out with the other dogs on one hunt. She made some error, and he administered the usual discipline for a mistake—a bit of bird shot. Sam was totally traumatized by this, and from then on would hide in the closet either at the sight of a gun, or when inclement weather produced thunder. In fact, she became a useful predictor of approaching rainstorms, for she could hear distant thunder before we could, and would dash for a closet and, trembling, put her head down in a back corner.

Sam lived a long, though apprehensive, life. When Mike got his first church, Sam went with him, and became well known among the members of his congregation. Sam came back to live with us when Mike married, and lived to the ripe old age of 18, at which point arthritis prevented her from ascending or descending the stairs in our split-level house on Holly Lane in Chapel Hill. Sam also had problems with flatulence, and although never permitted on the furniture, would sneak on when left unattended—and leaping off if we came into the room. When her arthritis reached the point that she would whine for a period, we had her put to sleep with some reluctance, and buried her under a large piece of granite in our back yard.

Our next pet was a Siamese cat that we named Gideon, after the bad cat in Pinocchio. Gideon proved to be anything but a bad cat: instead, he was loving and affectionate, and took great pleasure in laying in Pegge's lap and sniffing her perfume or dusting powder. These two bonded to the extent that when Gideon failed to come into the house one morning, and we found him dead in the gutter a block away, Pegge never quite recovered, and swore never to own a cat again.

But one day a huge Irish Wolfhound wandered into our yard, and indicated that it planned to stay. It had no collar but the remnant of a leash trailing, and although we tried to find the owner, we believe that it belonged to someone passing through town who had had to abandon it when it escaped. This dog, which we named "Shannon," quickly began to exhibit several unusual traits: it could leap over fences or walls that were eight feet high; it could climb trees to a point a dozen feet up, if prompted by a squirrel, and it could understand any command given: i.e., "Get the paper;" "Squirrel;" "Lie down and go to sleep;" "Get me when the pot starts to boil."

Shannon was a free spirit, and enjoyed roaming the neighborhood. She was picked up several times by the dogcatcher, but after deciding that she did not want to stay in the new emclosure, would simply climb or leap over the fence and come home. Shannon moved with my daughter Jill when she first left home and had a little house in the country, but either wandered away or was taken by someone (Jill had to leave Shannon alone at her house during the day).

The next animal was a Siberian Husky for Chris, that he named Tosha. We purchased her from a breeder in Cary, and I recall this little frightened puppy sleeping in Chris's lap as we drove home after picking her up. Tosha, however, quickly lost the puppy qualities, and proved to have a mind of her own to an extent that would have made Queen Elizabeth a pussy cat.

Tosha was too big to keep in the house, and once outside, she would disappear for five or more days, before returning. On one of these occasions, she was sighted five miles away. But she was arrogant, and seemed to consider us people inferior but necessary evils, who had to be put up with occasionally when hungry.

She demonstrated what she was nicely one time when I found her on Pegge's best comforter, asleep with muddy foot prints in abundance where she had first turned around three times. To get her attention, I beat her with a chain. She simply glared at me, and went to the door to be let out; I assumed that she would be gone for several days, and indeed she was—but first, she ate the ends off of the rubber bumpers on my Fiat X1-9 in retaliation. But when Chris moved out, he took Tosha with him.

With the children all gone and with our allergies, we have been petless since. But the quality of experiences we had with these pets may account in large part for the children's lifestyles now. Chris has maintained two dogs since marriage; Jill has had dogs and several cats, the latest a long haired cat named "PC" for "privileged character" and a large and very friendly white dog. Mike and Karen have a virtual menagerie, featuring birds and cats.

Chapter 29

My Love with Means of Movement

From the time my father brought home a new Ford four-door rag top touring car when I was two and a half years old in 1927, I have been addicted to means of transport. My grandfather had the desiccated remains of an early Model T in one of his barns on his Bladen County farm, and when he found me brushing the hay off the engine compartment in the early 1930s told me I could have it if I wanted it. I began to dream of vehicles I could make with the parts just as soon as I grew enough to know how to do it. In the meantime, I busied myself in school by drawing pictures of submarines, trains, and airplanes in my notebooks as the teachers lectured.

Throughout life, I had considerable empathy for the frog in the Walt Disney version of *The Wind in the Willows,* where the frog bounced vigorously on his bottom in uncontrollable glee with the anticipation that he would own a motorcar. Our next door neighbor in Graham had an eloquent garaged 12 cylinder Chrysler, and I used to sit in it and pretend I was driving all over the U.S.

There will be some replication in this section, for it deals with some events previously reported in other contexts, but which are assembled now in order to treat the topic adequately.

My first car was a well-worn 1927 Ford that I acquired in the summer of 1941 for the hefty sum of $25.00. It had some problems—for example, two or three complete revolutions of the steering wheel were required for a 90 degree turn—but it ran like a rabbit, and I was in seventh heaven owning my own car at the tender age of 16. Unfortunately, I ran it across a bridge at high speed (30 MPH) and hit a bump that threw the battery against the frame, shorting out the battery, and burning a dangerous appearing hole in the frame. This prompted me to sell it—for, you guessed it, $25.00.

For our planned honeymoon trip from Graham to Miami, I borrowed my father's 1937 Chevrolet. The year was 1946, and the wartime rubber shortage still affected tires. We started out on four retreads, each of which had to be replaced by the time we reached Atlanta, and only retreads were available as replacements. We decided at that point to honeymoon there, having spent the money we had counted on for expenses in Miami on black market retreads.

Our first car was a 1947 Ford—purchased new for something under $600. It served us faithfully in Atlanta, Greensboro, and Bainbridge, but proved to be a handicap when we moved in 1949 to NYC for graduate study. When we parked it outside our 3rd Avenue apartment, the neighborhood kids would break into it and play the radio until the battery ran down, and NYC enacted an alternate street parking law that meant one had to find a space on the other side of the street each evening for the following day, a process that sometime required hours. So, leaving Pegge in our apartment in early 1950, I bit the bullet and started driving South, stopping at each Ford dealership to try to sell it until I reached Graham, where Charlie Ivey, the hometown friend who sold us the car, agreed to take it off my hands for a reasonable amount. It left us stuck in New York City, and both of us began to long for the sight of a pine tree.

We replaced it after a carless year with a new 1951 Ford when we moved with my major professor in graduate study to Middletown, NY., where Pegge was the office secretary to Dr. Super, my Department Chairman, and I was a research assistant on his 20 year follow-up study of the vocational development of Middletown's eighth and ninth grade boys. This car provided reliable transportation around Middletown and on trips to family in North Carolina, surviving a series of driving lessons for a fellow student involved in the research project, one Harry Beilin, a very self-centered bachelor in his mid thirties, of Brooklyn origin, who simply could not start a turn until HE (and not the front of the car) was at the corner—resulting in many near misses of oncoming cars, telephone poles, and the like. But the car remained intact, and continued to serve us well when we moved to Princeton in 1952 and on into the fall of 1954. In that year, though protesting with half-hour needs for replenishment of the radiator, it provided a haul for the trailer that we used to move to Atlanta.

It was getting old and cranky, however, and one day on a whim I visited the Ford place in Decator, Georgia. When I started to leave, the old Ford would not start, and a crafty salesman offered to accept it in a trade for a beautiful special Ford in the showroom—one that had been built for the Atlanta Police Department in an agreement gone sour. Pegge was upset that I had made such a purchase without consulting her, but its uniqueness was an asset.

At that time, the Atlanta police had two vice squads, Squad "A" and Squad "B," that competed on weekends by racking up points for particular kinds of arrests—e.g., 10 points for floating crap games, 50 points for breaking and entering, 20 points for prostitution, etc. Records would be kept for a period of several months, and the team with the most points would be treated to a steak dinner by the team with the fewer points. The competition was indeed vigorous, for the team captains were found not only to be burning up the streets with cars at full throttle and burning out transmissions in the process, but also the captains had ordered two particularly "hot" cars to be built for them at the Ford Motor Company plant in nearby Hapeville. When the chief got wind of this, he "modified" the order, substituting two six cylinder standard Fords with automatic transmissions. One of the previously ordered cars was ready for delivery when the cancellation order went out, and this was the car I had purchased.

It was indeed a beauty—essentially a 1957 model, it would do 90 miles an hour in second gear without much effort. The engine was not only supercharged, but the transmission was specially built to withstand unusual stress. It would pass everything but a gas station, and proved to be great fun to drive. I kept it through the move to UNC-Greensboro and on to ETS-Princeton. It's demise came when I was alone and carelessly drove too fast in Bucks County, PA, one evening in a snow storm, and put it into a telephone pole at something like 50 MPH. The first contact was with a guy wire holding the pole up, and this sliced through the front bumper and radiator before it broke, making an entry for the pole to the engine compartment. The engine came in under my feet. It was night time, and the headlights were still on, but crossed like defective eyes, and I recall sitting in dead silence at the wheel with my feet on the engine, the soles on my shoes smelling of burning rubber, the telephone pole growing out of the hood, the broken guy wire swinging back and forth, and the snow flakes falling in the crazy X pattern formed by the headlights. Save for some bruises on my arms, I was unhurt.

I considered the car a total wreck, and sold it for $25.00 to a salvage firm in Trenton, N.J. I learned later that that firm had purchased a similar four-door 1957 Ford that had rear end damage, and had cut the two bodies in two and welded the undamaged parts together to form a drivable car. But like the Atlanta chief of police who had the vice squad captains accept something more modest, I purchased a four cylinder Canadian-built Studebaker which could go from zero to 30 miles an hour in 60 seconds. That car turned out to be the swan song for Studebaker, that only a few years before had produced the Avanti, a car I had lusted after.

After running the wheels off of the little Studebaker, I purchased a full size Dodge from the dealer in Langhorne, PA, with acres of cars. Pegge still had her trusty Falcon that we had purchased in Greensboro. The Dodge and Falcon shortly came back to North Carolina with us when I moved from ETS Princeton to the new ETS field office in Durham. I drove the Dodge down to North Carolina, and caught a bus back to Hopewell; there, we packed the family into the Falcon, and drove to the boat at Iggy's Marina. We moved to North Carolina on the boat, and I returned to New Jersey and retrieved the Falcon.

Work was such that I had little time for savoring cars in the following years in Chapel Hill. Pegge gave her Falcon to Mike when he left for college. We had a series of small cars now—(1) a Toyota (purchased with almost 100,000 miles on it, driven for a second 100,000, given to Mike to replace the Falcon, who drove it for another 50,000 miles, and then sold by Mike to a member of his church for more than I had paid for it; (2) a Dodge Colt, principally for Pegge, to replace the Falcon given to Mike; (3) a used Mazda, about which I remember only the plaid seat upholstery, and (4) back to self indulgence—an orange Fiat X-19, a mid-engine convertible.

The Fiat turned out to be a most reliable car, in spite of the intelligence that said "Fiat" meant "Fix it again, Tony,' with the major problem being its low to the ground characteristic—such that I joked that the only graceful way to get into it was to sit down on the pavement by the open door, and slide in. It took us to Canada, where we quickly found that there were no Fiats or Fiat dealers, and provided many happy top-down excursions. Accumulating 125,000 miles on it, and feeling that it was getting old, I sold it to a young lady who worked at RTI, who enjoyed it for a week or so before having an oil pump failure and trying to drive on in spite of it. I canceled the loan I had given her and took the car back, placing it in son Chris's garage in Raleigh, planning some day that he or I would replace or restore the engine. But we never got around to that.

Following was the purchase of a Pontiac Grand Am, which turned out to require more costly repairs to the windshield wipers than I had spent on the Fiat over the course of its 125,000 miles with us. I will never forget that when I took it to a Pontiac dealer in Durham for a problem with the transmission, I was billed $100 for the repair estimate (which came to several hundred dollars), but was promptly shown a new Grand Am that they would let me have in exchange—for an inflated price, of course. Wondering how the dealer's staff could believe that I was stupid enough to fall for this, I went back to Chapel Hill, and, after a brief search, purchased a silver Buick, a dealer demonstrator, that let me feel that we had indeed arrived in the world. Pegge in the meantime had acquired a new Chevrolet. The Buick served us well, although it had some defect that caused water to enter the car when it rained, and to puddle a couple inches deep on the rear seat floorboards. This problem persisted throughout a dozen trips to the nearest Buick dealer we would trust in Hillsborough for repair, and though we were not charged for the subsequent times, it was in the shop for attention to this problem for 105 days the last year I owned it. The water sloshing around was not the problem—rather, the carpet quickly soured, making the car smell like a Chatham County outhouse. I wrote a number of letters to the Buick headquarters, but never got a satisfactory response. The head of repair in the dealership where I had taken it told me that he had more money in that car than I did, which was probably no overstatement. But we never were able to remedy that defect. I had now retired, and Pegge had a relatively new Ford Taurus that would suffice for both our needs, so after trying briefly to sell the Buick, I gave it to a charity and took a tax break on its book value. We sold the Taurus in late 2006, and acquired a little Hyundai Accent which is our present means of transport.

These were our cars. Our two live-aboard boats were our true pride and joy.

Although cars were a love, boats were a passion. I had always wanted to have a boat with live-aboard, long distance cruising capability. On a trip to Barnegat Bay in 1966, we had found an old Elco, built in 1932, for sale at Iggy's Marina. It was 26 feet long, slept 5, had a head and galley, and a single engine. Iggy told us the owner wanted $1,500 for it. We had it surveyed, and the surveyor told us the bilge was full of whiskey bottles, and that the boat had not been out for a long time. "Offer him less—say, $1,200." We did, and the owner accepted. And we accepted the name already on the boat: the Beachcomber.

The Beachcomber, Figure 8 Island, NC: Randy Tomlinson, Jay Davis, and Chris Davis

The trip from Hopewell to Iggy's Marina involved back roads for about 40 miles. Our route to the boat took us through a little rural township where the two policemen, a father-son team, made their living by stopping speeders and fining them. In one of our first trips to the boat, we were caught, and thus helped improve the standard of living of the father-son team. It was on this route that we discovered, at a roadside stand, a New Jersey delicacy known as a meatball sandwich. This snack became traditional on our trips to the boat.

Although the Beachcomber was in reasonably good condition, we felt it needed paint—and not content with a quick cosmetic job, we decided to take it down to bare wood before repainting it. In this process, we discovered that it had no less than seventeen coats of paint, one on top of another, and we could count them because the paint remover removed only one coat at a time, and the succeeding underlying coats were different colors. This process took substantial time and a number of trips from Hopewell to Iggy's Marina. But we finally got it down to bare wood, painted, and in pristine condition.

The slip in which it was kept was the first just inside a dredged channel about 40 feet across, making the maneuvering of the boat into the slip on return from the bay to be precarious at best, for the length of the boat left only 10 or 12 feet as the turning area. Invariably, given the single engine, I had trouble with this.

But a number of returns brought practice and confidence, and one day when we came in, I handled the engine and rudder just right, and backed the boat perfectly into the slip. I turned to Pegge and said gleefully: "See? I did it perfectly!"

Pegge responded "That was really impressive. Now put it in our slip!" It was then that I realized that I had backed the boat into our neighbor's slip—the second in the line—alongside our space.

The Beachcomber was a classic, with a round bottom displacement hull. Planking was inch and a half thick mahogany. But there was some deterioration on some of the planking, and I made arrangements to have the boat hauled at a yard at Tom's River, some 12 miles north, for repair. We drove down from Hopewell, and I, Chris, and Jill boarded the boat to take it to the Tom's River yard, while Pegge and Mike were to drive up and meet us there to take us home.

It was a clear day, but the movement caused the leak from the bad planking to accelerate, and the boat began to take on too much water. I was frantically manning a hand bilge pump in addition to the automatic bilge pump which had more than it could handle, and trying to spot buoys for a channel I had never traveled before, when Jill began to say "Daddy, I am bored!" I have to admit that I wondered if she would still be bored if I threw her overboard... But we made the boatyard, in spite of the absence of some buoys that should have marked the entrance channel to the boatyard, and the repairs were completed the next week.

It was a crisp Sunday several weeks later that we decided to take a cruise up the bay. There were many boats out, and the water was calm, if cold (it was March as I recall). Suddenly, Jill came up out of the cabin and said "Where's Chris? I can't find him anywhere!" Quick inspection revealed that he indeed was no longer aboard, and then I looked astern, where a half mile or so back there was a small figure in an orange life jacket bobbing up and down in the middle of the bay. It was Chris, who had fallen overboard unnoticed, and whose cries, if any, had been drowned out by the old engine and faulty muffler.

We went back and retrieved him. His comment as we hauled him aboard: "It-t-t-s c-c-c-old!"

We decided that the old muffler had to come off and a new one installed. The muffler, however, was frozen onto the metal exhaust pipe from the engine, and was in the back of the bilge where space was too tight for me to access it. Mike, being smaller then, could get in, and I promised him a turkey club sandwich and a slice of lemon meringue pie if he would crawl down in the space with a hacksaw and cut the old muffler off.

This he did, but the space allowed strokes of only about four inches with the hacksaw. He labored a full hour before emerging triumphantly with the old muffler. I made good on my promise, and he has said several times later that that was the best turkey sandwich and lemon meringue pie that he ever had.

As indicated earlier: when time came to move to North Carolina, we made our major move itself on the Beachcomber.

It had become clear that the old engine was not sufficiently reliable for long trips, and just before moving to our new assignment in North Carolina, I purchased a used Gray Marine engine from McArthur's boatyard on the other side of the bay With the help of a carpenter recommended by Iggy, and the use of a boatyard crane to lift the old motor out and to lower the new motor in, we installed the new motor. But when we started it up for the first time, it began to spray water from a badly cracked cylinder head. McArthur had carefully concealed this flaw with paint. When I telephoned him about this, he laughed, suggesting that I should be more careful when I made such purchases, and that I should invest in a little paint as he had.

I found a replacement head for about what we had paid for the engine at a marine supply store in Newark, and went up and purchased it, and returned to Iggy's and installed it. The check to McArthur for the engine had not cleared, and when I suggested that we stop payment on the check, Pegge's chagrin over the situation vanished. This I did, a day or so before we left for North Carolina in the old Beachcomber.

We had left a car at Iggy's, and I flew back up in two weeks to retrieve it and bring it to North Carolina. Iggy and his wife had become good friends, and when I stopped to see them before returning to North Carolina, Iggy told me, laughing, that Mr. McArthur had come there hopping mad about some check the bank had returned, but stomped out when Iggy reported that we had left the state for somewhere further south.

The trip turned out to be an enormous adventure. We left the Marina July 3 in good weather, but it did not hold. Most of the days following were foggy, wet, and windy. The top speed of the old Beachcomber was about 6 knots, and the trip of some 600 miles required ten days of cruising and several more in boat yards. These days were not without incident.

When we came to the Delaware River, where a forty mile crossing to the entrance to a canal into the Chesapeake Bay was involved, we were beset with a fog so heavy we could see only some 50 yards ahead. The compass I had was erratic, and I kept the heading of the boat toward the canal entrance by staying at the angle required between our line of movement and the line of the current. It was a considerable relief to find after five anxious hours that we had come out only about fifty feet from dead center to the canal entrance.

As we proceeded down the bay, we inadvertently strayed into an off-limits area off the Aberdeen Proving Ground. This was off-limits because it was used as a firing range. About midway through, however, a copper tube oil line broke off where it entered the engine block, and our oil spilled out into the bilge. We had to stop and hail passing boats for assistance. A hardy soul in a 36 foot sailboat came to our rescue, and smirkingly towed us in to a marina where the line was drilled out, tapped, and replaced.

The fog came back as we continued down the bay. We moved cautiously because we could run aground on the east side of the Annapolis Bay Bridge, and I remember calculating that we should be either at the bridge or about to run aground, but I could see nothing in the fog. Just as I was about to stop and go back in the other direction, Pegge said "Look up!" and I did, and there above us was the center of the Annapolis Bay Bridge. Again, we had precisely maintained our intended course.

Having had enough excitement for the day, and having made our 60 miles, we turned in to a little marina at Pirates' Cove, about 10 miles below Annapolis. The unexpected repair off Aberdeen Proving Grounds had taken most of our ready cash, and we had found out earlier that no one would accept a check or credit card from a transient boat. We had just enough money for cab fare into Annapolis, a wire for money, and a movie, and into Annapolis we went, wiring Pegge's father for enough cash to get us back to Pirate's Cove and on the way again. We placed the wire request; went to the movie; prayed that the money would be at the Western Union office when the show was over—and it was! We bought groceries, and took a cab back to Pirates' Cove.

From there to Norfolk, through the Norfolk Navy Yard, and into the Inland Waterway canal, at the North Carolina line, we had no problems. The route took us close by many Navy ships of the line at Norfolk, which proved to be exciting for the children, particularly Mike. I lost my watch overboard at Coinjock, but the Alligator River and Albemarle Sound, reputed to be dangerous because of swells caused by the shallow water, were no problem, except for a nosy helicopter that hovered inexplicably over us for a few minutes as we crossed Albemarle Sound.

A particularly memorable overnight stop was at Bellhaven, NC. We tied up behind a cruising houseboat which was taking on fuel, and began to appreciate the Beachcomber when we found that the houseboat required over 1,000 gallons of gas for its day's run. The dockage was at a former hunting lodge which had, amazingly enough, a buffet that included chitlins but was also formally recommended by Duncan Hines. We ate very well, and swore to return some day.

The weather had turned mild and sunny, and the next day we were cruising nonchalantly into Morehead City when just as we exited the canal and were entering the Morehead City bay area all hell suddenly broke loose—high winds, blinding rain, and heavy swells. There was no hope of finding and following the dredged channel, and our charts showed the bay to be only 2 feet deep in places. I did not have to ask all aboard to don life jackets. But, the good Lord was with us, and we ended up in Morehead City, docking at the Sanitary Café and Fish Market, just as the weather cleared and returned to normal.

We were now only about 60 miles, or one day's run, to Wilmington, our destination. We set out the next morning in high spirits, but before getting out of sight of the Sanitary Cafe and Fish Market, ran aground at the edge of the channel with sufficient force to break our rudder and damage severely the wheel, or propeller. We were at the mouth of a creek just below Morehead City proper where a well equipped boatyard existed, and there had the boat hauled and got a new rudder and our wheel reconditioned. We had sufficient money to enjoy the local restaurants which were within walking distance, and after a day or so were on our way again. As we approached the Wrightsville Beach drawbridge over the waterway, we spied Pegge's mother and father, waving us in. Our new dockage was just on the other side of the drawbridge, and we were all happy to complete our adventure.

For the next several years, the boat provided a great get-away from the cares that accompanied work and child care, and we made many trips to fish just off shore or to the string of sand-finger islands that lined the southeastern NC coast. All three children became adept at handling the boat, although Jill seemed to have the edge in this respect: Mike let his mind wander, and Chris generally became bored after a short stint. And I used it for occasional business entertaining.

It was the latter purpose that led to its demise for us. As head of the North Carolina ETS research office at that time, I had a group of people coming in for a meeting which we arranged to have at Wrightsville Beach. We loaded the old Beachcomber with sufficient beer and booze to keep a large committee happy and comfortably nonproductive, and Graham Burkheimer and Susan Kerner of my staff came down the evening before the others were to arrive. It was a clear moonlit night, and we decided to sneak out the channel for an offshore joyride before the others came. But the tide was going out, and the channel tricky, and we went hard aground at Masonboro Inlet, about 300 yards from the Coast Guard Station.

The tide continued to fall, and each effort to dislodge only wedged us tighter. When the external rudder broke off, we knew we were stuck until help arrived. With a blinker light, we did make contact with the Coast Guard Station, and a series of exchanges that would make a good Laurel/Hardy comedy followed. Their form of communication was by a loud speaker. We were first asked if anyone aboard could handle Morse Code, and I responded in the affirmative with a blinker light. The question was repeated several times, until I simply gave up.

We were told to hold tight and that a boat would be dispatched in the morning to tow us to safety.

Graham Burkheimer was successful in yelling across the water to request that the Coast Guard call his wife and let her know he was all right. When he later called her himself, he found that the Coast Guard man had called Sophie, his wife, and told her that her husband was aground in the channel with a woman but would probably be all right when the tide rose. Thank goodness their marriage was sound, for we all got a good laugh out of this.

In about an hour after running aground, we accepted the fact that the Coast Guard was not coming to our rescue. Graham and I decided to avail ourselves of the copious supply of beverages aboard, and our principal suffering came from being out of cigarettes. Susan disgustingly left us to our brew and decided to sack in in the cabin.

We had not had a great deal to drink when Susan emerged from the cabin to tell us that there was a foot or two of water therein. Renewed efforts to contact the Coast Guard station were futile, but the tide began to rise, Graham was working the bilge pump, and we drifted loose. The boat was a single screw affair, and with no rudder could not be steered. But it spun around slowly as the tide came in, and I would give the engines a goose every time the bow was pointed in the right direction. We made it to the Coast Guard docks just as the sun was coming up. Rousing some sleepy members of this service, we found that their coxswain the night before was in no shape to come get us, and one acne-faced seaman confessed that he was the one on the megaphone the night before asking if we could handle Morse Code, but then realized that he could not.

Damage to the old Beachcomber was sufficient to make repair seem unreasonable, and we sold it to a boatyard that collected old relics. The keel, a piece of oak originally about 4" by 14", was riddled with marine worm holes, and it seemed best to let this piece of our lives get away from us. We vowed, however, to replace it at the earliest opportunity.

For the next two years, most of any time off was spend scouring boat yards up and down the east coast for a good buy in a used boat. We wanted one that would sleep the five of us, that was reasonably economical to operate, and that would require less maintenance than the old Beachcomber. We found one in little Washington, NC, a 30 foot Owens about 10 years old, and placed earnest money on it, but reneged based on the report of the marine surveyor we had hired to advise us.

I had a layover in Miami between flights to Puerto Rico on contract business, and checked the advertisements in the *Miami Herald* for boats. And, staying at the Hotel Columbus where I had lived during the ASW/Navy days in 1944, went out and across the park across the street to check out the boats at the Miami Marina. I was a bit shaken to find a Miami police car leaving the pavement and following me closely across the grassy area of the park. Miami had changed in the last 28 years!

I found no boats for sale at the city marina, but remembered a 30 foot twin engine Chris Craft advertised by a private party on one of the islands in Biscayne Bay. I went out to see what was involved. The seller was a retired wholesaler who had purchased another boat which he had to berth at the marina in downtown Miami, because his bay front house could accommodate only one boat. The boat was immaculate: it had a full galley, and was air conditioned. We took it for a spin around the bay, and it performed admirably—it would plane at about 12 knots, some 6 knots above the top speed of the old Beachcomber. I made an offer, which was accepted, and upon return to North Carolina went to the bank for the necessary loan. We had no trouble with this, and so Pegge, Jill, and Chris joined me in the flight to Miami to pick up and bring back our new boat (Mike was unable to take the time off from school).

We got into Miami late, and took our check to the seller. He needed to be sure the check was valid, so we stayed on the boat that night. The next morning he prepared breakfast for us, while his bank verified the check. His bank called as we were beginning to finish our coffee, and he scooped up the dishes, led us to the boat, and untied the lines. We were on the 604 mile trip to North Carolina before we knew it.

The boat performed beautifully. The weather was good; our charts proved to be reasonably accurate; and the only tense experience was the 100 mile distance between gasoline providers south of Charleston. Our anxiety was that our tanks' capacity was 100 gallons, and we had found that our fuel consumption was a mile per gallon. We cruised through the most desolate area between Savannah and Charleston at the most economical speeds, and made it into the public marina in Charleston without incident, and with a cup or two of gas left in the tanks.

This new boat, which we named the Sally Forth (from a song in the Gilbert and Sullivan operetta *Pirates of Penzance)*, was a total joy. We made many trips from the home marina at Wrightsville Beach. Morehead City was now only four or five hours away, and we could go down the waterway to the Cape Fear River and into Southport and back in a short day. It was also great sport to troll just off the coast for Spanish Mackerel. There were only three episodes of true adventure that we encountered with it. And all of these occurred on a vacation jaunt to Hilton Head Island at the Southeastern corner of South Carolina.

We had tied up at a little marina in wilderness type country on the Waccamaw River portion of the Inland Waterway in South Carolina, and the three children eagerly went through their ritual at the end of each day of cruising of donning their bathing suits for a dip off the stern. As they emerged so attired from the cabin, the dockmaster held up a hand, and asked them to wait a minute. He produced a loaf of bread from a cubicle on the dock, threw in into the water just astern of our boat, whereupon a huge alligator emerged from the brackish water of the river and snapped it up. Pegge and I have never seen those three move to dress so fast!

The Sally Forth, Inland Waterway, Wrightsville Beach

The second adventure was still on the Waccamaw River about 20 miles north of Georgetown when I noticed that the boat seemed to be hardly moving. Inspection revealed that a hose carrying cooling water to the port engine had ruptured, and the bilge was rapidly filling with water. We cut the engine, and augmented the automatic bilge pump with a hand pump and I and both boys bailing, and after an hour had the bilge reasonably back to normal. We then cruised into Georgetown on the starboard engine, and found an auto supply store that had a reasonable facsimile of the broken hose. This took us an extra day for the replacement, but we didn't mind—for Georgetown had convenient docks and was the locale of Victor's Restaurant, an establishment that served delicious food at reasonable prices, and which was in walking distance of the docks.

We reached Hilton Head marina with no further incident. We had purchased a little Sunfish sailboat which was lashed on top of the cabin, and which would accommodate two people. Chris and Jill decided to take it out into the sound the day after we arrived, as I had decided to change spark plugs in the two engines. Although I was involved in the task I had taken on, Pegge became aware that the two in the sailboat had been gone for some time. I went to the entrance of the marina with binoculars, and lo and behold found them to be a mere speck on the horizon, and obviously getting farther out to sea each minute.

I set a record putting the spark plugs back in, and we cruised out of the Marina, mooring lines trailing, at the maximum speed. We reached the Sunfish shortly, to find Chris and Jill in a heated discussion about the other's lack of sailing ability, and oblivious to the fact that they were several miles out to sea.

We learned later that the current in that area is sufficiently vicious that many boats have trouble with it.

We enjoyed fishing with Pegge's parents, and with our friends and friends of the children. We had great fun, as previously noted, trolling for Spanish mackeral just off shore, and recall one day when the sea trout were running in the Wrightsville Beach Bay, and we caught as many as we had hooks on the line within a few seconds of dropping the line, forcing us to stop after just a few minutes. On another occasion, Pegge hooked a small sand shark just off Figure Eight Island, which pulled like she had snagged a Mack truck. This trophy went back to Chapel Hill High School

This boat was well suited to business as well as social entertainment. I recall inviting, among others, the president and vice president of the American Association of Governing Boards, for whom I had done several studies, for a weekend of gentle cruising, and recall the evening after a day of cruising when we were docked and having drinks on the after deck. The usual cadre of tourists were walking the docks and looking at the yachts moored there. We were moored stern into the docks, so the passerbys were only a few feet away from our deck chairs. I remember full well the usually lugubrious president of the Association of Governing Boards calling out, after a second drink, to any female passing by: "Hi, pretty lady, come see our boat!" He was not taken up on this, and, I suspect, that if he had been, the situation would have been very much like Sam, our beagle hound for many years, finally catching a car he was chasing.

But all good things have to come to an end. I was employed by RTI at this time, and the Federal Fiscal year was changed to end not in June but in October, making the summer a busy one as Federal agencies rushed to utilize year-end funds in contracts. This kept us from the boat in the best season, and the engines were beginning to show signs of wear—four or five hundred hours in salt water is about the limit most marine engines will accommodate, and we had reached that point. Purchasing a new pair would have been more expensive than we felt was reasonable, so we sold the boat to an IBM executive—incidentally, for $2,000 more than we had paid for it.

Now, although I have found that Andrew Carnegie's definition of a boat is correct ("A boat is a hole in the water in which you pour money"), and although I have learned that ownership means several times more time in the bilge than cruising, I miss having a boat. Quite understandably, Pegge does not share this yearning, and given my creaking joints I would surely never get out of a bilge once I had entered it. But the sounds of the sea and the smell of salt water remain vivid in my memory.

Chapter 30

The Three Children as Adults

At this point in time—2007—the three are well into their adult lives.

Michael:

Although raised a Presbyterian, and taking his undergraduate study at a college affiliated with the Presbyterian church, Mike decided to be a Methodist minister, and chose a Baptist seminary for his theological training. He entered Southeastern Theological Seminary in the fall of 1975, after graduation from St. Andrews College in June. His first assignment was the Temperance Hall-McKendree Charge (Methodist) in Temperance Hall, NC, between Rocky Mount and Pinetops, where he began his ministry while still a student at Southeastern. While here, he married Karen Czerniakowski from nearby Rocky Mount on May 20, 1979, who brought with her six year old "Sam" or Michelle, a daughter from a previous marriage Mike moved almost immediately to a second assignment as Associate Pastor at the First United Methodist Church in Rockingham. Although assignments as Associate Pastor are generally for one or two years at most, he requested a move after one year because as Associate Pastor he missed the opportunity to preach regularly,.

In 1980, Mike was assigned to the North Gates Charge in Gates, NC. His son, John Caleb, was born in 1982 while Mike was serving this charge. In December of 1983, Mike moved to the Methodist Church in Moyock, where in the next two years his ministry was recognized by two Conference awards for Evangelism, making the Moyock church the only one in any Eastern North Carolina district to have double honors. These awards were presented formally at the Annual Conference in Fayetteville.

In 1986, Mike moved to Franklinton in the Raleigh district. Here he began with three churches, Franklinton Methodist, Wesley's Chapel, and Ebenezer, but through his efforts the Franklinton church became a "Station" appointment, meaning it had developed enough to sustain its own pastor. Because of this accomplishment, his church was selected as an "Exemplary Church," with recognition afforded Mike by having him address the Annual Conference Session at Methodist College in Fayetteville.

Stepdaughter Michelle graduated from high school in Franklinton, where she was valedictorian of her high school class, and nominated for many "bests." Although I have a list somewhere of the scholarships she was awarded, there were too many to mention, even including one for "Outstanding Student from the Air Force ROTC." In the fall, she entered the School of Pharmacy at the University of North Carolina in Chapel Hill.

At UNC, Michelle met Greg Pait from Bladenboro, NC, a former F-111 pilot who flew in Desert Storm and who was president of the pharmacy fraternity. After both she and Greg graduated, they were married and now live in Zebulon where Greg works for Nash General Hospital and Michelle for Wal-Mart in Wilson. In May 2007, they have two boys, Ryan and Matthew, and a new baby girl, Macy.

Christopher, Michael, and Jill—April, 1993

After six years in Franklinton, Mike was assigned to the Wake Forest Methodist Church. But although Mike felt he grew, the church had a reputation for being tough on its ministers, and there seemed to be substantial political intrigue among the lay leaders. And Karen's attempts to develop a handbell choir were rebuffed. After three years at Wake Forest, Mike placed his name on the moving list, and was assigned to Gardners Methodist Church in Fayetteville.

The year that Mike started at Gardners was 1995. Here he stayed for eight happy and productive years, the longest pastorate in the history of that church.

The "fit" extended to Karen, and John as well: Karen served as organist, led the choir, and helped to start a new handbell choir; John played in the handbell choir, and brought his trumpet to many services, Under Mike's ministry at Gardners, the church was recognized as the Outstanding Church of the Year for Evangelism in 1998. Mike was also active in civic activities, including serving as the (Boy) Scouting Coordinator for the Fayetteville District. His work with the local scout troop was instrumental in their earning the Bishop's Award for Excellence three years in a row.

John Caleb Davis, UNC-G A.B., December, 2006

John graduated from high school in Fayetteville, and during their last year at Gardiners, he entered the University of North Carolina at Greensboro on a music scholarship. He excelled in this area, with trumpet his primary instrument. He was also active in a choral group (the SPARTONES), whose creative treatment of vocal sounds took them to Radio City Music Hall in New York City his senior year. John graduated in December, 2006, and shortly gained employment in the Greensboro area with EB Games, a Fortune 500 company, in sales and management. He has shortly been promoted to Associate Manager of the EB Burlington Store.

With John now out of high school, Mike was again marked for reassignment, and in 2002 he moved to Trinity Methodist Church in Troy. Pegge and I reveled in this assignment, for Pegge's father and mother had grown up in Troy, and there were many of her relatives still in the area. Her maternal grandmother had been a member of that church, as was her favorite uncle Claude, and Mike relished his Friday evening suppers with Claude, his wife Villie, and other relatives that gathered at Asheboro restaurants each week on Friday. He found these regular family gatherings very special. In Troy, Mike also taught a course in world religions at Montgomery Community College, and had a monthly column in the local paper. And, his church was the church for the members of the Capel family, whose Oriental rug headquarters were in Troy, and with whose members, staunch supporters of Trinity Methodist, Mike got along with very well.

There were moments of special challenge as well. During Mike's ministry in Troy, Claude's son Otis died unexpectedly from a tragic accident (a horse he was riding fell on him), and Claude died at the age of 103, two weeks before his 104th birthday. Mike's funeral oration about this amazing man came from the heart, and is included in the appendix.

A second special challenge was the discovery, in 2005, by Mike that he had developed parotid cancer (cancer in the saliva gland in the cheek). But it was caught early and removed successfully, and for added insurance against reoccurrence, Mike took radiation therapy the first three months in 2006.

Although it was a tight year for reassignment, in June, 2006, Mike was promoted to Angier UMC, which brought him back closer to us and to his daughter and her family in Zebulon, NC. Mike had taken a strong stand at Trinity Methodist on a matter of principal involving church finances which led to an intolerable situation, but he left with much support from members of his congregation, and he felt greatly fulfilled by his opportunity to serve in Troy.

Karen had completed training as a pharmacy technician at Fayetteville Technical Community College in Fayetteville and had begun working for Eckerds Drugs in nearby Albemarle when Mike started his ministry at Troy. With quick promotions signaling success and attaining the role of lead technician at a new store there, she was loathe to leave her job when Mike moved to Angier, and took up residence in Albemarle, commuting to Angier and spending the weekends and vacation times with Mike.

In Angier, Mike is once again finding fulfillment in an active church. He serves as Secretary for two Conference committees: Church and Society, and Older Adult Ministries. He is also Secretary for the Clergy Friends Association at Methodist University in Fayetteville, and is Chairperson Elect of the Fayetteville District Circles on Ministry. And close to his old daddy's heart, he has just served on a committee that has prepared a strong resolution calling for an end to our involvement in Iraq, which was presented to the annual conference in June, 2007. It was not adopted, but set a precedent for later discussion and action.

Christopher

After graduation from Western Carolina University in 1979, Chris returned home and began work with the Village Advocate, but moved shortly to Disc Trading Company, an import/export record company in Chapel Hill with a lively overseas business. He shortly moved out of the house and into an apartment with one of his friends from high school and a recently divorced book store owner. With marriage in 1983 to Sherron Fairley, he moved to Brandt Industries in Fuquay Varina, a pneumatic process control manufacturer, again with responsibility for overseas shipments. He and his new wife Sherry rented a small house with a big yard in Raleigh near Cary township, where they lived until they purchased their first house, in Cary, in 1987.

From Brandt, he moved in 1984 to WTC Airfreight, a South African owned airfreight company with offices at the Raleigh-Durham Airport, staying with that firm when it was bought out by Burlington Air Express in 1988. From Burlington he moved to Kintetsu World Express in 1990, still at Raleigh-Durham Airport. When Kintetsu wanted to transfer him to Atlanta, he moved to Fritz Companies in 1992, still as an international air freight specialist and later ocean export manager.

Learning of a major opening with Novartis in Greensboro, with prime responsibility for international shipping of agricultural chemicals, he applied and was accepted in April, 1997, and moved quickly to major responsibilities. With this move, he and Sherry decided to build a house on acreage bordering a large lake near Mebane, from which Chris could commute to Greensboro some 40 miles away, and where Sherry could take a job with the post office in Graham, some 10 miles away. Their new house was finished in time for Christmas in 1997.

That part of Novartis in which Chris was employed was spun off from the pharmaceutical parent company and formed as Syngenta Crop Protection, Inc., in 2004. Although there were personnel changes of a belt-tightening nature, Chris was retained—with added responsibilities formerly assumed by displaced employees.

Chris and Sherry have not produced any heirs, but have had a close association with their pets. Tosha, the Siberian Husky, was with them through their residence in their rented house in Raleigh and their home in Cary. In their Mebane home, they have generally had a border collie and a large friendly mutt to provide companionship for the border collie. Their first border collie, named Keefer, has been followed by Cody, the current resident border collie, who shares their affections with Summer, a large friendly dog of varied heritage.

The love of cars has stayed with Chris, and he currently owns a 1965 Volkswagen Bug, a Subaru Outback, a Mitsubishi Montero, and a Dodge Intrepid. These are the current lot, with many hot forerunners that Chris and Sherry have literally run the wheels off of. A favorite avocation is automobile racing, especially NASCAR and Formula 1, and they frequently attend the stock car races in Charlotte.

Chris and Sherry have been avid international travelers. Chris started with gratis international trips as a perk with his transportation work, but at this point he and Sherry have variously traveled to Holland, Germany, France, Austria, the Czech Republic, England (including Wales and Scotland), and five times to Canada, which they particularly enjoy.

Jill

It was after Jill had bought a small house in Hillsborough that she met and married Larry Ballentine. They rented out, then sold, her house in Hillsborough, and purchased some 7 acres of pristine woodland on the banks of the Haw River just inside Chatham County. There, she and Larry camped while building their present home, and it was from there that Jill and Larry made a midnight dash to Siler City, where son Joseph was born two months early in 1989, weighing in at 3 pounds, 9 ounces.

Larry was a sort of Jack of all trades, which aided them immensely in building their house on the land they had purchased. They had the foundation laid before Joseph was born. Living temporarily but happily in a trailer on the property, they continued work on the house. Larry and Jill separated in 1992, at which time they had the roof and walls of their house up. Jill continued the work on the house to the point where she was able to obtain a Certificate of Occupancy just before Christmas in 1994. With characteristic ingenuity, Jill finished the house in the next several years. Larry had moved to Brevard, North Carolina, where his family lived, but returned after a period of time to live on a friend's property in Chatham County, a few miles from the house that Jill and Joseph were occupying. Their divorce became final in 2005, but the geographic propinquity permitted Joey to enjoy continuing contact with his father, which meant a great deal to both.

As previously noted, Jill had entered Alamance Community College, graduating in 1980 with an associate degree in early childhood development. From that date until late in 1989, she worked as a Nanny for two different families, endearing herself to both the children and their parents. Two weeks before Joseph was born in 1989 and continuing until 1993, she began work as a free lance proofreader for the UNC Press and for Carolina Academic Press, which was associated with Duke University. This permitted her to work at home while Joseph was little.

In 1993, she began work as a secretary and administrative assistant at Chapel Hill Reality, continuing there until October, 1995, when she joined a group of environmental engineers in Carrboro, where she managed the office and handled the accounting. In 2005 she resigned at the end of the year, and purchased some real estate in poor condition, renovated it, and sold it. She is currently investing in a second property.

Sailboating has been a passion for her and Joseph, and they have worked through a series beginning with a little green boat, a Compac 16' (a "weekender'), and currently a roomy 19 foot Hunter, large enough to live aboard, that she purchased several years ago. And like Chris, she enjoys traveling, and her long distance journeys since her trip with me to Puerto Rico when she was a little girl have included the Greek Isles, the Virgin Islands, Costa Rica, the Grand Canyon, Key West, and several trips to Canada and Niagara Falls and to New Orleans.

Jill's intellectual brilliance may be her worst enemy, for she learns very quickly and then is bored with the routine. She can take on literally anything and do it well, but she shortly becomes bored with it. Her insights into human nature and the way of the world constantly both delight and amaze me. Her unusual compassion for people and freedom from prejudice of any kind sometimes, I feel, interferes with her common sense. But she remains the exceptionally bright individual who can take on and succeed at any task, and who has amused herself and her son by such hobbies as sailing and travel as previously noted, and, among other things, by gourmet cooking (she has authored a very good cookbook with some unusual recipes of her creation).

Joey has in the meantime become something of a computer genius, and is able to do most anything but make coffee on a computer. He has built his own computer, to add to others that he has either purchased or been given by friends who were upgrading. And working primarily with duplicates from my collection, he has developed a quality collection of some 2,000 first day covers, including a number of high quality that he has designed and made himself, either by hand painting or with computer images or graphics, drawing on an unusual artistic talent. He graduated from high school in June, and is currently seeking options for summer work prior to entering higher education.

Chapter 31

Retirement

In the fall of 1988, having served 15 years at RTI and therefore qualified for their support of medical and dental insurance in retirement, and finding that I enjoyed coming and going to the office as it suited me (a benefit of seniority), I decided to take early retirement at the tender age of 63. I had ongoing projects, but I convinced RTI that I could complete the contractual commitments as a day to day consultant—an arrangement that the project sponsors approved. This cost the contract accounts less because of overhead considerations, and actually paid me more. RTI permitted me to retain my office and computer access, a deal that I took them up on for the next couple of years. During that time, I was also active as an independent consultant, an arrangement that returned about twice what I had been making with about half the time expenditure. The work I did was of little significance, for it involved generally inspecting and advising—usually activities in higher education management—but it did permit me to take Pegge on trips with me. One particularly memorable trip was to UNC-Asheville, where we dined at what historically was the famous Grove Park Inn with its active fireplace and rugged native stone construction, and where we visited the Thomas Wolfe house.

Some other trips afforded a joy for Pegge and me to be together, a marked contrast to many business trips I had had to make before. I agreed to give a paper on Black student athletes, in a panel at a meeting of the Southern College Personnel Association, in Fort Lauderdale, Florida, with Arthur Ashe a co-presenter. Even though Ashe was a no-show, we enjoyed the trip, dining elegantly in Savannah on the way down, and enjoying Epicot on the way back. We made a trip to the Shenandoah Valley area, taking in the campus of Washington and Lee University and the home of Stonewall Jackson in Lexington. We drove to a meeting of Americover, the annual convention of the American First Day Cover Society, in Falls Church, Virginia, and to stamp shows including one at Virginia Beach, Virginia.

Pegge Davis, 1990

But the signal joy of my retirement was the involvement with my grandson, Joey, who arrived in March of the year following my retirement. As previously reported, my daughter Jill had built a house on seven acres some 10 miles south, and worked at a variety of jobs over the next several years—delivery person for the *Chapel Hill Newspaper*, professional nanny for two Chapel Hill professional couples, proof reader for the Duke University and UNC presses, and office manager for a group of environmental science engineers. Joey became our constant companion during the day while his mother worked, and what a joy this was! In retirement, I had time that had been denied me while I worked to lavish on a little one, and Joey was exceptionally bright and responsive. In this regard, I recall inventorying some 500 words he was using by the time he was 30 months old; and I recall eating out with him at an Italian restaurant with a mural on the wall of the Parthenon when Joey was four, and of which he remarked, when he spied it "Boy! I'll bet that wasn't built in a day!" He was my constant companion when I went shopping, and even today, up to fifteen years later, it is not unusual to have a check-out clerk that I do not recognize ask me "How's Joey? He must be pretty big by now."

Grandpa ("Nonnie") and Joey Ballentine, 1992

    As is true of all children, there were things that he said that were particularly memorable. I will restrict my report of these to two: the first, at the age of 5, when in preschool, and the second, at the age of 6, while in the first grade. In the first instance: I always picked him up at the preschool after the day's activities were complete, and on one day rain had prevented them from enjoying recess outside. Instead, I found Joey in an auditorium holding area, equipped with a few toys to keep the children occupied in just such a circumstance. I helped Joey get out of the car he was pedaling around the hall and as we bid goodbye to the monitors, Joey said, in disgust for having missed outdoor recess, and in a voice loud enough to be heard by his teacher: *"This school is a piece of shit!"*

    The second comment I remember so well was made on the occasion of our waiting for a traffic light to change, and a Chapel Hill police cruiser, elaborately equipped,.pulling up alongside us in the other lane and waiting with us for the light. Joey looked at the car and its uniformed occupants, and then said "You know, I think I would like to be a policeman when I grow up." He was silent for a few seconds, then turned to me and said "For a little while, at least. Do you think they would let me keep the car when I quit?"

Joey had a particularly great preschool and first grade experience. His rural residence was partly responsible for his needing transportation to and from school, and his mother usually got him there on the way to work, and I usually picked him up. He played chess with his third grade teacher, generally giving him a tough game and winning. It was in the seventh grade at North Chatham Elementary School that he volunteered for work in the school library, and quickly became an indispensable assistant to the two librarians, who counted on him for computer applications. His move to Northside High School, serving Pittsboro and the surrounding area, involved school bus rides of a very considerable duration, so his high school years involved frequently meeting a school bus before 7 A.M., and not getting home until after 5 P.M.

Beyond Joey and grandparenting, I very soon found that there was not enough time in the day to do all the things I wanted to do. I enjoyed cooking, taking this on for all three meals each day because I wanted to do this, and became reasonably proficient with a good camera the children had given me (this taught me that when your kids give you a present you can't afford, you can legitimately assume that you have been successful!). And, I spent some time "messing around with Claudia, my squirrel friend," who was coaxed to eat from my hand, and, once emboldened, would come to the kitchen door several times a day, climb the screen, and protest that she was starving. But I quickly gravitated to three activities that have virtually become obsessions: philately; writing letters to corporation CEOs and to newspaper editors; and corresponding with friends on the Internet . . .

My interest in stamp and first day cover collecting was really prompted by Pegge, who had devoted some dozen years to building a very fine collection of stamps and covers. I started as her "purchasing agent," but quickly became so consumed by it that I may have crowded her out. In any event, she moved to spend her time largely in genealogical research, involving trips to many courthouses and search through old records, and work with the extensive files of the Mormon Church Family History Center and several on-line genealogical data bases in the hunt for elusive ancestors. We made painstaking searches of many cemeteries in Montgomery and Chatham counties. The courthouses visited included Chatham County, Montgomery County, Warren County, and Anson County. Many trips were made to the NC State Archives in Raleigh. Suffice it to say that her files now consume the equivalent of probably 12 standard file drawers, not counting hardback books or published family histories. She has been relentless in pursuing the actual facts in a field where data is traditionally infested with errors, and has experienced much pleasure from her activities.

As I began to find myself trapped with her basic collection of stamps and covers, I first decided to do what I could to get a mint copy of every U.S. Stamp that we could afford, attaining in perhaps the next 10 years a mint collection of almost all stamps beginning in 1900 (with the exception of the three dirigible stamps), and missing only earlier items available for $400 or more. Having fleshed out the collection of affordable U. S. singles, I moved to plate blocks, and again by careful shopping and taking the necessary time, built a collection to about the same standard as that I had established for singles. This work done, I realized that with first day covers, the options are virtually infinite—there can be as many as 500 different cachets for a given stamp, and for several favorites, we now have over 100 covers. The total collection at this point in time—July, 2007—is approximately 15,000 covers, requiring more than 100 volumes to contain them. The catalog value of the collection will approach $200,000, although I have seldom paid more than 20% of the current catalog value, and have found that letting the cachetmakers I like know how I feel frequently results in gifts of covers or greatly discounted prices. I realize, of course, that this is clearly not an investment, but it has been a great deal of fun and source of satisfaction.

In this activity, I have also become embroiled in activity with professional associations and philatelic venders. After purchasing covers and materials for more than a decade from Unicover, producers of the Fleetwood line of covers and supplies, I wrote the president and noted, gently, I felt, that his prices had escalated for some items over 200% in 7 years. The result: A response to an order for a substantial amount of cover albums was refused, with a notation that because I had been so ugly in what I had said to their staff I would have to go elsewhere for my supplies. This was no great handicap, of course, for all I had to do was to get some other person to order what I needed to maintain the consistency of storage, but it signaled how childish officers in a large organization can become with a good following in the market. The fact that over the years I had invested something over $5,000 in their covers and supplies told me that my letter to the president must really have bruised his ego.

I also became active in the struggle with the U.S. Postal Service to contest their permitting groups with property rights on the subjects depicted on stamps to charge licensing fees to cachetmakers, while requiring exemption for the USPS. Since only a handful of cachetmakers will make over 200 covers for a given stamp, a licensing fee of $2,500, a not atypical fee which was assessed by the property rights holders for the Marilyn Monroe stamp, is prohibitive. The solution to this problem seems to me to be a simple one: the Postal Service pays no fee for such use of images that are property righted, banking on the publicity and the free advertising given the subject. Requiring the same condition for the cachetmakers would not involve the loss of much money by the holders of the property rights. But working through the professional association, the American First Day Cover Society (AFDCS), was generally ineffective, I think principally because they did not want to appear to contest any activity by the U.S. Postal Service, and because they see their role restricted to publishing a journal and holding an annual convention giving cover dealers a market, and making minimal ends meet without jeopardizing their non-profit status. The result: an increasing ignoring of the licensing requirement (e.g., several hundred cachetmakers did covers for the Dr. Seuss Cat in the Hat stamp, despite a ruling by an official of Seuss enterprises that absolutely NO covers would be authorized). There has been minimal attention to this issue given by AFDCS now, but it is largely ineffective, and was most likely aimed principally at quieting vocal critics like myself who feel the organization should take stands on important issues affecting collectors, dealers, and this branch of philately.

In the meantime, it has become patently clear to me that the AFDCS is an organization that (1) holds an annual convention where dealers and collectors may get together, and (2) struggles to maintain itself financially and to preserve its tax-free status. This leaves no room to take stands to support the development of the hobby or the interests of the cachetmakers and philatelic dealers except in providing the national forum. I was nominated in the late 1990s to run for membership on their governing board, losing by a few votes (usually only about 10% of the members vote), and was asked to run again by the board chairman shortly thereafter but declined. I have felt that the organization could flex its muscles and truly represent the interests of it constituents, but it has become clear that anything beyond the publication of a journal and staging the annual convention is off limits as too risky or simply inane. Several good people have been elected to the board, but have quickly taken on the protective coloring that preserves the mediocrity of the organization. And sad to say, although there are exceptions, it has become simply a playground for a group of several dozen longtime cover collectors needing status by becoming involved as officers or other representatives of the Society.

Beyond the sheer pleasure of building an attractive collection, though, has been the contacts with dealers and other collectors. I found rather quickly that prominent cachetmakers are frequently exciting people in their own right. To date (mid 2007) two have been houseguests—Frank Murray, of Heritage Cachets, who stopped for a couple of days with his sister when returning to Bridgeport, NY from Florida, and Larry and Gloria Gassen from Downers Grove, Illinois. I have had frequent email and telephone contact with Doris Gold, who has to be God's most perfect creation; with Julian Pugh; an ardent Republican and dripping wet Baptist; with Fred Collins, who took much verbal punishment from me but remains cordial; with David Lipof, a remarkably capable artist who had had to stop work on covers because of encroaching blindness, but who is an excellent public school teacher; with kindly Lois Hamilton, for whom the perfect week was spent playing poker in Reno, with the return to a covered dish supper at her church the same week; with Joe Ryan, who was in and quickly out of cachetmaking but won several awards his first year; with Tom Dunne, an unusually good artist working for Colorano for many years and now living close by; with Tom O'Hagen, whose garage is full of old books with lithographs that he uses in his cachets; and some others. I have also had a lively association with a number of cover dealers who have become admired friends—this includes Ray Lattof in Davie, Florida; Frank Maasen, a formal rival in bidding who is now selling off his acquisitions; Dave Fletcher, of Hyannisport, Fort Lauderdale, and Dallas, the genial elder statesman of cover philately; Ed Lyons, a retired Army colonel in Tampa; Bob Patkin, of Georgetown, MA; Loraine Schmid, the wife of Paul Schmid of Colorano covers in Huntington, NY, who recognizes my voice when I telephone her; and many others who seem to put friendship first and business a distant second.

I also got much joy from interacting with several individuals who did remarkable work. Two of these—now deceased—were Tom Morrissey, a retired Navy petty officer in Reno, who painted ships in oils on covers in a corner of the lobby in the Reno post office, and Erwin Messiner, who, his wife Rusty tells me, was happiest when he was seated at the dining room table of their home in Philadelphia, working on covers with his water colors. And, believing that much of the best work is done by individuals for their own pleasure and is largely unknown by the philatelic public, I have sought out such people, with the most remarkable find being Joanne Bean, a preacher's wife in Fayetteville, NC, who has filled her time since 1988 making covers for every stamp issue, celebrating the members of her family or just expressing a remarkable good humor. Her work sufficiently impressed me and Doris Gold, with whom I shared some of her covers, that I did an article for Vol. 52, No. 1 (Jan. 2007) of the AFDCS journal *First Days* ("Joanne Bean: Closet Cachetmaker"). It must have impressed the editor as well, for in the edition cited he used an image of one of her covers to adorn the journal cover.

Another consuming passion has been writing letters on my formal personal letterhead to corporate heads on matters under their control which I felt were offensive, and writing letters, usually emails, to the editors of the local newspapers on matters of public concern.

In the first category, my favorite was a letter to the makers of the drug Detrol LA, which was advertised on TV by showing adults in a tizzy to get to a bathroom when running water intruded on their consciousness—a golf course sprinkler, a glass of water being poured at a conference table, or the like. In my letter, I said that every time their commercials came on TV, I peed on the couch, and that they should buy me a new one. I never had a written response, but the offensive commercials disappeared almost immediately. After a time, new commercials began to appear for Detrol LA, but there was no water flowing

I also believe I got an offensive commercial by Nabisco pulled. This one advertised Grey Poupon mustard by showing an old gentleman making himself a sandwich in the back of his Rolls Royce, but with the noise from the squeeze bottle of mustard sounding so much like the expulsion of flattus that the chauffeur raises his eyebrows. I wrote the Vice President for Marketing that my six year old grandson, having seen this many times with the six o'clock news, frequently asked for "Grey Poop-On" at the dinner table, and once receiving it, would amaze us with a sonorous fart. This commercial was also pulled shortly thereafter.

Another triumph which turned out to have an unusual twist in the corporate response was a letter to the Vice President for Marketing of Ford Motor Company in Hapeville, Ga. I wrote that seeing his advertisement "Have you driven a Ford lately?" so frequently, and having driven most other Fords from the Thunderbird to the Mustang, I had never driven a Ford Lately. When I went to a dealer and asked to drive one, I said that I was ridiculed instead of given the courtesy of a test drive. I later heard their commercial with the adenoidal country singer singing "If I had the money, tell you what I'd do, I'd go into town, and buy me a Ford truck or two," and needing a truck, decided to ask the local Ford dealer to show me the new Ford Truckertoo. Again, I wrote, I was shamelessly ridiculed. The outcome: I received a telephone call from a local Ford dealer making profuse apologies for the insults I had received from sales staff, and when I confessed what I was up to, he laughed, but said that there was one Vice President in Hapeville who did not see the humor in the matter. But both of these Ford Company commercials were immediately removed from TV.

There were also failures. The most significant one was writing the president of CBS in New York City that we enjoyed "The CBS Evening News with Dan Is Off Tonight." Absolutely nothing happened, and Dan Rather continued to be frequently absent from the "CBS Evening News with Dan Rather." I then wrote Dan Rather and suggested he open his evening newscast with "Good Evening—This is the CBS News with Dan is On Tonight." Again, no response. And Dan continued in his on-again, off-again mode until his account of President Bush's Air Force service got him displaced as anchor.

I also struck out on a variety of letters to physicians, the AMA, congressional sources, and pharmaceutical manufacturers about the high prices of prescription drugs, and particularly the role that the costs of TV advertising, PAC contributions, free samples to physicians, and lobbying expenses played in the prices. These prices, of course, permitted the pharmaceutical industries to enjoy the highest net profits of any industrial group in recent years. In several exchanges with a U.S. Congressman representing my district and with whom I was on a first name basis, I wrote that I had just seen a bumper sticker in his home town that read: "Invest in America—Buy a Congressman!" This gentleman had, of course, profited heavily from campaign contributions by the drug companies, and my letter obviously hit scar tissue, for he responded with considerable vigor about his integrity. But he maintained that TV advertising for prescription drugs could not be touched because of the Freedom of Information Act.

Frequently, those letters written in good sport were received and returned the same way. Pegge, like her father, is an avid sports fan, with basketball her favorite spectator sport, and the UNC Tar Heels her favorite team. At one point in time when the Tar Heels had lost a game or two that they should have won, I wrote then Coach Dean Smith that my wife was an ardent fan, and that every time the team lost, I had to sleep on the couch with our smelly dog (this was the Irish Wolf Hound)—and that if he lost one more, I was sending the dog to him. He answered that this was the best incentive he had received, and that he would try very hard to win the remaining games in the season.

Although the letters of the sort mentioned above were generally written in jest, my letters to the editors took on more serious personal concerns. There are too many of these for efficient comment here, but a sample of these letters is included in the appendix.

I have chronicled elsewhere the several family deaths we sustained in retirement: my mother's death in 1991 at the age of 93 (my father had died in 1964), and the traumatic loss of both Pegge's parents in 1999. Pegge had always been very close to her parents, and this was most difficult for her; it was not incidental for me, either, for the two of them had been great friends with whom many enjoyable days had been spent—from bridge games in the years after we were married, to fishing with her mother on the piers of Wrightsville Beach and to hunts with her father and the amazing pack of dogs that he had trained.

One other member of my in-laws' family is a major involvement in my later life. Nell's younger sister, Elizabeth (or "Libby") is a widow who had worked as a secretary for a government office in Washington, DC. When she lost her husband, she returned to Burlington and lived with her mother. She worked as a secretary for the Western Electric plant in Burlington, but retired in the late 1970s. When her mother died at the age of 96, she moved to Raleigh, where she lived alone in a small apartment. In the mid 1990s, it became apparent that she needed assistance, and I began to help her with housing, budgeting, investing, and health related needs. Libby is an exceptionally sweet and loving person, and this has been a joy.

We moved her to an assisted living home in Chapel Hill in 1999 where we could keep a closer eye on her, but a year and a half later she fell and broke a hip. This was treated successfully at UNC Hospitals, but resulted in Libby requiring a higher order of care. We placed her at Britthaven of Chapel Hill, a nursing home only a few blocks away from where we live. There, at 93 years of age (in July of 2007), she maintains the sweet disposition she has always exhibited.

Libby had given money over the last two decades to many charitable and/or evangelical groups, and her sweet and charitable disposition had attracted many entities of questionable integrity as well as some that were quite legitimate, and where the appeal was to her need to give rather than to a need to remediate something. For example, I found canceled checks from ACLU to support recognition of homosexuals' rights, the same month that she had written checks to one or another of the Jerry Falwell enterprises to help old Jerry combat the grievous sin of homosexuality.

Her rampant giving had attracted many solicitors, and dealing with them turned out to be a major activity: at the time she went on Medicaid, I had a list of some forty groups that were constantly asking her for money, and that persisted in spite of letters explaining her status and asking that her name be removed from their mailing lists. Many of these were finally dissuaded (after the fifth request had been ignored) by using their postage paid return envelopes to enclose and mail a brick, but some who did not provide postage paid return envelopes were persistent. The myriad Jerry Falwell enterprises were particularly resistant to my requests to cease and desist, even after enlisting the help of the Consumer Advocate Group in the N.C. Department of Justice. The Department of Justice representative finally flushed out a representative of the Falwell group who kept telling us that Libby's name had been removed, with a communication invariably following in a week or two with another plea from one of Jerry's enterprises for some cash. I finally telephoned the representative that it seemed only prudent that we both give up, and I will never forget her "Oh, thank you, sir!" Old Jerry must have been hard on his contact people.

This experience has been a revelation in how enterprises of questionable integrity prey upon old people for money. I have recently had to get the help of the NC Department of Justice to stop appeals from an entity by the name of "Save Jerusalem," which asked her for money to support appeals to President Bush to take a kind view of Israel. She still gets mail from the many Falwell "causes," where the most notorious was one during the Clinton administration asking for "$100, $200, or the most you can prayerfully afford," to support Falwell's proposed legal action against Clinton and Janet Reno for establishing a secret dossier on Falwell. A very little investigation found that the money was needed to pay Falwell's lawyer son for handling the case. But now, some ten years after starting to deter the appeals her rampant contributions had spurred, I am down to only a couple of appeals a month. Those that have hung on this long are pretty weird causes., like the "Save Jerusalem" enterprise mentioned.

It was about the turn of the century when Pegge and I both realized that the house at 405 Holly Lane, in which we had lived since 1967, had stairs that were increasingly difficult for us to negotiate. We began to feel like poor Sam, our golden beagle, who at 19 years of age was so arthritic that she could not negotiate the stairs, and had to cry to be taken up or down by one of us when she wanted to move to another level. We also discovered that we had more space (some 2,200 square feet) and clutter from the last 30 plus years than was reasonable. We purchased a much smaller (1590 square feet) single level house a few blocks away that had belonged to the chairperson of the Chapel Hill Garden Club. The magnificent flora at our new address (with something blooming at all periods throughout the year) compensated for the loss of book shelves (from 212 running feet at Holly Lane to less than 100, after building additional shelving, at our new house, and the Durham County Library becoming some 2,000 volumes richer). Our piano and guest bedroom were also victims, though we relished the thought that any overnight guests would be relegated to a motel rather than accommodated at our house. Our new house, although still in Chapel Hill, is just over the Orange County line in Durham County, where our annual property tax is considerably less.

It was also this period—beginning in 2000—that we began to feel the loss of many dear friends. For Pegge, still deeply touched by the loss of her parents in 1999, a particular void was created by the sudden death of her friend Dorothy Zehner in 2003, a couple years before a good friend of mine, retired English professor Charles Edge, died. Our relationships with both of these people had been very meaningful, and the void was deeply felt. It also brought starkly into consciousness the number of good friends we have lost in death: such people as Jack Bardon, a friend from Princeton University Days; Bob Glover, former colleague and friend from ETS and Regional Lab days; Becky Green, to whom Pegge felt particularly close; Clyde and Margaret Davis. and Margie Clark from our church days; Bill Bevan, Dick Goodling, and the Cliff Wings from Duke; a number of classmates and shipmates—enough to leave too few of us for continuation of class or ship reunions.

My friend Charles Edge had asked me to promise to speak at his funeral, and what is said on that occasion may tell something of what this kindly man meant to me. Those comments are provided in Appendix C.

We now—in 2007—spend our days more comfortably than we probably deserve. Pegge continues her genealogical research and her reading, and I spend time talking about cleaning up my study, and communicating with a menagerie of friends on the Internet. This includes Junius Duard Greene, the retired sheriff of Orange County, California, and William Sanders, the retired chief of the California State Highway Patrol; David Moorshead, a philatelic friend, who not only is very intelligent but who harnesses that intelligence very well, if sometimes caustically; Doris Gold, the gracious and wholesome first day cover artist; Howard Dennis, a fellow cover collector in Michigan who helped me assemble a complete set of Billie Jo Wilson's first day covers; Frank Edge, Charles' robust brother, a retired school superintendent with a sharp wit and good sense of humor; Richard Cannopp, a stamp dealer with a Playboy taste; Ray Lattof, a retired public school teacher and now cover dealer in Florida; Jim Thompson, retired owner of a chicken processing business in South Carolina, and part owner of the Panthers, a pro football team in Charlotte; Pegge's genial cousin, Jim Tucker, a bachelor who lives with his dog Pete in Bennettsville, S.C.; Masu Sasajima, a former research associate now retired in Seattle, Washington, who spent the WWII years in a Japanese internment camp in Colorado, and who was a principal in the team creating Sesame Street; Amanda Taylor, a very dear friend who views the world very much as I do; Gwen Fortune, the brilliant Black (she would say "woman of color") thinker, author and critic of the foibles of man, now in Florida; Andi Irby, a Goddaughter with more hits on Google than the Chancellor at N.C. State University where she is on the administrative staff, and her son James; John Rhodes, a writer employed by the University whose sharp responses are quick to rebut effectively letters to the editors that praise Bush or bash liberals, Christian fundamentalists, and corporate officials who take advantage of the little man; and, of course, the other philatelic dealers and cachetmakers already mentioned.

And a final delight: in writing and editing this statement, I have frequently taken recourse to Google, the computer search engine, for information on people that I have named. A great many have been found to be deceased. It was a considerable delight in this search to find my old and very dear friend, Marty Hamburger, in Miami (I had lost contact with him some 20 years ago). Marty is currently 87 and a widower, and is aflicted with Parkinson's. But telephone and email contact reveals the same lively wit and keen intelligence that so endeared him to me.

Now, as I write this, I have experienced my 82nd birthday, which I described to those who wished me a happy one that it was like wetting one's pants—uncomfortable as hell, and you hope no one will notice. There are many things that I would do differently, could I but start over. But I really can't complain.

Somehow it seems as if I have aged several decades in the last two years—I now have to walk with a cane; I get winded when I come up the handicapped ramp at the back of our new house. There is a magnificent magnolia tree in our front yard, that goes 40 or so feet up in the air, and that begs to be climbed, but it remains virginal. And all I have to do if I want to live dangerously is to go out to the mailbox at the street without my cane.

And this brings me to the present, and to the statement by T. S. Eliot:

> This is the way the world ends—
> This is the way the world ends—
> This is the way the world ends—
>
> Not with a bang, but a whimper.

Appendices

A. Resume for J. A. Davis

B. Paper: "How to Succeed at ETS"

C. Remarks, Memorial Service for Charles Edge

D. Funeral Sermon for Claude Morris by the Rev. Mike Davis

E. Selected Published Letters to the Editor

    E1. Letters Concerning Preparation of Teachers

    E2. Letters Concerning Educational Tests and Measurements

    E3. The Duke Lacrosse Fiasco, and the NAACP

    E4. Factors that Drive Up Medical Costs

    E5. The Presidency of George W. Bush

    E6. Letters about Irritants

    E7. Letters Responding to Letters

A. RESUME

The resume for Junius A. Davis following is drawn from an up-dated master used as a basis, with less appropriate publications or professional activities deleted, for appending to proposals for Federal contracts at the Research Triangle Institute. Many of the dates have been forgotten; many of the co-authors for the publications are people I do not remember. And although the findings of the research studies impressed me highly at the time the work was completed, I cannot recall the conclusions of many now—and in fact, cannot remember conducting some of the studies. This attests the genius of my long-time friend, Dr. Martin Hamburger, who once introduced me as the "author of many widely non-read publications in psychology."

RESUME

Junius A. Davis, Ph. D.
500 Colony Woods Drive
Chapel Hill, NC 27517
(919) 942-3630

Personal Information
Date of Birth: February 4, 1925
Marital Status: Married (to Pegge M. Davis; 3 Adult Children)
Citizenship: U.S.

Education

    A.B., Mathematics, University of North Carolina at Chapel Hill, 1946
    A.M. Vocational Guidance, Teachers College, Columbia University, New York, NY, 1950
    Ph.D. Counseling Psychology, Columbia University, New York, NY, 1956

Dissertation: ***Returns Sought from Adult Work by Early Adolescents, in Relation to Sociometric Status among Peers.*** Columbia University, 1956

Professional Experience

October, 1988 to Present: Independent Consultant in Higher Education and in Education Research

November, 1980, to September, 1988: Principal Scientist, Center for Educational Studies, Research Triangle Institute, (Retired September 30, 1988).

(Concurrent Appointment: Associate Member of Graduate Faculty, Department of Psychology, School of Education, NC State University. Graduate instruction in educational research, and tests and measurement. Membership on doctoral dissertation committees.)

Recent Activities for RTI (1986-88): Director (beginning in fall, 1987) of a major evaluation of the impact of federal support (through Section 780 of the Public Health Act) on the development and establishment of departments of family medicine in the nation's schools of allopathic and osteopathic medicine. This work follows similar responsibility for a 1986-87 study of the impact of federal support (through Section 786a of the Public Health Act on Predoctoral family medicine programs. These studies involve the assessment of the impact of the programs on fiscal trends, curricular content, clinical training, family medicine departmental development, and organizational change in medical schools from 1978 to the present, and on numbers of family medicine graduates. Also, direction of a task concerned with assessment of Schools of Nursing in terms of adequacy of program content against role demands for baccalaureate degree nurses in official public health agencies; and a case study of family medicine residency training centers. Preparation of concept papers, for state—level governance or administrative offices, on remedial courses at the postsecondary level, funding formulas for public 2-year institutions, and governance for postsecondary vocational training systems.

Directed (1985-86) a design study for a longitudinal analysis of curricular materials in reading over the kindergarten-grade 8 period; a study of black students in traditionally white colleges; and, a study of mission, staffing, and enrollment trends, governance, and fiscal allocation procedures in the N.C. Community College System.

Directed (1980-83) a major inquiry into management of the institutional development program created by Title III of the Higher Education Act of 1965, using evaluability assessment techniques; directed a national study of the impact of Title III on the dynamics of institutional development and the attainment of independence from federal support. The latter study involved intensive case studies of 51 "developing" institutions of higher education, with particular attention to the nature and extent of federal investment, five year fiscal trends, administrative organization and functioning, fiscal management, and programmatic change against current assessments of institutional vitality and viability.

1973-1980: Director, Center for Educational Research and Evaluation, Research Triangle Institute.

Directed the overall development of RTI's new Center for Educational Research and Evaluation; recruited professional and support staff (peaking at 45 members); directed and participated in marketing and proposal development activities; established facilitation and technical/clerical support resources; managed the fiscal aspects of the cost center; coordinated work with other Centers on contracts involving interdisciplinary efforts; and initiated and maintained quality control procedures. Authored or co-authored over 100 proposals resulting in competitive awards of approximately $17,000,000 from federal, state, and private sources; achieved from 23 to 92 percent of dollar value of proposals annually bid.

Directed initial RTI project activity for the follow-up of 23,000 young people involved in the National Longitudinal Study of the High School Class of 1972, for the National Center for Education Statistics; directed a national study of the functioning of college and university governing boards, for the Association of Governing Boards; director of a student market survey, for a community college in Texas; directed a study of remedial programs in the 16 universities of the University of North Carolina System; directed or served as senior advisor for studies of college drop-outs for the Ontario Ministry of Education and the Inter-American University in Puerto Rico.

Collaborated with RTI professional staff in the design, analysis, and reporting of research and evaluation studies, with particular emphasis on policy implications of findings. Major contracts over this period held by the Center for Educational Research and Evaluation included work sponsored by the National Science Foundation; in the U.S. Department of Health, Education, and Welfare, the National Institute of Education, the Office of Special Education, the Office of Planning, Budgeting, and Evaluation, and the National Center for Education Statistics; the Ford Foundation; the Charles Steward Mott Foundation; and various states, including Connecticut, Maine, Ohio, Texas, North Carolina, and Minnesota.

1967-1973: Director, Southeastern Office, Educational Testing Service, Durham, NC.

(*Concurrent Appointments*: Lecturer in Psychology, and Adjunct Professor of Education, Duke University; Adjunct Member of the Graduate Faculty, University of North Carolina at Chapel Hill; Adjunct Graduate Faculty Member, University of Massachusetts; served on doctoral dissertation committees in education, psychology, and public health; taught psychology of adolescence, tests and measurements, principles of guidance, research seminar in higher education, and history of higher education. Also: Director of Research, Regional Education Laboratories for the Carolinas and Virginia, 1967-68 (on half-time leave from ETS). Served as senior author for the initial successful proposal creating the Regional Education Laboratory for the Carolinas and Virginia.)

Directed the establishment and development of a field research office for ETS, focusing on minority education issues; responsible for developing a variety of models for researcher-practitioner collaboration in education research. Directed ETS contracts for: a national evaluation of the Special Services Program of the U.S. Department of Education, for the Office of Planning, Budgeting, and Evaluation of the U.S. Department of Education; technical support and evaluation of the physicians' retraining program at the University of Puerto Rico, for the National Institutes of Health; development of an advanced placement test for LPNs entering baccalaureate programs of nursing, for the N.C. Regional Medical Program; various studies of minority students in traditionally white colleges and universities, for the College Entrance Examination Board, and for the N.C. Board of Higher Education; directed other special studies for higher education institutions or state departments of education on the admissions process, student life, teaching effectiveness, and programmed instruction; and directed a study of member perceptions of the Association of Governing Boards, for that Association. Supervised the principal investigators for national studies concerned with the "Individually Guided Education Program-Mathematics," for the Office of Education; the application of the Delphi technique to higher education decision making (as an ETS developmental activity); a study of the impact of "Sesame Street," and pilot work for "The Electric Company," for the U. S. Office of Education; field work for the Head Start Longitudinal Study, for the Office of Economic Opportunity, and an evaluation of the Educational Improvement Program of the Durham, NC public schools, for the Ford Foundation, the program sponsor.

1961-1967: Assistant to the President; Senior Research Psychologist; and Head, Educational Sociology Group (1962-64), Guidance Research Group (1963-65), and Higher Education Research Group (1964-67).

(Concurrent Appointments: Lecturer or Adjunct Professor, Graduate Schools of Education at New York University, Rutgers University, the University of North Carolina at Chapel Hill, Brooklyn College, and Teachers College, Columbia University. Taught: educational guidance, vocational counseling, and tests and measurements.)

Directed, as Assistant to the President, special studies of non-cognitive student traits valued by faculty at highly selective institutions; directed validity research and manual preparation for a number of psychometric instruments including the College and University Environment Scales and the Myers-Briggs Type Indicator; served as a senior technical host for a variety of external senior researchers or educational practitioners visiting or serving as consultants to ETS; prepared special reports or presentations, including speech-writing for the president of ETS.

Initiated and directed, successively, the Educational Sociology, Guidance, and Higher Education Research Groups in ETS' Developmental Research Division. These groups conducted developmental work for ETS programs and for external sponsors, including the College Entrance Examination Board, the U.S. Office of Education, and the Danforth, Jacobs, Ford, and Kettering Foundations. Work included initial studies of the student protest movement of the 1960s; pioneer work in the application of various factor-analytic procedures for the establishment of measurement dimensions useful for different purposes; development of models, procedures, and instrumentation for institutional research, including standard student biographical data forms, faculty evaluation procedures and instrumentation, environmental assessment measures, and automated guidance procedures.

1958-1961: Graduate Dean, and Professor of Psychology and Education, University of North Carolina at Greensboro.

Directed the early development of the graduate program of the former Woman's College of the University of North Carolina, including the establishment of the first Ph.D. Program at that institution; developed and established basic graduate school regulations and procedures that stand relatively unchanged today; served as chair of various institutional or all-university committees, including the UNC-G Graduate Administrative Board and the All-University Admissions Research Committee; taught in the undergraduate program in psychology (social psychology, personality theory), and in the graduate program in education (tests and measurement; educational and vocational guidance; introductory statistics).

Served as organizer of or participant in a number of special symposia on women's role, including a special conference on the emerging role of women sponsored by the Women's Bureau, U. S. Department of Labor; launched, with an *ad hoc* faculty committee, a scholarly journal (*Analects*) devoted to creative endeavor in art and writing.

1957-1958: Director of Testing and Guidance, Board of Regents, University System of Georgia.

Directed basic research for the establishment of procedures for admissions counseling in the secondary schools, and for student selection and placement procedures for the institutions of the University System; developed a validity studies service for the Georgia institutions (which later became the model for a similar service provided nationally by ETS); lobbied successfully for the disclosure, by the College Board, of test scores to testees and for emphasis by the College Board on guidance procedures and materials; developed procedures for translating high school rank-in-class or grade average into a standard score (later adopted by the College Board), to permit ready incorporation of this datum into admissions formulas.

1954-1957: Instructor, Assistant Professor, Department of Psychology, Emory University.

Taught, at graduate and undergraduate levels, courses in statistics, industrial psychology, theory of vocational development, counseling, tests and measurements, and mental hygiene. Developed remedial study programs for undergraduates and professional school students; served as counselor in the Student Counseling Service; directed University admissions and placement research programs.

1952-1954: Assistant Director of the Counseling Service, and Instructor, Department of Psychology, Princeton University.

Served as clinical, educational, and vocational counselor to students; developed and directed a remedial reading and study skills program for students; directed the University's Student Tutoring Service. Conducted basic admissions research for the University, including special studies of performance in college as a function of secondary school attended, and of performance of public *vs.* private school graduates at the University (with N. Frederiksen).

1951-1952: Research Associate, the Career Pattern Study, Horace Mann-Lincoln Institute of School Experimentation; and Instructor of Sociology, Orange County Community College, Middletown, NY.

Served as member of the design and first-year data collection team for Professor Donald Super's Career Pattern Study, the first major longitudinal study of educational and vocational development. Taught Introduction to Sociology at Orange County Community College, the nation's first community college (and then in its second year of operation).

1950-1951: Graduate Assistant, Department of Counseling Psychology, Teachers College, Columbia University. Teaching Assistant for Professors Donald E. Super, Albert A. Thompson, and Harry D. Kitson.

1948-1949: Instructor (English), U. S. Naval Academy Preparatory School, Bainbridge,. Maryland (on active duty, U.S.N.R.).

Co-authored review texts, English and American literature; taught English grammar and literature to fleet appointees to the U.S. Naval Academy. Assistant Coach, Swimming.

1946-48: Control Buyer (men's furnishings), Sears, Roebuck and Company.

Estimated mail order sales and bought men's furnishings for Sears' Greensboro (NC) mail order plant; managed inventory control procedures.

1943-1946: Active duty as Ensign, Lieutenant Junior Grade, U. S. Naval Reserve. (retired in 1964 after 22 years of active and inactive duty).

Served in Caribbean and Pacific Ocean areas, including the Saipan and Okinawa campaigns, as Communications Officer, Gunnery Officer, Anti-Submarine Warfare Officer, Navigator, Deck Watch Officer, and Executive Officer for service force vessels (patrol and escort craft; aviation gasoline tanker).

Other Professional Experience: Special Appointments and Activities

Special Evaluation Consultant to the Minority Recruitment/Retention Grants Program, South Carolina Commission on Higher Education, 1987; 1988.

Member, Inter-Institutional Research Group, Institute on Desegregation, North Carolina Central University, 1987-1988.

Member, Advisory Council (and its Research Sub-Committee), Wake County (NC) Public School System Dropout Prevention Program, 1986-1988.

Invited member of the York River Round Table, a select group of educational institution, foundation, and government representatives concerned with current higher education issues., 1985-87.

Chairman, American Educational Research Association Research Training Committee, 1979-1982.

Gubernatorial appointee to the Corrections Planning Committee, State of North Carolina (technical advisory board for the N.C. Prison System), 1978-1984.

Active participant in the first organizational meeting of the International Association for Educational Assessment, in Geneva, Switzerland, 1974.

Special consultant on curriculum evaluation and administration to Harvard Medical School (1972), to the Medical Sciences Campus of the University of Tennessee (1971), and the University of Puerto Rico Medical School (1973-75).

Developed instrumentation and designs for market surveys of prospective college students, as consultant to McFarlane and Associates, Broad Run, VA, 1972.

Director of Title 1 (ESEA) Summer Workshop, Alabama Department of Education, Auburn University, 1971.

Program Chairman, special conference on "Developments and Assessments in Education Centers and Laboratories," the Eighteenth Annual Western Regional Conference on Testing Problems, San Francisco, California, May 9, 1969 (and Editor of *Proceedings:* Princeton, NJ: ETS, 1969).

Member, Board of Cooperating Editors, *Educational and Psychological Measurement,* 1968-1985.

Member, Organizing and Planning Committee (chaired by Dr. W. Roy Niblett, University of London), and for a special British/Canadian/U.S. Conference on the Relevance of Higher Education, held at Quail Roost, NC, December 8-14, 1958 (supported by a British foundation).

Organizer and Director of a summer workshop for institutional researchers and educational developmental officers, Regional Education Laboratory for the Carolinas and Virginia, at Montreat Anderson Junior College, 1968.

Director of a conference on Research-Based Planning and Development, for the Regional Education Laboratory for the Carolinas and Virginia, Durham, NC, July 27-30, 1968 (and editor of *Proceedings:* Durham, NC, RELCV, 1968).

Director of a major symposium (supported by the Kettering Foundation) on institutional vitality, reported in *Conversations toward a Definition of Institutional Vitality.* Princeton, NJ: ETS, 1967.

Member (1964-65) and Chairman (1966) of the Program Committee, Division 17, American Psychological Association.

Organizer, with Joseph Lins, John Stecklein, and others, of the Association for Institutional Research ; and, with Dr. Earl McGrath of Teachers College, Columbia University, and Vice Chancellor Charles Carter of the University of Lancaster (Lancaster, England), of a British-American Conference on Research and Evaluation in Higher Education, in 1966.

Program Chairman, Southern College Personnel Association Annual Meeting, Washington, DC, 1965.

Instructor: Origins of Prejudice, and Riot Control, in special State-sponsored seminars for law enforcement officers in the State of New Jersey, 1965-1967.

Consultant (Counseling Psychology): Department of Veteran Benefits, USVA, 1964-1985.

Consultant to the American Institutes for Research, and field studies liaison activity for *Project Talent*, a longitudinal study of personal and educational development (1960-1961).

Instructor for the U.S. Naval Reserve Officer Training Program at Georgia Institute of Technology, with responsibility for courses in Basic Seamanship, Navigation, and the Uniform Code of Military Justice (1955-1958).

Developer and Director of a special summer educational guidance program for high school students at Emory University, for the United Methodist Church, 1955-1957.

Psychological Appraiser (of missionaries on leave from foreign service): Board of Missions, United Methodist Church, 1955-1957.

Psychological Appraiser, Airline Pilot Testing Program. American Institutes for Research, 1950-1953.

Selected Publications

"Academic Performance of Public and Private School Graduates at Princeton." *ETS Research Bulletin*, 1954, 54-61. (With N. Frederiksen.)

"Public and Private School Graduates in College." *Journal of Teacher Education*, 1955, VI, 18-22. (With N. Frederiksen.)

"A Validity Study of the Iowa Legal Aptitude Test." *Educational and Psychological Measurement*, 1955, 15, 499-501. (With C. Gray and K.T. Duncan.)

"The College Teacher as Counselor." *Journal of Teacher Education*, 1955, VI, 281-285.

"Differential Academic Achievement of Public Vs. Private School Graduates." *Journal of Counseling Psychology*, 1956, 3, 72-73.

"ABACs as an Aid in Test Interpretation." *Journal of Counseling Psychology,* 1956, 4, 145-147. (With N. Frederiksen.)

"What Workers Mean by Security." *Personnel Psychology,* 1956, 9, 229-241 (With A. A. Thompson.)

"Differential College Achievement of Public vs. Private School Graduates." *The Reporter,* 1957, X, 7-9.

"Reliability, Validity, and Stability of Sociometric Ratings." *Journal of Social Psychology,* 1957, 43, 111-121, (With C. F. Warnath.)

"Prediction of Grades from Pre-Admissions Indices in Georgia Tax-Supported Colleges."

Educational and Psychological Measurement, 1958, 841-844. (With Gretchen Franz and Delores Garcia.)

Distributions of 1975 Entering Freshmen on Pre-Admissions Indices. Atlanta: Regents, University System of Georgia, 1958.

"Georgia's Search for Solutions." *College Board Review,* 1958, *36,* 29-32.

"Non-Apparent Limitations of Normative Data." *Personnel and Guidance Journal,* 1959, *Research in Planning. 37,* 656-659.

"Contributions of Sociology to Research in Child Development and Family Life." In Ashby, Helen (ed.) *Research in Child Development and Family Life.* Greensboro, NC: Institute for Child and Family Development, 1961, 107-111.

"Cooperative College Admissions Research." Institutional Research on College Students. Atlanta: Southern Regional Education Board, 1962, pp. 181-193.

"Comments on Student Follow-up Studies." In Lins, Joseph (ed.), *The Role of Institutional Research in Planning.* Madison, Wisconsin: National Institutional Research Forum, 1963, 137-140.

"Non-Intellectual Factors in College Student Achievement." In *High School to College: Readings for Counselors.* New York: The College Entrance Examination\ Board, 1965.

"The Criterion Problem in College Admissions Research." In *Research in Higher Education: Readings for Counselors.* New York: The College Entrance Examination Board, 1965.

"The American College Student." *Purple and Gold* Chi Psi Quarterly). Winter, 1965.

"What College Teachers Value in Students." *College Board Review,* Spring, 1965.

A Guide to Research Design. Princeton: Educational Testing Service, 1965 (With R. L. Linn and Patrica Cross.)

"Today's College Student: Egghead, Bohemian, Skill Seeker, or Joe College?" In Voorhes, R. V., et al. (ed.), *The Aim of Higher Education: Social Adjustment or Human Liberation.* St. Louis: UMHF/UCCF Publications, 1966. (With Frank Coakley.)

"Applications of the Science of Measurement to Higher Education." In Hopkins, E. H. (ed.), *New Dimensions in Higher Education (32).* Washington, DC: USOE, 1968.

"Organized Student Protest and Institutional Climate." *American Educational Research Journal,* Vol. 5, No. 3, May 1968, pp. 291-304. (With Masu Sasajima and R. E. Peterson.)

"The College and University Trustee in North Carolina." *Higher Education in North Carolina,* Vol. IV, No. 10, December 11, 1969.

"Who and What is a College Trustee?" *Chapel Hill Weekly,* December 21, 1969. (Also: in *Proceedings* of the Governor's 1969 Conference on the University Trusteeship, Institute of Government, University of North Carolina.

"The Interaction of Learning, Personality Traits, Ability, and Environment: a Preliminary Study." *Educational and Psychological Measurement,* Vol. XXX, No. 2, Summer 1970, pp. 337-347. (With B. J. Romine and W. S. Geyman.)

"The Use of Measurement in Student Planning and Guidance." In Thorndike, R. L. (ed.), *Educational Measurement* (rev. ed). Washington, DC: American Council on Education, 1971.

"Is the SAT Biased Against Black Students?" *College Board Review,* 1971, 81, pp. 4-9.

"The Desegregation/Integration Dilemma in Higher Education: Implications for Research from Minority Group Experiences." In *Educational Research-Prospects and Priorities* (Appendix 1 to *Hearings on HR 3606, Committee on Education and Labor, U.S. House of Representatives*). Washington, DC: U.S. Government Printing Office, January, 1972.

Black Students in Predominantly White North Carolina Colleges and Universities: Research Report #2. New York: College Entrance Examination Board, 1973 (With Anne Borders-Patterson.)

"Institutional Evaluation." In Anderson, Scarvia, et al (ed.) *Encyclopedia of Educational Evaluation.* San Francisco: Jossey-Bass, 1975.

"The NLS Study of the High School Class of 1972: A Resource for Educational and Human Development Researchers." In Milholland, J. E. (ed.), *New Directions for Testing and Measurement: Insights from Large Scale Surveys.* San Francisco: Jossey-Bass, 1979 (With J. Levinsohn.)

Black Students in Predominantly White North Carolina Colleges and Universities, 1986: A Replication of a 1970 Study (College Board Report No. 86-7). New York: College Entrance Examination Board, 1986 (With Anne Borders-Patterson.)

"Blacks on Predominantly White Southern Campuses." In *The Admissions Strategist*, Vol. 10 (1987). New York: College Entrance Examination Board, 1987. (With Anne Borders-Patterson.)

"BSN Education and PHN Practice: Good Fit or Mismatch?" *Nursing Outlook*, Vol. 36, No. 5, 1988. (With Patricia Deiman and B. Jones.)

"Assessment of the Federal Grant Program for the Establishment of Departments of Family Medicine." *Family Medicine*, Vol. 22, No. 5 (September 1990), pp. 343-349. (With Frank M. Lawler.)

"A classification of Developmental Activities of Academic Family Medicine Supported by Federal Grants." *Academic Medicine*, Vol. 66, No. 3 (March 1991), pp. 166-168. (With Frank H. Lawler and Jane Berkhof.)

"Corresponding with the USPS about Cachet Licensing Fees." *First Days*, Vol. 41, No. 4, (June One, 1996), pp. 284-285.

"Nominations: 1998-2000 AFDCS Board of Directors." In *First Days*, Vol. 42, No. 6, (September One, 1977), pp. 458-460 (E. Lyons, Ed.).

"Cachetmaking in North Carolina: A Search for Hidden Treasure." *First Days*, Vol. 43, No. 3 (April 15, 1998). pp. 190-193. (With R.W. Masto.)

"Joanne Beane: Closet Cachetmaker." *First Days*, Vol. 58 No. 1, (January 15, 2007), pp. 9-12.

Presentations and Papers

Over 150 presentations and papers at special purpose symposia or annual meetings of professional associations, including the American Psychological Association, the American Personnel and Guidance Association, the Sociedad InterAmericana de Psicologia, the Association for Institutional Research, the American Higher Education Association, the American Council on Education, the Southern College Personnel Association, the Southern Society for Philosophy and Psychology, the Southeastern Psychological Association, the National Vocational Guidance Association, the Georgia Association of Colleges and Universities, the Southern Regional Education Board, the North Carolina College Conference, the North Carolina Association for Institutional Research, the Southern Association for Institutional Research, and the Society for College and University Planning. Representative presentations and papers include:

"The Coming Role of the Admissions Officer: His Technical and Ethical Responsibilities." *Proceedings, Second Annual Admissions Conference.* Atlanta: Regents, University System of Georgia, 1957, pp. 8-14.

"Factors to be Considered in Determining Cut-Off Scores." *Proceedings, Second Annual Admissions Conference.* Atlanta: Regents, University System of Georgia, 1957, pp. 22-29.

"Current Research in Non-Intellectual and Non-Interest Factors in Academic Achievement" Much Ado about Nothing?" Paper presented at the Third Annual Meeting, Southeastern Psychological Association, Nashville, 1957.

"The Selection, Admission, and Placement of College Students." Paper presented at the Thirty-Fifth Annual Meeting of the Southern Association of Colleges for Women, 1958 (Published in the Association *Proceedings* for that year.)

"Admissions Research in the N.C. College Conference." Committee Report to the 40th Annual Meeting of the North Carolina College Conference, November, 1960 (Published in Conference *Proceedings*, 1960, pp. 48-53.)

"The Design of Admissions Research." Paper presented at the Southern Regional Meeting of the College Entrance Examination Board, in New Orleans, February 3, 1961.

"The College Student Characteristics Study." Paper presented at a symposium on Institutional Research on College Students (the "Swannanoa Conference"), sponsored by the Southern College Personnel Association and the Southern Regional Educational Board with support from the Carnegie Corporation, March, 1962 (In Wilson, K. (ed.) *Proceedings*. Atlanta, Ga., 1962.

"Desirable Characteristics of College Students: the Criterion Problem." Paper presented at the annual meeting of the American Psychological Association, August 31, 1963.

"Relation of the Medical Students' Psychological Type to their Specialties Twelve Years Later." Paper presented at the annual meeting of the American Psychological Association, Los Angeles, 1964. (*ETS Research Memorandum RM 65-13*.) (With Isabel Myers.)

"The Student Revolution." Keynote Address for the Annual Meeting of the Southern College Personnel Association. Lexington, KY, 1965.

"Look Upon Ayodha: A Critique of Project Essay Grade." Paper presented at the annual meeting of the American Psychological Association, Chicago, September, 1965. (*ETS Research Memorandum RM 65-13.*)

"An Institutional Research Program for Developing Institutions." A working paper for the Regional Education Laboratory for the Carolinas and Virginia, January 15, 1967.

"Selection of Students for Higher Education in the United States." Paper presented at a conference on Purposes and Assessment Methods in Higher Education, sponsored by the University of Lancaster (England) and the Institute of Higher Education of Teachers College, Columbia University, at Grasmere, England, April 1967.

"Student Sub-Cultures: A Factor in Campus Stress. Paper presented at the 23rd National Conference on Higher Education of the American Association for Higher Education, Chicago, 1968.

"Objectives, Design, and History of the National Longitudinal Study." Paper presented at the annual meeting of the American Educational Research Association, Washington, DC, April 1975. (With Elmer Collins.)

"Requirements for a Holy State Assessment." Paper presented at the Southeastern Conference on Educational Measurement, Blacksburg, VA, 1975.

"Characteristics of Successful Federally Supported Special Service Programs in Higher Education." Paper presented at the Pennsylvania Association of Trio Project Directors, March 25, 1976.

"Problems in the Evaluation of the Trio Programs." Paper presented at the 1976 Annual Meeting of the American Educational Research Association, April, 1976, San Francisco. (With G. J. Burkheimer and J. N. Pyecha.)

"Impact of Financial Aid on Postsecondary Entrance and Persistence." Paper presented at the annual meeting of the American Educational Research Association, New York City, April, 1977 (With S. B. Corrallo.)

"Hazards in Research Involving Minorities." Paper presented at the 11th Invitational Conference on Measurement in Education. Athens, Georgia, Dec. 8, 1972

"El Estudio Longitudinal Nacional de Los Estados Unidos de America: Un Conjunto de Datos sin Precedente para la Exploracion." Paper presented at the annual meeting of the Sociedad InterAmericana de Psicologia in Lima, Peru, July 4, 1979.

"The Achievement of Institutional Viability." Paper presented at the annual meeting of the National Association of Title III Administrators, Norfolk, VA, October 27, 1983. (Published in *Proceedings*, Third Annual Conference, NATTA.) (With Rose Mary Healy.)

"The Emerging Mission in Strong Historically Black Colleges and Universities." Paper presented at the Second National Conference on Desegregation in Postsecondary Education. Durham, NC, October 11, 1987.

"The Issue of Developmental Studies in Higher Education." A commissioned paper for the South Carolina Commission on Higher Education. RTI Concept Paper, July, 1986.

"Allocating Institutional Funds through an Enrollment-Based Formula," and "Administration and Governance for Public Postsecondary Vocational Education." Summaries of issues, and reviews of experience in selected states, for the Louisiana Board of Elementary and Secondary Education. (Published as Appendix C.1, pp. C.1-2-C.1-23 and Appendix C.2, pp. C.2-2-C.2-17 in *Postsecondary Vocational—Technical Training in Louisiana*. Baton Rouge, LA: Gulf South Research Institute, May, 1987.)

"The Developmental Proposition for Departments of Family Medicine: A View from Outside." Paper presented at a special session sponsored by the Division of Medicine, Health Resources and Services Administration, in Baltimore, MD, April 24, 1988.

"Research Issues and Strategies in Regard to the Educational Treatment of the Black Athlete." Paper presented at the 1990 Conference of the Southern Association for Institutional Research and the Society for College and University Planning, Ft. Lauderdale, FL, October, 1990 (available from ERIC Clearinghouse on Higher Education as ED 332642).

Project Reports

"Faculty Perceptions of Students—1: The Development of the Student Rating Form." *ETS Research Bulletin RB-64-10*, February, 1964.

"Faculty Perceptions of Students—II: Faculty Definition of Desirable Student Traits." *ETS Research Bulletin RB-64-11*, March, 1964.

"Faculty Perceptions of Students—III: Structure of Faculty Characterizations." *ETS Research Bulletin RB-64-12*, April, 1964.

"Faculty Perceptions of Students—IV: Desirability and Perceptions of Academic Performance. *ETS Research Bulletin RB-64-13*, March, 1964.

"Faculty Perceptions of Students—V: A Second-Order Structure for Faculty Characterizations." *ETS Research Bulletin RB-65-12*, May, 1965.

"Faculty Perceptions of Students—VI: Characteristics of Students for Whom There Is Faculty Agreement on Desirability." *ETS Research Bulletin RB-66-28*, June, 1966.

"Correlates of Academic Performance of Community College Students in Career or Transfer Programs." *ETS Research Bulletin RM-66-35*, July, 1966. (With R. L. Linn.)

"Organized Student Protest and Institutional Climate." *ETS Research Bulletin RB-67-15*, March, 1967.

"Admission of Athletes with Grants-in-Aid in the ACC Institutions: A Confidential Report to the Chancellors and Presidents." Durham, NC: Educational Testing Service, 1971.

"Validity of Pre-Admissions Indices for Blacks and Whites in Six Traditionally White Public Universities in North Carolina." *Project Report 71-15*. Princeton: Educational Testing Service, 1971.

"The Validity of Tests and Achievement in High School for Predicting Performance in Public Universities in North Carolina, with Special Attention to Black Students." *Project Report 71-3*. Princeton: Educational Testing Service, 1971.

"The Stringency of Licensing Standards for Medical Practice in Puerto Rico." Special report to the Puerto Rico Board of Medical Examiners. Educational Testing Service, 1971.

"Comparison of Performance of Spanish-Speaking Physicians on the University of Puerto Rico Medical Knowledge Exams with Their Performance on the ECFMG Examination." Special ETS Report, February, 1972 (With Susan Kerner-Hoag and G. Burkheimer.)

"The Potential of the National Academy of Voluntarism of the United Way of America." *Project Report 72-20*. Princeton: Educational Testing Service, September, 1972.

"What Is, or Should Be, the AGB?—A Report from the Membership." *Project Report 72-28*. An ETS Project Report submitted to the Association of Governing Boards. Princeton: Educational Testing Service, September, 1972.

"Impact of the Curso de Perfeccionamiento: An Audit of the Effectiveness of the Physician Retraining Program at the University of Puerto Rico." *Project Report 73-22*. Princeton: Educational Testing Service, 1973.

"A Census of Special Support Programs for 'Disadvantaged' Students in American Institutions of Higher Education., 1971-71." An ETS Project Report submitted to the Office of Planning, Budgeting and Evaluation, U.S. Office of Education. *Project Report 73-16*. Princeton: Educational Testing Service, April, 1973.

"Dropouts at InterAmerican University." A special research report to the President, InterAmerican University, San Germain, Puerto Rico, 1974.

"The Effective College and University Board: A Report of a National Survey of Trustees and Presidents." An RTI project report submitted to the Association of Governing Boards. Research Triangle Park, NC: Research Triangle Institute, 1974.

"The Impact of Special Services Programs in Higher Education for 'Disadvantaged' Students." An ETS project report submitted to the Office of Planning, Budgeting and Evaluation of the U.S. Office of Education. *Project Report 75-14*. Princeton: Educational Testing Service, June, 1975.

"Accountability at the College of the Mainland: A Report on External Evaluation." Special report to the President, College of the Mainland, Texas City, TX, 1976. (With W. McFarlane.)

A Study of the National Upward Bound and Talent Search Programs, Vol. 1: Review of the Literature Relevant to the Upward Bound and Talent Search Programs. An RTI report to the Office of Planning, Budgeting and Evaluation of the U.S. Office of Education. April, 1976 (With Cynthia A. Kenyon.)

Remedial Educational Activities of the University of North Carolina: 1976. A special report to the University of North Carolina General Administration. Research Triangle Park, NC: Research Triangle Institute, June, 1977.

Actualizing Policy Implications of the National Longitudinal Study. An RTI project report submitted to the National Center for Education Statistics. Research Triangle Park, NC: Research Triangle Institute, January, 1978.

Evaluability Assessment of the Strengthening Developing Institutions Program. An RTI project report submitted to the Office of Planning, Budgeting and Evaluation, of the U.S. Office of Education. Research Triangle Park, NC: Research Triangle Institute, September, 1981 (With R. A. Ironside.)

Institutional Development: Implications for Institutions of Higher Education. An RTI project report submitted to the Office of Planning, Budgeting and Evaluation, of the U.S. Office of Education. Research Triangle Park, NC: Research Triangle Institute, October, 1983. (With R. A. Ironside and J. VanSant.)

Factors Associated with Successful Developmental Investment in Title III Eligible Institutions: A Special Report to Program Managers in the U.S. Department of Education. An RTI project report submitted to the Office of Planning, Budgeting and Evaluation, of the U.S. Office of Education. Research Triangle Park, NC: Research Triangle Institute, October, 1983. (With R. A. Ironside and J. VanSant.)

The Anatomy of Institutional Development for Higher Education Institutions Serving Students from Low Income Backgrounds. An RTI project report submitted to the Office of Planning, Budgeting and Evaluation of the U.S. Office of Education. Research Triangle Park, NC: Research Triangle Institute, October, 1983. (With R. A. Ironside and J. VanSant.)

The North Carolina Community College Study: Mission, Enrollment and Staffing Patterns, Funding Procedures, and Administration and Governance. An RTI project report for the North Carolina State Board of Community Colleges. Research Triangle Park, NC: Research Triangle Institute, May, 1986. (With A. M. Cruze, J.E.S. Lawrence, and Karla Cosgrove.)

Black Students in Predominantly White North Carolina Colleges and Universities, 1986: A Replication of a 1970 Study. An RTI project report for the College Entrance Examination Board. Research Triangle Park, NC: Research Triangle Institute, July, 1986. (With Anne Borders-Patterson.).

Impact of Federal Support on the Family Medicine Predoctoral Training Program. An RTI project report to the Division of Medicine, Bureau of Health Professions, Health Resources and Services Administration, Department of Health and Human Services. Research Triangle Park, NC: Research Triangle Institute, August, 1986. (With S. H. Gelbach.)

Vocational Education Study: Final Report An RTI project report for the Joint Legislative Commission on Governmental Operations, State of North Carolina. Research Triangle Park, NC: Research Triangle Institute, November, 1986 (With J. L. Cox, Judy Holley, J. E. S. Lawrence, and D. W. Drewes.)

Study of the Postsecondary Vocational Technical School System of Louisiana. Baton Rouge, LA: Gulf South Research Institute, 1987. (With L. Cox, Judy Holley, and others.)

Public Health Nursing: Education and Practice. Washington, DC: U. S. Department of Health and Human Services, October, 1987. (With D. C. Jones and Madora C. Davis.)

An Assessment of the Development and Support of the Family Medicine Departments Program. An RTI project report to the Division of Medicine, Bureau of Health Professions, Health Resources and Service Administration, Department of Health and Human Services. Research Triangle Park, NC: Research Triangle Institute, March, 1989. (With Frank Lawler.)

Present or Past Professional Association Memberships

American Educational Research Association
American Psychological Association
American Personnel and Guidance Association
Southeastern Psychological Association
Southern Society for Philosophy and Psychology
Southern College Personnel Association
Phi Delta Kappa
Kappa Delta Pi
Sigma Xi
Association for Institutional Research
International Association for Educational Assessment
American First Day Cover Society
American Philatelic Society

May, 2007

B. Paper: "How to Succeed at ETS

As is so frequently the case when a change in corporate objectives creates a situation that incumbents cannot tolerate, company loyalty goes out the window. This may or may not have been the case when pressures to close the ETS Field Research Office that I had created were made, but I began to see ETS in a very different light from that which had guided my conduct there for 12 Years.

Primarily, then, for therapy, I put together a paper that dealt with all the little skeletons that could be invoked. In this paper, "p/j" means "project/job," which referred to the numerical code for accounting purposes of any activity; "WAR" is "Work Activity Record," the name of a form used to record activity for accounting purposes; and "CEEB" stood for the College Entrance Examination Board, a separate organization, but for which ETS was contractually the operational arm for all testing activity.

This paper dealt frequently with events or names that were quite sensitive at that time, and a copy was shared only with a confidante and the then executive vice president, now deceased. Most if not all of the problems treated so facetiously in this paper have long since been remedied, and it is best considered as indicative of my mood at that time under the circumstances I faced.

HOW TO SUCCEED AT ETS

A Guide for Program, Project, and Cost Center Directors

1. *Financial and Support Considerations.*

   1. Never permit anyone from another cost center to charge your p/j. Instead, pad your own WAR with as many charges to p/js outside your cost center as possible. Your personal success is judged not on how much business you attract, but by the proportion of your time you can charge to an outside or inside source. Avoid overhead, which has been declared inappropriate for almost everyone except the officers (they need all they can get to maintain their accustomed style of life).
   2. Recognize that if you must go outside your cost center for necessary services, there will be pressure to choose the most expensive alternative within ETS. You will receive no personal credit for this while you are on this earth, but you can have the satisfaction of knowing that you are contributing to the support of your organization. In particular, never be misled by cheaper costs outside the organization. This sustains our competitors, who are generally profit-making corporations, and who, by doing work for less, threaten to take business away from us.
   3. Before agreeing to any activity, figure out exactly how much it will cost. Then double (or better yet, triple) that figure. This holds particularly when fixed price contracts can be negotiated. The world is still full of suckers like CEEB that cannot challenge the defense of "ETS quality is expensive." Also, our cost accountants are usually bigger, crookeder, and smarter than theirs.
   4. In test development activities, insist on ETS copyright for materials produced, no matter if the sponsor who supports the activity is willing or not. Remember that with CEEB revenue down, we need to find legal ways of underwriting development costs. This applies to questions such as "What is your sex?" as well as to achievement test items.
   5. Spend a lot of time on the telephone. This is not only an income-producing activity (as long as you have something to charge time to), but also ties up someone else who, if he is worth his salt, will find new ways to charge for the work he could have been doing instead of talking with you.
   6. Never, never argue with anyone in the Financial Division. They believe that ETS survives as a function of their great skill in using cost accounting formulas to eliminate cost centers or activities that do not abide by the above rules. Arguments for tempering decisions on the educational

(or social) significance of an idea or program with future potential for supporting ETS will be neither understood nor heeded. First, these people are concerned only with staying out of trouble now, not next year, when they may loaned to Washington. Second, their task is to set cost rates so that such costs as for, say, a modest conference center, can be retrieved, and our non-profit status comfortably maintained even under the scrutiny of Nader's Raiders. Third, they have no basis to judge potential except from the history of an existing project with a rich income over the years with some low-cost clown (i.e., not John Carroll) in charge.

7. Pad your department or program with low-salaried people, but insist that their cost rate be computed by averaging their costs in with your costs. Then, when asked for help, use these people to do the work.
8. Should you have a chance contact with a foundation or federal representative that reveals need for a job you can handle, use self-hypnosis to forget you ever heard. The danger of doing otherwise is that you may unwittingly disrupt the clandestine efforts of someone else at ETS above you who has for several years trying to sell something else they or ETS wants to that agency, which, though the agency neither wants nor needs it, could provide income for ETS for years to come.
9. Consider parolees from prison with prior records of stock frauds and swindles in choosing a budget representative. The internal auditors, in their conviction that only employees filling out travel vouchers are inherently dishonest, will never catch them.
10. Never let a research project answer the initial question. This disposes of the problem. Instead, learn how to let research lead to new, more expensive-to-answer questions. If any trouble with this, point out that what you have achieved is what any good research accomplishes.
11. The notion that the nation's wealth comes from increased productivity and efficiency does not generalize to ETS. *Increased wealth for ETS comes most precisely from increased charging.* No one has found how to get away with this at the organizational level except by creating a monopoly, then spreading the additional costs among several million test takers. Our success is attested by the fact that no one else, save the largest foundations and federal enterprises, can afford us.
12. Remember: ETS grew large and great by taking a simple idea from Brigham, adding a little polish by employing a better printer than he could afford, and then finding new things to charge for, without commensurate productivity or costly change in the original product. (Look how long we got away without a test manual for SAT!) Those who understand and practice this principle will receive the eventual reward of being allowed to charge all their costs to overhead.

II. *Care and Feeding of Officers*

1. If you have an action-oriented VP, wriggle around until you're assigned to one of those never replaced but never active. They leave you alone to practice your craft unhindered.
2, If your VP is active and interferes with life as you prefer it, arm him with material to use against other VPs. This is an excellent way to keep the officers too busy to interfere with you.
3. Never disagree with anyone above you. This forces them underground where they practice Relationship with Other ETS Staff rule # 5, particularly disastrous to the target when practiced between consenting officers.
4. If of the opposite sex, sleep with your VP. If of the same sex, recognize that the best channel is through the mistress. Work on her, for she is more likely to listen and be listened to.
5. If you have grievances, find a way to make them known anonymously. Putting your name with them interferes with having them judged on their merit, and permits them to be interpreted as "Old _____ is on his kick again." Look what happened to Bill Coffman, John Hemphill, and Dave Nolan, who took forceful stands as matters of principle.
6. In any research project—but particularly for those federally supported—do what you can to alienate your project officer. This not only keeps him out of your hair, but also, because his need is to protect his own job by having you do a successful project, is likely to get him consigned as a part-time lecturer to the Graduate School of Education at Indiana University, where he belongs.
7. Remember that something that costs a great deal (i.e., a computer terminal or a conference center) is easier to acquire than something that is cheap (i.e., a slide rule, or access to Dining Room 4-C for a staff meeting). Recognize this in requests. Winning one or two of these larger requests keeps the organization efficiency-minded, as finance has to deny the day-to-day necessities to acquire the large sums required to support the ongoing activities of the organization.

III. *Work Efficiency*

1., Get rid quickly and completely of any request that requires handling. As a last resort, do the work yourself.
2. Learn how to PERT. With this tool, in two months you can show anyone a better way to do what they completed 45 days ago.

3. Don't lose too much time producing quality reports. The sponsor won't understand them, no one internally will read them (be thankful, for the ETS game is to knock each other's work).
4. Never, never publish. Such destroys your chance to use the material again in a speech or subsequent report. Remember some of our most successful people have been givimg the same paper for 15 or 20 years.
5. Never go to any superior with a problem—or even with a solution. Just solve the problem instead. The inviolate and supreme criterion of effective problem resolution is that no physical or mental energy by anyone else will be required. This holds even if the consequence is a gross, public misstep by ETS. Another program or project will always come along. Particularly dangerous is any controversy between two professional staff that is forced on superiors to resolve. As one upwardly mobile VP recently remarked: "This puts me in the middle, and you know I can't afford that."
6. On receiving a troublesome inquiry by phone from outside, refer the caller to someone else. A secretary with a firm and hostile attitude with anyone can be a great asset.
7. Once you've delegated a responsibility, never waste time checking up on progress. This not only requires your time and threatens a clash with a prima donna who's now building his own empire, but also reveals you to be Wood Hall supervisor material, rather than Division Head or Officer material. The latter types have, of course, ideas of such excellence that nothing could go wrong, and no further attention is needed. Develop that kind of image, Baby!

IV. *Blameavoidance*

1. If the sponsor of a grant or contract complains, or if a subgroup of program benefactors attack, blame the problem on the outside party.
2. Upon sustaining cost overruns that can't be hidden by charging to someone else's p/j, pad your next p/j. This can be avoided if each new proposal is a duplicate of a past proposal, and you recharge as if the work really has been done.
3. Add a minority group staff member. Given any complaint, you can state that he or she did this, and that the complainer is obviously prejudiced. This has the added advantage of convincing the minority employee that ETS and the outside world *are* prejudiced.
4. If your activity is charged with cultural bias, appoint a token minority member to staff. If trouble persists, convince CEEB to fund a conference for finding constructive ways around the problem. That is good, of course,

but leaves CEEB with nothing else to do but come back and raise hell with us.
5. Do not sustain any personal confrontation with minority groups except at some site far remote from the Princeton Office. Should the report ever get back, it will be so garbled no one will recognize your part in it, and you can say it was probably something CEEB stirred up.
6. Remember Henry V's advice to young Prince Hal: "Busy giddy minds with foreign quarrels." Thus, England had a magnificent war with France, and attention was drawn away from England's internal domestic problems. Ronald Reagan and the seasoned ETS program director make good use of this.

V. *On Initiative and Creativity*

1. Never take on a new chore—program, proposal, or project—suggested by an officer. They have to become involved with the losers no one will take. Instead, work on those that everyone else wants; let them do the dirty work of writing the proposals. Then, inflate price and get yourself to the bidder's conference; when proposed budget is cut, you can return reporting the sponsor only wants and can pay for what *you* are willing to provide.
2. Don't make suggestions. Remember that the ETS policy has never tolerated the Suggestion Box; instead, the concept of the Objection Box is supported. At ETS, one proves his ability and great intelligence by finding fault with suggestions, or pointing out situations where years ago they were tried and failed.
3. Don't waste time on technical creativity, unless it is costly—see Financial and Support Consideration # 11. Remember, ETS technical excellence depends on having a facade of consultants like Ledyard Tucker, or John Perkins, who can be bought, and avoiding fools like Ralph Tyler and David Reissman who cannot be bought. The maudlin, simplistic world outside isn't ready for anything but maudlin, simplistic answers.

VI. *Use of Job Role to Achieve the Good Life*

1. Get yourself appointed to one of the new committees. You need the chance to nap undetected and rest from your other strenuous activities
2. If wage-increase guidelines call for a 7% increase, recommend increases for your staff totaling only about 4%. The person reviewing you must then make a final recommendation on your salary that will bring the total group to 6.5%, keeping the other .5% to be applied to his own salary. This gives you both a nice raise.

3. Have an affair with your secretary or assistant; this proves your masculinity or femininity in long-standing ETS style. Avoid affairs with clients; you can never be sure who else at ETS, ACT, or CEEB they are sleeping with.
4. Remember you can eat well while traveling by inviting a guest to dinner. The $7.50 limitation now does not apply. A local school teacher or passing American Legionnaire will do nicely.
5. Join a carpool to get to and from work. This means you have a constant excuse to leave promptly five minutes early, no matter what the activity underway at the time. If you were with outside visitors, treat the pool to cocktails on the way home, and turn in an entertainment report naming the outside guests who, witnesses can attest, were in town that evening.

VII. *Relationships with Other ETS Staff*

1. Never make the mistake of being explicit about the success of your program or project. ETS consists of a sophisticated group of bastards who know you are guilt-ridden and trying to hide something. Excellence of your program is best shown by simply ignoring the possibility that any other program may exist.
2. A sign of great weakness is accepting any suggestion from anyone outside your program or project (this excludes officers, who tend to make no suggestions anyway). You should know that you have thought of all the good ideas yourself. Admitting another idea is as good is not only inherently offensive, but also is likely to be parlayed by the one who suggested it into a competing empire that could destroy your own.
3. Come to work a dignified hour or so late; leave precisely on time. Remember that a frequent two-martini lunch can equip you to meet the afternoon challenges with the non-concern and glassy stare they deserve.
4. Never write a memo. In particular, never write a memo answering another memo. This reveals weakness or defensiveness. If not convinced, note the scarcity of memos from the officers.
5. Do away with enemies by whispering. Should a memo be necessary, send no copy to the person involved, or mark it confidential, showing a copy to the person charged, but be sure that copy is burned before transmission. A hushed word over lunch to a VP, like "I can't understand why so and so is fighting you behind your back, but you know how he is" is better than 10 documentations.
6. If a researcher, consider your sacred mission to be the investment of ETS' non-profits in studies no one would pay for. This keeps you pure in the

eyes of your colleagues. If your work should prove something someone else had done at ETS is wrong or if you find fault with programs, this is excellent, too, for you maintain organizational integrity (even if the other guy was right).
7. Get a picture in the *Examiner* of you accepting a brownie from one of Lou Kozma's staff.
8. Pictures from the centerfold of *Playboy* or *Penthouse* are good, too, for they make the hanger a leader and a hero in the popular revolt against Kay Sharp. When caught, press the matter angrily as a case of jeopardy to academic freedom.
9. If nothing else works: hang a picture of Lee Cronbach in your office. Inscribe it

With affection and gratitude
for finding a way to compute

$$\rho^2 t_\cdot x_{\cdot f} = \delta^2 t_\cdot / \delta^2 x_{\cdot f}$$

—Lee

Grateful acknowledgment is made to P/Js 035-01 and 581-13, to which the 46 man-days necessary to produce this report were charged.

C. Remarks: Memorial Service for Charles Edge

Throughout my professional life, I felt that social contacts with those with whom I worked was hardly proper. Although I went to great lengths to support my associates and staffs, and insisted that we operate on a first name basis, I felt that off the job was a private or personal matter for all of us. That I was able to carry this off was attested by my successor on the occasion of my retirement: I was recognized in a speech by my successor for being fiercely loyal to and supportive of my staff, even when so doing was personally damaging to me.

Upon retirement, this restriction no longer held, but the patterns had been set with the people with whom I worked. Close friendships, for both Pegge and myself, became people with whom we came into contact in our daily life other than former work associates.

One such person was Charles Edge. For four years before his death from heart problems that were (in my opinion) improperly treated by the hospital and its physicians, he was a close and dear friend. We talked or emailed each other daily, and frequently had lunch together. He asked me to speak at his memorial service, should he predecease me, and this I did. I provide here a copy of what I said because so much of what was exemplary in his life are things I value highly.

Comments at the Memorial Service for Charles E. Edge, Ph.D.

June 10, 2005
Junius A. "Jay" Davis

My dear friend Charles: a most remarkable man. He starred in one of the toughest, most excellent, and deservedly arrogant departments in this or any other University for three decades, achieving the unique distinction denied many excellent teachers—not one, but two Tanner awards for excellence in undergraduate instruction. But his colleague Erika Lindemann has just provided a sensitive and excellent summary of his substantial contributions during his tenure there.

It must have been a decade ago that I received a note from a Charles Edge that began "You don't know me, but . . ." The note dealt with a matter concerning stamps that the American Philatelic Society had asked him to forward to me. I looked him up in the UNC telephone directory, finding him to be a retired professor of English. My interest in Charles was immediately piqued by his life in a career I would have chosen, had I thought I was good enough and had I thought I could make a reasonable living at it, for my happiest days at the University in the early 1940s were my classes in English Literature and Creative Writing. Although he started as a hero figure, I found quickly not only a warmth, but also a remarkable fit with my other interests and values. (Little did I realize then that others who were quite different from me felt the same way about Charles.)

What was he like in retirement? Again, Erika has provided an excellent summary of his life both before and after the classroom. A prime characteristic was that he was fiercely independent and self-sufficient, and proud of it. He spent his time productively with his computer, reading newspapers, reviews, emailing, etc. He relished the opera as a hungry man would view a perfectly grilled fillet mignon, but he also relished his soaps, recording them when one of us took him away for lunch. He did not miss a political opinion piece in the *Washington Post*, the *New York Times*, the *Boston Globe*, the *Los Angeles Times*, or the verbally prolific bloggers. He amassed a distinguished collection of stamps; donated them to a youth philatelic association; then built a distinguished collection of First Day Covers that qualified as "miniature works of art." But dearest of all to him was his noble cat, Dixie, and the friends who visited him, emailed him, or went to lunch with him a close second. In his relationships, he was cautious and discreet to a fault, and took special pains not to offend others.

But my views—and those of Erika—could be biased, for we dearly loved this man. He had asked me on the way to the hospital to let some of his philatelic friends know why he could not respond to them, and as his hospital stay became extended, I contacted others in responding to email messages in his computer mailbox. I did not ask them to tell me what they thought of him, but their responses frequently included some words that helped define what Charles was to them. Let me share some of these with you. Although I have not sought permission from anyone, these are actual quotes:

1. Doris Betts (Distinguished novelist, fellow Professor Emeritus of English, UNC)

    "My friend and gentle person."

    "A teacher who made even the most recalcitrant male students open up to Victorian novels."

    "A superb teacher, a kindly colleague, an altogether good man. I miss him."

    "I am so sorry Charles is gone from us. What a lovely person."

2. Bob Z. (A Professor of English at another major university, who was a fellow graduate student with Charles at Duke University)

    "The death of an old friend, such a good guy, has a finality not easy to accept or know what to do about."

3. Preston F. (A Professor of English at Butler University in Kansas; Charles was on his dissertation committee

    "He was my greatest teacher ever."

4. Joey B. (My teen-age grandson; frequent lunch partner with Charles and me, and an ardent debater on political issues)

    "He was a real cool guy. Neat, you know."

5. Kathie Vaughan (Talented artist who painted portrait of Dixie)

    "Both children loved to go to lunch with him, and he was always eager to hear about their lives."

6. Mickey C. (Then an aide at the Copy Center who helped him with his FDCs)

"Please tell him I am praying for him—he is such a wonderful man."
"Heaven will be a kinder and gentler place—Look out, ladies, here he comes!"

7. Amanda T. (Administrative Staff Member in the UNC Dental School)

"I am so saddened by the news. I know how much Dr. Edge wanted to go home to Dixie."

8. Cheryl (Receptionist for the Ophthalmologist treating his macular degeneration. Her voice broke when I called her to cancel Charles' appointment. She had heard of his demise from staff at the office of Dr. Wood, his regular ophthalmologist).

"We all were horrified to learn of his heart attack He is held in great affection there."

9. Kathy V. (Previously quoted)

"I am sad for those whose lives he touched—we shall miss Charles very much."

"He encouraged me to new literary discoveries."

10. Sarah F. (Graduate student in English who served as his driver)

"He is very important to me. I haven't had a living grandfather for many years .... has been a great friend to me since I met him."

11. Frank M. (Retired GE Salesman and cachetmaker in upstate New York)

"I'm really so sorry to hear about Charles. We are losing a lot of good people lately."

12. Doris G. (Nationally distinguished artist living in Southern California, whose Jewish husband said prayers for Charles every morning at 6 A.M. beginning May 2)

"Here I am in La Mesa, and tears come to my eyes when I think of what he is going through. (Response to a progress report when Charles was in the hospital)

"Charles was esteemed by so many, and his memory will be kept alive by those who cared so much for him."

"I don't think he was aware that so many people cared."

13. Ray L. (Retired English teacher; fellow bachelor and pet lover, philatelic friend)

"There are just so many people who care for Charles."

"I'm relieved to know that Dixie is doing well. She was the center of Charles' life."

"I'm devastated. I have really been down."

"Although I never met Charles personally, I felt a genuine connection with him from our numerous email correspondences. I could sense what a genuinely decent person he is."

14. Dave F. (Retired Real Estate Investment Trust owner, of Dallas, Hyannisport, and Fort Lauderdale, and philatelic friend)

"Dr. Edge has been much on my mind today—I don't know why, but he is important to me just a nice guy, I guess."

"The man was loved. You can ask for no more than that."

"He was not just a great guy. He was a smart and accomplished guy."

"I'll miss him."

Now that you know I am not alone in my regard for Charles, let me say what I admired about him.

He cared deeply about other people—not because he wanted to be liked, but because he liked them, and was genuinely interested in them. He refused to rank other people by such things as level of education or intelligence, degree of wealth, social caste and class, ethnicity, age, sex—and as one consequence, children knew instinctively and instantly that he genuinely liked them.

He gave, not because he wanted to receive or to be loved for the act, but because he genuinely wanted to impart something of value to others.

And: he was so unassuming that most of us did not realize the depth and stature of this man until we lost him.

Several years ago Charles asked me if I would be willing to speak at his memorial service. I asked him why in the world would he want me to do this. I will never forget his reply: "I am quite sure you will say something scandalous about me!" I can't disappoint him. So, in closing, I would like to paraphrase e e cummings' comment about Buffalo Bill:

> *"Charles Edge is defunct.*
> *Jesus he was a handsome man . . ."*

Let us all be thankful that this remarkable man touched our lives.

D. Funeral Sermon for Claude Morris by the Rev. Mike Davis

Claude Morris, who lived a physically active life for nigh on to 104 years, was my wife's favorite uncle, my father-in-law's favorite brother, and my favorite of all of my in-laws kith and kin. When he died, my minister son Mike was the pastor of his church in Troy, N.C., and Mike shared his parent's deep admiration and affection for this man. The sermon he preached for his funeral documents many of the important things for which our families have stood, and is respectfully appended here.

Text: 2 Timothy 4:6-8

*"The time of my departure has come. I have fought the good fight,
I have finished the race, I have kept the faith. From now on there
is reserved for me the crown of righteousness, which the Lord,
the righteous judge, will give me on that day, and not only to
me but also to all who have longed for His appearing."*

We are here today to remember and celebrate the life of **Claude Edward Morris,** who went home to be with the Lord on Tuesday afternoon.

Claude was blessed to be with us for almost 104 years.

He saw Haley's Comet twice;
He watched the Hindenburg fly overhead on its way to Lakehurst, N. J.
He remembers people and places that he had been, and stories he had heard. And if you were from Montgomery County could tell you something about your grandfather, where people gathered, what they did, and what they talked about.
Every bride that married into the Morris family was given a tour of the county by Claude: to Low Water Bridge, the jumping off rock, Indian Hole or Beans Mill. He could make you see and feel a special connection here.
Ex. Even Matt (Neal's oldest boy) remembers Claude taking him to Low Water Bridge when he was 3 years old. Matt went too close to the river and fell in. On the way home he told his parents the best part of the trip was "falling in the river."
Claude loved our community and he loved LIFE.

He waited until he was 38 years old to ask Villie to marry him. She thought he was never going to ask her. Now 66 years later . . . we all know that they have shared a special love . . . a wonderful home, with strong family values and a solid faith that has carried them through good times and bad.

They have been blessed to see children, grandchildren, and great grandchildren come into the family.

Ex. And Claude even when he was 80 years old would be down on the floor playing with the children. Putting a smile on their faces. Telling a story or a joke and making them laugh, or listening to his grandchildren play music.

He set an example for all of us. He didn't hold a grudge. He accepted people where they were. He treated them with kindness, and he helped people when it was within his power to bless them.

He gave a poor man a chicken when he had nothing to eat.

He brought home apples from the mountain to share with others.

He made me an apple pie. When I walked in to see Claude and Villie, Claude was worn out and lying down in a chair. He was covered in flour from his waist down. "What have you been up to?" I asked. He went on to tell me that he had made me an apple pie. He got about half of it done, when he asked Villie to finish the rest.

Claude organized our family reunions . . . and they have been going on for 65 years.

He always made sure that everyone had plenty to eat. Mashed potatoes, biscuits, were always on the table. Many times there was homemade ice cream. During our Friday night family gatherings we had a great time. Leona and Grace always said Claude was the best brother ever.

When they were growing up, Claude's family remembers Wednesday night picnics with Vienna Sausage, Pork and Beans, Sardines, and a Coke. They said it was the only junk food they were allowed growing up. But it seemed like a feast for the King and Queen of England when you sat out on a lovely day and had a meal together. Claude knew how to help everyone have a good time.

Claude loved his animals, too . . . .

He raised foxhounds, and doctored peoples' pets.

He could tell you the name of some one's dog, and even that dog's birthday!

He could tell you the names of every mule a man with 13 had, and jokingly replied when someone asked what the man's name was who owned them: "I don't remember."

Claude had a good sense of humor, and he passed it on to his family.

Ex. His children jokingly said that "Daddy loved his dogs more than he did them!"

If you knew Claude Morris you can probably remember a good joke he told you. If it brightened your day, made you smile or laugh, then it was all worth it. God puts people here who know how to help us enjoy life.

Claude was a member of Trinity Church . . .

He sang in the choir for 15 years . . . and went through the county with the Trinity Quartet.

Claude was the groundskeeper and custodian for the Church.

Ex. We once found a heavy piano up on the third floor and wondered how it got there. The Church has tiny stairwells, and the piano had been lifted up three flights of stairs. Taking it back down took many men and this after we had taken the piano apart, with the metal section in the middle still intact. I asked Uncle Claude about it, and he said, "My boys and I carried it upstairs." With Uncle Claude, he always found a way.

Claude was active in our United Methodist Men's Fellowship—cooking, and attending the Men's Class at Trinity.

Our text today proclaims the joys of keeping the faith that keeps . . .

Claude had a faith that kept him.

Those 'in' Christ . . . who have run the race, and finished the course . . . and kept the faith, will receive the crown of righteousness.

Ex. One day there will be a great and mighty congregation wearing crowns. It will be made up of those who loved the Lord and lived for Him. This we can look forward to . . . because we have a faith that keeps us and has promised this.

Faith is never simply saying, "I believe . . ." Real faith implies intimate fellowship with God in Christ.

Ex. The Apostle Paul looking back on his life could see the covenant his soul had kept with Christ. He felt the strength his faith had given him and the ways it had molded and blessed who he became.

It is not wealth or intellect that makes us. It is faith that can fit us for heaven—faith working within us to draw us nearer to God Himself every day.

Ex. Enoch was the first man reported to go home to God.

He and God often walked together. The ancients say that one day as Enoch and God were walking, God said "Enoch, you are much closer to my house than yours. Come and stay with me." That day Enoch went home with the Lord.

In the end it is our hope in Christ that assures each of us the chance to walk with God forever, and to wear the crown of righteousness.

Ex. They tell a story of a man walking by a cathedral as it was being built. A stone mason was working on a block of marble sculpting it. The man asked the mason what he was doing. He pointed to a place up top where the stone would fit perfectly if he did his job right, and the mason said, "I'm shaping it down here, so it will fit in up there!"

Claude Morris has gone home to be with the Lord . . .

We give thanks for his life . . . because God has shaped him down here so that he can fit in up there.
And God's mercy and grace are so wide, that if we will let him . . . He will shape us too—down here—so that we can fit in up there!

Rev. Michael A. Davis
Trinity Methodist Church
Troy, North Carolina
May 12, 2006

E. Selected Published "Letters to the Editor"

I have forgotten where it was, but in one of the first *Who's Who* kind of publications in which I was listed, "writing angry letters" was described as a hobby. Although the majority of such letters that I have written were to individuals—usually corporation heads, political figures, or (a favorite target) evangelists that write me for "the largest amount I can prayerfully afford"—I have frequently found that letters to the editor are sometimes more likely to reach their target than letters sent directly. And, I find that thinking people read editorials, columnists, and submitted letters, when they would skip major news items. Pegge believes simply that I like the notoriety, and she just may be right—she usually is.

The letters included in this section have been selected from letters that were actually published, usually in a local paper (I have not had much luck with national newspapers other than the *Atlanta Constitution*, and those letters, written when I was at Emory University or the Board of Regents of the University System of Georgia, have long since been lost in my files. Some of the letters selected may seem trivial to the reader, but my selection criteria have to do with matters that seemed then and now impor- tant to me. And somehow, I cannot escape the feeling that maybe—just maybe—some of these may have had more impact that any of my many carefully crafted research reports.

The letters and editorial presented in this section are copyrighted by the respective newspapers, and are reproduced here by permission of the copyright owners.

E1. Letters Concerning Preparation of Teachers

When I assumed the graduate deanship at the University of North Carolina at Greensboro, I had hoped to have some impact on the quality of teacher training at that institution. That I failed was attested by a grade report turned in the last semester I was in residence by a Professor of Education for a first graduate course in education: there were 29 students in her class, and all 29 received a final grade of "A".

I should have just shut up, of course, but now removed from the University payroll, I turned to the *Greensboro Daily News* to provide a forum. My credentials as former dean of the graduate school surely were instrumental in making my statements appear credible. The letters attracted comment, as expected, from some of the faculty and students, and unexpectedly, a supporting editorial.

It would be tenuous at best to claim that the letters were related to any improvements in teacher education. It was clear, however, that they prompted a productive dialog among the citizens in the community. And, I am sure they were read and understood by the faculty in other departments at the Woman's College, who in turn may have exerted a variety of positive influences. The Dean of the School of Education, who had winced when our Graduate Administrative Board failed to approve his efforts to introduce a new course entitled "Introducing Children to the World," and to be taught by TV's Ms. Frances Horowitz of Ding Dong School, had breathed a discernible sigh of relief when he learned that I had resigned. Nevertheless, he left the following year, and there were some significant additions to the faculty—Dr. Jack Bardon, for instance, whom we had known in Princeton.

All letters and other material included in this first part of Appendix E were published in the *Greensboro Daily News* at various dates in the fall of 1961 and 1962 (I did not keep an accurate record of the date of publication). The copies provided in the following pages are transcribed from xerox copies of the actual news clippings.

Our incompetent teachers?

Editor of the Daily News
 In our concern for better public education, it would be well to look carefully at the kinds of young people we attract to and distract from career plans as teachers, and who may be found in the teacher preparatory programs in the colleges of the state and nation.
 In a recent study involving analysis of almost 5,000 students in eight colleges on every trait or aptitude that modern testing research has found useful in describing college students, the researcher concluded: "Expected patterns of scores appear . . . engineers and physical scientists are good at mathematical reasoning,

the English majors are good at verbal comprehension, and the education majors are outstandingly poor at everything intellectual." It is significant both that the education majors did poorly, and that this was expected.

Studies such as the Ginsberg analysis of students who failed to pass the draft deferment test, or the classic study of the Thurstones in the 1930s, have long given objective evidence to support what every college staff member knows: Students who cannot do well in conventional subject matter in the arts and sciences can change their major to education, and usually survive with distinction.

At one quite reputable local college in Greensboro, the average education major (as a junior) stands in the bottom 10 percent among peers majoring in history in general intelligence, yet education majors "achieve" higher grade averages than do history majors. I know of no institution of higher education where similar situations have not prevailed.

The same situation is found in programs at the graduate level. An adjoining state found in requiring teachers applying for graduate study to meet current intellectual requirements for admission as freshmen that almost half of these applicants were excluded.

When I was graduate dean at the Woman's College and insisted that teachers applying for graduate courses meet the same test minima required by the university for entering freshmen (as well as to produce a transcript with better than a C average and to make no more than two errors of spelling or grammatical usage on their application), I was accused by one program director of trying to ruin his program, and by a higher administrative official of unreasonably attempting to turn W.C. into a "little Harvard," and of being unsympathetic to the needs of the state for more and better trained teachers and of the college for larger numbers of graduate students, a factor in its budget.

Such facts, though long common knowledge among college officials as well as among students seeking easy programs, have been suppressed for obvious reasons. When confronted with these facts, professional educators argue that intelligence or scholastic ability alone is not a sure criterion of teaching ability, and indeed this is true. But these same educators have failed to produce, in their years of fervent practical work and concern with the "whole child", any reliable and valid criterion of teaching ability. It would seem that a major stock in trade, in the absence of any measurable teaching ability, would be learning ability (intelligence), or the ability to read with understanding and to comprehend, remember, and manipulate verbal and mathematical symbols.

The outlook in North Carolina and other states is bleak not only because of years of prostitution of standards which attract mediocre students and frighten away capable ones, but also because generations of college education faculty have taught to this less capable group, and have lost the ability to provide much of real substance in their education courses. One popular local graduate course for teachers in service employs as its text a third grade mathematics text, and students are led through it page by page. The instructor of this course would have difficulty shifting to a challenging and useful consideration of, say, the concept of probability or the theory of numbers.

Thus, to obtain a public school teacher as intellectually competent as her average pre-college pupil, courses and faculty in professional education may have to be by-passed (1962 legislation in California provides for such) not because methods or other professional courses are not useful for prospective teachers, but because work in these courses has been watered down to a point where recovery in a decade or two is highly unlikely.

As Dean Howe at the Woman's College has recently pointed out in this column, the state of North Carolina is fortunately moving away from categorical professional education requirements to a system of institutional approval. But those of us with children in the public schools or who depend in economic survival on the products of our schools must still ask this question: Who in the colleges may control the criteria for admission to training permitting certification as teachers, the general faculty or the education faculty: and, in either event, will these faculty have the courage after a century of precedent to take the necessary risks?

With the survival of a nation at stake, the glib rationalizations or pretty speeches developed in the many years of concealing the real facts from self and others may no longer protect the professional educators; they certainly do not protect you and me.

Junius A. Davis
Princeton, New Jersey
Published in the Greensboro Daily News in August, 1961

The letter just provided ("Our Incompetent Teachers?") provoked an editorial that appeared in the *Greensboro Daily News* with that letter. That editorial follows.

Teacher Training and Quality Education

Dr. Junius A. Davis, formerly dean of the graduate school at Woman's College and now assistant to the president of the Educational Testing Service in Princeton, N. J., has written a letter to the Public Pulse which speaks for itself.

Its substance: The more poorly equipped students invariably go into teaching and teacher training is woefully substandard.

These charges have been made before, but seldom by individuals directly connected with professional education. Former Chancellor E. K. Graham, Jr., of Woman's College campaigned openly and candidly for changes in teacher certification, but he has long since departed these environs.

The indictment must have validity since it remains so persistent. Professional educators invariably reply that intelligence or scholastic ability alone is not a sure criterion of teaching ability. And Dr. Davis agrees. A teacher's ability to get the subject across to his pupils, to inspire and challenge them, can mean more than intelligence alone. Some of the greatest minds have no ability to impart knowledge.

But then Dr. Davis challenges the professional educators to produce some "reliable and valid criterion of teaching ability." Is there one, and can it be established?

The outlook for education, indeed, is bleak, as the former W.C. dean foresees, if the teaching profession continues to attract largely mediocre minds and scares away capable ones. Certainly, too, the whole education hierarchy is laced with over-the-years output of mediocre schools of education. If these professional leaders are inadequate, they will not likely inspire or challenge the teachers now expected to produce quality education in North Carolina.

Money, of course, will not do the job alone. It will not eliminate the educational gobbledy-gook now being handed out in some teacher training institutions. It will not necessarily give a new generation of teachers a firmer foundation in basic disciplines.

But it will break the vicious cycle. It will begin to retain and attract more capable individuals. This stimulated competition should lead to sounder teacher training standards and cut out some of the "crip" courses which now make teacher training courses attractive to the less competent.

Dr. Davis' indictment may be harsh. It may speak up too partisanly (sic) for the testing systems which now provide his bread and meat

But few will deny he makes his point. And those who seek quality education for North Carolina, from Governor Sanford on down, would do well to heed his advice that a thorough study be made of the criteria controlling teacher education. The preceding basic letter and editorial elicited heated or hurt responses from faculty in the School of Education. One such letter, from Dr. Anna Kremeier, appeared quickly, and I felt that a response was mandatory. This response, "For Rigorous Standards," was published in the next several days.

For Rigorous Standards

Editor of the Daily News

The letter from Anna M. Kreimeier, published in this column on August 21, is a typical but discouraging example of what those who deal with professional educators have to cope with. My statement which provoked her answer (this column, August 12) made two basic points: (1) teacher candidates for public school positions represent an inferior campus group in terms of general intelligence; and (2) this fact must produce a watering down of courses contrived exclusively for teachers or teacher prospects, as well as the stultification of faculty in teacher education. Dr. Kreimeier answers that I should study Earl McGrath's report which finds that teachers are more liberally educated than "many other professionally trained people." I have no quarrel with the McGrath conclusions, but they have nothing to do with the present level of students in teacher training programs, nor little to do with the impact of these students on courses designed for them.

Incidentally, the McGrath survey found that a number of the "liberalizing" courses were taught in education departments. Could this be because education majors cannot cope with psychology in the psychology department, philosophy in the philosophy department, statistics in the mathematics department, etc.? Or because faculty in these departments find teacher candidates as a group too gross to meet reasonable standards of performance? This is my conjecture, and I should be happy to cite data to substantiate it.

Dr. Kreimeier's quotation implies that critics of teacher education base their criticism on misinformation, or have vested interests in their own academic areas. Perhaps we "critics" would not appear misinformed if our arguments were comprehended, or adequately answered rather than dodged. The other explanation hits more closely home: I am a professional educator, and my vested interest is for substantive courses and rigorous standards.

Junius A. Davis
Educational Testing Service
Princeton, N.J.

Published in the Greensboro Daily News in late August, 1961.

Another letter protesting the stand that I expressed was purportedly written by an education major at the Woman's College, Ann Bird Adams, signed by 24 other education majors, and published on Oct. 9, 1961. The tone, not surprisingly, was that the girls considered themselves "thoughtful and dedicated persons who are preparing themselves to be successful and highly qualified teachers."

This prompted another letter to the editor, which was published by the *Greensboro Daily News,* on November 9, 1961, under the title "Who Are the Good Teachers?" The text of this letter follows.

Who Are the Good Teachers?

Editor of the Daily News

In browsing through a library, I have come across two items, three decades apart, which seem to carry some lessons for those concerned with the quality of education in our public schools.

The first is from "The Student and His Knowledge," a classic study supported by the Carnegie Foundation for the Advancement of Teaching, focused on the subject matter achievement of high school and college students in Pennsylvania over the period 1928-1932. Comparing prospective teachers with other college groups, it states (p. 343) "... The majority of the group (preparing to teach) are most at home in the lower half of the total college distributions; they exhibit inferiority in contrast with the non-teachers in nearly every department of study; and they show up badly when compared in the same tests with students four years below them who represent the educational problems with which they must be prepared to deal." Of one teaching specialization, the report reads (p. 302) "The group is parasitic; as an integral part of a collegiate enterprise its curriculum should be abolished, if it cannot be radically altered. These persons have a minimum of ideas or interests in common with educated men and women; it were better to secure from time to time such of their service as may be needed and discontinue the grotesque policy of decorating them with gratuitous college degrees."

But that was three decades ago. In the spring, 1961 issue of the Harvard Graduate School of Education Association Bulletin, Paul Diederich reports an experiment carried on in various parts of the country concerned with utilizing the reservoir of talent among college educated housewives as "readers, aides, and technicians"—or assistants—for public school teachers. He states (p. 31) "As a test case, we tried out Bound Brook, New Jersey, ... It is a town of 8,600 people, not a suburb, not a college town, and not very wealthy. We placed a brief story about the employment of readers in the neighboring New Brunswick Home News, indicating that a college degree and a good background in English was essential and that most readers could not expect to earn more than $15 or $20 in an average week.

"The story appeared on a Saturday; by the following Tuesday, we had 67 applications for the eight available jobs. Wishing to discourage as many as possible, we sent out postcards at once, inviting those with respectable credentials ... to learn more about the work and to take four tests: a verbal intelligence test, a paper-grading test, a paper correcting test, and an essay test of their own writing ability.

"... Forty nine appeared. Half of these came within six points of a perfect score on the verbal intelligence test, and a quarter within three points. The highest 20 on all four tests were called in for interviews, and none of these stood below the 90th percentile on college sophomore norms—the highest table of norms in our book. I had previously given the same intelligence test to about 300 teachers in my measurement courses at Rutgers, and only a quarter of them stood that high."

Miss Adams (Public Pulse, October 9) and her friends should, of course, not trust the excerpts, but seek out the originals.

Junius A. Davis
Educational Testing Service
Princeton, N.J.
Published in the Greensboro Daily News November 9, 1961

E2. Letters Concerning Educational Tests and Measurements

The following letter needs a bit of explanation. Shortly before this letter was published, I wrote a scathing letter about a new teacher evaluation test that had been adopted by the Department of Public Instruction, and that included such items as the cleanliness of finger nails. It was published in a Sunday edition of the Raleigh *News and Observer*, and early that morning I had a phone call from my friend, Craig Phillips, the Superintendent of Public Instruction, who said, between obvious sobs, "Jay, how could you have done this?" In my next letter, critical of the governor as well as of the Department, I chose to use the pseudonym "Craig Pobouy," and the UNC School of Education address. The paper accepted and printed it. If "Po" Craig guessed who wrote it, he kept his tears this time to himself.

Reader says test results should "irritate"

To the Editor: The Jan. 26 story "Hunt denies competency test scores," states that Governor Hunt was "obviously irritated at reports the state's high school competency test had been made easier."

I am irritated, and he should be, too. The tests, made easier or not, confirm that a significant number of our 11th graders cannot perform some very simple mental tasks applicable to everyday life and work.

The tests confirm that blacks, Indians, and other minorities, after 11 years in our school system, still have substantially larger deficits than whites in these skills.

North Carolina has chosen to apply a competency test as a graduation requirement late in the public school grade sequence, when 11th grade performance in the tests could have been almost perfectly predicted (and hence recognized) at sixth or seventh grade levels (and when there would have been time for an honest attempt at remediation).

The party line in the governor's office and in the Department of Public Instruction is to twist these pathetic results to "prove" that our schools are doing a good job, rather than to focus on the enduring problems they outline.

Twelfth-grade teachers over the state are necessarily being diverted from preparing more able groups for post-secondary education to coaching young people who failed the tests, so that when the self-same test is next administered the schools and the governor can once again point to our rather astonishing excellence.

And, the proposition that setting cutting scores or casting items into difficulty levels could not have been influenced by normative considerations is patently absurd.

Is Governor Hunt really anxious to see improvement in our public schools, or is he more concerned with some minimal competency testing, Today Show and all, as a springboard for political ambitions? Time will tell this, as well as what kind of politician he is.

CRAIG POBOUY
Chapel Hill
Published in the Raleigh News and Observer February 5, 1979

The 1970s and 1980s saw a ground swell of hostility toward standardized tests. This movement was fed by concerns that tests, when used as a part of selection procedures, would unduly restrict individual opportunity. And, because cultural minority groups tended to score lower that cultural majorities, the outcry that they were biased against minorities was rampant. My research, replicated by others with the same results, found that Black students made lower grades than white students with the same test scores, suggesting that if there were a bias in the application of tests in selection of Blacks, it was a bias *for*, not *against* Blacks. A more sophisticated interpretation of this finding is, of course, that it is the instructional system and its performance evaluation procedures that are biased.

Be that as it may, Ralph Nader decided to turn brief attention to the criticism of testing. It this area, he was clearly in something well over his head., and refutation came easy.

Educator defends standardized tests

To the Editor: The Associated Press story, "College tests like roulette, study charges," is a good example of how bright, rabble-rousing people parading as reformers and watchdogs can both become more concerned about shock value than about truth, and dupe well-meaning journalists into accepting their biases.

For example, the story says about President Turnbull of Educational Testing Service that "He acknowledged a student's past grades as a better predictor of future grades, but he said the test scores enhance that prediction." The word "acknowledged" implies subtly that when confronted with the Ralph Nader charges, the ETS president admitted that, after all, tests may be of limited value.

Not so. From the beginning in 1948, ETS competent researchers have stressed the fact that past performance is the best indicator of future performance, and also that a standard test improves that prediction. This is not only the result of five decades of research, but is also infinitely logical, considering differences in grading systems from school to school, grade inflation and other aspects of the inevitable differences in past performance gained in 50,000 different settings.

Nader charges that "tests do a poor job in predicting college performance." Drawing from the findings stated above, tests do a poor job compared to, say, rank in high school class of graduation or grade average. They do an excellent job, however, in improving the prediction from performance measures alone—probably in large part because they place all students on a standard base. Nader also ignores the fact that most states have higher education institutions where a technical institute of distinction and a major university draw students with the same mean high school average grades, but where the College Board score average of one institution is significantly higher than at the other—guess which way?

Nader also climbs vigorously on the popular but erroneous bandwagon that tests are "biased against minorities." This appears to be so if one only examines test performance of minority groups against that of majority groups. But various painstaking research, including some of my own, has shown consistently that cultural minorities perform less well than a subgroup of the cultural majority with the same test scores. For predicting performance, carefully constructed tests like those of ETS and the American College Testing Program are biased, but they are biased in favor of, not against, cultural minorities.

It is exceedingly curious that this modern McCarthy, so ostensibly concerned with standards of excellence, is playing to those who fear, probably for good reason, that the application of standards may restrict their opportunities. With or without tests, the educational system and its own standards of performance will.

I think, Mr. Nader, I'll go buy myself a Corvair!

J. A. Davis, Ph.D.
Chairman
Research Training Committee
American Educational Research Association
Published in the Raleigh News and Observer January 31, 1980

A persistent myth in regard to the 16 institutions in the University of North Carolina System is that all maintain the same academic standards. This is useful when students transfer from one institution to another, for there is no question as to the acceptance of credit for courses already taken. And only a very few realize that they can gain admittance to the most selective institution by getting accepted at another, making adequate grades for a term, and then applying for a transfer.

In reality, the institutions serve a hierarchy of student capabilities as reflected by their academic credentials. Not recognizing this is considerably face-saving to the less selective institutions, and particularly the traditionally black institutions. But it also causes some difficulties. The letter "Solutions oversimplified" dealt with this problem.

Solutions oversimplified

The Perkins-Stith series on remedial classes in the University of North Carolina system and the SAT score drop are pure genius of investigative reporting.

The subsequent editorials do not come off as well. As is frequently the case, it is not a matter of the validity of the basic data, but of erroneously presumptive solutions to the problems revealed by it.

The major flaw in what you call the "challenge for the UNC board" is that the 16 institutions are so diverse that what is appropriately "remedial" in one institution is "honors' level in another. Those who would bell the cat by setting a minimal standard on SAT for admissions would have to decide whether to close out some institutions (principally, those traditionally black), or set standards virtually as low as the minimal competency test requirements of the public schools.

If you believe there is a middle ground, look at the data. And, of the two solutions, one would not fly in the face of federal and public pressures, as well as reduce the diversity of higher education opportunity; the other would serve to authenticate and stamp in the low standards in the public school system that both of us are concerned about.

The SAT, so central to your argument, is not a particularly good measure of what has been learned in high school, though it may serve to examine grade inflation. Another issue is what is the proper role of the Board of Governors—to set policy in this regard, which encompasses such diverse issues as access and opportunity, standards and the well-being of the state as a whole, or to prescribe what each institution should do? You state "Surely the UNC board can enact an immediate policy that only work in college-level courses may be credited toward graduation." Barring remedial work for credit isn't the answer; courses would simply reemerge under other titles and classifications. What is college-level work? Can the board legitimately assume to control what the faculties define as qualitatively adequate? We have, in expanding access to higher education, gone rather far; we do need to stop paying the colleges to do what the high schools should have done. We need to recognize the roles played as well by our community college system.

I suspect the actions taken by the board, and the strategies that President C. D. Spangler Jr. is quoted as emphasizing, represent a better approach than you recognize.

J. A. Davis, Ph.D.
Center for Educational Studies
Research Triangle Institute
Research Triangle Park.
Published in the Raleigh News and Observer of June 5, 1986

E3 The Duke Lacrosse Fiasco and the NAACP

The Duke lacrosse case, where three players were formally charged with raping a black female stripper hired for a party at an off-campus residence by Durham County's DA anxious to win votes from the black segment of the county, had the charges finally dismissed by the State Attorney General on the basis of an unbelievable number of serious flaws by the prosecutor, who has now (June, 2007) been put out of his office and lost his license to practice law. In the one year interim between the incident provoking the charges and action by the State Attorney General, many individuals became involved: the Duke University president immediately caused the winning lacrosse team coach to resign and canceled the remainder of the season; the accused students were suspended; a Duke University group of 88 faculty rushed to proclaim themselves blacker than the stripper; the police investigators cut corners in gathering evidence; the defense attorneys found that the D.A. had suppressed evidence favorable to the defense; the attention of the national media, notably the New York Times and CBS' 60 Minutes, was attracted; and several hundred letters to the editors of the local papers were published.

I contributed to these letters a number of times. However, I will reproduce here only two. The first expressed concern that the Duke president had ignored the basic tenet "innocent until proven guilty" and taken immediate punitive action against the coach and the team; this was given the title "Brodhead shares blame." Although this letter and several others were critical of the Duke University president, I figured that I had nothing to lose, since I had been blacklisted years earlier for flunking their basketball center. And, these letters had impact: a letter of strong support for Brodhead appeared very shortly after my letter by a descendant of James B. Duke and former chairperson of the Duke Endowment, stating emphatically that Brodhead had acted properly.

The second letter was prompted by a letter by the Rev. Curtis Gatewood, Vice President of the North Carolina Chapter of the NAACP, which threatened to "demand justice in the streets" when the N.C. Bar Association "join(ed) the mobs in Durham who have verbally lynched and sought to politically assassinate District Attorney Mike Niforng for seeking to prosecute three white Duke students accused of raping a black NCCU student." I was much upset by this diatribe, for (1) it had become quite clear that the accuser was simply not credible, (2) that the charges were groundless (as later attested by the N.C. Attorney General), and (3) I felt that the language of the Rev. Gatewood impeded substantially any progress made in the desegregation movement.

This letter, a copy of which I sent to Julian Bond, Board Chairman for the National NAACP, may have been influential in prompting a more reasonable response. I never heard from the Rev. Gatewood on this and had only a *pro forma* acknowledgment from Julian Bond, but when the N.C. Attorney General's investigation found no basis in fact for the charges against the Duke lacrosse team members and declared them innocent, and cited the many irregularities in the work of the Durham DA and police department investigators, the press noted that the NC Chapter of the NAACP now accepted the findings without comment.

These two letters follow.

Brodhead shares blame

Professor Joe Dibono's letter of June 17 stated that he feels Duke University President Richard Brodhead's actions in response to the lacrosse affair show his inability to lead the university. This letter drew two critiques in your June 22 edition. Beth Brown, in "Blame Nifong, not Duke or President Brodhead" correctly places the major criticism on District Attorney Mike Nifong.

Yet it was Brodhead who put concern for image above the basic principle of innocence until proven guilty, by canceling the team's season and causing the resignation of a capable and loyal coach. This action made Duke a full party to Nifong's desperate attempt to win votes at whatever cost to other individuals or institutions. It also added to, rather than distracted from, the notoriety for Duke in the nation's media.

Reinstating the schedule of the lacrosse team, though an admission of earlier mistakes, was again a decision based on image considerations rather that principle. Doris Ondek, whose June 22 letter revealed she felt Dibono was critical of Brodhead because Brodhead supported college athletics, missed the point. Duke has become a great university in large part because of leaders who put principle above more frivolous bases for decision. Dibono showed something of the same mettle in taking the stand he did.

Junius A. Davis
Published in the Durham Herald-Sun of June 26, 2006

Gatewood's big leap

The January 28 letter by Curtis Gatewood takes the rather remarkable view that the N.C. Bar Association's concerns about District Attorney Mike Nifong are a "conspiracy to disrupt justice, "an attack (on) the integrity of a prosecutor who is prosecuting a case which has the potential to challenge racism, classism, and sexism simultaneously."

Even more remarkable is the fact that Gatewood is a minister and an officer of the North Carolina Chapter of the NAACP.

The sacrificial lamb for Gatewood? A black female stripper with semen from four different males, but none from the accused, on her panties or in her body immediately after making the initial charge. His champion and hers? A prosecutor who, among other things, illegally withheld evidence favorable to the defense and who promoted his biases by early pronouncements to the press that the accused are "hooligans."

There has been remarkable progress in addressing racial injustice since the 1960s. And, although there is still much room for improvement, this will not occur if Gatewood's closing threat, a quote from Malcolm X, is taken seriously: He wrote: "If black people can't get justice in the courts, we have to demand justice in the streets."

It is such irrational rhetoric as that that threatens the progress so many of us have fought for. Besides, we can't compensate Rev. Gatewood and his people for all the ills done in the past, such as giving them land and offering settlements, because it is not ours to give. It belongs, of course, to the Native Americans.

J. A. Davis
Chapel Hill
Published in the Durham Herald-Sun of February 3, 2007

E4. Factors That Drive Up Medical Costs

We have experienced annual costs of prescription drugs for Pegge and me in excess of $5,000 after insurance the last several years, and we have found that a trip to the Emergency Room at the state-supported University hospital starts at something over $1,200 before the inevitable extras, such as physician's fees, are added on, and after a four mile $525 ride in the (public contribution supported) Orange County Rescue Squad ambulance. Any two hour TV segment is now punctuated with a dozen different "Ask your doctor if Flooflab is right for you." Knowing how the pharmaceutical companies support this cost of advertising, and mindful of the other "investments" pharmaceutical companies make (i.e., lobbying, PAC costs), I have felt that all factors that inflate medical costs are fair game for letters to the editor.

Of many letters written and published, I have selected four for inclusion here. The first, "Expensive Medicine," was a 2002 attack on a pharmaceutical firm with its headquarters in the Research Triangle Park nearby. The second, published in October of 2006 ("Well-Cared-For Pay") was in response to a news story about bonuses paid to UNC health system executives. The third, published in March of 2007 ("Now we get it"), was in response to a news story about the 2006 salary and bonus paid to the head of the North Carlina Blue Cross/Blue Shield health insurance organization. The fourth, published in April of 2007 ("Those poor CEOs"), took advantage of an item in the News and Observer reporting a national survey of equity-based compensation paid to chief executives for repetition of my concerns about the role of exorbitant salaries in inflating health care costs.

Expensive Medicine

Having just paid $168 for a 30-day supply of a GlaxoSmithKline inhalant for allergies, your July 23 front-page article about Bob Ingram, chairman of GSK, was most revealing.

Ingram was quoted as saying that GSK "is always going to be a convenient political target because we make money off people not feeling well." True, but it would be more accurate to say GSK is a target because it makes more money by investing huge sums in contributions to politicians, to lobbying, and to TV advertising of prescription drugs, and adding these costs to what we pay for prescriptions in such a way that profits are not eroded but remain the highest of any industrial group.

Yet, prices are usually defended by alleging that costs of needed research are high, without reference to the other costs cited.

For example: You report GSK contributions to a recent "political gala" of $250,000, and more than $490,000 to congressional candidates during the 2002 election cycle alone.

It is also reported that Ingram finds U.S. Sen. John Edward's involvement in legislation to speed the availability of generic drugs "disappointing." Why? Ingram is reported as saying that GSK typically loses 80 percent to 90 percent of its profits on a drug after a generic maker is able to replicate it. Those lost profits are the result of sick people being able to get prescribed medication at more affordable costs. Right on, Senator!

J. A. Davis,. Ph.D.
Chapel Hill

Published in the Raleigh News and Observer of Wednesday, July 31, 2002

Well Cared For Pay

UNC health system executive William Roper's base salary last year was only $489,030, so that paltry sum was augmented by a bonus of $110,010 (news story, Oct. 13). At least two other administrators reportedly received bonuses of over $100,000.

It is no mystery as to where such monies come from. One of us was referred there for X-Ray studies, which were completed on an out-patient basis in a half-day; the bill was $1,560, of which $1029 was for "ER" (we did not get near that part of the hospital). A bit later, for outpatient back surgery, the charge was $351 for a 15 minute meeting pre-surgery meeting with the physician and blood work, and $11,722 for the subsequent out-patient surgery a week later (which involved being held in the hospital for seven whole hours). The hospital's aggressive collection policies, well known from previous articles, add insurance to the institution's capability to support its administrative staff.

It is nice to know that our state hospital includes its own executives in its mission to care for the people of North Carolina.

Junius A. and Pegge M. Davis
Chapel Hill

Published in the Raleigh News and Observer of October 18, 2006

Now we get it

With our principal wage earner retiring over two decades ago, we have experienced the double-whammy of rampant inflation and rising medical care costs. In 2006, our after-insurance costs for medical and dental service and pharmaceuticals exceeded $12,000, and charges to Medicare on our behalf ran close to $100,000.

We had trouble understanding this, until the News and Observer item of October 13 revealed that UNC Health Care System bonuses in 2006 ran to more than $2.5 million. This item reported that Dr. William Roper, CEO of the

UNC Health Care System, had his 2006 salary of $489,030 augmented with a bonus of $110,010.

But now we see "Blue Cross CEO gets hefty raise" in the N&O on March 3, with "hefty" defined in the article as a 22 percent raise for CEO Robert J. Greczyn, Jr., yielding a 2006 income for him of $3.1 million. Of that figure, $2.2 million constituted a bonus. This may not seem out of line when one considers the net profit this non-profit organization gained in 2006, which amounted to $167.6 million.

This helps us understand the February 20 letter that we received from the BCBS Vice President Marianetia Perdomo that informs us that BSBS supplementary insurance rates are increasing effective April 1. Given that we are only two of the 3.4 million North Carolinians with BCBS coverage, it also helps to explain the rampant profiteering that is encapsulated in the ever-increasing health care costs.

J. A. and Pegge M. Davis
Chapel Hill
Published in the Raleigh News and Observer of March 6, 2007

Those poor CEOs

Almost buried in the April 6 News and Observer is a brief reporting a Watson Wyatt Worldwide report that equity-based compensation paid to chief executives increased by 48 percent in 2006. Median annual bonuses reportedly grew to $2.2 million.

Thus, the bonus last year for Blue Cross/Blue Shield's CEO, Robert Greczyn, of $2.2 million was only average. We now understand why our BCBS rates increased effective April 1—our boy has got to do better than average!

And we worry about poor Dr. Bill Roper, CEO of the UNC Health Care System, whose bonus last year was only $110,010. Perhaps this explains why we have just gotten a first-time report of still another charge for hospital services in August—he has got to do better!

But it is Bob McGehee, CEO of Progress Energy, who keeps North Carolina among the best crowd. Progress Energy reported his 2005 compensation as $4.2 million but reported in a filing to the Securities and Exchange Commission that his compensation package rose to "nearly $9.9 million" in 2006.

We are beginning to understand why so many companies have mass firings or outsourcing of jobs when business gets a little tough. They have to, to keep food on the tables of their CEOs.

J. A. and Pegge Davis
Chapel Hill
Published in the Raleigh News and Observer of April 10, 2007

E5. Letters to the President, VIA Letters to the Editors

Finding that President Bush's actions were as obnoxious to me as his posturings on TV (which some wit likened to the expression on a young child's face after his first successful use of the potty), I felt I should share my very great intelligence by writing him personal letters or emails. But my experience in this regard, reported in a letter to the editor of the Raleigh *News and Observer* that was published January 10, explained why I abandoned any attempts to communicate directly with the White House.

A work in progress

I was pleased to note that President Bush encourages comments from citizens, and has established a Web page to facilitate communication.

Several days ago I sent him a five-word message which said simply "Don't mess with Social Security!" Receipt of this message was acknowledged, and a page and a half reply followed shortly.

It began "On behalf of President Bush, thank you for your letter about Afghanistan . . ." It was signed by Heidi Marquez, special assistant to the president and director of presidential correspondence.

I replied, using the Web page again, that my comments were about Social Security and had nothing to do with Afghanistan. This time I got an almost immediate response. The letter, again a page and a half in length and signed by Ms. Marquez, began: "On behalf of President Bush, thank you for our letter about the issue of abortion . . ."

May we all take comfort in the fact that our president listens to what we say, and uses some of our tax money to respond thoughtfully.

J. A. Davis, Ph.D.
Chapel Hill

This letter was published in the Raleigh News and Observer of January 10, 2005

(It should be noted that twice again after this, I wrote the president, proclaiming that my last message was not about the topic of his response, and twice again I got an answer from Ms. Marquez, thanking me on behalf of President Bush for my letter on some other topic than the one on which I had written.)

Finding the formal channels of communication directed without notice, like raw sewage, to an obscure location, I decided to try to communicate more publicly.

In the furor over the leak about Valery Plame which was purportedly by a source within the White House, the *Chapel Hill Newspaper* on July 27, 2005 published a number of letters critical of the White House. Under the caption "Readers weigh in on White House leaks" were letters with titles "Bush should target White House leakers," "What is the real story behind leaks?" "Lies have propped up Bush and his allies," and "Bush without Rove is unthinkable." A copy of my entry is provided below.

Bush deflects gaze with court nominee

Political activity has gotten uglier and more sophisticated than when Will Smith, running against UNC President Frank Porter Graham for the U.S. Senate, accused him of "practicing nepotism with his sister."

Karl Rove has perfected such deception for political purposes as an art form, for he destroys any opponent with absolutely no regard for what it will do to our nation and way of life.

Now that his true nature and modus operandi have become apparent, the White House strategy is to obfuscate accounts of his criminal activity in the press with activity that will displace press attention to him, e.g., an instant Supreme Court nominee.

This strategy has worked so many times in the past for the Bush administration. Will it work once again?

J. A. Davis
Chapel Hill
Published in the Chapel Hill News on July 27, 2005

The damage done to the president and his administration in their response to Hurricane Katrina is probably second only to the damage the hurricane dealt to New Orleans. Posturing to try to nullify the tragedy of errors was rampant, attracting me to submit the letter "Fox to investigate the hen house."

Fox to investigate the hen house

U. S. Sen. Bill Frist has called for an investigation into the federal response to Katrina that is "bipartisan" only in the name he gives it.

And our president, who said "Brownie, you are doing one heck of a job" before public outcry forced him to send "Brownie" back to Washington, has said that he will personally lead an investigation to find out "what went right and what went wrong."

Wonderful! The foxes are going to investigate and report to us what happened to all those chickens!

Junius A. Davis
Chapel Hill
Published in the Chapel Hill News September 14, 2005

Although at first I was surprised by President Bush's continuing attempts in the spring of 2005 to sell his plan for privatization of Social Security when even kindergarten children could see that he was beating a dead horse, these efforts began to become consistent with other behavior by this president. I felt that this explanation of what passed for tenacity was appropriate.

President ignores evidence

As my British friends would say, it is extremely "curious" that our president persists in trying to sell his plan for privatization of Social Security, in spite of the burgeoning evidence that the Congress and the people are not buying it. But that is to be expected, when we have a president who does not read, tolerates aides only who tell him what he wants to hear, and has his secret service goons screen out those with opposing views when he speaks to audiences in selected states.

Vinegar Joe Stillwell had advice for his young officers that Mr. Bush would do well to heed:

> "The higher the monkey climbs on the flagpole, the more he exposes his rear."

J. A. Davis
Chapel Hill
Published in the Chapel Hill News March 22, 2005

In October, 2005, an acquaintance who once told me that she felt God had put Bush in the White House told me that I was wrong in any criticism of the President. The increasingly frequent use of the argument that any criticism of Bush was treasonable because we "should support our president because he is our president." as well as the belief that he represented the core values of the Republican party, needed an effective rebuttal. I believe I found it in words written in 1918 by former Republican president Theodore Roosevelt.

Remember words of TR

I note that the not infrequent criticisms of President Bush in these letters are matched by the rebuttals, many of which take the form of stating that we should support our president because he is, after all, our president. I find that if I voice some concern about our president to a Bush fanatic, I am accused of committing treason

Time was when Republicans were true Republicans. A former Republican president, Theodore Roosevelt, stated in 1918:

"The president is merely the most important among a large number of public servants. He should be supported or opposed exactly to the degree which is warranted by his good conduct or bad conduct, his efficiency or inefficiency in rendering loyal, able, and disinterested service to the nation as a whole.

"Therefore it is absolutely necessary that there should be full liberty to tell the truth about his acts, and this means that it is exactly necessary to blame him when he does wrong as to praise him when he does right. Any other attitude in an American citizen is both base and servile.

"To announce that there must be no criticism of the president, or that we are to stand by the president right or wrong, is not only unpatriotic and servile, but is morally treasonable to the American public. Nothing but the truth should be spoken about him or anyone else. But it is even more important to tell the truth, pleasant or unpleasant, about him than about any one else."

J. A. Davis
Chapel Hill
Published in the Durham Herald-Sun on October 31, 2005

The following letter was submitted through Moveon.org, in response to their request to write a letter to the newspapers about the president's stand on his wiretapping. It was published by two area newspapers on the same day.

Law-breaking Bush has climbed too high

Although the most significant aspects in Mr. Bush's State of the Union address were about what he failed to recognize (as subsequent comment has clearly confirmed), his adamant insistence that his wire-tapping was not only legal but necessary for our protection was as true to form as was his scheme a year ago to overhaul Social Security, or his fantasy, after putting on his Air Force costume, of "Mission Accomplished."

What he is really saying is "I are the president, so hesh yo' mouth—believe what I tell you, not what you see or hear."

Our imperial president is not only violating one of our most sacred traditions of personal privacy, he is also breaking the law. This is all the more grievous when existing law already offers the president the power to wiretap suspected terrorists immediately with the only proviso that he gets a court order up to three days later.

Vinegar Joe Stillwell used to advise his young officers: "Remember, the higher the monkey climbs on the flagpole, the more he exposes his rear." Our president seems to be gaining considerable altitude. (In fact, some observers are detecting nose bleed.)

Will our courts, our Congress, our media and the increasing chorus of enlightened citizens bring him down a notch or two? There is so very much at stake.

Junius A. Davis
Chapel Hill

Published in the Chapel Hill News on February 19, 2006, and with a minor variation (parenthetical comment in first sentence omitted) in the Durham Herald-Sun of February 19, 2006

Immune to evidence

In his April 20 letter, "What was Bush's crime/" James B. Smith makes such assertions as Iraq did attempt to buy yellowcake, that Al Quida and Iraq were connected, that Bush never claimed that Iraq was an immediate threat to the U.S., etc. He concludes with the following statement: "I have no more faith in the words of the FBI that I do with those of Gov. Mike Easley, or almost any other politician at any level, including Bush, the head of Duke University, Congressman David Price and Senators Elizabeth Dole and Richard Burr, or prosecutors Michael Nifong and Patrick Fitzgerald." This revealing statement is th best built-in proof that I have seen as to why some people believe only what they want to believe: they persist and reject all information and evidence to the the contrary of their preconceived biases, and are hopelessly immune to any further evidence, pro or con.

Junius A. Davis
Durham

Published in the Durham Herald Sun of April 24, 2006

E6 Letters about Irritants

This group of letters in this section are about a variety of things that, in one way or another, have irritated us. Some irritants on which I have ventilated include: the pervasive stench of thousands of hogs that pervades the air in some counties ("Albertson's excess"); some evils that are evoked by progress that is profit-driven ("Does 'village' have to be this way?"); political absurdities ("China only one factor"); failure to recognize that prisoner abuse is wrong ("Abuse of prisoners confirms perceptions"); tolerance of a legislator who was repeatedly and openly exposed by his actions that he was a crook ("Way of the world"); the difference between December 7, 1941, and 9/11 ("Memories of Dec. 7th"); use of the Holy Scripture to justify ugly personal convictions ("Multifaceted Bible"); letting political bias color judgment of legal actions ("Not like Nifong"); and finally, three letters about failure of drivers to observe speed limits.

Alberson's excess

State Senator Charlie Albertson's paragraphs inserted in the state budget exempt Duplin County hog farms from inspections by water quality regulators (news story, Oct. 14), and substitute an agency charged with "assisting" farmers. His explanation ("People with the right attitude will accomplish a lot working with farmers") is an insult to even ordinary intelligence: the word "farmers" is, as we have come to learn from the TV ads by "Farmers for Fairness," simply a euphemism for Wendell Murphy and his cohorts.

Once again, these "farmers" have the "assistance" of the General Assembly. And Alberson epitomizes those in our legislature who would sell all of us out, including most of the displaced and stench impacted real farmers in Duplin County for the big money interests rather than for the state and public good.

It is a formidable task for ordinary citizens to vote out of office those who are paid big money for deceiving us, but excesses like those of Albertson will surely help us in the long run.

J. A. and Pegge Davis
Chapel Hill
Published in the Raleigh News and Observer on October 21, 1997

(It is interesting to note that this letter solicited a very well-written, two page Shakespeare quoting personal response from an official in a Duplin County Chamber of Commerce office, stating that he had driven over the county with his car windows open, and had not detected any odor suggesting pig farms. He invited us to visit him and the county. Having driven through it on Interstate U.S. 40 several times and becoming nauseous from the stench, we declined.)

Several letters over the past 30 or so years have taken one or another aspect of life in Chapel Hill to task. One letter noted the little girls, ages 5 or 6, who had erected a lemonade stand on Pinehurst Drive (an area of million dollar plus homes) with a huge sign reading "Lemonade, Two Dollars." Another, of which I am very proud because I believe it was influential in removing panhandlers from busy intersections inside the city limits, was a letter noting the several hundred cigarette butts on the ground at the corner of Ephesus Church Road and the 15-501 By-Pass where a man stood daily with a cardboard sign reading "Homeless—Need Money for Food—God Bless." Calling attention to this particular debris, I suggested that donations of at least $3.00, the cost of a pack of cigarettes, be made. These letters were published in the *Chapel Hill Newspaper*, but I apparently failed to keep copies.

Another concern has been the building boom including a pricey nursing home "Chapel Hill House") and the destruction of woodland south of Chapel Hill for the a community of several thousand very expensive homes and shops ("Southern Village"). Such changes, I believe, take advantage of the characteristics they then destroy for profit, and prompted the following letter:.

Does 'village' have to be this way?

My father, UNC Class of '17, felt the village had lost its simple charm when Franklin Street was paved. I began to feel the same way when the quickie mart Texaco station went up on the corner of Estes and East Franklin, in methodical defiance of protective covenants at that time and vigorous opposition from councilwoman Mae McClendon.

But nothing prepared me for Hideous House, the strange new structure hanging over the U.S. 15-501 bypass at N.C. 54, or for Ugly Village just south of town with its $400,000 monuments to bad taste crowded one on top of another. My old friend, Elliot Cramer, has recently in a letter to the CHN editor lauded local development as a positive aspect of progress, an easier interpretation, to be sure, from Crawford Dairy Road than from the Timberlyne or Eastgate areas.

Nevertheless, we still have the comfort of sharing space with a great university. Or do we? Chancellor Hooker has told the faculty that the acceptance of the money from Nike is a complex matter, but that is about the same answer (and the same logic) that any successful prostitute struggling for the semblance of integrity would give if trying to provide a socially acceptable answer to why she is so comfortable financially. And with what is "Ram Road" paved, and where is it really heading?

What cruelties and obscenities can be evoked by "progress!" 'Tis sad, but I can't believe it had to be this way.

J. A. Davis
Chapel Hill
Published in the Chapel Hill News of September 26, 1997

China only one factor

Your front page Oct. 14 headline "Dole blames China for N.C. trade woes" referred to a speech in Winston-Salem in which Sen. Elizabeth Dole said she plans to push a bill to slap a 27.5 percent tariff on Chinese imports if China persists in what she calls unfair trade practices.

Will China persist in the face of such fierce opposition?

I am reminded of the man with a car hopelessly mired in deep mud, and who was found by a passerby to be hitching a kitten to the front bumper with a chain. "You're not going to try to make that kitten pull that car out, are you?" asked the passerby. The reply: "I've got a whip!"

Dole is probably correct in that because China is undervaluing its currency, the resulting undercutting of U.S. prices has had some impact on jobs in North Carolina. But although her party has a whip, her chain is still tied to the kitten. I am sure that the China trade barons are trembling in their boots.

Dole conveniently ignores the likelihood that our state's job problem may have something to do with the fact that in three short years the nation has gone from a record surplus to a record deficit, that our once booming economy is in shambles, and that as far as the deficit is concerned, we "ain't seen nothin' yet." Maybe she can deviate from those in the Bush administration who blame the usual scapegoat for such problems, former President Clinton, by attributing this to China, too.

J. A. Davis, Ph.D.
Chapel Hill
Published in the Raleigh News and Observer on October 18, 2003.

Abuse of prisoners confirms perceptions

The horrendous acts of prisoner abuse seem to confirm to the Arab world that we are indeed evil, that our platitudes about democracy are deceptive, that our national motto is "Videri quam esse," or "to seem, rather than to be."

So? Our president affirms Rumsfeld, and apologizes on Arab-language TV only after PR damage. Vice President Cheney, the warrior who has always let others fight his battles, proclaims Rumsfeld to be the best secretary of defense we have ever had.

Then some congressional members of the hearings to explore with Rumsfeld how the abuses could have occurred use their time instead to make political speeches about how much the Iraqis love us for what we have done for them (e.g., Elizabeth Dole's speech about "incredible breakthroughs"). On May 11, when it came Maj. Gen. Antonio Taguba's turn to testify, a stooge from the Department of Defense linked to responsibility for the abuses by some reputable journalists, Steven Cambone, was not only granted permission to attend but allowed to interrupt and contradict Taguba's testimony.

And when Republican Sen. James Inhofe states he is more disturbed over the level of attention given to the abuse than to the abuse itself, he becomes a national hero: Mark Leibovich, in the May 13 edition of the Washington Post, reports "Inhofe's office received 5,500 emails (May 11)—up from about 100 on a typical day—and about 70 percent of those were supportive, he says. "One of the consistent strains was, it's about time someone said something," Inhoffe says. The fact that Inhofe is reputed to be considered the "dumbest senator" by his congressional colleagues doesn't get as much publicity.

I believe I can understand how we can be seen by the Muslim world not for our moral integrity but as "the Great Satan."

J. A. Davis
Chapel Hill
Published in the Chapel Hill News June 2, 2004

Jim Black, Speaker of the House, N.C. General Assembly, was found to be connected with a number of abuses of his position—notably for a variety of payola schemes. The exposure went on for a considerable period of time before mounting pressures forced him to resign and face criminal charges (he was ultimately convicted). One of the snippets of exposure in the *News and Observer* had to do with his use of his position to influence award of a state job to a friend. This account, published in the *N & O's* edition of December 1, 2005, prompted a letter of two sentences, a supreme example of my capacity for sarcasm. It appeared the next day in the *N & O* as follows:

Way of the world

Regarding your Dec. 1 headline: "Black helped friend get state job." That's what friends are for.

J. A. Davis, Ph.D.
Chapel Hill
Published in the Raleigh News and Observer of December 2, 2005

Most letters to the editor that I have written are a reaction to a popular absurdity that spoils my attempt to view all things romantically. Occasionally, however, I simply have an emotion that cannot be restrained. On December 7, 2005, the local papers were replete with items about various individual's perceptions of the anniversary of the Japanese attack on Pearl Harbor, with many comments attempting to draw a parallel between our response to the attack on Pearl Harbor and our response to 9/11. This I considered a hideous travesty, possible only for the generations that had not been involved in WWII. So, I fired off a letter to the Durham *Herald Sun*, which, though written quickly and without revision, was stated by the editor who called to verity its origin as the "best letter we have received in some time." The letter:

Memories of December 7

Sixty four years ago on December 7, for a radio program for WUNC from 1:00 to 1:30 p.m., I was a UNC freshman on the controls for a panel discussion among four political science professors.—two from UNC, and two from Duke. Their topic was "Are we likely to go to war with Japan?" At 1:12 the station manager at a Durham station, which was handling our feed, came on to say that news had just come in that Pearl Harbor was being attacked by the Japanese.

The panelists were unable to interpret my gestures from behind the observation glass, so I went in and told them. After a long silence, one uttered one word, "S—t." The group quickly rallied, and turned to speculate on what would be involved in our inevitable national response. At 1:30, we turned off the equipment and went to Danziger's for coffee.

It took me 30 days to enlist in the Navy. That was a war to take seriously, to be proud of, to worry more about losing the war than about losing one's life. The technology has improved, but somehow our political leadership, whether Johnson and Viet Nam or Bush and Iraq, seems to have gone the other way.

I hated to lose friends in WWII, but I was proud of them and of what they were doing. For the more than 2,100 killed in Iraq—some 1,000 after our president declared "Mission accomplished"—I can only grieve. Pray for our nation, and for its young men and women.

Junius A. Davis

Published in the Durham Herald-Sun on December 12, 2005.

I have problems with people who use professions of faith or constantly cite scripture, ostensibly for some noble purpose, but actually to prove to others (and to themselves) that they are, after all, true Christians. These people I call

"Jesusholics." Such a lady from Clayton had a letter published in the *News and Observer* of March 24, 2006, which attacked another letter writer for citing, two days earlier, "Thou shalt not kill" as an argument against the death penalty. She rebutted this with the following quotes:

> "Numbers: "And if he smite him with an instrument of iron, so that he die, he is a murderer; the murderer shall surely be put to death."

> Genesis: Who so sheddeth man's blood, by man shall his blood be shed: for the image of God made he man."

> Exodus: " . . . then thou shalt give life for life, eye for eye, tooth for tooth . . ."

I am afraid I could not resist making a brief response, which was published the next day:

Multifaced Bible

The writer of the March 24 People's Forum letter captioned "Biblical penalty" cited references from the Bible that she feels justify the death penalty. Unremarkedly, the scripture she cited is from the books of Genesis, Exodus, and Numbers.
Perhaps she was saving money and purchased a Bible marked down because the New Testament portion was missing. Or perhaps she just hadn't gotten that far yet.
Junius A. Davis
Chapel Hill
Published in the Raleigh News and Observer of March 25, 2005

A frequent letter writer to the local papers is an outspoken advocate of anything President Bush does, and who can never see any merit in those he classifies as liberals or Democrats. In a letter that was published by the Raleigh *News and Observer* of January 25, 2007, he likened Special Prosecutor Patrick Fitzgerald, whom I consider the paradigm of bipartisan and vigorous adherence to the law, to the Durham D.A., Michael Nifong, who by that time had been thoroughly and unmistakably exposed as playing loose with the law for personal advantage in connection with the Duke University lacrosse case.
When no rebuttal appeared in several days, I wrote a brief letter I considered strong, and submitted it through a contact on the paper to insure that it was published. It appeared on Valentine's Day, 2007.

Not like Nifong

The writer of the January 25 People's Forum letter captioned "No case at all" exposed himself as one who, like those in the Bush administration, would like us to believe that there was nothing wrong about the exposure of the CIA's Valerie Plaim—which ignores the fact that the administration has gone to such great lengths to conceal the source of the leak.

But what is utterly despicable is not only to make prosecutor Patrick Fitzgerald a scapegoat, but also to infer that somehow he is more culpable than Durham District Attorney Nifong—to write that "At least Nifong, at the very beginning of the case, had some reason to believe a crime had been committed. Not so with Fitzgerald."

But then, if the current administration in Washington can get away with such blatant deceptions, why not their supporters? Sadly, that is why we need selfless and apolitical prosecutors of the caliber of Patrick Fitzgerald who respect the law, rather than use it for personal gain.

J. A. Davis
Published in the Raleigh News and Observer February 14, 2007

One of the trivial things that has bugged me in my later years is the fact that drivers on our highways seem completely oblivious to speed limits, with the result that I find it hazardous on the local interstate to drive only at the posted limit, which is 65 MPH. This has occasioned several letters.

The News and Observer published, in May, 1996, a collection of letters having to do with the rampant disregard of speed limits on North Carolina highways and on city streets. The heading for this group of letters was "State of the automobile." The following letter was the lead letter in the group presented, together with a sketch of a distraught man behind a steering wheel. That letter follows.

Our Triangle 500

I can remember when I was a young driver 50 years ago. I would occasionally get caught in traffic behind some old person loafing along at 10 miles per hour below the speed limit. Old fogies with nothing to do, I said.

Now I am that old person. I drive frequently in the Raleigh area. One day recently, about noon when traffic was relatively sparse, I set my cruise control on the speed limit and in the drive on Interstate 40 from Ridge Road to Exit 273 to Chapel Hill, passed one car but was passed by 54 others. Passing drivers were angry enough to cut in front of me too closely, give me the finger, flash their lights incessantly or grimace expletives at me when they should have been watching the road. I think that the one driver that I passed with an out-of-state license plate was lost.

I find the Raleigh Beltline even worse, particularly in the construction zones around rush hours. The "$100 Fine" signs aren't working.

Speeding in heavy traffic has become endemic in these parts. I hear that we have an active Highway Patrol, but at what are they active? It is getting hazardous to drive at less than 10 to 20 miles over the speed limit, and one is apparently quite safe in these parts from citations for speeding if they simply keep up with traffic.

J. A. Davis, Ph.D.
Chapel Hill

This letter was published in the Raleigh News and Observer May 25, 1996

The second letter selected was published in the *News and Observer* of November 8, 1996. It read:

The Speeders' Edge

Regarding your October 31 item "State declines to lower speed for I-95 zone":

This brief article quoted a state Department of Transportation engineer as saying that lowering the speed limit in an Interstate 85 work zone (to 45 mph) "would create a larger speed differential between operators obeying and those exceeding the posted speed limit, thus creating the potential for increased and more severe incidents."

(Didn't we just have a rather severe "incident" in this same work zone near Durham? It's good to know that the state was without sin, and that the problem was simply that some drivers obey the traffic laws and some don't.)

But it is also apparent that a state transportation official seems to believe that drivers obeying the speed limits only create traffic hazards for the rest of us. This seems to suggest that the state Highway Patrol's motto should be, "To Stay Alive, Drive 85."

J. A. Davis
Chapel Hill

Published in the Raleigh News and Observer on November 8, 1996

Fast forward a decade and a year to May, 2007: the *News and Observer* then began a series of articles by investigative reporter Pat Stith and associates on the speeding problem. Although the emphasis was on lenient judges, who, for example, were found to administer only a slap on the wrist for repeat offenders exceeding

100 MPH, I could not resist an "I told you so" letter to the *N & O*. This letter, given the title "A decade of demons," was published on May 25, 2007.

A decade of demons

I note, with much interest, the able investigation and reporting of Pat Stith and the N & O team of the speeding problem on our highways.

I recall my letter published by the N&O over a decade ago—on May 25, 1996—in which I reported: "One day recently, about noon when traffic was relatively sparse, I set my cruise control at the speed limit and, in the drive on Interstate 40 from Ridge Road to Exit 273 in Chapel Hill, passed one car, but was passed by 54 others. Passing drivers were angry enough to cut in front of me too closely, give me the finger, flash their lights incessantly, or grimace expletives at me when they should have been watching the road."

I would replicate the experiment, except that I have found driving on Interstate 40 at the posted speed limit of 65 mph is now much too hazardous. Suffice it to say that reckless speeding in North Carolina is long-standing.

I had hoped change at the top of our N.C. State Highway Patrol would help, but I believe the problem has gotten worse. Your probing analysis of the lenient treatment of repeat offenders by the courts seems to be getting closer to the cause.

Good luck in this campaign—many lives, including some who are reading this letter, depend on it.

J. A. Davis, Ph. D.
Chapel Hill
This letter was published in the Raleigh News and Observer on May 25, 2007

E7. Letters Responding to Letters

Generally when I see a letter to the editor expressing a view I applaud or consider totally inane, I search for the writer's regular mail address and take issue with him or her in private. Occasionally, however, there will be a letter so blatant that a public response seems mandatory. In this final section, I will share a part of one exchange that appeared in the Durham *Herald Sun* in August, 2006.

The writer I entered into public dialog with then was a Jamie Huff, a UNC Pharmacy graduate employed by Wal-Mart, living in Oxford, N.C., who frequently wrote letters heaping high praise on President Bush and Conservatives, and finding endless fault with any and all Democrats and liberals. To one of his characteristic letters in the Durham *Herald Sun*, I wrote:

Keep it coming, Huff

The mouth of the ever-decreasing minority for the Bush/Cheney camp and their many mistakes, Jamie Huff, writes in his August 14th letter: "I don't hate anyone. I just like exposing liberal hypocrisy."

Keep those letters coming. Huff is doing a heckuva job exposing himself and his kind and affirming that liberals, after all, may be right on some things such as rigid and narrow-minded people who call themselves "conservatives." Keep those letters coming, Jamie!

Junius A. Davis
Chapel Hill
Published in the Durham Herald Sun of August 19, 2006

I was quite serious in trying to tell this man that his letters hurt more than helped the causes he espoused. But the letter quoted above elicited a reply as follows:

Terrorism against U.S. didn't begin in 2000

First, I would like to acknowledge the razor-sharp insight of Junius A. Davis' letter of August 19th. I will continue to contribute letters so that others like him can benefit from by boundless knowledge. Davis should remember that reading is fundamental.

Next, it appears John Rhodes (Letters, Aug. 17) is obsessed with me. He accuses me of "distracting the readers' attention" by focusing on the past. If he chooses to believe that American history began in the year 2000 that is certainly his right. A wiser person might look to the past to gain understanding of the situation we find ourselves in today.

Terrorist aggression against this country began over 25 years ago when Jimmy Carter's brilliant foreign policy allowed Islamic fanaticism to take root in the Middle East. Muslim extremists held American hostages in Iran for 444 days. They released them on the day Ronald Reagan took office upon realizing someone other than a cowering apologist was in charge.

Since then Americans have been killed in 15 separate attacks in a 25-year span culminating in the horrific attacks of 9/11. The sight of innocent Americans jumping to their deaths led George Bush to decide that appeasement was no longer a viable strategy.

Meanwhile, the left has been engaged in it's (sic) own Jihad to destroy Bush and regain political power in America. What they fail to grasp is that there won't be an electorate to rule if the terrorists win.

Jamie Huff
Durham

Published in the Durham Herald Sun on August 24, 2006

I should have heeded my maternal grandmother's advice about arguing with a skunk, but the letter quoted above was irresistible. Thus:

"Boundless knowledge?"

I thank Jamie Huff for his letter of August 24 in which he continues to share his "boundless knowledge" for us true conservatives and all liberals. But if his knowledge were really boundless as he claims, he would have noted the more than 2,600 American service personnel and untold thousands of Iraqi men, women, and children slaughtered after Bush so blatantly lied about WMDs.

He states that I "should remember that reading is fundamental." Yes, reading is important—it is a major objective of elementary school education. Instruction in the processes of thinking and judgment comes later. An arch-conservative, General Vinegar Joe Stillwell, used to tell his young officers: "Remember that the higher the monkey climbs on the flagpole, the more he exposes his rear." Huff either missed that or failed to accept the essential wisdom therein.

Junius A. Davis
Chapel Hill

Published in the Durham Herald Sun of August 26, 2006